£2-50

THE SAME OLD GAME
Volume One: Before Codification

Mike Roberts

"Alan the hayward of Hertil and William of Wyndhul were playing at ball;
and both running together, trying to get the ball first, each caught the other
on the shoulder and fell to the ground. Alan falling on Walter's knife,
which was in its sheath, received a wound between the shoulder and the elbow,
by no fault of Walter's. They got up and went on playing, as Alan
did not feel much hurt, and afterwards went to the tavern,
drank new ale together and went peacefully home. The next day,
the arm swelled up and Alan, saying this was due to the new ale,
asked Walter to send for a leech to heal his arm. Treatment was applied,
but he died the following Saturday; and Walter, seeing that he had died
of the wound, absconded and has not returned."
Calendar of Inquisitions, Staffordshire, 1266

Alan and Walter, this book is for you

**ROBERTSBCN
PUBLICATIONS**
2011

First published 2011
By RobertsBCN Publications
Rogent 47, 2° 2ª
Barcelona 08029
Spain

www.sameoldgame.com

ISBN-13: 978-1461093190

Cover images:
Front:
The foot-ball play by Alexander Carse (c1830)
Back:
Football at Rugby by E Harwood (1859)
Emperor Taizu plays Cuju (c1300 AD, Yuan Dynasty)

CONTENTS

PROLOGUE

Welcome to the weird and wonderful world of the origins of football. It all began as a pagan ritual, a fertility rite in which the ball symbolised the earth and the scoring of goals ensured a good harvest. Originally invented in the Far East, it is the Ancient Romans we have to thank for spreading their barbaric mock-battles over a ball around Europe, eventually introducing it to Britain, where it was neatly combined with the local tradition of kicking around the heads of vanquished foes. Some of these games are still played annually today, and remind us of the wildness of medieval mob football, a deadly game played village against village. It was so violent that it was outlawed, and by the 19th century barely existed anywhere other than the public schools, where it was refined and given structure.

Football had always been about kicking the ball until an extraordinary incident at Rugby School, when a boy called William Webb Ellis picked it up and ran. His goal was disallowed, even though the teacher agreed that it had been a 'pretty good try'. So good that he decided to change the game to allow handling, and rugby football was born. Both the kicking and handling codes were eventually standardised by public school old boys in London when they formed the Football Association and Rugby Football Union and created the games we know today.

But these new forms of football were not met with the same enthusiasm in Ireland. There, they had been playing their own form of the game for even longer than the English in which the ball could be both carried and kicked. This ancient game was eventually codified by the Gaelic Athletic Association and was the same game that Irish gold diggers took with them to Australia. Combined with elements borrowed from Aboriginal ball games, that game led to Australian rules football.

Little of this affected the settlers in North America, who had long been enjoying a football game of their own. It vaguely resembled rugby, but American football also included elements that were learned from the natives and the ferocious mock-battle football games they played on the prairies. The Canadians copied the game, but were so uncomfortable with the idea of playing something created in the USA that they made some token changes, such as having three downs instead of four, and playing with twelve-man teams, which they marketed as a different sport of their own.

The story of the origins of the world's different football codes is plagued with myths, folk legends and downright lies. It may come as surprise that practically none of the above is likely to be true.

Anthropologists may have some great theories about sun-worship, head kicking and fertility rites, yet nobody has ever managed to produce a 3rd century manuscript to back any of these assertions up. The Romans? Are we so sure they played football at all? Was medieval mob football as chaotic as we've been led to believe? How much did the public schools really 'refine' a plebeian ball game, and did Webb Ellis really invent rugby football? Did Gaelic football even exist when the first games of Australian football were played? And how native an idea was American football, or are there much closer associations to British and Canadian games that are too frequently ignored?

Football unites the world but also divides it. Even now we are feeling the effects of the heated rivalries that led one basic idea, football, to go off at so many tangents. As each code seeks to glorify itself ahead of the others, so too do their histories get distorted to cover up for some uncomfortable truths.

Rugby and soccer have led an uneasy coexistence for a century and a half. The subjects of the soccer empire mock the egg-chasers and their game that was still claiming to be amateur until as late as 1995, by which time it was doomed to play the commercial second fiddle. Meanwhile rugby union, the bastion of middle class amateurs donning their old school ties and playing a game that combines muscle with sophistication, looks derisorily down upon the overpaid working class prima donnas that squeal around on the floor after nothing worse than a brush on the shoulder.

But shamateurism aside, rugby did have its professionals in the form of the breakaway code of rugby league, and the scorn rugby union players felt towards soccer was nothing compared to their utter contempt for the Northern Union's bastardisation of their game, and for a player to switch to the professional code was enough reason for ostracism by family and friends.

But where all three come together is in their ridicule of a stop-start sport they cannot fathom in which Americans play *foot*ball with their hands and pelt about in their helmets, shoulder pads and spandex pants. Yet the Americans in turn condemn soccer as a dull, unwanted European import for women and children. And as for Canadian football? It's just American football with pointlessly different rules for NFL rejects to play.

Irish, and especially Irish Catholics, take pride in their national form of football, which only recently allowed Croke Park to be used for soccer and rugby matches, and even then just as a temporary measure. 'Foreign' games haven't always been made overly welcome in Ireland, and in return, you will hear the Irish one being rebuffed as more of a nationalistic pageant than a proper game.

Australia is divided by football. Soccer, or wogball, is for the ethnic minorities, yet neither is Australian rules quite the national game outsiders think. In many parts of the country, aerial ping-pong has never managed to dethrone rugby league as the local passion.

But as we delve into the past, we gradually find all these different codes merging together to the extent that it is hard to pinpoint exactly when one form of football broke away and became another. Like the revelation to Luke Skywalker that Darth Vadar is his father, like Charlton Heston seeing the beached Statue of Liberty and realising he had been on Earth all along, it turns out that each of these sports, with their apparently distinct histories, all stem from the same root.

This is not the story of soccer. Or of rugby, be it union or league. Or of the American, Australian, Canadian or Gaelic rules. This is the story of football. It's the same old game.

1 A WHOLE NEW BALL GAME
What is football?

Common grounds

From the Scilly Isles off the coast of Cornwall, where the local league has only two clubs that play each other seventeen times a season and also compete in a couple of somewhat two-dimensional cups … To NCAA Division 1A, where over 30 million spectators a year make it the most attended sports league in the world.

From the tiny Tiwi Islands off the coast of Darwin, where over 3000 people watch the local Grand Final, more than the local population, 35% of whom are regular players … To the 82,500 capacity Croke Park in Dublin, the fourth largest stadium in Europe, and which can fill to capacity to watch the strictly amateur GAA in action.

From the CFL in Canada, where the temperatures for games can hit double figures – below zero that is, without even counting the wind chill factor … To Stellenbosch University in South Africa, which has, depending on who you listen to, anything from fifty to over a hundred teams, and more pitches than anybody has seemingly ever managed to count accurately, but is considered the largest club in the world.

From the microstate of Andorra in the Pyrenees, population just 70,000, but which has thrashed the likes of Norway, Slovenia and Sweden in World Cup qualifiers … to American Samoa, at the time of writing 205th and last in the world rankings, having only ever won one game, against the Wallis and Futuna Islands in 1983, and once, in 2001 suffering the humiliation of 31-0 defeat to Australia in the World Cup qualifiers.

Two teams, one field, one ball. It's a global concept called football. Or not.

In a fabulous book to which we shall be referring intermittently throughout much of this humble attempt to expand upon such impressive groundwork, Montagu Shearman wrote in 1888 that "the accounts … which come to hand of the gradual establishment of the game in Canada, the United States, New Zealand, and Australia, seem to indicate clearly that before many years have passed football will be, like cricket, a common pastime for all the English-speaking nations of the globe."

Montagu was right and Montagu was wrong. One and a quarter centuries have passed, and football is indeed a common pastime not just in those countries but also in many more, whatever language they choose to speak. But football does not always come packaged in quite the same form.

To start with, we have association football, to give it its 'proper' name, or soccer[1], as it is also widely known. This is unarguably the most widespread team sport in the world. It is often noted that FIFA, the world's governing body, has more members than the United Nations. Sixteen more in fact[2].

Yet when the word 'football' comes up in trans-national conversation, we often find ourselves having to clarify which kind of football we're talking about.

From England, the birthplace of soccer in its modern form, it is only a short hop across the water to Ireland. And here, especially in more rural parts, and there are a lot of those in Ireland, talk of 'football' primarily refers to the Gaelic version, where touching the ball with the hands is not only legal, but is a fundamental part of a fast-moving game.

The use of the hands over the feet also vies for popularity back in the UK, where rugby football is the handling alternative. The word 'football' is rarely used in conversation to describe the sport any more, although most governing bodies are still known as Rugby *Football* Unions, and there was a time when the Rugby rules were considered just one of the many overlapping varieties of what was generally termed football. Of course, to confound the issue further, there are two conflicting versions of what was once the same game: rugby union and rugby league.

It was the handling code that triumphed in North America, in a parallel universe where what the world knows as American football but the locals simply call 'football' features eligible receivers, first downs, special teams and rushing yards. British rugby players generally fail to make neither head nor tail of the rules of what they mistakenly dub 'gridiron', and Americans often find rugby equally confusing, yet strange as it might seem, both games were based on the same original set of rules.

To add to the web of complexities, north of the 49th parallel, we find the Canadians playing something else. Canadian football is similar to the game played in the States not just in many ways, but in most ways. It is quite common for players to compete at both sports, and there are many who scoff at the pedantic differences in the CFL's rules and might even argue that it doesn't deserve to be considered a different code at all. But the game has a very separate history, and every right to claim an identity of its own.

---

[1] We'll be coming back to the football v soccer argument later on, but to avoid confusion in a book dealing with several different sports that all go by the same name of 'football', we'll be using the word 'football' when referring to all of the different codes in general, or when there is no need to specify any particular code, and 'soccer' when needing to make it specifically clear that we are referring to the 'Association' game (except when the word 'football' appears in official titles or quotations). If it's any consolation, I hate calling it 'soccer' too, but if it helps to make things clearer…

[2] This is not because it is considered more important in some parts to have a national soccer team than to have a country. It is because FIFA recognises no fewer than 29 teams that the UN does not. New Caledonia, for example, is actually a French dependency. Hong Kong, Taipei and Macao are politically part of China, and of course England, Wales, Scotland and Northern Ireland are not independent states as such but, whether they like it or not, form the United Kingdom.

And then there's Australia. The debate over how the Aussies came to develop their native form of footy, the most popular sport in the country in terms of spectator figures, is a fascinating one. Other than being played on a huge oval pitch and with an oval ball, it shares so many similarities to Gaelic football that the two countries are able to play an annual series using composite rules. But as we shall see later, the theory that the Aussie code was developed from the Irish game is at best questionable, and at worst nonsensical.

So, how did essentially the same game evolve into such diverse forms? From William Web Ellis picking up a soccer ball and single handedly inventing the game of rugby to the Australians adapting European football to an Aboriginal game called *marngrook* it can be hard to separate myth from reality. Which is precisely what this book hopes to do.

Ruling it out

It's important to understand that football culture before the late 19th century was very different to now. It did not have anything like the formal structures we are used to, with international federations governing the laws, and television coverage helping to make sure the whole world knows the proper way to abide by them.

Nowadays, it is easy to conjure up images of games in bygone days being played just like we play them today. Two teams turning up at the delegated time, deciding upon the starting line ups, shaking hands with the referee, and getting down to it.

But less than 150 years ago, even the most senior teams were still arriving for matches and then having to sort out how many players were on each team, how long they would play and how they would decide who wins … and also whether you were able to use your hands, if kicking in the shins was acceptable, and even what you had to do to score a goal.

Why didn't it occur to anybody to decide on a set of rules? It did. The first known written rules for any kind of football are said to be those written at Rugby School in 1845, but this surely can't have been the first time that something like that had been done. In fact, *calcio storico* in the Italian city of Florence had a rudimentary written code many centuries before that, while countless other football-like games had been played over the years by such far-flung cultures as Pre-Columbian America, Ancient China and Aboriginal Australia. We have little hope of knowing whether any of those jotted the regulations down on papyrus, carved them into a stone tablet or painted them next to the buffalo on their cave walls, for those early attempts to define the complexities of the Neolithic offside rule have long since been lost in time. But it was not by the written word but by word of mouth that these traditions were conserved, and historians are left to pick up clues from what little evidence has survived.

Said academics may have a more scientific name for the period, but back in what we shall call 'the olden days', sports were generally played by whatever systems the locals agreed to on any given day. And no matter how refined those games were, they were highly localised with no ambitions of being played beyond the small communities that enjoyed them. There is no evidence before the mid 19th century of any form of football that was in any way standardised over any particularly large geographical expanse.

It was not really until then that several factors, including an increase in leisure time and the development of new methods of transport, gave teams the opportunity to play anybody other than their mates from the other side of the village. Sports clubs starting bonding together and rather than informal gatherings on public holidays, they started arranging proper fixtures and tournaments. Rather than matches between different school houses, matches could be held between different schools. And that led to the need to set up local committees and federations, whose most important job was going to be deciding what rules they were all going to play by.

The Football Association was formed in 1863. Soccer eventually settled rules for such concepts as offside and corner kicks and outlawed hacking and handling, but that did not mean that every footballer the world over was in the mood to be bossed around by a bunch of London toffs. Getting people to agree to play by the FA's rules took a lot longer than most of us imagine, and the rival Rugby Football Union was particularly unimpressed. But by that time, the footballing diaspora was already well under way. Football had long set sail from Britain to far-flung corners of its Empire and beyond, where others would conjure up ideas of their own: downs, behinds and overs, scrimmages, rouges and marks. And that's where it all starts getting complicated, and a unified football code was never to be.

Schools of thought

We can draw parallels with modern day sports to understand how the chaotic nature of early football would not have seemed quite so odd at the time. FIFA has tried to standardise 'downsized' variants of soccer as what is now known around the world as futsal, but only with limited success. Five-a-side games are still played semi-officially in the UK, for example, with (a) fluffy balls (b) long, low goalposts and (c) no kicking the ball over head height, none of which exist in futsal, with its horrible non-bouncy ball and the option of calling basketball-style time-outs.

Move things down to school playground level, and there is still an incalculable variety of different games being played around the world today, adapted to local whims and the conditions of whatever plots of land and other equipment can be found.

If lacking proper soccer goalposts, schoolbags, dustbins or piles of jackets make for suitable alternatives as long as they stay put, which they invariably do not, with the expression "somebody moved the goalposts" being the source of infinite teenage controversies.

Numbers are determined by how many kids are there are at the time, though there may be some weeding out of the ones nobody likes. Teams are decided by lots, shirt colours or, worst of all, the utterly humiliating system of captains picking one player in turn until only the skinny git nobody wants is left. If there is an odd number, then this can easily be compensated by awarding one of the teams the right to a 'rush goalie'.

In the absence of a ball, a Coke tin will often suffice, and if there are no definite pitch boundaries then play can be spread as far as you like until it meets a natural hazard such as a river or picnicking family (or when dribbling the ball any further away defies all tactical or athletic logic). Positions on the pitch are generally defined as the crappest players in defence (when bothering with a defence at all) and the fattest ones in goal.

The penalty area, if any, is of the 'as far as that bush' variety, while referees are conspicuous only by their absence, and decisions are made mutually by each team, inevitably ending in the kind of arguments that lead to the oft-quoted "I'm going home, and I'm taking my ball."

For purposes of keeping the only ball in use for as long as possible before Johnny takes it home in a sulk, the offside law is generally ignored. Otherwise games would never last longer than five minutes.

That is not to mention such intricacies as taking throw-ins with the feet and corners with the hands, keepers not being able to come out of their area, or the ball being able to bounce back off walls into the field (or yard, garden or parking lot) of play.

The duration of the game is generally until the bell rings to go back to class, or if playing outside school hours, you just stop when it has got too dark, everybody is knackered, mum calls you in for dinner, or when you have all lost count of the score and simply decide (usually by a complete travesty of sporting justice) that the next goal wins.

And that's soccer, a game generally heralded for its sheer simplicity, yet the intricacies of transferring it to anything other than a standard eleven-a-side full-size scenario are often so complicated that many efforts are aborted and you just play three-and-in or heads-and-volleys instead.

Trying to sort out a playground game of rugby generally leads to games that aren't really rugby at all. With conversions and drop goals being almost impossible to recreate without the proper goals and equipment, you have to improvise by finding a suitably rugby-goal shaped tree or handily placed set of scaffolding.

Having players tackling despite different levels of strength and experience is a recipe for disaster, especially when the only surface you can find is tarmac. The usual solution is touch rugby (or 'six down' as they call it in South Africa), for which the Federation of International Touch even offers a set of rules and organises competitions. And there is also 'tag rugby', which informal rugby league players in Australia have taken to the next level as the fully institutionalised 'oztag', which involves pulling Velcro strips off the players' bodies instead of tackling. The Aussies seem keener than anybody to standardise social versions of field sports, and the softened down version of Australian rules, 'rec footy', has been taken under the auspices of the AFL.

But at playground level you are unlikely to find a kid who's heard of or cares about any of this, and getting a pick-up game of rugby off the asphalted ground is often like a trip back to the bygone era with teams deciding on the rules before each match, and the likes of scrums, line-outs and rucks usually looking about as structured as the street football games of medieval times.

And if trying to get an impromptu game of rugby off the ground was hard enough, an accurate NFL-style rendition of American football on the school playground is as good as impossible. Touch football fills the gap, but even the touching itself is a source of controversy, because whether playing the one or two-hand variety, it is often as good as impossible to judge whether a touch has really been made.

Anything from three to eleven or more players can be on a side, most or all of whom are eligible receivers, and if there are an odd number, you might go for the 'all-time quarterback', who just switches from one team to the other. And because your average American is pretty inept when it comes to kicking any kind of ball, many games decide to do away with the idea entirely, having a throw-off instead of a kick-off, and eliminating field goals and extra points.

But despite the arguments about whether to allow a 'steamboat' or 'blitz' count to give the quarterback time to make a pass, given that little Chet and Kyle Juniors' blocking is hardly going to provide him much protection, and whether there should be a special rule to protect Uncle Hank from his heart condition, the games get played, everybody enjoys it, and Turkey Bowl matches between family and friends are as much a Thanksgiving institution in the US as Dallas and Denver games on TV. It never occurs to anybody that there should be a need to write down the rules.

The authorities may have standardised official codes for football, but 'playground rules football' is still a law unto its own. And may it stay that way forever.

Home rules

That was much the sentiment shared by many when the rules-making bodies of the 19th century sought to convince them of the need for official regulations. Laying down the law was never going to be an easy task, because everywhere you went, people were quite happy with football the way they knew it, taking great pride in their local methods and reluctant to see them modified for the sake of folk they had never met before and probably never would.

In times when the pre-match discussion and trading of rules was often part of the fun, football was an improvised affair rather than a precise science. Even in our modern day and age, with i-phones, e-mail and SMS to communicate, and with cars, trains and busses to get from house A to pitch B and pub C, amateur, social, Sunday League and pub teams around the world still struggle to get the right number of people together for a game of any code of football at the right time, on the right pitch and with the right kit. Any captain knows the frustration of staring down the road and praying for those two missing players to appear around the corner, trying to remember who washed the kit last week and whether or not he is likely to have recovered from his hangover in time, or arriving an hour late only to discover that the opposition has got tired of waiting and buggered off home.

It's hard to imagine these days how we even managed without mobile phones, so one can only be filled with admiration that games got played at all in centuries gone by, when the only way of announcing fixtures to the rest of the town was through the town crier, and when kick-off times were a nightmare because the nearest clock was on the church tower in a village that was five miles away.

The quality of the ball was limited by the players' own ability to craft a reasonably durable sphere out of whatever materials could be found. The council didn't lay on any nice flat fields with the lines marked out in white paint. Games were played on whatever patch of land could be found, and if there did so happen to be a ditch in the middle of it, you just invented a rule to deal with it. If the opposition decided that they wanted to use their hands, well, you just buckled down and used your hands too. And if somebody decided to hack you down with a thump on the shins, you jolly well hacked him back.

Pool players will be familiar with this kind of logic today. Even before games between people that drink in the same pub, you inevitably have to establish a few ground rules before you start. Is it two shots for a foul, and if so does the second shot carry? Or do you get 'ball in hand' and can put the cueball anywhere you like? Is it a foul to pot one of your opponent's balls after you have potted one of your own? Does a foul on the black end the game? Is it only one shot on the black, and do you have to nominate the pocket you are going to pot it in?

Just for eight-ball pool there are a frightening number of house rules that vary from one establishment to the next – and rival attempts to standardise the game are generally being met with deaf ears at the 'down the pub with your mates' level. But the quibbles about what's right and what's wrong and the scoffing at daft local rules are part and parcel of the occasion.

And so while one kind of football was being played as the haggises grazed in the heathery Highland glens, in between the cricket and clotted cream on a quaint Westcountry village green, the vicar was dipping biscuits in his tea while watching something totally different. And in the absence of any live television coverage of each other's matches, nobody was any the wiser.

And if the differences could be so marked between one British county and the next, then it can hardly be surprising that when football was taken as far afield as North America and Australia, it soon metamorphosed into something barely recognisable from any of the remotely standardised origins it probably never had.

Origin of the species

Tracing the origins of anything often comes down to a chicken and the egg type conundrum that is nigh on impossible to solve. John Logie Baird is often credited as being the creator of television, but how far would he have got without the help of a wee disk invented by Paul Gottlieb Nipkow? And although Karl Friedrich Benz goes down as the original brain behind the automobile, his petrol-powered contamination device would never have rolled very far without the help of the unknown masterminds of five or six millennia earlier that came up with the clever little concept of the wheel.

Scientists can say what they like about the 'big bang', but people find it easier to understand and identify with Adam and Eve and other creation myths. No matter how developed our brains might be, we humans still like a nice, simple explanation for where things come from, and so much the better if we can put a face or a nation to their origin.

William Smith warned us of this way back in 1875 when he said that "the ancients were fond of attributing the invention of all games to particular persons or occasions … but such statements do not deserve attention[3]." One of the examples he uses to illustrate his point was that of Herodotus in his *Histories* of around 430 BC, who claimed that in Lydia, in modern day Turkey, there had once been "great scarcity of food … they looked for remedies, and different plans were devised by different men. Then it was that they invented the games of … ball and all other forms of game except dice, which the Lydians do not claim to have discovered. Then, using their discovery to lighten the famine, every other day they would play for the whole day, so that they would not have to look for food, and the next day they quit their play and ate."

Even if the Lydians did dream up ball games as a way of beating hunger, it is as preposterous to believe that ball games *per se* were their invention as it is to say that football was invented when somebody kicked a dead Viking's head. We are guilty of the same thing today. Former Mexican soccer international Hugo Sanchez opens Fremantle Media's excellent *History of Football* movie by saying that we should erect a statue of whoever it was that invented football, and "worship him like a God." It's a silly comment. There was no 'one man' who invented football.

19th century visionaries like Ebenezer Cobb Morely, Walter Camp and Michael Cusack did wonders to promote the widespread acceptance of certain interpretations of the game and its rules, but ultimately these were no more than modifications to something that had been evolving not just for centuries, but for millennia.

In that respect, football is said to be different to another sport that was indeed created out of the blue by a specific person at a specific time. In 1891, a Canadian called James Naismith, who was teaching in Springfield, Massachusetts, came up with an indoor pursuit to cheer up the cold New England winters. It's perhaps a good thing that the man himself stood in the way of the idea of calling it Naismith Ball. Instead, that event marked the birth of basketball.

However, although Naismith and the boys hanging out at the YMCA had come up with a brand new way of having a good time, all they really did was take elements of other games and mould them into something new. Naismith was a keen gymnast and rugby player, so had plenty of knowledge of different sports to draw upon. As it happens, a good fifteen years earlier, OH Kluge had come up with a strikingly similar game in Germany called *korbball*.

---

[3] Sir William Smith *Dictionary of Greek and Roman Antiquities* (1875).

And the ancient Mesoamerican ballgames played thousands of years before shared many characteristics with Naismith's apparent brainchild[4].

However far back you go in history, you can go back further still. Basketball was another take on the time-honoured idea of two teams attempting to get a ball or similar object to one end of a playing area and score, while at the same time trying to prevent the opposing team from doing likewise at the other end. From there it's just a case of changing the size and shape of the goals, ball and playing area, limiting what you can and can't do with different parts of the body, and also deciding whether or not some kind of instrument can be used to propel the ball...

Stick to it

We tend to look at the origins of ball sports the wrong way round. We want to identify the moment when people first started kicking the ball, first started carrying it or first started hitting it with an object. But all of these are basic actions that humans have been able to perform for as long as we have been climbing trees and swimming. Modern ball sports did not develop as people learned to do these things; they developed as people started making them illegal.

The basic concepts of football are the same as those of hockey, hurling, lacrosse and even polo, the only real difference being that in the latter the ball is struck with some kind of stick. The borders were probably even less defined in the past. In France, they played a game called *soule*, where either the stick or the hands were used to propel the ball. Ireland has hurling, but in southwest England the same name was used for a game that, to the best of our knowledge, never featured anything like the *camán*. Likewise, the North American Indians had similar games that did or did not use sticks depending on where you happened to be.

Stick-based ball sports are usually ignored in football histories because they appear to belong to a different family. But the pattern of football and how it spread around the world is often disjointed, being prevalent in one culture, yet absent in the next. The pieces fit together far more logically when we also include stick-based games in the equation.

Stickball games probably set many of the standards that football was only later able to follow. That's to do with the development of sports equipment. For most of history, football as we know it today was as good as impossible due to the absence of decent balls to play it with. They had existed – the Chinese used a fairly decent model for centuries, in Central America they had produced a very satisfactory rubber ball, the Polynesians found coconuts did the trick, and the Romans came up with something they called a *follis*. But large fruit, strips of hide stuffed with hay, inflated bladders and perhaps even human heads were all well and good, but they still only made for a very rudimentary game.

---

[4] Four years later, at another YMCA in neighbouring Holyoke, Massachusetts, William G Morgan, created a new game called Mintonette, which soon became volleyball. Again, although it was a new game, it was based on concepts recorded as far back as Ancient Greece and China.

We imagine footballs from a modern perspective, when they are as easy to obtain as a loaf of bread. But that was not always the case. Even when the technology was there, ball-making was a craft that took time and skill. In Medieval times, the presentation of a ball to the townspeople by an important dignitary was often an occasion of great ceremony. We are usually told this indicates the symbolic significance attached to the ball, but it more likely reflects how much the villagers appreciated the rare opportunity to play with a properly crafted ball. Even so, it was unlikely to have been durable enough to withstand more than a few hours' play at the very most, and it was often a long wait before they saw another one.

It was far easier to mould small but more resilient balls out of stone, bone, wood or clay. These did not lend themselves too well to the kind of football we play now. So, rather than kick or throw the ball, it made more sense to play games that involved hitting it with some kind of stick, bat, club or racket. Following that evolutionary logic, games resembling hockey, cricket or golf would have come first. It was only when ball technology had improved to the extent that you could satisfactorily kick, throw or punch the things without them bursting open every five minutes that people were finally able to throw away their sticks and start giving some serious attention to football. And that process was not really complete until the revolutionary developments in the galvanised rubber industry of the mid 19th century, which is precisely when stickball games started going out of favour and football took off in their place. And so this history shall also be honouring the role of stickball games in footballing evolution.

The name of the game

Englishman Montagu Shearman wrote that "it is hardly to be believed that it should never have occurred to a man playing with the *follis* to kick it with his foot when his arms were tired" though he also added "but be that as it may, we know of no mention of a game played by the Romans where the feet were used to kick the ball, and of the game known from the middle ages to the present time as football no trace can be found in any country but our own."

As 'football', maybe not, for 'football' was an English word unlikely to be used by cultures that had other words for feet and balls – but as this book shows, there were plenty of games played outside of England that did involve kicking a ball with the feet. But we might also have to question Shearman's belief that kicking is the defining trait we should be looking for.

Football. Such a simple name. There can be no doubting where it comes from. A nice, simple compound noun. Foot and ball. If only. It's the 'foot' bit that confuses the issue.

Americans living in Europe have their Super Bowl parties ruined on an annual basis by Smart Alec limeys tapping on their shoulders and insisting on this point *ad nausea*. 'Ho, ho, ho. You call it football but you don't use your feet!' they jeer, always as if they were the first to spot that hilarious inconsistency in the name of the game those weird Americans find so kinda like awesome.

But as is so often the case, maybe it is the mockers themselves who are the fools. After all, in basketball, you don't hit the ball with a basket (if anything it's the other way round) so how can we be so sure that the 'foot' bit even refers to the idea of kicking the ball at all? It's not just in American football, but also in rugby, Gaelic and Australian football that the hands generally come into far more contact with the ball than the feet ever do, and throughout history there are further references to games called 'football' where the ball was carried and thrown. So where did the name come from?

Etymologists have pondered this lexical issue for years, and some of these wizened folk have come to the conclusion that rather than any kicking action, the word is actually referring to the notion of playing the game 'on foot'. The argument is that 'football' was a derisory term for a game played by the common mob on their feet as opposed to on horseback, which was the *modus operandi* for the sports played by the aristocratic classes of medieval times. Shearman points out that "for many centuries in England any pedestrian sport which was not immediately connected with knightly skill was considered unworthy of a gentleman of equestrian rank, and this will account in a great measure for the adverse criticisms of football which proceed from writers of aristocratic position."

But the not-on-horseback theory falls a bit flat when we observe that although there were indeed plenty of equine activities in the English-speaking world of the Middle Ages, these were not ball sports that involved teams trying to score goals in any way comparable to football. In the British Isles, there is no evidence of ball games being played on anything other than the feet until cavalrymen returning from India taught the good people of Aldershot, Hampshire about polo in 1834[5].

Another group of our etymologist friends, when not busy settling Scrabble disputes, have argued that the term originally had nothing to do with the actions, but the ball itself. We'll begin the story with the 15th century *Book of St Albans* by Dame Juliana Barnes[6]. If you can excuse her rather rudimentary English, she told us "this terme *pila* is take for a certan rounde instrument to play with, the wich instrument servys other while to the hande and then is calde in Latyn *pila manualis* as here. And other while it is an instrument for the foote and then it is calde in Latyn *pila pedalis* a 'fote bal'."

---

[5] The English were also said to have been impressed by the *pato* played by the Gauchos of Argentina, a far earlier form of the 20th century European invention of horseball. *Pato* in the 17th century involved battling over a duck in a bag. It was regularly banned in Argentina due to the violence, not so much to the poor duck as among the players, before being revived with new rules and a ball instead of a bird in 1937.

[6] There are doubts as to who this woman really was (she is said to have been prioress of Sopwell nunnery near St Albans), but if she really did write this book, then she has a very good case for being the world's first female sportswriter. It was written sometime in the 1480s, and contained three essays on the field sports of the times, which in those days meant hawking, hunting, and heraldry. A chapter on fishing was added later, rather cutely called "fysshynge wyth an angle."

Latin was the lingo for official purposes back then, which included the common practice of banning football, and such scribings of the times do indeed use the term *pila pedalis*, as does William Robertson in his Latin-English dictionary of 1693, *Phraseologia Generalis*.

The curious thing, however, is that *pila pedalis* (think pills and pedicures) does not actually mean a ball that is struck with the foot at all. Of course, you don't need me to tell you that that is a *pila pedarius*, a term that was never used. *Pila pedalis* actually means something more akin to 'foot-like ball'.

It seems very odd that there was no better way to describe a ball than the fact that it was similar to a foot, rather than *pila porcus bladderus*, for example, but Latin had not been used in everyday communication for over a millennium, so we probably shouldn't read too much into something that probably tells us more about 15th century difficulties with Latin declensions than where football got its name from. After all, Dame Barnes was clearly making a distinction between balls that were thrown (*manualis*) and struck with the foot (*pedalis*), even if the grammar was wrong. It is nevertheless curious that the error, if that is what it was, was not corrected.

Thankfully, people gradually came to their senses and started using a language they actually spoke when they needed to write things, and so along came *futeball, footebaule, foot a ball, fotebale* and countless other spellings of the word in the good old days before Bill Gates gave us his spell-check[7]. At least by 1780, a 'football' was being defined as "a ball driven by the foot[8]," while it seems games that were more about carrying the ball were given different names[9]. Not until the 19th century do we come across clear evidence of a carrying game being called 'football', and that was the one at Rugby School, which was originally a kicking game but later evolved, and with that came the gradual use of 'football' as a catch-all for all such games that didn't involve striking the ball with an instrument.

We shouldn't bog ourselves down with too much with the feet and kicking issue, in much the same way as we need not waste too much time wondering why there is no water involved in a game of pool, there are no horses in water polo, there are no camp costumes in drag racing, there are no cardboard containers in boxing, why angling involves little or no geometry and fencing does not involve the demarcation of plots of land using wooden stakes and barbed wire.

For that matter, does football have to use a ball? Empty cans and bottles are often fine for an impromptu kickabout in the car park, the Afghan sport of *bushkazi* is played on horseback as the players compete, of all things, over a headless goat, and two of England's oldest surviving 'folk football' traditions have nothing to envy of Royal Shrovetide Football just because they don't involve anything spheroid.

---

[7] Though I still insist Diego Maradona is Argentinian and not Argentinean.
[8] Thomas Sheridan *A general dictionary of the English language* (1780).
[9] Such as camp-ball in East Anglia, hurling in Cornwall, *cnapan* in Wales, *caid* in Ireland and hails or simply the ba' game in Scotland.

The Haxey Hood in Lincolnshire is said to go back seven centuries[10], but the hood would make for almost as poor a football as it would an item of headwear, for it is a cylindrical tube of leather containing a length of rope. And in Leicestershire, the village of Hallaton goes in for bottle-kicking[11].

All of this shows that our search for football's origins has to be much wider than merely looking for moments in history when men kicked things that were round.

And we'll start that search by going all the way back to the very beginning...

---

[10] The evidence is based on the rather hazy local legend of Lady de Mowbray, who graced the land in the 14th century and was dismayed to see her hood fly off as she rode by the village of Haxey. But so charmed was she by the sight of thirteen local lads battling to retrieve it for her that she granted them all a plot of land. The Haxey Hood is a re-enactment of those events. The oldest solid reference to the game goes back to 1815 and William R Peck's *Topographical Account of the Isle of Axholme* where it is told how January 6th "is devoted to throwing the hood; an amusement, tradition reports, to have been instituted by the Mowbrays." The build-up to Haxey Hood involves a medley of manic rituals, including twelve 'boggins' touring the local pubs for days singing songs associated to the game, and the 'fool' being 'smoked', which thankfully no longer employs the old method of swinging the jester upside-down on a rope above smouldering straw to the point of near death by suffocation. The game itself is a battle to get the hood to your pub of choice, but this is not done by simply carrying it. It has to be 'swayed' by a massive scrum that spends the evening heaving one way and another in a claustrophobic mass.

[11] They're not bottles in the modern sense, they're small barrels, and although they call it bottle-kicking, unless you're wearing a particularly well-cobbled pair of steel toe-caps, you wouldn't really want to use your feet on the things. It's actually a relatively modern development, which evolved sometime around the 1890s out of an old Easter Monday tradition whereby bottles of beer and slices of hare pie were thrown to the crowds. Somewhere along the way, the battle for the bottles developed into a game, possibly influenced by football or rugby, possibly influenced by other folk football traditions. It's more like rugby without the rules, and it's still played today between Hallaton and neighbouring Medbourne. The aim is for the teams to get the bottles back over their respective rivers, with a mile-wide area of countryside in between. With thorny hedgerows, barbed wire and plenty of dung to deal with, it can get frighteningly brutal – and this got especially out of hand in the late 20th century, when a folk tradition got more tangled up with soccer hooliganism culture than it deserved to. It's calmed down a bit of late, but is still one of the most radical displays of peacetime violence you can hope to see.

2 SETTING THE BALL ROLLING
Football in prehistory

Rolling bones

I'd like Montagu Shearman to introduce this chapter. Perhaps it's a sense of guilt for contradicting everything he has said so far when he really doesn't deserve such treatment. In 1888, Monty wrote that "if men have run races ever since the creation, it may almost be said that they have played at ball since the same date ... As balls and clubs are provided with the slightest exercise of skill and trouble from the resources of nature, we may be certain upon abstract reasoning that ballplay became popular as soon as the aboriginal man had time and leisure to amuse himself."

Picture the scene. Ug and Og are sitting outside the cave on a cool summer evening. The carcass of the boar the tribe hunted earlier that day is now little more than a pile of bones, the fruit they foraged from the woods has been eaten, and the women have been dealt with as only a good caveman knows.

There are cave paintings of bison killings to be finished, but they can wait for now. And there they sit, grunting at each other in a primitive form of language, and frankly, cave-life isn't what it's cracked up to be.

Ug breaks off the boar's head and starts idly tossing it in the air. Og watches, and decides that, as there are several million years to wait before television is invented and they haven't got any sockets to plug a set into anyway, what Ug is doing looks like fun. He looks around for something to toss in the air, but none of the rocks, bones and apple cores lying around look half as much fun as the head that Ug is throwing about. Og wants to play with it too.

So, when Ug's attention seems to be waning, he quickly leaps to his feet, grabs it mid-flight, and runs to a corner, chased by an angry Ug, who dives at his waist, pulls him to the ground, and wrenches the object of their mutual desire from his grasp. Wrestling over a boar's head is great fun, and it is not long before the whole tribe is joining in with what becomes a regular evening ritual.

We chuckle at the seemingly ridiculous idea of Stone Age man playing football. But it is by no means an implausible theory. Not football as we know it, but our prehistoric ancestors quite feasibly got amusement out of fighting for possession of some kind of object. And the original idea would probably have been just that, maintaining possession for as long as possible, something that is still a common enough exercise in football training today.

By logic, the earliest kind of ball sport was probably something akin to what we know as Piggy in the Middle, Keep Away, Monkey in the Middle, Pickle in a Dish or any number of colourful names. Another game that would hardly have required too many imaginative design skills would have been early dodgeball[1].

Primitive man was not so primitive that he couldn't grasp concepts like those. Tim Harris notes that humans were able to produce their own garments from anywhere between 72,000 and 42,000 years ago, made simple weapons at about the same time and invented watercraft just a few thousand years later. 20,000 year old ice skates have been unearthed in Heinola in Finland, people were tanning leather about 10,000 years ago and were weaving cloth around 6,000 BC. If early man could do all this, and bake bread, hunt animals, make clay pots and form small armies, it is hugely patronising on our part to feel he was incapable of inventing games that resembled the football we play today.

In fact, when we note that even the humanoid forms that predated *homo sapiens* had vastly better developed brains than any other creature we know to have ever walked this earth, it might not be unreasonable to suggest that forms of football were being played long before our race even existed. So it might not be a question of when did humans start playing football, but at which stage of our evolution did we start playing it? Yes, football is older than mankind itself!

Early humans were hunters, and spears were a common element of daily life. Spearing a wild animal is a tricky enough skill at the best of times, and there can be little doubt that our distant forefathers practiced the art by throwing spears at makeshift targets in their spare time. There would surely have been a competitive element as they demonstrated their superior spearing skills over those of their companions. And what better way to show off to the caveladies?

These target games would have spawned early forms of bowling, often believed to be the oldest sport in the world simply on the grounds of anthropological logic than any solid evidence. The Flintstones certainly enjoyed the game, although Hannah Barbera cartoons are not the most reliable way of explaining ancient history. However, the skittles found by Sir Flinders Petrie in the 1930s in a child's tomb in the Nile Delta of Egypt and dated to around 3200 BC have been claimed to be the oldest items of sports equipment ever found, although our prehistoric ancestors were probably sharp enough to have devised something similar thousands of years before that.

Be it a golf green, a dartboard, a basketball hoop or a cricket stump, competing to get objects to hit some kind of target forms the basis of a large number of forms of human amusement. From two Neanderthals competing to hit a dodo with a stone, all the way through to people all around the world playing *Call of Duty* online together, it's the same

---

[1] A game popular at North American schools, in which rather than trying to keep the ball away from other players, the object is to hit them with it. The potential for violence is certainly there too, as picked up on so brilliantly by the South Park team in 1998! The earliest known mention of a game like this appeared in *The New York Times* in June 1903, where the claim was made that it had been around since 1892. But so simple is the concept that it could quite feasibly have been around in some shape or form for a good many thousands, even millions, of years before that.

concept taken to different extremes. Evolutionary logic suggests forms of football lie in between.

In the family of sports that includes anything from football to hockey or waterpolo, rather than orderly turns, the players wrestle or jostle for possession as they compete to hit the same object at the some kind of target(s). Battles with neighbouring tribes would have given early man plenty of experience of the concept of attacking an objective while defending one's own, so the application of the same idea to their games in the form of respective 'goals' would have been a logical reflection of the kind of contests that were a part of human survival.

Historians and anthropologists will spend time immemorial trying to work out where and when these ideas first developed, but it's nigh on mission impossible. Written records of any nature don't go back any further than about 6000 years, but ball games are almost certainly older than that, which by definition makes them prehistoric. As we shall see in the next few chapters, there is plenty of evidence of this, but that evidence is just a drop in the ocean compared to eons of history that the tides have since washed away beyond recall.

The PRFA describes how "anthropologists, archaeologists, and other ologists concerned with matters ancient have pieced together an interesting theory from pottery shards, fossilized grain, old ashes, splintered bones, dusty doohickeys, and the customs of primitive people who still exist in the world today," but it is very hard to trace the tracks of ancient football. We need hard evidence, but due to its sheer simplicity, football doesn't really leave us much to work with. The objects they used as balls were so simple that even if they had survived until today, we would have no way of knowing that they were ever used for a game. But what about the goalposts? Who is to say that some of the many standing stones and monoliths that litter our world are what historians claim them to be? It actually seems closer to human nature for at least some of these not to have been erected in honour of the gods, or to mark burial sites, but to have been put there simply as goalposts for an early form of football. Stonehenge a Bronze Age football stadium? It may well sound ridiculous, until we learn about the Mesoamerican ballparks...

Animal magic

We can get some help out of observing what animals do. Amazingly, scientists are still asking whether animals play or not, despite anybody knowing that if you throw a ball, a dog will take delight out of running to fetch it, and a cat can get endless pleasure out of a ball of string.

Observers of animals have generally agreed that the more intelligent a life-form is, the more likely it is to play, and that this is usually done by the young, and mainly males. They are preparing themselves for adult life, so while the female young of the species have been observed to hone their child-rearing skills, the males practice hunting and self-defence. It's the same thing as human girls playing with dolls and boys with guns. Alex Hawes explains it nicely: "Juvenile cubs obviously can't practice hunting and killing prey upon each other without moderating aspects of hunting techniques. Social play must differ from real dominance competition, or else it would escalate into actual aggression. Ungulates can't practice escape with real predators, for obvious reasons. Play therefore seems to serve as relatively risk-free motor training for behaviors normally carried out only in life-threatening or otherwise serious occasions[2]."

And so we have young deer working out what their antlers are for, zebra foals kicking their hind legs to practice self-defence, and even chicks trying to catch twigs and feathers as they prepare for adult life, when their lot in life will involve hunting insects or fish.

But then we have birds that will use stones to make largely pointless noises, young penguins that happily knock each other off blocks of ice and then climb back up to do it again, monkeys and dolphins doing acrobatics, and a whole menagerie of other forms of largely pointless, but fun, fauna pastimes.

Here we can bring in 19th century philosopher Herbert Spencer's 'surplus energy theory'. Spencer argues that the higher up the food chain a species lies, the less time it needs to spend foraging and hunting, and so instead such creatures burn off all that extra energy playing games. When our own lifestyles don't satisfy our innate impulses, we do so artificially instead. Take an animal out of its natural context, and keep it as a pet or stick it in a zoo, and they will come up with all kinds of different ways of doing what Mother Nature originally intended them to do. No matter how much you fatten the cat on Whiskas, it'll still go chasing after that mouse. Stick a man behind an office desk for umpteen hours a day, and within days he will be feeling that something in his life is missing. He'll be signing up for the gym or the squash club in no time. He may not actually do any gym or squash, but the intention is there at least.

Animal games are rarely all that complex, but they should not be snubbed just because we humans have set such high standards with the complexity of our own sports that anything our furry, feathered or scaly friends do pales in comparison. When humans throw Frisbees, they are satisfying the same instincts as dogs catching sticks, and arm-wrestling in the pub is same expression of macho prowess as a battle of strength between humpback whales to earn the right to mate with a female. We have no right to consider ourselves that much different. In fact, compared to most animals, we humans are pretty crap at anything athletic. Even a little rabbit can easily outrun us, we're pretty hopeless when it comes to swimming, all of our fellow primates are far better climbers, and as for combat, we have none of the fangs, claws or horns that give so many other creatures the upper hand. A human betting he can kill an elephant with his bare hands is onto a bit of a loser. But we are *homo sapiens*, the 'knowing man'. We have speedboats, we have elevators, and we have Kalashnikov rifles. We have the brainpower to overcome our physical shortcomings, and have also applied that know-how to

[2] Alex Hawes *Jungle Gyms: The Evolution of Animal Play* (*Zoogoer*, February 1996).

our pastimes, meaning even the simplest of sports, such as boxing, sprinting and javelin throwing, now involve complex rules and sophisticated equipment.

But elephant polo players, for instance, have noted that their mounts soon pick up the basic idea of what they have to do and will give the ball the occasional tactical kick if need be, while in Gaelic football there seems to be an unwritten law that any big match must be interrupted by a dog running onto the pitch.

Zoologist and ethnologist Desmond Morris sees a parallel between human games and hunting. "A game of football becomes a reciprocal hunt" he writes. "Each team of players, or 'hunting pack', tries to score a goal by aiming a ball, or 'weapon' at a defended goal-mouth, or 'prey'... The essence of the ancient hunting pattern was that it involved a great deal of physical exercise combined with risk and excitement. It involved a long sequence with a build-up, with strategy and planning, with skill and daring and ultimately with a grand climax and a moment of triumph[3]."

A similar analogy is that of football as a re-enactment of war. The terminology of the battlefield is frequently transferred to the sports field: we attack, we defend, we shoot, and the coach is the general strategically positioning his troops. Sadly, there are few things more natural to the human race than the need to bond with other members of our peer group, village, tribe, race or nation to gang up on our neighbour. Whether for survival or through fascination, we seem to have an innate need to demonstrate the superiority of our combat skills, strength and athleticism over others.

It is no coincidence that the human desire for group combat has so often found itself associated with football in the form of hooliganism. When there are no real battles to be fought, football provides a perfect alternative to quench that thirst for conquest – some are content to limit their battle to a struggle over an inanimate object played by some form of agreed rules, others prefer to simply kick the faeces out of their opponent, but both sets of people are satisfying the same basic desires.

So, football could well have its origins in ancient forms of mock combat. Staged fights have a long history, the Romans of course turned them into a fine art in the gladiator arena, and it is hard to find any culture anywhere in the world that does not have some traditional form of wrestling, combat sport or martial art. For one of the finest and earliest examples, we turn to Herodotus. Born around 500 BC, he was one of the earliest Greek historians, although some of his stories, such as the one about gold-digging, camel-devouring ants, have led scholars to view his words with justifiable suspicion. He tells of a custom among the Aures tribe of Libya in which they held a kind of Miss Aures beauty pageant, where the winner was paraded around the lake. All very nice, until we learn that the festivities ended with her and several other ladies being given sticks and stones to fight each other with.

---

[3] Desmond Morris *Manwatching: A Field Guide to Human Behaviour* (Triad/Granada, 1978).

In the 4th century, the Bishop of Hippo in modern day Algeria, and better known to us as Saint Augustine, was horrified by the tradition he witnessed in Caesarea, in what is now Israel, whereby the people would divide into two groups and go at each other with sticks and stones, brother against brother, and fight to the death. The story goes that the eloquent cleric was able to teach them the error of their ways, and although this is obviously an extreme case, this is just the kind of tradition that would have eventually developed into games like football, as humans became more civilised and discovered there were ways one group of men could demonstrate their superior speed, strength and dexterity over that of another without having to go quite so far as killing them.

Physical strength in the form of trial by combat, duels, and team sport too, has often been reported as a form of settling disputes. The North American Indians are a prime example, where their early forms of lacrosse were often used to settle inter-tribal arguments without the need for anybody to die in the process, while in our modern world, football matches between nations or cities with a 'history' are often regarded as continuations of previous, and more fatal, conflicts. We could cite matches between FC Barcelona and Real Madrid as one example, which especially for the former is treated as a symbolic prolongation of years of political and military animosity, and matches between Celtic and Rangers still evoke references to the Battle of the Boyne in 1690.

Pagan origins

Sports historians seem obsessed with telling us that different games were originally related to pagan ceremonies, fertility rites, the spring equinox, lay lines and other spiritual connotations. These meanings are often taken as read, although factual evidence is a bit thin on the ground.

The pagan theory is frequently based around the notion that the ball was round not because that is the logical shape for a ball to be, but because it symbolised the sun. The PRFA tells us, admittedly with tongue firmly in cheek, that "in some cases, a team tried to move the sun toward a goal, such as a tree, which symbolized growing things. If a goal could be hit with the sun, it meant all that grew would be impregnated with the source of warmth and life. Sometimes the object of the game was to bring the sun into contact with the soil by dropping it into a hole in the ground. But even the throwing of the sun back and forth had magical results. Merely handling the symbol of fertility correctly brought virility and fruitfulness to those who needed it[4]."

---

[4] The symbolism of the soccer ball portraying the globe or the sun is a popular one. This may seem very ahead-of-its-time considering people still thought the world was flat, but this is another example of our misconceptions regarding our ancestors. Long before Christ was born there were academics that could show that the world was round, and the flat-earth theory was old hat by the 14th century. It was much later books like Washington Irving's *The Life and Voyages of Christopher Columbus* of 1828 that suggested his sailors threatened mutiny for fear of falling off the edge of the world and getting devoured by monsters. They did nothing of the sort, and knew perfectly well that the world was spherical.

The PRFA later points out, probably quite correctly, that "these speculations on ancient origins hold a certain fascination and, indeed, may contain more than a kernel of truth. And yet, we should remember that jock antiquarians often compete with each other in assigning earlier and still earlier origins to their favourite games."

Picture the scene. A Bronze Age village sits deliberating how it is going to improve the crop yield. And it suddenly occurs to one of them to invent a game-cum-ceremony in which the spherical ball represents the sun, or even that the game should be played east to west in honour of its movements. The trees used as goalposts symbolise growth, the playing field symbolises the soil, and each goal scored represents a day of plentiful harvests. Yeah, that'll work.

Maybe the ancients did believe that the best way to ensure flourishing crops was to chuck a ball around. We may now guffaw at such ridiculous beliefs, but perhaps if we could turn time around, it would be the ancients that would be laughing at our own stereotypical images of our ancestors all being sun-worshipping heathens that based their agricultural science on such a preposterous principle. If the farmers of the Dark Ages had really put their faith in such ideas, then it is hard to imagine how the human race ever survived. In fact, agriculture was already surprisingly well developed by that point, when manure, cinder and ironmaking slag were certainly used to fertilize crops.

Other than old wives' tales passed from village to village over the last two hundred years, there very little properly sourced substantiation of ball sports serving the same purpose, yet the 'pagan' theory invariably provides the introduction to football histories. FIFA are as guilty as anyone. Their website tells us that "it is certain that in many cases, pagan customs, especially fertility rites, played a major role. The ball symbolised the sun, which had to be conquered in order to secure a bountiful harvest. The ball had to be propelled around, or across, a field so that the crops would flourish and the attacks of the opponents had to be warded off."

Did it really? Or have too many people been duped by the likes of Janet and Colin Bord, who write that "the customs may become clearer if we instead describe them as magical rites performed to raise energy, which is then directed to the desired goal, which is usually the fructification of crops, cattle, people and the well-being of the land itself. When these magical rites are performed at prehistoric sites which themselves may already produce or store energy, then the rites are adding to the energies present at the site and available for use[5]."

The Bords are enthusiasts of the paranormal and unexplained, having written extensively on the existence or not of fairies and Bigfoot, so the idea of football being associated to magic is right up their street. It is tempting to write their claims off as a load of cobblers, but the Bords were mightily impressed by Jeremy Harte's revelation that "the Alnwick Shrove

---

[5] Janet and Colin Bord *Earth Rites: Fertility Practices in Pre-Industrial Britain* (Granada, London, 1982).

Tuesday football game takes place along the main street, the A1068, which aligns with a church, an abbey and Eglingham church, while part of the A351 road in Corfe Castle, Dorset, again where Shrovetide football is played, aligns with the castle and a tumulus." It sounds like they're reading far more into this than they need to. Surely it was normal enough for ancient football games to pick a couple of well-known local landmarks as the goals, and the gates to a castle or church would have been ideal, more for a practical than any symbolic purpose. Maybe the A1068 and A351 were designed with some kind of spiritualistic reason in mind, but even if they were, one wonders whether any medieval footballers even knew, let alone cared.

Bigfoot and Henderson

The real champion of the fertility theory is Robert Henderson and his 1947 classic *Bat, Ball and Bishop: The Origin of Ball Games*, a book that would have gone largely unnoticed had he not dedicated a large chunk of it to questioning the widely-accepted truth that baseball had all been the doing of a New Yorker called Abner Doubleday. Instead, he quite rightly suggested it originated from cricket and rounders in England.

But Henderson's main argument was not that. He wanted to show that baseball, and by extension other sports, shared a common origin. He claims that "the major purpose in the minds of the millions of people who play games is that of personal enjoyment" but "that attitude does not go very far back in history." Elsewhere he does agree that "a spontaneous origin appears at first to be a reasonable guess. It is natural to throw things – stones, apples or any round object, and what more natural than to throw it back? And what more natural that some form of ball games should be developed?" It would indeed seem a logical explanation for the origins of football, but Henderson muses that "strangely enough, there is little evidence to support the theory." He says this as if he expects the apples that prehistoric ball-players used in their games to still be sitting there now, next to the one that fell on Isaac Newton's head. Having cast aside the most obvious explanation due to a lack of solid evidence, he then announces that the purpose of his book is "to show that all modern games played with bat and ball descend from one common source: an ancient fertility rite observed by the Priest-Kings in the Egypt of the Pyramids." That's an impressively sweeping generalisation.

He actually goes further than that, for other sports he considers in his work, football included, don't use bats at all, but he is convinced that all of those came from his Egyptian source too. But although he does turn out a most impressive study for his time, he doesn't really show us anything of the sort. He merely explores the origins of different games, and then tells us, usually on the back of no particular evidence other than his own imagination, that they were in fact re-enacting this supposed Egyptian rite. Describing team ball games, he says "there are various theories as to how the ball was introduced as a 'bone of contention' between the opposing sides. There is no doubt as to what it symbolises: the idea of fertility." Got that? No doubt. Categorical.

Describing early polo, he refuses to accept that people rode around on horses hitting balls for fun, exercise, preparation for battle or simply because of an innate competitive spirit. No, "in Persia, when the Egyptian rites were being translated into traditions adapted to a nation of horsemen, the 'players' did not participate in the activities as games and sports are understood today … the opposing sides were merely observing the traditional dualistic ceremonies, which reverted either consciously or unconsciously to the ancient fertility springtime rite … which called for the magical rebirth of the earth's vegetation, and which can be traced back to the very early times in the texts found in the pyramids … As they became the common heritage of the people their religious significance gradually disappeared and a meaningless 'custom' survived or a skilful game developed."

Texts found in the pyramids? What texts? These are not facts. This is just Henderson inventing stuff. Maybe early games did involve some kind of ritual, but these associations were almost certainly thought up far later than the games themselves. Eric Midwinter makes the same point. "There is apparently an innate desire in some of these scholastic quarters to attach the highest degree of symbolic significance to the games of past societies" he writes. "Could the pundits be putting the symbolic cart before the authentic horse? If one examines the anthropology of sport in recent generations, one discerns that the game normally came before the encrustation of portentous justification." Quite right. Football existed long before it became a tradition to sing *Abide by Me* before the FA Cup Final or *The Star Spangled Banner* before the Super Bowl, for the All Blacks to do the Haka, or for FC Barcelona to offer their trophies to the Virgin Mary on the audacious assumption that she was a fan of theirs and not of Ahi Nazareth.

To put things in a different perspective, we could imagine what explanations the archaeologists of the future might come up with when they unearth our own football stadiums. There may be a huge crescent over Wembley Stadium, but it has nothing to do with Londoners being moon-worshippers, but will future texts write of how "the 21st century people of the region then known as Florida revered a now extinct form of aquatic mammal called the dolphin. Great temples were built in its honour, such as one discovered on the site of the ancient city of Miami. A primitive form of zorkball was played here. The players wore dolphin images on their helmets and the supporters also carried different dolphin-related imagery. In this game, the ball was struck using a bat, although some zoologists have observed that this game may not have been played in honour of the dolphin, but a fish called the marlin, which was similar in appearance to the dolphin and hence considered sacred in much the same way[6]."

Throughout history, football has been associated with feast days. In Britain, for example, games were often played on Christmas Day or Shrove Tuesday. All kinds of symbolic reasons for this have been suggested, forgetting the obvious one that these were the only days

---

[6] Pila Futoria *Origins of Zorkball* (Alpha Centauri University Press, 2245).

30

when people didn't have to work and could instead enjoy life's simple pleasures. Owing to the festivities going on around them, the games would naturally get soaked into the traditions and symbolism of the holiday. It's no different to wearing a Santa hat at a Boxing Day soccer match, but the games didn't develop out these traditional beliefs, the traditional beliefs were incorporated into the games.

But although it seems unlikely that Bronze Age man believed he would only become fertile if he scored a couple of prehistoric touchdowns, let's not totally ignore the arguments for a ritualistic origin of football. Henderson finds one example from 12th century Auxerre in France where "it was the custom of the Dean of the Chapter and other church officials, properly robed for the occasion, with amices on their heads, to form in a processional. The ball was handed to the Dean by a clerical student, after which … they proceeded down the aisle of the Church, while the Dean, taking the ball in his left hand, danced to the rhythm of the Easter hymn. The others, skilfully moving in dance steps, swung with the music, as hand clasped hand, alternating with the ball as it was passed from dancer to dancer."

It is all too easy to scoff that one aside, for we all know that religious folk are prone to get excited about revering all kinds of bizarre objects, and some kind of orb is not an unusual feature of religious ceremonies. But the plot thickens when Henderson also points out that in Vienne near Lyon, the archbishop "threw a ball amongst the people, who promptly played a game of ball."

We can take these two very isolated incidents from medieval France and with a little imagination, conjure up whatever fanciful theory we like. Henderson did that, and later quotes Francis Peabody Magoun, who he considers to have been "commendably cautious" when he said that "we cannot, if we would, deny the possibility that one of these same prehistoric footballs symbolised the fertilising sun, or that the game itself represented a once bitter intertribal contest. Yet, were this demonstrable, it would shed but little light on the origin either of ordinary popular football, or of the Shrove Tuesday game still played in England, and for just this reason: that there would not be one scrap of evidence pointing to a continuity between such a prehistoric heathen past and our games as they first appear on record[7]." Henderson goes on to argue against this claim, but nothing he says stops you thinking that the point Magoun made was actually quite a good one.

Let's not patronise our ancestors too much. They may have been more 'primitive' than we are now, but their brains were biologically the same. Yet now, because we have the benefit of modern technology, though most of us have no clue whatsoever how it works (apart from pressing a switch to make it come on), we feel we can write off the people of centuries gone by as so heathen that they could only invent football as a symbolic way of getting the Gods to be nice to them. Sorry, but let's not even go down that road.

---

[7] Francis Peabody Magoun, a scholar of an amazing variety of subjects from Germanic nomenclature, to Finnish folk legends and also football in *Shrove Tuesday football (Harvard studies and notes in philology and literature)* (1931).

When we explain the history of the cosmos, there are two main conflicting arguments. On the one hand we have mythical and religious explanations, and on the other the scientific or evolutionary view. We could make the same distinction between the two traditional views of the history of football. On the one hand, the belief that the game grew out of pagan rites, tree-hugging and sun-worship, and on the other, the belief that games developed naturally along with human evolution and the desire to play, compete and exercise. And that's reason enough to play football, is it not?

Heads and volleys

But ask anyone in an English pub where football came from and the chances are they will either ask you to stop bothering them with silly questions or they will explain how football developed from kicking or throwing heads around. But we have to be very careful to distinguish between folklore and verifiable history. Not surprisingly, our fanatics of the bizarre mysteries of the earth, Janet and Colin Bord, edge towards the former. They write that "a most important aspect of Celtic religion was the head cult … The Celts were head-hunters … the head was the most important part of the body, symbolizing the divine power, and they venerated the head as the source of all the attributes they most admired[8]."

More recently, David Terry told us that among the Ancient Celts "when an enemy champion was defeated in battle, the head was removed. The brain was extracted and mixed with lime to harden and made into balls. Such a ball was considered magical and supposedly more powerful than a stone. The brain-ball was occasionally used in games of hockey and kicked about as in a game of football; and here we may reflect on similar myths around the world relating to the origin of football[9]."

The story goes that the Druids refereed these matches, and the brain was considered the centre of a person's will. It's all great stuff, to be sure. Let's just hope Terry didn't do too much of his research in the local pub too. The Druids refereed the matches? Please… It's not to say that they didn't, but there is a big difference between the kind of history based on evidence, and the kind of history that people just make up. Be prepared, we've got chapters and chapters more of this kind of thing to come! Still, the use of the word 'myths' suggests Terry may not be too impressed with the theory either. Much as brain-balls appear in Celtic sagas, we have little way of telling what parts of these fairy tales were really part of ancestral society.

William Shakespeare's contemporary, John Webster, wrote in his most famous work, *The White Devil* of 1612 that: "Like the wild Irish I'll ne'er think thee dead,

Till I can play at football with thy head."

---

[8] Janet and Colin Bord *Sacred Waters* (Paladin 1986).
[9] David Terry *Sport and Health of the Ancient Celts: Illustrating a 2000 year Old European Community* (Sant Augusten, 1998).

But great playwright as he may have been, it is unlikely Webster was much of an expert on the matter of the Irish head-cult, and this quote tells us more about the stereotypical view of Celtic barbarianism than anything else.

There are few more reputable experts on ancient pagan culture than Ronald Hutton, and he insists that it's a load of poppycock, for "there is no firm evidence of a 'Cult of the Human Head' in the Iron Age British Isles as was once asserted … The frequency with which human heads appear upon Celtic metalwork proves nothing more than that they were a favourite decorative motif[10]."

It is tempting to go along with Wojciech Lipoński here, who observes how "historians question those legends as actual evidence. The stories mentioned might have been the combinations of Celtic traditions, actual military events, folk imagination and wishful thinking."

Where we do find an interesting example of head-ball is not in Britain, but in Central Africa, noted by none other than Henry Morton Stanley on his famous search for the missing missionary and explorer David Livingstone. Henderson provides the gruesome details: "When it was considered necessary to make a human sacrifice, an unfortunate slave was firmly tied to stakes in a sitting posture. The flexible sapling was planted in front of him, from the top of which was suspended, by a number of cords, a bamboo ring. The pole was bent over and the ring put around the slave's neck, kept rigid by the tension of the sapling. Then came the ceremony, dancing and drunken mimicry, the climax being reached when the executioner, with one stroke of a keen-edged weapon, sliced the head from the body. The tension released, away flew the head, catapulted for some distance, to fall amongst the waiting tribesmen. A ghastly, bloody struggle followed; for the rest of the day the head passed from man to man, until one retained it in undisputed possession. Thus is established the right to be recognised as the bravest man in the village." So there you have it – football was born in Africa[11].

Of course it wasn't. Football didn't start anywhere in particular. It was a long and geographically complex Darwinian process, and one of the few things we can be sure of is that the idea of kicking things was not something that the Chinese invented out of the blue two or three thousand years ago.

But that is where FIFA have officially placed the dawn of football as we know it, so it makes sense for our journey through football to make its first stop in the Far East.

---

[10] Ronald Hutton *The Pagan Religions of the Ancient British Isles* (Wiley-Blackwel, 1993).

[11] It is also said that in ancient India, polo was played using human heads wrapped in muslin.

3 EASTERN PROMISE
Ball games of the ancient Far East

Chinese whispers

The Ancient Chinese played a game that could be transcribed roughly from Chinese into our own alphabet as *tsuchu, cuqiu, zhuqiu, cuyuan* or any number of other possible spellings. We'll go for *cuju* here. Its origins are unknown, but the term first appears in a manuscript that was unearthed in 1973 from a Han Dynasty (206 BC–220 AD) tomb in Hunan province. A chapter entitled *Political Chaos* documents how the legendary Yellow Emperor, who was said to reign around 2650 BC, defeated his enemy, Chiyou, beheaded him and "stripped off his skin and made it into an archery target. He had his men shoot at it and rewarded those who had the most hits. He cut off his hair … stuffed his stomach and made it into a ball. He had men kick it and rewarded those who scored the most. He fermented his bones and flesh, threw them into a bitter stew, and had the men drink it." It's all rather macabre, and more mythology than fact, but it does at least insinuate that the Han, who wrote the account some 2000 years after the events supposedly happened, were aware of a kicking game that involved keeping some kind of score.

This should come as no surprise, for football (or soccer at least) began in China[1]. We know this because in July 2004, at the Third International Football Expo in Beijing, the only slightly controversial president of soccer's global governing body FIFA, Joseph Blatter, made an official announcement stating it so. *Cu* means to kick, and a *ju* was a kind of ball, and although little is known about the actual rules, the fact that the word 'kick' appears next to 'ball' was enough for FIFA to pounce upon this as the immaculate conception of the beautiful game.

They even have a place, Linzi in the Shandong Province, which was the capital of the Qi Kingdom (1046 BC–221 BC), and one of the biggest cities in the world at the time. It is here that some kind of ball game is mentioned in two separate texts. The first is *Zhan Guo Ce* (the 'Strategies of the Warring States'), compiled between the 3rd to 1st centuries BC, and the second is *Shiji* (the 'Records of the Grand Historian'), written from 109 BC to 91 BC by Sima Qian, and which was his attempt to record roughly 2500 years of Chinese history. That was some feat, and scholars are rightly reluctant to take Qian's word too literally, but he does cite a speech made during the reign of King Xuan (319 BC–301 BC) in which it was observed that "Linzi is rich and well supplied. Not one of her people does not play the flute, strum the zither, strike the harp, beat the drum, play cock fighting and dog racing, gamble at *liubo*[2] or kick a ball." *Shiji* also tells the story of Xiang Chu, who "Doctor Chun Yuyi

---

[1] A country where stone balls have been discovered that date back to the 6th millennium BC.
[2] A board game played by the Han whose exact rules are no longer known.

examined and urged not to overexert; but Xiang Chu did not listen and went out to play *cuju*. As a result he vomited blood and died." You just don't get that kind of commitment these days.

What the Han were probably doing was using their own sporting traditions as a plot device in their myth-tories. But *cuju* was a big deal to the Han, for whom it was a popular pastime among the courts and nobility, and was often played by the military as a way of loosening up the leg muscles after long expeditions. As archivist Liu Xiang (77 BC–6 BC) noted, "kickball deals with the power of circumstances in the military. It is a means to train warriors and recognise those who have talents."

Riordan and Jones explain that "the emperor Gaozu built a huge football pitch (*cujong*) in his palace, and in the preface of Luji's *Cugehang* he mentions that football pitches were not only built at the imperial court, but that the nobles and wealthy citizens also had private pitches … The historian Pan Gu (AD 32–92) recorded that when Huo Qubling, a general in the Han army, led his soldiers to the northern borders, he allowed his soldiers to construct a field to play *cuju*[3]."

So what exactly did *cuju* entail? It must be remembered that we are describing a game that was played over several centuries and one heck of a wide area, so we are better off thinking of *cuju* as the generic name for a number of similar yet different ball sports in much the same way that we use the word 'football' for different codes today. Riordan and Jones are convinced it bore some kind of resemblance to our football, in which "the forms of *cuju* developed in the army had strong competitive characteristics in which teams attacked and defended their goals" and the History Channel's *Ancient Chinese Sports* documentary claims Han players were forbidden from using their hands, since "the belief at the time was that the ball symbolised dignity." If one Han general could be persuaded that chess would make for a "similar but not tiring[4]" alternative form of training to *cuju*, then there must have been a huge amount of strategy involved. The truth is, there is very little we know about it for sure and the best we can do is puzzle over the meaning of the cryptic description offered by Han writer Li You (55–135 AD) in *Ju Cheng Ming*:

"A round ball and a square wall,
Just like the Yin and Yang,
Moon-shaped goals are opposite each other,
Each side has six in equal number.
Select the captains and appoint the referee(s),
Based on the unchangeable regulations,
Don't regard relatives and friends,
Keep away from partiality,

---

[3] Allowed? This differs from Sima Qian's version that Huo Qubing's troops were almost dying through lack of food but were still ordered to build a *cuju* court on which to continue their training.

[4] Cited in Mark Edward Lewis *Sanctioned violence in early China* (State University of New York, 1990).

Maintain fairness and peace,
Don't complain of others' faults,
Such is the matter of *cuju*.
If all this is necessary for *cuju*,
How much more for the business of life?"

The little Li You tells us could quite feasibly be describing something like football. There were six players on a team, some historians have asserted, so that the total was twelve in representation of the months of the year, for "the movement of the ball from one side of the field to the other would thus have formed a cycle of yin and yang that corresponded to that of Heaven and Earth[5]." However, another popular interpretation claims that Li You wasn't even saying that there were six players on each team, but that each team had to defend six goals formed by moon-shaped holes in the ground or in a wall. Another interpretation is that moon-shapes had nothing to do with the goals at all, and in fact the players were "imitating the moons and rushing against each other," which is another reference to the twelve months, or 'moons', of the year. The fact is that the details are so sketchy that all we can really do is speculate, and the many ideas that can be found floating around the Internet are best not taken too seriously.

Net interest

To make their balls, the Han had just sewn together two halves of leather and stuffed them with feathers, a heavy old thing with very little bounce and that couldn't be kicked very high. But dynasties followed dynasties, and *cuju* developed with them. It is under the Tang (618-906) that inflatable balls made of patches of leather were sewn together and immediately inflated and then shrunk in cold water to make them airtight. Growing up these days simply has to involve blowing up a condom at some point, while Tang adolescents got their giggles from blowing up pig bladders and one spotted that it made an excellent inside for a football. Pictures of the game being played around the 10th and 11th centuries show something that isn't all that different in appearance to the modern day soccer ball, and indeed, this 'technology' would remain state of the art, at least in the Old World, right up until the 19th century and the invention of rubber bladdered balls.

A whole new field of opportunities was opened up thanks to the lighter, bouncier thing the Tang were playing with, and if their game was a development of the Han one, then it had morphed into something very different in which the teams gathered on either side of a huge net (the *wangzi*) strung up between two bamboo poles at a height of between 10 and 30 metres. Somewhere near the top there was a hole (the *fengliuyan* or 'prominent eye') of something between 30 and 80 centimetres in diameter (one set of official measurements states three *zhangs* high, and one *chi* wide, but we'll stick to metric for simplicity's sake).

---

[5] Mark Edward Lewis *Sanctioned violence in early China* (State University of New York, 1990).

Under the Tang, whose capital Chang'an was apparently awash with courts, *cuju* was now more about juggling skills and we also find pictures of women, the Emperor's own concubines, playing the game around the 9th century AD. One story tells of a seventeen year old girl taking on and beating an entire army team single handed.

This is the variant that has been adopted by *cuju* revivalists, mainly because there are surviving pictures that at least give them something to work with, although the exact nature of the rules remain an unsolved mystery. The idea seems to have been a kind of foot-volley in which the ball could not touch the ground and rather than over the net, teams had to kick the ball through the hole.

The Tang went out and the Song (960–1279) came in, and the founder himself (Emperor Tàizǔ, who reigned from 960–976) was an avid ball player who was painted playing *cuju* with Prime Minister Zhao Pu[6]. This and other artwork of the time, including *One Hundred Children in the Long Spring* by Song artist Su Hanchen (1130–1160) suggest that the Tang's net had disappeared and what they now called *baida* was basically modern day hacky-sack. The players stood in a circle and played a form of keepy-uppy with a remarkably complicated scoring system based on the number of mistakes made. Points were deducted for not kicking the ball far enough, not kicking it high enough, kicking it too hard or for punting it out of the enclosure.

One of the four great Chinese masterpieces, *Tale of Water Margin*, includes a famous illustration of the Song game, and the text tells how street urchin Gao Qiu ('great ball') happened to be passing by carrying a large box just as Prince Duan was playing *cuju* with his servants and a loose ball was heading out of the court. Despite his hands being full, Gao Qiu managed to catch it with his feet, and so impressed was the Prince that he made the passing scamp his personal servant. Shortly after, Duan ascended to the throne as Emperor Huizong and his new servant was promoted to Grand Marshal. Gao Qiu would eventually be exposed as a tyrannical villain, but before that one of his tasks was organising the *cuju* displays for Huizong, who particularly enjoyed watching a game as a birthday treat, and to add to the fun, would see to it that the losers got a good flogging or, even worse, faced the utter humiliation of having their faces painted in yellow and white chalk.

There was money to be made out of *cuju*, but professionalism seems to have ultimately brought about its decline. What had once been a competitive sport became more of a performing art, and playing to win was no longer the vogue thing. Decent performers could make a living for themselves, and elite groups were trained up to perform for the royal courts. Professional players would commonly set up guilds in their cities and potential newcomers would pay them to be their teachers.

And so it continued through the Yuan (1279–1368) and Ming (1368–1644) dynasties, appearing, for example in a famous painting of the Yongle Emperor (1402–1424 AD) watching eunuchs playing the game. But as *cuju* was transformed from sport to circus act,

---

[6] Albeit two centuries later by Qian Xuan (1235-1305) in the Yuan Dynasty.

stickball games and particularly the version on horseback called *jiqiu* relegated it to the second division in terms of popularity. The Qing Dynasty (1644–1911) led to a major shift in Chinese culture, far removed from the ancient Han, and the game was no longer passed down the generations or even considered by some to be part of the new Chinese heritage.

Despite once being a national obsession, *cuju* faded from public consciousness, and if it was still around in the 17th and 18th centuries, we don't know anything about it.

Cuju believe it?

And that, FIFA are adamant, is the story of how football began. It is interesting to note the words of Peter Velappan, president of the Asian Football Confederation, and in attendance as Blatter gave his blessing to China as the birthplace of football. He commented at that same event that "football started in China and its future is in Asia. China has so much potential to develop football. I hope the Asian Cup will help highlight the truth that China has the most football potential in the world."

China does indeed offer amazing potential as one of soccer's few undertapped markets, and what better for FIFA than to 'officially' designate it as the cradle of the sport? Perhaps one of the reasons soccer is still underdeveloped in Asia is because the people do not see the game as part of their culture or history. So Blatter and his corporate cronies fly off to China and make a big thing of the fact that soccer is actually very much part of their culture, because they were the very folks that invented it. And they should still be playing it, and, more importantly, they should be putting lots and lots of money into it. There's nothing like a bit of manipulation of history for one's own ends. The Chinese aren't likely to say no. Hell, we invented the compass, gunpowder, paper-making and printing, and now they're saying we invented soccer too!

But FIFA propaganda aside, can we really say that China and its *cuju* was the true origin of football? Certainly, we are talking about a team ball game that bears certain semblances to it. But there are far fewer similarities to soccer than Blatter would have us believe, and even less to games like rugby, from which soccer branched.

There is very little plausible evidence that the foot-volley games played by the Chinese around the start of the second millennium travelled down the Silk Road and inspired Europe's medieval football. Europe and China knew next to nothing about each other until the time of Marco Polo's expeditions around 1260, by which time football-like games already existed in Europe[7] and it is telling that it would be another 300 years before the Europeans could craft a similar ball to the Chinese.

It's curious how *cuju*, once such a national obsession, disappeared from the Chinese sporting psyche. Some say the demise had something to do with the 19th century, when

---

[7] Some historians take a dim view of the Marco Polo thing full stop. So many elements are not mentioned in his accounts (tea, Chinese writing, the Great Wall and chopsticks, to name just four) that it is widely assumed that most of what he learned was picked up from travelling traders, and that he never set foot in China at all.

China, so powerful in Asia, found itself invaded with astonishing efficacy by British and other European forces, which provoked an alarming need for China to move with the times and develop western technology, customs and military methods. There was an overwhelming sense of shame that the Chinese were no longer at the forefront of modern thinking.

Native Chinese sports were more about displaying prowess and technique than winning or losing. For many years China struggled with its sporting identity. As western sporting ideals spread around the world, China didn't quite fit in. They lagged behind in the early years of 'modern' sport, but by the late 20th century suddenly started shooting up the Olympic medals table, epitomised by their stunning display at the 2008 Beijing Games. China is now part of mainstream sporting culture, and only now, as if the point has finally been proven, seems ready to turn back and start exploring its own sporting past. *Cuju* revivalists tour the country trying to reignite the passion for the game that got lost in history. Ren Hai, director of the Olympic Research Center in Beijing says "China is looking for a new cultural identity, a new national image. Traditional sports are part of that process … If you want to be a truly strong country you have to have your own culture. Where does that come from? It must come from history[8]."

Korea moves

As much as *cuju* was a major development in the history of sport, it is hard to claim it was the direct ancestor of football. FIFA have modified their own assertion, and its website now more cautiously calls the Chinese game "the very earliest form of the game for which there is scientific evidence." But we don't have to travel too far from China to find claims to sports that may well challenge *cuju* in the vintage stakes.

Some kind of game was played in neighbouring Mongolia, where the Buriat people were known to create balls out of bundles of rags, leather and bristles, and balls feature in children's folk tales, where losing a ball is apparently a signal of sickness or misfortune. However, Iwona Kabzinska-Stawarz made an extensive study of *Games of Mongolian Shepherds* (Warsaw 1991), which mainly involve wrestling, and came to the conclusion that "I have not met anybody who would list ball games as Mongolian national sports, although there may be some of that opinion."

The Koreans had a game called *chukguk* ('kick-a-ball') which was strikingly similar to *cuju* and Shim Seung-ku notes that one text written during the Chinese Song dynasty even noted that "the Korean people are good at kicking balls[9]." The professor writes that Kim Daemun's 8th century AD *Hwarang Segi* contains a reference that "the Kingdom's 23rd king (AD 514–540) kicked a ball with a son of his sister in the courtyard of the royal palace. It is highly likely to have referred to *chukguk* in the form of kicking a shuttlecock." These shuttlecocks

---

[8] Cited by Jason Dean in the *Wall Street Journal* (August 2008).
[9] A professor at the Korean National University in *The History and Characteristics of Korean Chuk-guk*, published in *Tradition & Today* (2002).

were made by stuffing strips of paper through a small metal ring and then fluffing them into a roundish shape.

We don't know an awful lot about *chukguk*, but we can read in *Samguk Sagi*[10] that while playing the game, the ruler of the Chilla Kingdom, Kim Yousin (AD 654–661), once got his foot tangled in his opponent's trousers and they fell down. Useful to know, although these events were being described in a text written some 500 years later.

Seung-ku concludes that "in the late 19th century when modern western football was introduced to Korea, the traditional form of kicking balls disappeared and only a kicking brass coin game survived. There were once a straw ball kicking game and a bladder ball kicking game. Kicking a paper cup, which is popular in domestic universities, is influenced by such a traditional culture of kicking balls."

Made in Japan

Kemari (also known as *kenatt*) was a similar ball game that was played in Japan around the same time as *cuju*. An expert on the matter, Yasuyoshi Oonishi, claims "it started around 1400 years ago. It was introduced into Japan from China at the same time as Buddhism[11]." However, that's just one version of the story. There are sufficient differences between China and Japan's games to make it plausible that they both had entirely different histories, while another theory claims *kemari* was imported from Korea in the 6th century and thus takes us back to *chukguk* and the sorry trouser-falling episode. It is generally assumed that *kemari* has a much shorter history, but that is simply because there is no documentary evidence to suggest otherwise. It is very possible that the game dates back even further[12].

Kemari was remarkably sedate. Oonishi explains that "before playing a game the players must have the ball blessed at the shrine. Afterwards, in the garden that is called *mariniwa*, they all take part in a ceremony called *tokimari*. A man called *Edayaku* prays for prosperity and world peace. After this they start playing." It may sound ceremonial, and Guttmann & Thompson note instances of the ball symbolising the sun, of the duality of yin and yang, and of a match played as a kind of rain dance, but it seems *kemari* was normally a secular affair.

Rather like *cuju* it has precious little in common with any modern day football codes other than the fact that the feet rather than the hands are used to propel the ball, which was called a *mari* and was about eight to ten centimetres in diameter, generally made of deer skin with the

---

[10] Or *Chronicles of the Three Kingdoms*, completed in 1115 and detailing the history of the Three Kingdoms of Korea: Goguryeo, Baekje and Silla.

[11] Speaking on *History of Football: The Beautiful Game* (Fremantle Home Entertainment, 2004).

[12] A 'recently discovered text' suggests that a game was played around 50 AD between Japanese *kemari* players and Chinese *cuju* players. Perhaps this qualifies as the first international football match, although the evidence is ambiguous at best. 'Recently discovered texts' should always be treated with caution, and this one seems to have been 'discovered' not in an ancient tomb, but an Internet blog. The tale now seems to have found its way into *kemari* folklore, but it would be nice to see it substantiated.

furry side inwards and the hide facing out, which was then stuffed with sawdust, grain or a similar material.

Like the Tang and Song games in China, it's basically keepy-uppy with remarkably simple rules, the idea being for players (called *keashi* or *mareashi*) to pass the ball to each other without it ever touching the ground, the kind of thing the Brazilians are so good at doing on Copacabana beach.

In traditional *kemari*, any number of players from two to about twelve could take part, although it could also be practiced alone. A game would start with one player tossing the ball in the air and kicking it up and down with his feet. Maybe there was a limit on the number times a single player could kick the ball (Guttmann and Thompson reckon three was the generally accepted maximum), and kicks were accompanied by different calls of "*Ooh!*", "*Ariyaaa!*" and "*Ari!*" as the players' communicated strategies. And you just keep doing that until some mug makes a mistake and the ball hits the ground, the aim simply being to keep the ball airborne for as many kicks as possible.

It was played on a pitch called a *kikutsubo* that was about 15 metres wide and had a tree planted in each corner (which strictly speaking had to be a cherry tree, a maple, a willow, and a pine). Many Japanese nobles would have these courts laid out in their yards so that they could play at any time. The trees were not merely decorative – the ball was actually kicked into them and reading the way it tumbled down the branches was one of the skills of the game.

The many 13th century paintings of *kemari* show the players kitted out in *hitatare* robes, with ridiculously baggy sleeves, and the pointed *eboshi* hat. The curious thing is that this kind of clothing had already gone well out of fashion by the time, so the *kemari* players were presumably well aware that rather than a modern day sport, they were re-enacting a tradition that was already ancient by their time.

The first solid evidence of the game dates back to 611 AD, although it was not until the Heian era (781-1180 AD) that it really started to catch on. There are even scoring records from the time of Emperor Daigo (around 900 AD), where we learn that a decent *kemari* team could hope to keep the ball up for about 50 kicks, although the best known score was 206, which would be dwarfed by later generations of *kemari* wizards, perhaps assisted by a rule that the scorekeeper could sometimes add a bonus for especially clever kicking.

In the early days, the game was only played by the ruling classes, but during the Kamakura era (1192-1333) it had spread down to the warrior classes, which was when Fujiwara Narimichi gained his status as the Patron Saint of the sport. In *Koden Nikki* (1197) this player claimed to have practised almost non-stop for two decades, and "during this time, when I was unwell, I kicked the ball while lying down … was there ever anyone who loved the game as much as I do?" He could even juggle the ball while walking along a handrail on the Kiyomizi temple's balcony, and wrote a treatise on the subject called *Sanju Kajo Shiki*.

Kemari was huge for several centuries. We are told that Shogun Minamoto no Yoriie (1182–1204) was so avid a player that he neglected his duties to such an extent that an economic depression ensued and he was ousted from his position. And in what is probably folk legend, Emperor Gotoba (1180–1239) played in a team that kept the ball up for more than 2000 kicks. The ball, which in the words of a poet claiming to have witnessed the achievement "seemed suspended, hanging in the sky," was retired from duty and awarded the rank of viscount in the Japanese court. Yes, the ball, not the players. A strange destiny indeed for an inanimate object. Gotoba's real intention was to raise the courtly status of the game, and it was he who issued regulations that the colours of the players' stockings should indicate their status and level of skill – an idea that only managed to produce bitter resentment among certain groups. The different houses quarrelled over the traditional property of *kemari*, and it would take more than three centuries before the Asukai finally won the battle to control the 'texts of transmission'. But although there is a wealth of historical anecdotes about the debates over stocking patterns and the arrangements of the trees, Guttmann and Thompson are alarmed at how little was ever written about how the game was actually played.

By the Muromachi Period (1392–1573) it was popular in the streets of the whole country and features prominently in the art and literature of the times. In 1683, there are claims that a team managed to keep the ball up for a whopping 5188 kicks. You can bet the geezer responsible for kick 5189 was unpopular that evening. The way the *kemari* community was so aware of the latest hi-scores suggests the first ever instance of a sporting world record being statistically measured.

It was still going strong in the 18th century, when over a period of 65 years, diarist Sejimo Yoshitada regularly mentions the game, including the construction of five courts in the village of Nozawa and the coaching he once received from one of the Asukai overseers.

But then, rather like *cuju*, the sport started going out of fashion. Just why is unclear, but it was probably the result of 19th century shifts towards the western modernity that Japan would so openly embrace. The Kemari Preservation Society was set up as early as 1903 by Emperor Meiji and it is played to this day in Japan, with the basic rules (not there are that many of them) still intact after well over a thousand years.

Although sumo enthusiasts might beg to differ, it is regarded by many as Japan's national sport, and it is not unusual to see three generations of people playing the game together, and keeping score is generally far less important than the pure aesthetics of the game.

Two of the most important annual meetings are what is known as 'first kick' on New Year's Day at Shimogamo Jinja Shinto in Kyoto and the Kemari Festival in November at Danzan Jinja in the ancient capital of Nara, both of which attract sizeable crowds and plenty of media interest. With *kemari* players decked out in full Asukai period gear, modern matches may be more cultural displays than true sporting contests, but it is great to see that the game still survives. And long may it prosper.

Sepak Takraw

The Chinese, Korean and Japanese games quite possibly share a common root with the footbag-like games played throughout Southeast Asia, and that have varying origins in the countries we know today as Thailand (*takraw*), the Philippines (*sipa*), Malaysia (*sepak raga*), Vietnam (*cầu mây*) and possibly Laos (*kator*), Indonesia (*raga*) and Myanmar (*chinlone*), too. There was no historically standard set of rules, and it was only in 1965 that they were all amalgamated into the modern composite code of *sepak takraw* for the sake of international play. Even its name is a combination of two of its names of origin, *sepak* meaning 'kick' in Malay and *takraw* meaning 'ball' in Thai (the two nations where the game is most popular).

It plays to similar rules as volleyball or badminton, the main difference being that the ball is only struck with the feet. And it is rapidly gaining (or perhaps better put, regaining) popularity in the region, having become part of the mainstream, with televised coverage and inclusion in the Asian Games.

The earliest evidence appears in the 14th century Malay Annals, or *Sejarah Melayu*, when an unfortunate accident during a game led to a major political reshuffle. The sultan's son, Raja Muhammad, was struck on the head by a ball delivered by the son of Tun Perak, a famous *bendahara* (minister). Having had not just his head but also his dignity hurt, Raja Muhammad's response was perhaps a little over the top. He stabbed and killed the *bendahara*'s son, and as a result of his actions would end up being banished from the sultanate.

Such a game was observed by an English expedition around 1775. "They often play at football, if so may be called a kind of spherical basket about the size of a man's head, made of split rattans. About ten or twelve persons make a ring, and toss the ball from one to another: sometimes they kick it with the foot, sometimes with the shoulder, and often with the knee, keeping it up as long as they can[13]."

Over in Thailand, the earliest accounts date back to King Naresuan (1590–1605) of Ayutthaya, where there are vague references to a game played in a circle that involved keeping the ball off the ground for as long as possible. Murals at Wat Phra Kaeo in Bangkok, built in 1785, show the Hindu god Hanuman playing what would seem to be the same game with a troop of monkeys.

The early Thai and Malay games sound very like the Chinese and Japanese games, but although the traditional game of keepy-uppy always remained a popular but informal game among the working classes, it was increasingly diluted by ideas brought to Southeast Asia by British and French colonisers. Most poignantly, there does not seem to have been any net until 1870, when it was probably added as a direct imitation of European games.

The exact origins of *sepak takraw* are still pending more detailed research, but it seems very likely that they had something to do with the other oriental ballgames. However, and for the same reasons stated about *cuju*, it would take a wild imagination to suggest that *kemari* or the

---

[13] Thomas Forrest *A voyage to New Guinea, and the Moluccas, from Balambangan* (1774-1776).

forerunners of *sepak takraw* had any connection whatsoever to our modern day varieties of football, mainly because by the time the Far East was able to influence western culture, very different forms of football had already existed for centuries in Europe.

But what these games do show us is how different cultures, however distant, tend to come up with the same kind of ideas. Why, even in Pre-Colombian America they had ball games, as we shall see in the next two chapters.

4 THE HIP PARADE
Ball games in Pre-Colombian Central and Caribbean America

Go west

Native Americans were playing ball games long before Christopher Columbus set anchor off San Salvador in 1492, and the Spaniards were the first Europeans to come into contact with what is collectively known as the 'Mesoamerican ballgame'. It has often been categorised as an early form of football, although the foot versus hands argument doesn't even come into it. They managed to get by without using either!

When the Spanish arrived in Central America, the Aztec Empire was at its height, having subdued the surrounding tribes and still expanding rapidly. But Montezuma II (1466–1520), their last ruler, would have to cope with the most unexpected twist of fates. It has been said that he saw it coming. Montezuma knew that the white skinned god Quetzalcoatl would one day return to claim his kingdom, black beard and robes and all. That man would be the Spanish conquistador Hernán Cortés, although whether there really was an ancient prophesy is questioned by many historians that believe this was 'post-conquest rationalisation' by the Aztec, who made a scapegoat of Montezuma, and unceremoniously stoned him to death for giving in so easily to the Europeans. Cortés himself apparently wept over the death, which he saw as the loss of a good man.

The Spanish conquistadores generally paid scant regard for the cultures they as good as wiped off the face of the earth, seeing them more as a source of gold to be pillaged and slaves to be subdued. Native games were almost universally deemed unhealthy pagan rituals, and even when a few more open-minded travellers did take the trouble to study the games, it does not seem that any of them stooped as low as to play them.

The conquistadores' interest was usually more focused on the amazingly bouncy substance (rubber) that the ball was made of than any of the finer details of the rules or cultural context, which they usually condemned as pagan frivolity, banning the games outright in 1595, thus driving them underground to the extent that they soon disappeared entirely from the local culture.

However, we do know that Cortés was inspired enough to bring a group of ballplayers back to Spain, where they were ordered to perform for Carlos V's royal court in Toledo in 1528, and were famously painted by German artist Cristoph Weiditz. Their amazing skills certainly raised an eyebrow or two, and so it is unlikely but certainly plausible that some of the Native American skills, rules and tactics may have been borrowed by European sports somewhere down the line, although the suggestion that they had anything to do with the development of modern day football codes is probably stretching things a bit too far.

Rubber matches

From the wide range of differences observed it seems clear that rather than one specific early form of football, there were countless variants played all around the continent and developing into new forms all the time. As different tribes and civilisations went about conquering each other, they assimilated different elements of their respective cultures, including ball games. So, rather than put the pieces of the jigsaw together and learn about one game, we are really talking about a whole family of games, which would have been as similar yet different to each other as soccer and rugby are now.

The hotbed for such games in what for the settlers was the New World is the area known as Mesoamerica, roughly coinciding with Mexico and Central America, and home to some of the most developed civilisations on the ancient continent[1]. The Olmec civilization (1400 BC–400 BC) is the first for which we have extensive historical details, and that means for ball games too. 'Olmec' itself was a word the Aztec used to describe their ancestors as the 'rubber-people', in honour of their predilection for using latex to produce anything from shoes to swaddling for babies, and what interests us most here, balls. The earliest found to date were discovered in an Olmec sacrificial bog at El Manatí, and have been dated to around 1650 BC, making them as old as any evidence there is for inhabitation of that place.

Although we know next to nothing about what the Olmec games might have entailed, football figurines found not too far away at San Lorenzo Tenochtitlán, including some of women, have been radiocarbon-dated as far back as 1250 BC. This should not be interpreted as meaning that this was either when or where the ballgame was created. It is just that any older evidence has long since been withered away to nothing by the forces of nature and human development.

Unlike their ancient footballing cousins around the world, who almost universally played ball games on improvised pitches, the Mesoamericans built huge arenas, many of which can still be visited today. They were often built close to major temples or pyramids, not unlike the way our modern day sports stadiums are attached to commercial centres. About 1400 courts have been found to date, which is a higher total than has been found either for Greek or Roman sporting arenas, and with more than half of those only having been discovered in the last twenty years or so, there could be many more where those came from. Of these, some 450 have been excavated, and many are in remarkably good shape. And these are just the arenas, but it can be assumed that the ballgame was also played on a more informal basis just like street football today.

---

[1] Here we shall focus mainly on the Olmec, Maya and Aztec but there is evidence of other cultures also playing the game, the Zapotec, for instance, who built the Dainzu pyramid in Oaxaca where fifty stone pictographs clearly show people playing a ball game, decked out in knee pads and gloves, and being watched by deities or clerics with jaguars. The Toltec, the Mixtec and Totonac all played the game too, so I can only apologise for any rash generalisations on the following pages.

The oldest ballpark is believed to be the one found in 1995 at Paso de la Amada, Chiapas, dated to around 1300 BC in the Olmec period. The arenas built by the Olmec lack the splendour of the ones that would come in later cultures, and oddly enough there is no evidence of such courts being built by the Teotihuacan culture that followed (110 BC– 600 AD), although the Tepantitla murals do show people playing ball games both with and without sticks.

It is also revealing that it was after the fall of the city of Teotihuacan that the Mesoamerican ballgame really took off, and mainly in the neighbouring and longer lived Maya civilisation (200 AD to 1200 AD), most specifically its Post-Classic Period after 900 AD, which was when games such as one known as *pokyah* (or *pok-ta-pok*) enjoyed particular popularity – and we know that because of the proliferation of ballcourts.

The most famous and impressive site is at Chichen Itza, measuring almost 100 by 30 metres, and built by the Maya around 600 AD. It is now one of Mexico's most famous tourist attractions and as essential on any Cancun holidaymaker's itinerary as tequila shots, tacos and toilet paper. Its many attractions include the amazing acoustics – a whisper at one end can be heard at the other and to this day scientists have not managed to work out how.

About 13 different types and shape of court have been found, which suggests plenty of regional, cultural and temporal differences, and sizes vary from the immense Chichen Itza to others that are as many as five times smaller. But they all share enough generic traits to imply that they were more or less the same thing. The H shaped playing area is a common factor to almost all of them, and they were usually decorated with images of Maya Gods of such essential elements of life as fire, plants and fertility.

Ball tales

Popol Vuh (the 'Book of the People') is one mighty tome. Its survival was all thanks to a Dominican priest named Francisco Ximénez (1666–1729). At a time when most conquistadores were doing their best to cover all tracks of the civilizations they were devastating, Ximénez opted to transcribe for posterity the oral traditions of the Maya Quiché kingdom in Guatemala. *Popol Vuh* does contain plenty of 'true' history, but it doesn't take an academic to realise that the older legends may take more than a few 'biblical' liberties with the truth.

Popol Vuh says its bit about the ball play of the ancients, the most revealing being the legend of the Maya hero twins, Hunahpu and Xbalanque, who were Gods from the period before they had invented humans. These two were the sons of Hun-Hunahpu, who was at odds with the lords of the underworld, the Xibalba, who seemed to take exception to being bothered by the noise his ball playing was causing. He ended up being decapitated and his head was hung from a tree, where it somehow turned into a calabash (a skull-like fruit common in Central America). As one of the daughters of the lords, Xquic, happened to be passing by the suspended gourd, out jetted a flow of sperm-juice from the fruit, and Xquic now had a little Maya bun in the oven. You were warned that separating fact from fiction wouldn't be too testing on the grey matter.

And so it was that Hunahpu and Xbalanque were born, who would go on to have many adventures and eventually stumble across their father's ball game equipment, and take up the sport themselves. Soon it was time for them to be summoned to the underworld to play ball for their father's honour against the wicked Xibalba. It's too long a story to tell in full here, but basically the Xibalba were dirty players, using a ball with a hidden blade and other such dastardly deeds, but the twins actually lost each of the games deliberately and were punished for doing so by being sent on a number of quests that wouldn't be out of place in a PlayStation game. They were despatched to the Dark House, the Razor House, the Jaguar House and then the Fire House, each time outwitting the Xibalba until their encounter with the Bat House, where Hunahpu let the side down and got decapitated by a bat. But his brother Xbalanque was no fool, and when he went into the next challenge alone, in which Hunahpu's head was to be used as a ball, he came up with the clever idea that he could use a gourd instead and thus recover Hunahpu's head and bring him back to life. Taking huge liberties with poetic licence, the plan worked, and Hunahpu was whole again!

But that was just the start of it. By now, the twins had this coming back to life thing down to a fine art, and allowed themselves to be burned alive and for their remains to be ground to dust and cast into the river. Silly Xibalba. That of course only served to regenerate the twins as catfish, and eventually humans. Impressed by this peculiar adeptness at self-reincarnation, the Lords summoned the amazing duo to perform their tricks before them.

Not only did they kill a dog and then bring it back to life, but Hunahpu willingly offered himself as a sacrifice, yet returned from the dead immediately after. The two highest lords liked that a lot, so much so that they asked if these amazing twins could do the trick on them too. They really should have seen this one coming! Yep, the highest lords dead, Hunahpu and Xbalanque revealed their true identity to the others. Ha, ha, fooled you, and no, we are not bringing those two bastards back to life! The lords begged for mercy, confessed to all their sins and promised to stop being nasty to humans from that day on. The hero twins returned to the real world, but didn't stop there, on they went up into the sky, and still look down upon us today. They are the sun and the moon, and are there to look after us and make sure those nasty Xibalba never come bothering us again.

However, much as the hero twins are forever associated to the legend of the ball game, *Popol Vuh* doesn't really tell us anything of much use in explaining how the game worked. And Alexandre Tokovinine explains how "a famed K'ekchi performance of the hero twins story celebrating the foundation of San Juan Chamelco in 1543, for instance, has not a single reference to the ball game" which suggests that *Popol Vuh* was just one telling of the tale, and the ballgame was really no more a key element of the story than Widow Twankey is to Aladdin.

He advises caution when drawing too many conclusions from the legends and engravings. "Several legends with 'strong ball game presence' are known: a version of Huitzilopochtli myth recorded by Tezozomoc; a story of Topiltzin and a *tlachtli* model as written by Ixtlilxochitl; the ball game of Quetzalcoatl versus Tezcatlipoca (when the latter turned into a 'tiger') recorded by Mendieta; the ball game between Huemac and the Tlalocs as told in the codex Chimalpopoca …What is universal for these and other ball game occurrences in Aztec sources, pictographic codices included, is that the ball game may be a 'framework' for any story involving competition, engagement, and that the ball court is a special, often magic location for it."

The argument is that the ball game was used as a plot device or background setting for legends and myths, which were then reflected in the many images found decorating the ballcourts. There is a big difference between games played by mythological beings and games played by the ordinary man in the Mesoamerican street.

Aztec cameras

The Aztec later conquered much of Mesoamerica, and seemingly inherited the ballgame from previous cultures, adapted it to their own and called it *ullamaliztli.* We again find the H-shaped court, now called a *tlatchtli,* but this may be because they simply played it on the same courts that the Maya had used for *pokyah.* However, we know more about this game than any other because it was still in vogue when the conquistadores made their unexpected appearance and changed the shape of the continent forever.

From ancient engravings, we can tell that matches involved teams of anything from 2 to 11 players, and the rubber balls measured around 20 to 30 centimetres in diameter. The basic idea was to move the ball around using some of the most bizarrely inappropriate parts of the body for the task, namely the hips, chest, shoulders, knees and/or elbows. Strange as it seems, the two most logical actions, throwing and kicking, seem to have been universally forbidden, but this was helped by the nature of the ball they used. Fray Bartolomé de las Casas, one of the most outspoken critics of the cruelty to which the Indian peoples were subjected, wrote in the 16th century of "a rubber they call *ulli* … out of which they make the balls they play with, and which bounce six times higher than our wind balls and don't stop bouncing as if they were full of mercury."

Of the few contemporary descriptions of the game in action, Franciscan missionary Bernardino de Sahagún provides one of the most useful. In his immense 12-volume project to document 'New Spain' in the late 16th century, he wrote that "at other times the lord played ball for his pastime, and for this balls of *ulli* were kept; these balls were about the size of some large balls for bowling, they were solid, of a certain resin or gum which they called *ulli*, which is very light and bounces like an inflated ball; and he also brought with him good ball players who played before him and other principal men played on the opposite team and they won gold and *chalchiguites* and beads of gold, and turquoise, and slaves, and rich mantles, and *maxtles*, and cornfields and houses, feathers, cacao, feather cloaks … the ballcourt was called *tlachtli* and consisted of two walls, twenty or thirty feet apart, and were up to forty or fifty feet in length; the walls and the floor were whitewashed, and were about eight and a half feet high, and in the middle of the court was a line which was used in the game. In the middle of the walls, in the centre of the court, were two stones, like millstones hollowed out, opposite each other, and each one had a hole wide enough to contain the ball. And the one who put the ball in it won the game; they did not play with their hands, but instead struck the ball with their buttocks; for playing, they wore gloves on their hands and a belt of leather on their buttocks, with which to strike the ball[2]."

Further information is provided by Diego Durán (1537–1588), a Dominican friar who got into all kinds of trouble for his writings on native culture and history because rather than demonise their heathen society, he seemed to think there were aspects of it that were worth admiring and even maintaining.

Durán provides by far the best description of the ballgame we have, although there is a clear suggestion in his words that by the time the conquistadores arrived, the game was already in decline. "It was a highly entertaining game and amusement for the people … Among them there were those who played it with such skill and cunning that in one hour the ball did not stop bouncing from one end to the other, without a miss, the players using only their buttocks and knees, never touching it with the hand, foot, calf, or arm. Both teams were so alert in keeping the ball bouncing that it was amazing. If watching a handball game among Spaniards gives us such pleasure and amazement on seeing the skill and lightness with which some play it, how much more are to be praised those who with such cunning, trickery, and nimbleness play it with their backsides or knees! It was considered a foul to touch the ball with the hand or any other part of the body except the parts I have mentioned – buttocks and knees…

"… Many a time have I seen this game played, and to find out why the elders still extol it I asked them to play it in the ancient way. But the most important factor was lacking, namely the enclosure where the contest took place, within which it was played, and the rings through which they cast and passed the ball. And it was a foolish insistence of mine to try to see today something which existed in ancient times, as different as the real thing from a picture. So that we can understand its form and begin to appreciate the skill and dexterity with which this game was played, it must he noted that ball courts existed in all the illustrious, civilized, and powerful cities and towns, in those ruled by either the community or the lords, the latter stressing the game inordinately. A regular competition existed between the two types of communities. The ball courts were enclosed with ornate and handsomely carved walls. The interior floor was of stucco, finely polished and decorated with figures of the god and

---

[2] Bernardino de Sahagún *La Historia General de las Cosas de Nueva España* (written between 1545 and 1590).

demons to whom the game was dedicated and whom the players held to be patrons in that sport[3]."

Durán makes it clear that rather than depictions of the games as they were played, these were images of the game in legends, and just like we should be with regard to European games, we should be wary of the usual theories that the ball may have symbolised the journeys of the sun or moon towards the underworld, and that that the game itself was a ritualistic re-enactment of the duality of the feuds between good and evil, summer and winter, day and night.

All of this typical ancient ball-sport spiel could be true, but many of these associations may also be claptrap cooked up by later theorists. Spiritual beliefs played a huge role in Mesoamerican culture, but the connotations may have been no more important to the global picture than the symbolism in modern day football club crests.

It has been suggested that the H-shaped court may have symbolised the 4 cardinal points worn by the God Quetzalcoatl, or maybe had something to do with the positioning of the stars. But Durán offers a far less cosmic explanation for choosing that shape. An illustration accompanies his text, which shows two players, each with leather wrapped around their waists and forearms, at each end of the H-shaped court, with play being conducted down the 'crossbar' of the H, which had a stone ring hung on each side. Durán explains that "the corners were built on purpose so that if the player's ball fell into one it was lost and was considered a foul."

He continues by saying that "because of heathen custom, around the wall were planted wild palms or trees which give red seeds, whose wood is soft and light. Crucifixes and carved images are made of it today. The surrounding walls were adorned with merlons or stone statues, all spaced out. These places became filled to bursting when there was a game of all the lords, when warlike activities ceased, owing to truces or other causes, thus permitting the games.

"The ball courts were anywhere between 100, 150 and 200 feet long. In the square corners (which served as ends or goals) a great number of players stood on guard to see that the ball did not penetrate. The main players stood in the centre facing the ball, and so did the opponents, since the game was carried out similarly to the way they fought in battle or in special contests…

"… In the middle of the walls of this enclosure were fixed two stones facing one another, and each had a hole in the centre. Each hole was surrounded by a carved image of the deity of the game. Its face was that of a monkey. One team put the ball through the hole of the stone on one side while the other side was used by the other team. The first to pass its ball through the hole won the prize. These stones also served as a division, for between them, on

---

[3] Diego Durán *Historia de las Indias de Nueva España e Islas de Tierra Firme* (not published until between 1867 and 1880).

the floor, was a black or green stripe. This was done with a certain herb and no other, which is a sign of pagan belief.

"The ball always had to be passed across this line to win the game, because if the ball, projected by the backsides or by the knee, went bouncing along the floor and passed the stripe the width of two fingers, no fault was committed; but if it did not pass, it was considered a foul play."

Ballpark figures

Scoring through rings, which predated the Aztec period, is not massively unlike basketball, and provides plenty of ammunition for those who dispute the idea that James Naismith's invention in 1891 was quite as new as he claimed. However, scores didn't flow quite as rapidly in the Aztec ballcourts as they do at the Staples Center.

Toribio de Benavente Motolinia wrote that "a man throwing it by hand at close range could not put it in once in one hundred tries, nor in two hundred[4]." That was by hand, but in *ullamaliztli*, of course, they had to do it from long range with their bum! Most games probably ended without the ball going through the ring at all, for when it did, this was a very rare and special occasion. Rather like catching the snitch in Harry Potter's quidditch matches, it was a kind of *deus ex machina* that rendered all other scoring meaningless, while the outcome of most games seems to have depended on a complex scoring system that has never quite been deciphered, but drawings of games in progress show people keeping score with grass leaves, green for one team and dyed black for the other.

The system was probably based on counting the number of 'fouls' a team committed, as described by Durán. These seemed to include letting the ball into your endzone or failing to get it across the line in the middle of the court. We can only have fun guessing what other rules there might have been[5].

The copious figurines provide further clues. They often wear helmets that are not unlike those that American footballers wear today, while they sometimes donned leather or rubber eye patches, so we can assume things could get pretty violent out there. Imagine a cricket ball hitting you full pelt in the face, and you'll appreciate that Mesoamerican balls were not to be messed with.

Some kind of gauntlet often appears on the hands, frequently a kind of disk with finger holes. Both De Sahagún and Durán mention these gloves, the latter explaining that "they wore gloves so as not to injure their hands when supporting themselves against the ground."

De Sahagún explained that the players wore "a belt of leather on their buttocks, with which to strike the ball" and these yoke-belts also feature prominently on the figurines. There is

---

[4] Toribio de Benavente Motolinia *Historia de los Indios de la Nueva España* (written in the 16th century but not published until 1858).
[5] Although the modern game of *ulama*, which we'll be meeting later on in this chapter, does provide a few clues.

evidence of them being made from rubber, wood, leather and even stone, which may have just been a case of individual or regional preferences and developments. In ancient Mesoamerica, producing decent ballgame yokes would have been as important as golf club and football boot technology are today. Yokes were things to be proud of, and usually bore decorations, including images of the animals that symbolised different gods.

Ullamaliztli was certainly a way of sorting the men out from the mice. It was probably a non-stop sport without time-outs or substitutions. We have no idea how long games lasted, but they must have gone on for quite a while, for Durán wrote that "some of these men were taken out dead from that place for the following reason. Tired and without having rested, they ran after the ball from end to end, seeing it descending from above, in haste and hurry to reach it first, but the ball bounced and hit them in the mouth or the stomach or the intestines, so that they fell to the floor instantly. Some died of the blow on the spot because they had been too eager to touch the ball before anyone else. Some … got their haunches so mangled that they had those places cut with a small knife to extract blood which the blows of the ball had gathered."

Such descriptions make one wonder why anybody would have wanted to go into the ballcourt out of choice. It has even been postulated that the stars of the full-on blood-and-guts matches were actually slaves and captured warriors who were forced, gladiator style, into playing for the entertainment of the ruling classes.

But if that was the case, it seems odd that there are of tales of Aztec noblemen playing ball games. The warlike imagery on some ball courts supports the suggestion that it may have often been used for duelling among leaders to settle disputes[6]. Fray Juan de Torquemada, the 16th century Spanish missionary who played a major role in prohibiting the ballgame, claiming it to be the work of the devil, was shocked that Emperor Axayacatl once played neighbouring ruler Xihuitlemoc, betting the marketplace in his capital city against one of his rival's gardens. Axayacatl lost the game, but took defeat so badly that he sent his soldiers to Xihuitlemoc's palace, under pretence of offering him a floral tribute, but in reality to have him murdered. Texcoco chief Nezahualpilli once challenged Montezuma II to a game, staking his entire kingdom of Acolhua against three of his rival's turkeys. A pretty poor bet that, but Nezahualpilli's confidence paid off. He won the game and Montezuma's public image took a severe bashing.

Fernando de Alva Cortés Ixtlilxochitl[7] notes that Topiltzin, the Toltec king, took on three rivals, and once again, it was his kingdom that was at stake.

---

[6] Some historians have even gone as far as to conclude that there is a direct ratio between the number of ballcourts and the amount of political stability in a given region, which fits with Durán's comment that it was only in peacetime that the games were played

[7] In his *Relación histórica de la nación tulteca* written between 1600 and 1608. As his name suggests, Fernando de Alva Cortés Ixtlilxochitl was part Spanish, part native, and had the sadly misguided belief that the potential market for writing about the native culture would be a way out of his dire poverty.

Headless Chichens?

But death through wounds and exhaustion was not the only way players were said to meet their fate on the Tlatchtli court, and what the game is most famous for now in *1001 Amazing Sports Facts* books is its association with sacrifices and executions.

Human sacrifices as part of public events were nothing unusual in Mesoamerica. There are images from as far back as 2000 BC that show that the Olmec were at it long before the Aztec appeared on the scene, and it was also an integral part of Maya culture. Human blood offered to the gods was considered a fair exchange for rain, fertility and several other benefits.

Important games did seem to involve some kind of human sacrifice to the gods (and in particular Huitzilopochtli, the god of war, and Amapan and Uappatzin, the patron deities of *ullamaliztli*). There are pictures like the one at Chichen Itza that shows snakes and squash plants crawling out of a dead player's body, presumably symbolising fertility, while another holds his late opponent's head aloft as if it were the Vince Lombardi Trophy.

From such evidence, it has been famously concluded that after the game, the losing captain suffered the ultimate indignity of having his bonce removed. But there is another argument that this would be completely out of keeping with the Aztec way of thinking. We are told that the Aztec felt that the ultimate honour was to celebrate victory by offering your life in tribute to the gods. This may sound decidedly odd to us but, unlike the Aztec, we are generally agreed that after death you do not have to go through a 13-stage ordeal before you can enter heaven. If being executed for leading your team to victory was a way of getting out of having to suffer that kind of purgatory, then you wouldn't have the slightest qualm with this somewhat unfair sounding clause in the rulebook.

Bodies lacking skulls have often been found around the sites of former courts, but as they were commonly situated close to temples, these may have people killed under entirely different circumstances. It has been suggested that, in fact, neither of the captains were put to the axe after the game, but merely prisoners or slaves that were not directly involved in the game at all. Sahagún wrote of an instance whereby "when the Chieftain arrived … at the *tlachtli* court … they killed two slaves in front of him, who were the images of the Gods named Amapantzitzin, and many other prisoners." Here we have two slaves being sacrificed in a ballpark, but not in any way associated to the actual game.

As Alexandre Tokovinine suggests "the human sacrifices mentioned or depicted could be in fact dedicatory, that is, associated with the ball court and its specific functions as a locus for the game (of this such a special form of sacrifice), but not with the ball game itself. The holy king would perform that sacrifice as a 'symbolic ball game' in a sequence of various dedicatory ceremonies. If this is true, was there a proper ball game sacrifice at all?" In America they get the half-time show at the Super Bowl, in the English FA Cup Final you have to make do with a marching band, while the Aztec would have been quite comfortable watching the heart being ripped out of some poor spectator and being offered to the Gods.

Bernardino de Sahagún describes a 'gladiatorial sacrifice' in which captives were armed and forced to fight on a huge circular stone. Similar to the amphitheatres of Ancient Rome, the ballparks were likely to have been multipurpose venues, and we have to be careful before assuming that the relics found in them had anything to do with the ballgame at all. There are pictures of anything from wrestlers to musicians performing in ballcourts, and whistles, ocarinas and drums have been found at Tenochtitlan.

Unfortunately, when it comes to understanding the culture of the ancient Mesoamericans, our prime source of data are the records left by the conquistadores, and these were generally anything but praiseworthy of anything they witnessed the locals doing. Instead, they took great pleasure in vilifying the barbaric, heathen and misguided nature of their savage practices and beliefs. In no small measure, this was done to justify the eradication and enslavement of the native people. The Spanish could probably have learned an awful lot from the American natives, but that was something they rarely had the slightest intention of doing, and the darker the image of these people's cultures was presented to the folk back home in Spain, the less opposition there would be to their genocide.

The stories of players having their heads chopped off as told by Mexican tour guides masquerading as university professors at historic sites are just the kind of thing to keep their customers interested and earn a few extra dollars-worth of tips, but are not necessarily to be taken too literally.

Contradicting reports suggest that winning a game in the *tlatchtli* was a far more pleasant affair. The victorious teams were entitled to help themselves to the spectators' clothes and valuables, and top players were rewarded with gifts, adulation and high ranking positions in society. Certainly Diego Durán's description is of a game that was pleasant fun for all and sundry, and everybody went home with their heads intact. "Through this demanding sport excellent players were formed, and, aside from being esteemed by the sovereigns, they were given notable dignities, were made intimates of the royal house and court, and were honoured with special insignia … the man who sent the ball through the stone ring was surrounded by all. They honoured him, sang songs of praise to him and joined him in dancing. He was given a very special reward of feathers or mantles and breech-cloths, something highly prized. But what he most prized was the honour involved; that was his great wealth. For he was honoured as a man who had vanquished many and had won a battle."

Of more concern to Durán were the less sanctimonious arts of drinking and gambling that he witnessed. Betting was rife in Aztec culture, and he notes how onlookers "gambled their homes, their fields, their corn granaries, their maguey plants. They sold their children in order to bet and even staked themselves and became slaves, to be sacrificed later if they were not ransomed."

It was there, rather than the violence, where the conquistadores' problem mainly lay, and why they vowed to see the game removed along with so many other aspects of the native culture. Something they were remarkably efficient at achieving.

Fighting for survival

Spanish colonialism was undoubtedly the cause for the demise of the Mesoamerican ballgame, and as the peoples of the New World were subdued, their sporting traditions rapidly became a thing of the past. But they never died out entirely. The traditional ball game of *ulama* is still played among the indigenous people in the Sinaloa province of Mexico today and is unquestionably a direct descendant. Its name is surely a derivative of the Aztec *ullamaliztli*, and the name of the court, *taste*, surely comes from the Aztec *tlachtli*. And, let's face it, how many other ballgames are there in this world where players are limited to only using their hips and buttocks?

Folk researching the ancient Mesoamerican ballgames share a fascination for *ulama*, as it provides some of the few clues as to what the original games might have entailed, even though it has surely been modified quite a bit since its pre-Colombian days.

Modern *ulama* is played on a variable sized court of about 50m in length and 4m wide, with a dividing line in the middle. Local rules vary, but it is usually played three-a-side and the general idea is to hit the ball to and fro using only the hips, with points being won and lost for a complex variety of different reasons. These include failing to hit the ball back, knocking it out of bounds, allowing it to stop moving, or touching it with the wrong part of the body. So, although the game is usually won by the first team to score eight *rayas* (stripes), games can actually go on for hours due to points not only being won, but deducted too.

There's no contact in this sport. In fact, players are penalised for touching their team-mates, although if you ever get the chance to try thumping 4kg of flying rubber with your hip, you will soon realise that this is no game for cissies. The players' bodies have the bruises to prove it. Also, and perhaps reminiscent of the ancient games, although the hip-based version of *ulama* (*ulama de cadera*) is by far the most common, there are other popular variants. Female players most commonly play a version using a smaller ball in which the forearm is used to propel the ball (*ulama de brazo*), while there is also a form of the game played using a wooden bat or mace (*ulama de palo* or *de mazo*).

Sadly, and like so many traditional games, *ulama* went out of fashion in the last century, when most Mexican sportspeople turned their attention to soccer, baseball and other imported games. If it weren't for a handful of hardcore players in Sinaloa, it would probably have disappeared entirely.

But there is another reason: balls. *Ulama* is such a minority activity that there is absolutely no commercial sense in marketing the rubber orbs used to play it. You want an *ulama* ball, you make it yourself, and in Sinaloa that is not the easiest of things to do, and that's not just because of the complex process of boiling and vulcanising rubber sap. To clear land for modern developments, rubber trees in the region have been all but polished off, and the nearest place to find the stuff is the increasingly drug-baron controlled Durango province, which is several hundred miles away. The upshot of it all is that an *ulama* ball will set you back something in the region of $1,000, and that's more than the typical Sinaloan's annual salary. No wonder so many stick to soccer.

At first the situation sounds ridiculous. Surely they don't need to be such perfectionists? If they can't get natural rubber, surely some kind of artificial substitute, latex say, could be just as good, or failing that, a soccer ball? Not so. Mazatlán businessman Jesús Gómez has tried all that, and none of his experiments have produced the right results, although he is still optimistic that one day he will come up trumps and find a rubber substitute that works for *ulama*. Speaking in 2006, he said "if we can't get natural rubber, we need to find another way. Otherwise, *ulama* will not survive. It's that simple[8]."

But the University of Zurich and California State University, together with the Mazatlan Historic Society, may have come to the rescue of Gómez and his beloved game. With their help, a number of rubber balls have been produced and distributed to the many *ulama* playing communities of Sinaloa. In the town of Los Llanitos, one of the hotbeds of the game, there are now more than twenty children, some as young as six years old, playing *ulama*. If all goes to plan, and in keeping with the recent craze in so many far-flung corners of the world to use long-lost sports as a vindication of national or indigenous identity, a major revival may be upon us in a Mexico that is keener than ever to reassert its pre-colonial past.

The next step for *ulama* could be the wider institutionalisation of the game, but the purists would rather that was not be left in the hands of the entrepreneurs on the Mexican coasts who would love to dress the players up in ancient costumes, face paints, drums and all, and get them performing for the tourists. The response from the *ulama* community has been a resounding 'no'. Much as it would offer the opportunity to push the game into the public eye, they don't want it to descend into some kind of exploitative Disney-esque display of questionable historic veracity. Admirably, they much prefer to play a real and modern sport than to re-enact an ancient ritual.

Whether *ulama* can survive is something that only time can tell. But it is pleasantly reassuring to know that somewhere in Mexico the long-lost ballgames of the Mesoamericans have managed to survive to this day.

Going batey

Although the ballgame is generally associated to the Mesoamerican region, for that is where the vast majority of the surviving evidence of it can be found, khaki clad archaeologists have dug up enough clues over the years to show that that the game was far more widespread than we were originally led to believe. In fact, the ancient games played as far north as Arizona by the Hohokam Indians, and as far south as Venezuela by the Otomaco were probably all part of the same family.

One non-Mesoamerican region where the ballgame certainly thrived was the Caribbean, where something very similar featured among the Taíno, the indigenous inhabitants of the

---

[8] To John Fox for *Students of the Game* which appeared in *Smithsonian Institute Magazine* in April 2006.

Bahamas, Greater Antilles, and some of the Lesser Antilles, whose society was as good as wiped out by the arrival of the Spaniards. If the European diseases didn't get them first, the Taíno were rounded up for use as slaves in the plantation economy along with scores of others shipped in from Africa. The Spanish settlers were never big on bringing women with them to the New World, but the Taíno ladies made for far more exotic alternatives, and the ensuing mestizo population further diluted what little remained of the local culture. One thing that the Spanish settlers showed negligible interest in was a ballgame the islanders played, and which would very soon be becoming a thing of the past.

Thankfully not all of the new arrivals were quite so impressed by the holocaust of the native civilisation. Somebody who took a profound interest in the rights of the newly discovered people was 16th century Dominican priest Bartolome de Las Casas[9].

Las Casas was at loggerheads with the renowned historian of the time, Gonzalo Fernandes de Oviedo (1478–1557), whose *General History of the Indies* of 1535 he described as "containing almost as many lies as pages." While Las Casas was making an admirable effort to do something to save the natives from genocide, Oviedo went to great pains to depict the heroic exploits of the Spanish settlers in these heathen lands. But, for better or worse, it is mainly thanks to the accounts provided by these two men that we know anything at all about the games played by the Taíno people.

That information has now been complemented by the discovery of several ball courts in the Antilles, the most fascinating of which are in Ponce, Puerto Rico. Discovered in 1975, the ruins have been dated back to AD 25, and no fewer than nine ballparks have been found in the area ranging from 12 to 35 metres in length.

The game's existence has been cited as definite evidence of contact between the ancient Mesoamerican and Taíno civilisations. After all, the Taíno called their game *batey* (which is what the courts were called) or *batu* (which was the ball), the same name ethnographer Ralph Beals observed that the Acaxee tribe of western Mexico, where modern *ulama* is played today, used to describe a ballgame played in "a small plaza, very flat, with walls at the sides[10]."

As was the case with his peers in modern-day Mexico, most of Oviedo's fascination with *batey* relates to the amazing bouncy substance called rubber that the balls were made out of. Yet he does take the time to also provide us with a few general outlines as to what the game itself entailed.

The courts were usually paved areas in the centres of villages. The ones found in the Caribbean are generally U shaped or triangular, often decorated extensively with petroglyphs (carved standing stones) depicting geometric designs and images of humans and animals,

---

[9] His *Short Account of the Destruction of the Indies* (1542) is a vivid description of the cruel atrocities he witnessed.

[10] Ralph J Beals *The Acaxe, A Mountain Tribe of Durango and Sinaloa* (University of California Press, Berkeley, 1933).

which have been interpreted as revealing the symbolic nature of the game, but may just have been put there because they looked nice.

It was a team game, played by anything from around ten to thirty players, and judging by the layout of the courts, there was a predilection for playing the game between west and east, which does suggest some kind of solar symbolism. The Taíno apparently also played games between fathers and sons, and had no qualms about mixed-gender games, while there was also a curious tradition of match-ups between teams of married women against the virgins. The only difference seems to be that the ladies wore a shawl around their bodies, while the men were considerably less shy about the affair, and played in their birthday suits. Although the nonchalant extermination and forced labour of the Taíno barely raised an eyebrow among Oviedo and his cronies, such nudity, female athletics and, even worse, the gambling and other debauchery surrounding this sport were very worthy of condemnation.

Las Casas describes how "one team served the ball and the other team returned it, using anything but the hands. If the ball arrived at shoulder height, it was returned like lightning. When it came in near the ground, the player rapidly hit the ground, striking the ball with his buttocks. Play continued from side to side until an error was made." Although Las Casas says nothing about it, one assumes kicking was illegal too. In fact, it is extraordinarily similar to modern-day *ulama*, with the ball being knocked back and forth and teams gaining points whenever the opposition failed to return the ball, knocked it out of bounds (marked by stone boundaries) or the ball stopped dead. Also like *ulama*, the idea of the game was to score a predetermined number of points.

Stone elbow and neck collars have been found at the sites of ancient courts in Puerto Rico, where relics of the game are particularly rife. These are often ornately decorated, with owls and bats figuring prominently, which rather ominously were the Taíno symbols of death. These collars may have been used to strike the ball in similar fashion to the Mesoamericans, but they are sporting garments of such inappropriateness that it is tempting to believe they were only worn for ceremonial purposes.

Las Casas described how "on this island what I could understand was that their songs which they call *areytos* were their history passed from person to person, fathers to sons from the present to the future, as here uniting many Indians … passing three or four hours or more until the teacher or guide of the dance finished the history, and sometimes they went from one day to the next." The *areytos* was a major festive period that shows that the Greeks may not have had such an original idea with their Olympics, for it was at this event that different communities would come together not only to exchange the aforementioned tales, songs and dances, but also to indulge in a bit of political diplomacy, and then play each other at sports. And as was common throughout North America, the ballgame may have been used as a non-aggressive way of settling disputes between different chiefdoms. We know that mock battles were also held during the *areytos*, which may have been related to a similar idea, or were perhaps something akin to Roman gladiator fights.

The Taíno civilisation was all but wiped off the map by the Spanish conquest, but particularly over the last fifty years or so it has witnessed a revival, especially in Puerto Rico, where a recent study makes the rather broad claim that 61% of the population has Taíno DNA. This all comes as part of the wider resurgence of indigenous self-identification in the Caribbean as a backlash against what are considered Europe-imposed nationalities. And as the modern-day Taíno do all they can to resuscitate the lost elements of their heritage, the ancient sport of *batey*, which has not been played for centuries, is undergoing a long-awaited comeback in Puerto Rico and the Dominican Republic. When the United Confederation of Taíno People (UCTP) was established in 1998, it immediately stated that one of its aims was to get people playing the ancient game once more. It was the driving force behind the establishment of the First Annual Caribbean International Batu Games, which were held in Borikén (Puerto Rico) in July 2007 "to return the game's focus to its original intention as a unifying ceremonial force, which will promote our culture in a meaningful and respectful way."

The next step might be for the *ulama* and *batey* revivalists to realise that they are both on a very similar mission and to join forces. There is certainly plenty of leeway for some kind of composite rules to be developed, and from there on, the future is suddenly starting to look very bright indeed for the hip-based ball games that were so very nearly condemned to dust.

But although the Mesoamerican ballgame and to a lesser extent its Caribbean cousin have tended to get all the limelight, this was by no means the only early form of ball play going on in the Americas before the Europeans landed and brought the indigenous civilisation to ruin. Further north in the Americas we find another family of ancient ball sports, and a modern-day adaptation is alive and kicking in the 21st century.

5 LITTLE BROTHERS OF WAR
Ball games in Pre-Colombian North America

Indian file

The Mesoamerican ballgame is perhaps the best known of the Pre-Columbian sports, but it was anything but the only one. Further north, in what are now the USA and Canada, the natives had their own ball games in which they used their hands, feet and sticks in ways far more similar to modern day football than any game we know the Maya or Aztec ever played.

Trying to describe those games in a few simple words is no easy matter, in much the same way as it is a huge misconception to simply bundle all of the people of North America together as Indians[1]. North America had, and still has, a complex patchwork of native nations, with vast differences in terms of appearance, language and culture. Ethnographers commonly classify the natives of the USA and Canada into ten general groups, although within these there are numerous other nations and tribes. From the Inuit and Aleut in the Arctic, to the Algonquian, Mohican, Massachusett and Micmac in the northeast woodlands, the Sioux, Apache and Cheyenne of the Great Plains, the Cherokee, Choctaw and Creek of the southeast, the Chinook and Kalapuya of the northwest and the Apache and Mohave of the southwest to name but a few, there are as many differences between Indian nations as there are between the people of Britain, Russia, Turkey and Spain.

There was never such a thing as the 'Native American ballgame', but rather a miscellany of different games indulged in by different people in different places, which often shared characteristics and traditions with those played elsewhere, but just as often did not.

Having warned against generalisations, we shall now make one. While bygone Mesoamerican civilisations have left us all kinds of evidence of majestic ballcourts and ornate figurines, there are far fewer physical remains of the games played further north, where people were more inclined towards games in the big, wild open. Little physical

---

[1] Native Americans are not Indians. That is a term that takes us back to Christopher Columbus, who never did find out that he had discovered a new continent, but believed until the day he died in 1506 that he had 'merely' found a new shipping route to the East Indies that avoided the inconvenient trek around Africa or through the not always over-welcoming Ottoman territories. Nevertheless, calling a Native American an Indian is not, generally speaking, considered derogatory, and in fact, a 1995 US Census Bureau survey revealed that most indigenous people in the USA actually preferred being called an American Indian than a Native American. The main problem with the term 'Indian' is that is factually wrong and particularly confusing when you add Indian Americans to the mix, i.e. Americans that come from the real India, the one Columbus *thought* he had discovered. Although Original Americans, First Nations, Aborigines, Indigenous Peoples, Amerindians and other suggestions have been up for discussion (and Redskins sent way off the PC scale), there is no blanket term that everybody is comfortable with. We'll go for Native Americans here, and make our apologies now for any offence caused, but we have to call them something!

evidence remains, but thankfully some colonists saw the natives as something more than savages to be quashed as they moved west in search of potential *lebensraum*, and took the time to write about their culture and traditions.

Seldom quarrelling

And those included a ball game tradition to rival anything Europe had at the time. "Foot racing, swimming and archery may have rivalled ball games in breadth of participation, but none compared in terms of group interest" writes Joseph B Oxendine[2].

In some form or other, there is evidence of native ball games being played in just about every corner of the continent, but the ones that most resemble modern-day football were those played by the different peoples that are grouped together as the Algonquian. They dominated a huge area stretching from New England on the East Coast, as far west as Michigan and Wisconsin, and as far south as Kentucky, and at least a dozen of these tribes, including the Lenape, Micmac, Abenaki, Wolastoqiyik, Massachusett and Narragansett played the sport.

The earliest written reference to it has often been misinterpreted as meaning that the early settlers played football in Jamestown, Virginia in 1609. They may well have done, but the source of this was the experiences of Henry Spelman, an English teenager who was sent to spend two years with the Lenape Indians and learn about their language and way of life. He made no insinuation in his *Relation of Virginia* (1609) that the European settlers actually played the game with the natives when he wrote "when they meet at feasts or otherwise, they use sports much like to ours here in England, as their dancing, which is like our Derbyshire hornpipe … They make their goals as ours, only they never fight nor pull one another down. The men play with a little ball, letting it fall out of their hand, and striketh it with the top of his foot. And he that can strike the ball furthest wins that they play for."

William Strachey is another of the primary sources for information on early Virginia. He is best remembered for being one of the survivors of the shipwrecked Sea Venture off the coast of Bermuda, and his account was said to have inspired Shakespeare's *The Tempest*. His classic *Historie of Travaile Into Virginia Britannia* (1612) provides pages and pages of invaluable observations of every detail of the native peoples he encountered, and he too was impressed by their organised sports. He writes that "they have the exercise of footeball, in which yet they only forcibly encounter with the foote to carry the ball the one from the other, and spyrne yt to the goale with a kynde of dexterity and swift footmanshippe, which is the honour of yt; but they never strike up one another's heeles, as we doe, not accompting that praiseworthy to purchase a goale by such advantage."

---

[2] Oxendine is a member of the Lumbee tribe of North Carolina, and was writing here in his *American Indian Sports Heritage* (1995).

Not long after, Roger Williams, the theologian who founded the colony of Rhode Island and who was also a staunch supporter of Native American rights, famously described the delightfully unpronounceable *pasuckuakohowog* (meaning 'they gather to play with the foot') as "great meetings of foot-balle playing, only in summer, town against town, upon some broad sandy shore, free from stone, or upon some soft heathie plot, because of their naked feet, at which they have great stakings, but seldom quarrel[3]."

In 1634, William Wood's *New England's Prospect* also mentioned enormous pitches on the beach in a game played by the Massachusett. He wrote that "their goals be a mile long, placed on the sands, which are even as a board; their ball is no bigger than a hand-ball, which sometimes they mount in the air with their naked feet, sometimes it is swayed by the multitude, sometimes also it is two days before they get a goal; then they mark the ground they win and begin there the next day."

He too was fascinated by the gentlemanliness of it all, whereby "in sports of activity at football (though they play never so fiercely to outward appearance, yet angrier boiling blood never streams in their cooler veins), if any man be thrown he laughs at his foil, there is no seeking of revenge, no quarrelling, no bloody noses, scratched faces, black eyes, broken shins, no bruised members, or bruised ribs, the lamentable effects of rage; but the goal being won, the goods on the other side lost; friends they were at football."

That's four quotes so far, and all of the observers were surprised at how jovial and good-spirited it all was. So why all these websites describing Native American football as an extremely violent practice in which there were injuries and often deaths? In which the players were heavily disguised in war costumes, making it impossible after the game to tell who had committed what unsavoury act out on the field, and therefore meaning there were few recriminations despite the bloodshed?

That idea probably comes from William Wood's 1634 musings, where we have just seen that he was actually amazed at the tameness of it all. His misinterpreted words were: "before they come to this sport they paint themselves, even as when they go to war, in policy to prevent future mischief, because no man should know him that moved his patience or accidentally hurt his person, taking away the occasion of studying revenge." 'Accidentally' is the key word here. Rather than suggesting there was any deliberate violence, Wood was implying quite the opposite. But perhaps he's also showing some ignorance of his own, for Eisen and Wiggins accuse him of typical Puritan "impromptu interpretations of their neighbor's customs. The painting of the face and body, in fact, had religious overtones; the game itself carried religious, magical and medicinal significance in Indian cultures."

Wood also sets something of a precedent when he was unimpressed with these fancy-dan Johnny foreigners that didn't like it up 'em. It is plain that he didn't see much of a future for European soccer scouts in the Americas. "It is most delightful to see them play in smaller

---

[3] Roger Williams *A Key into the Language of America. An help to the Language of the Natives in that part of America called New England* (1643).

companies, when men may view their swift footmanship, their curious tossings of their ball, their flouncing into the water, their lubberlike wrestling, having no cunning at all in that kind, one English being able to beat ten Indians at football."

The contemporary evidence doesn't dwell on the violence of the game. William Bartram said that "football is likewise a favorite, manly diversion with them. Feasting and dancing in the square at evening aids their games[4]." Reverend George Patterson describes the Micmac game of *wolchamaadijik* in which the ball was "knocked along on the ground. Did they not wrestle? I enquired of my friend Peter. Oh no, was the reply. Wrestling is apt to lead to a quarrel, and they would not, under the circumstances, run any risk on that score[5]." It all seems like harmless fun.

Stansbury Hagar does mention how in another Micmac game called *tooadijik* "in more recent times a player may catch his opponent by the neck and thus hold him back until he can obtain the ball himself, but scalping was anciently employed as a means of disposing of an opponent[6]" and over in California, JW Hudson tells how in the Nishinam game of *pasko* "rough play was the rule, as a player is allowed to run with the ball in his hands and interference is possible[7]" but that's about as 'bad' as it gets, and hardly sounds like mortal combat.

Just for kicks

Down in Central America they may have been making their balls out of rubber, but there is very little evidence of that in the North. The simplest solution was a suitable rock, while others carved balls out of wood or bone, or used animal hides stuffed with whatever materials the local environment could provide. Like in Britain, there were kicking and carrying codes. JW Hudson mentions the *tanasukwitokoin* of the Shoshonean that "is played with one ball, 7 inches in diameter, which is dropped in the center of the field and kicked or carried in almost the same manner as modern football. The goals are pairs of upright poles, 5 feet between and 400 yards apart."

He also tells us about the Paiute of Nevada, who had a ball "called *wutsimo* and used in a football game by men, say, four on a side. The object is to kick the ball between two goals, *tubi*, made of willow sticks, and some 8 or 10 feet high" and also the Topinagugim game in which "no interference or handling of the ball is allowed." Meanwhile, in Hagar's *tooadijik* "the goals were of two sticks placed slantingly across each other like the poles of the traditional wigwam … and the object of the game was to kick it between the goal posts."

---

[4] Describing a Cherokee game in his *Travels through North and South Carolina, Georgia, East and West Florida, the Cherokee Country, etc* (1791).
[5] In his *History of the County of Pictou* (1877).
[6] In *Micmac Customs and Traditions* published in *The American Anthropologist* (1895).
[7] Cited in Stewart Culin's astoundingly comprehensive *Games of the North American Indians* (1907), and probably the finest in-depth study ever made of the subject.

But while European football was generally the domain of the male of the species, North American football was unusual in that the ladies often played just as big a part. In the Topinagugim game of *umta*, JW Hudson said "the men are stationed in a line on one side and the women on the other … At a word, a man casts down the ball and each side tries to secure it. The women must advance the ball with their hands, or with a handled basket, *amata*, while the men can kick only, and must not throw or touch the ball with their hands, nor can they interfere with their hands. The women are very expert and throw the ball long distances."

Henry Spelman reckoned the Lenape 'football play' was one "which women and young boys do much play at, the men never," but one of the leading scholars of Lenape history, the late Nora Thompson Dean[8], argues that *pahsaheman* was played by men against women. She told of how an oblong shaped ball was made from deerskin stuffed with fur for play on what was essentially a rustic soccer field. Here again, concessions were made to the ladies. While the men's team was not allowed to move with the ball, and could only kick it either at goal or to an opponent, the women were free to run with it, and throw it about as much as they liked. Also, the women were allowed to tackle rugby-style at will, but the men could only block the ladies with their bodies or attempt to knock the ball out of their hands.

The men had it difficult already, but there are accounts that if, even with all that against them, they were still on top, one man would be elected to join the women's team. And when needing a timely goal, the women had a neat trick of handing the ball to an elderly lady who the men would never dream of tackling, and the crinkly dame would hobble through to score unchallenged.

But although some of the Native sports resembled football, others applied the same basic notions to very different games. In a Micmac game described by Reverend George Patterson in 1877, "a pole is raised at the edge of a void space, some three hundred yards across. The parties arrange themselves four or five on each side. The ball is thrown into the air, and all hands dart toward it to catch it. He who succeeds in catching it before it strikes the ground darts away to the pole, all on the opposite side pursuing him, and if they can catch him before he reaches the pole, his party loses … the excitement is kept up amid shouts and bursts of laughter, until the game is finished[9]."

This is similar to a Winnebago pastime where a ball was kicked up and "as it falls they kick it back again, so as to send it up as much as possible without letting it hit the ground[10]." That is hacky-sack or keepy-uppy, which in Winnebago eyes, was a game for girls to play.

But if it's ball-kicking you want, then it doesn't come much better than what such south-western tribes as the Mandan, Zuni, Pima and Hopi got up to, which was something more akin to 'football races' than football matches.

---

[8] In an account given to the Lenape Land Association in Pennsylvania (1971).
[9] Rev George Patterson *A History of the County of Pictou, Nova Scotia* (Pictou Advocate, 1877).
[10] Louis Meeker *Siouan Mythological Tales* (Journal of American Folklore, 1901).

From the 18th century onwards, several American ethnographers describe these races, which all had their individual quirks, but generally involved racing while kicking a small, hard ball (or similarly foot-propellable object) over courses of varying lengths. It is believed to be one of these balls that is currently on display at the Smithsonian Institute in Washington DC.

A very basic example is that of the Chukchansi of Fresno County, California, in which JW Hudson informs us that "two or more men play on a side, using a stone ball, *shelel olol*. At a signal each captain kicks his respective ball forward to his partners, who forward it in the same manner to a goal line 400 yards distant. The one whose ball is first over the line wins."

Using a ball that could be kicked much further, these races were run over considerable distances, becoming major endurance tests, especially when played barefoot through rocks and prickly vegetation. In Mexico, the Tarahumara are still running ball races today, where their incredible feats of stamina constantly leave the athletics world in awe. They say the art descended from their ancient practice of hunting by running after their prey until it collapsed with exhaustion and what they call *rajalipame* once reportedly involved kicking balls over distances of up to 100 miles! Norwegian explorer Carl Lumholz, who considered the Tarahumara "many times better off, morally, mentally, and economically, than his civilised brother," described how "a peculiar feature is that the men toss along a small ball as they run, each party having one of their own. These balls are about two and a half inches in diameter and carved from the root of the oak. The foremost runner kicks it with the toes of his right foot, so as to make it bound along as far as 100 yards, and he and all the men behind him follow in the same trot as before. The first man reaching it again kicks it onward. It must never be touched by the hand, unless it happens to fall in some awkward place, as between stones or in a water-pool, when it is picked up and kicked on[11]."

Not surprisingly, westerners took an interest in testing the Tarahumara against 'mainstream' distance athletes. But although there have been success stories, there have been cultural boundaries to cross. Tarahumara running is more about endurance than speed. Peter Nabrakov writes how several Tarahumara were persuaded to overcome their fears of 'a river that takes seven moons to cross' and represent Mexico at the 1928 Olympics in Amsterdam. Unfortunately "no one made it clear to them that marathons were only 26 miles, 385 yards long. Minutes behind the frontrunners, the Tarahumara crossed the finish line and continued running until halted by officials. 'Too short, too short' they complained[12]."

For an original take on the football theme, there are few as impressive as the Iroquois game of fireball, and considering its spectacular nature, it's surprising there have not been more attempts to reignite the passion like they do at the Tuscarora Indian Reservation in Niagara County, where a game is played as an annual 'ritual'. Essentially it is football played on a

---

[11] Carl Lumholtz *Unknown Mexico - A Record of Five Years' Exploration Among the Tribes of the Western Sierra Madre; In the Tierra Caliente of Tepic and Jalisco; and Among the Tarascos of Michoacán* (Macmillan and Co Ltd, 1902).

[12] Peter Nabrakov *Indian Running: Native American History and Tradition* (Ancient City Press, 1987).

field with goals at either end, where the ball can be held, although understandably enough, it is far more common practice to kick the thing. And that's because, as its name implies, the ball is set on fire!

The ball is soaked in any kind of flammable fluid (we are informed that melted fat was used before more modern liquids like oil and kerosene appeared) and then teams battle to score as many goals as they can before the flames die out, which is usually after twenty minutes or so. It is quite some sight, being played by night in total darkness other than the torches around the goalposts.

But we might have to tread carefully here, and not just because of the risk of getting razed. Although the Iroquois elders claim the game has been a tradition longer than anyone can remember and the Tuscarora game in 2010 was advertised as the 165th, while fireball was described in 1896[13], it is still doubtful whether it really was a pre-Colombian ancient game.

The same could be said of something played down in Mexico, and particularly in the state of Michoacán, called *uarhujkua* or 'burning ball'. The claim is that it originated from a ceremony in honour of the sun, and it is now played by hitting the ball hockey-style with sticks. But the Chinese might have something even older still. In this case its *beikou*, a form of field hockey played among the Daur people of the Inner Mongolia region, who number little more than 100,000, yet on the basis of their local passion supplied a third of the Chinese men's field hockey team at the 2008 Olympics. Their local game has apparently been around for 1000 years or more, and there is an alternative variant played at night, when the ball is covered in felt and set alight.

Play ball, not war

So, football was a reasonably innocent game amongst most Native American tribes, and often more appropriate for the children's playground and not even considered particularly masculine. But when sticks were used, the whole thing turned nastier. There were many variants of such games, and it is impossible to do justice to all of them and their unpronounceable names here, but for starters there were the Mohawk *tewaarathon* ('little brother of war'), the Choctaw *toli* ('stick ball'), the Cherokee *danahwahuwsdi* ('little war'), the Iroquois *baggataway* ('bump hips') and the Onondaga *guhjeegwahai* ('men hit a rounded object').

Stewart Culin notes that having two erect posts at either end of a field was probably the most widespread method for goalposts, but others, such as the Miami, Chinook and Chippewa used single goals that both teams played towards. The Muskogee aimed for a square mat on the ground, and others just went for a simple tree or rock.

The settlers wrote plentiful accounts of something so impressive that it couldn't possibly be ignored. We'll begin with James Mooney, who explained that "the Indian game of the ball play is common to all the tribes from Maine to California, and from the sunlit waters of the

---

[13] William M Beauchamp *Iroquois Games* (Journal of American Folk-Lore, IX, 1896).

Gulf of Mexico to the frozen shores of Hudson Bay. When or where the Indian first obtained the game it is not our province to inquire, but we may safely assume that he shaped the pliant hickory staff with his knife and flint and twisted the net of bear sinew ages before visions of a western world began to float through the brain of the Italian dreamer.

"In its general features, Indian ball play was the same all over the country, with this important exception, that among the northern and western tribes the player used but one ball stick, while in the Gulf States each contestant carried two and caught the ball between them. In California men and women played together, while among most of the more warlike tribes to the eastward it was pre-eminently a manly game, and it was believed to insure defeat to a party if a woman even so much as touched a ball stick[14]."

Albert James Pickett provides a cracking description of how it was played by the Creek of Mississippi. "It was the most exciting and interesting game imaginable, and was the admiration of all the curious and learned travellers who witnessed it. The warriors of one town challenged those of another … The players were all nearly naked, wearing only a piece of cloth called 'flap'. They advanced towards the immense plain upon which they were presently to exhibit astonishing feats of strength and agility. From eighty to a hundred men were usually on a side … In the centre were erected two poles, between which the ball must pass to count one. Every warrior was provided with two rackets or hurls, of singular construction, resembling a ladle or hoop-net with handles nearly three feet long … The play was commenced by a ball, covered with buckskin, being thrown in the air … They seized hold of each other's limbs and hair, tumbled each other over, first trampled upon those that were down, and did every thing to obtain the ball, and afterwards to make him who had it drop it before he could make a successful throw … It was kept up for hours, and during the time the players used the greatest exertions, exhibited the most infatuated devotion to their side, were often severely hurt, and sometimes killed in the rough and unfeeling scramble which prevailed[15]."

This game is still played today by the Creek, and although the violence has been almost completely eliminated, it is essentially the same game that Pickett witnessed way back in 1851.

Injuries, maiming and even death were common features in the stickball games of many Indian nations. Specifically describing the Cherokee game of *anetsâ*, Mooney says "it is a very exciting game as well as a very rough one, and in its general features is a combination of base ball, football, and the old-fashioned shinny. Almost everything short of murder is allowable in the game, and both parties sometimes go into the contest with the deliberate purpose of crippling or otherwise disabling the best players on the opposing side. Serious accidents are common. In the last game which I witnessed one man was seized around the

---

[14] James Mooney *The Cherokee Ball Play* (American Anthropologist vol. iii, 1890).
[15] Albert James Pickett *History of Alabama: and incidentally of Georgia and Mississippi, from the earliest period* (1851).

waist by a powerfully built adversary, raised up in the air and hurled down upon the ground with such force as to break his collar-bone. His friends pulled him out to one side and the game went on."

Along similar lines, Culin cites George Starr, who saw a Choctaw game where "in wrestling, the players seize each other by the belts, dropping the ball sticks. With the exception of the prohibited butting, almost everything is permitted. At the present game five men were crippled, of whom two died."

The 'Little Brother of War' name came about because the sport was often used to settle disputes between tribes, an only slightly less harm-inflicting alternative to full-on warfare. Violent as it is, it actually suggests quite a civilised approach to deciding feuds. Rather than going into battle, they did something that was a very accurate simulation of it, and although the game was bitterly savage, if there was any body count at all, it was far lower that it would have been in the case of open warfare. Mooney provides one example whereby "there is a tradition among the few old traders still living in upper Georgia, to the effect that a large tract in this part of the state was won by the Cherokee from the Creeks in a ball play. There are no Cherokee now living in Georgia to substantiate the story, but I am inclined to put some faith in it." Maybe we should learn from that and use it as the solution to all the world's modern day conflicts. Lay down our weapons, and just play ball instead. That said, maybe not, or Australia and Brazil would conquer the world in a week.

Great as it was as an alternative for war, in 1763 we come across a priceless example of the game being used as a military tactic by the Chippewa to defy the European settlers at the fort of Michilimackinac (in modern day Michigan). Alexander Henry explains how, seeing as their siege of the fort was not going as well as they had planned, the natives seemingly gave up on their efforts and started playing *baggataway* instead. But this was just a decoy. The white settlers were so intrigued by the game that they left the fort to get a closer look, not realising that a second group of Chippewa had sneaked off round the back and captured the undefended fort while the Europeans were all gawping at the ball game[16].

The earliest, and finest, pictorial record of the game comes in the form of *The Indian Ball-Play* by George Catlin (now at the Smithsonian American Art Museum) that shows the Choctaw of Oklahoma in the late 1840s. What looks like an Indian battle scene features huge rugby-like goalposts, teams that must have a good hundred players each, and crowds watching from the sidelines. Speaking on his inspiration to paint the piece, Catlin once said

---

[16] Alexander Henry *Travels and Adventures in Canada and the Indian Territories between the Years 1760 and 1776.* But it was a suspiciously similar story to one described in the same part of the world by Anne Grant in her *Memoirs of an American Lady* (1836), whereby "there was at length a day fixed, on which a great match at foot-ball was to be decided between two parties of Indians, and all the garrison were invited to be spectators. It was to be played on the esplanade opposite to the fort. At a given signal the ball was to be driven over the wall of the fort … The Indians were to run hastily in, on pretence of recovering the ball, and shut the gate against the soldiers, whom Pondiac and his people were to tomahawk immediately."

the game was "a school for the painter or sculptor, equal to any of those which ever inspired the hand of the artist in the Olympian Games or the Roman forum."

A picture may tell a thousand words, but words are always handy too, and Catlin wrote that "in these desperate struggles for the ball … there are rapid successions of feats, and of incidents that astonish and amuse far beyond the conception of anyone who has not had the singular good luck to witness them … every mode is used that can be devised to oppose the progress of the foremost, who is likely to get the ball, and these obstructions often meet desperate individual resistance, which terminates in a violent scuffle … when the condensed mass of ball sticks, and shins, and bloody noses is carried around the different parts of the ground for a quarter of an hour at a time without any one of the mass being able to see the ball; and which they are often thus scuffling for several minutes after it has been thrown off and played over another part of the ground[17]." It might sound barbaric, but this portrayal, even with scuffles when the ball is nowhere in the vicinity, is almost identical to the kind of thing we will be finding later to describe rugby football well into the late 19th century.

Catlin noted that when fist-fights broke out, the normal practice was not to interfere but just leave the hoodlums to it and carry on with the game, but Oxendine notes reports of games elsewhere in which 'umpires' with whips went around sorting out any fisticuffs, and players were strictly told to leave any weapons at the side of the field before the game started.

Colonel Willett was witness to a game played by the Muskogee in Georgia in 1831, which he says was "conducted with as much order and decorum as the nature of things would admit … the whole night before the play is employed by the parties in dancing, and some other ceremonial preparations." On the day of the game, the teams (of about eighty each) head to the field and "when they get within about half a mile, in a direction opposite to each other, you hear the sound of a war song … as if fiercely about to encounter in fight. The play is commenced by the ball being thrown up in the air, from the centre, every player then, with his rackets, of which he has two, endeavours to catch the ball and throw it between the poles … and every time this can be accomplished, it counts one … Throughout the whole of the game the women are constantly on the alert with bottles and gourds filled with drink, watching every opportunity to supply the players[18]."

On the last few pages, we have committed the same crime as so many before by picking out the juiciest, nastiest comments about Native American stickball games, simply because they provide an epic, barbaric image that frankly makes more interesting reading. The more mundane and perhaps less exaggerated texts suggest the games were usually quite civilised affairs.

For a start, Oxendine is not convinced by the theories that Indian stickball primarily served for readying warriors for the battlefield. "To depict the ball game primarily as overt training

---

[17] George Catlin *North American Indians* (Wiley & Putnam, 1841).
[18] *A Narrative of the Military Actions of Colonel Marinus Willett, Taken Chiefly from His Own Manuscript.* Prepared by His Son, William M Willett (1831).

for war is to distort the character of the Indian people" he writes. It was "primarily a game for enjoyment and social significance, not a training regimen."

John Long tells of the Chippewa, who play "with great good humour and even when one of them happens in the heat of the game to strike another with his stick, it is not resented. But these actions are cautiously avoided, as the violence with which they strike has been known to break an arm or leg[19]." And Jonathan Craver claimed the same Chippewa people "play with so much vehemence that they frequently wound each other, and sometimes a bone is broken; but notwithstanding these accidents there never appears to be any spite or wanton exertions of strength to effect them, nor do any disputes ever happen between the parties[20]."

Girl power

Oxendine cites Catlin observing another game played in the Mississippi basin in the 1830s in which "they have two balls attached to the end of strings, each about a foot and a half long, and each woman has a short stick in each hand on which she catches the string with the two balls and throws them, endeavouring to force them over the goals of her own party."

Yes, women. This game, often known as 'maiden's ball' or 'double ball' and played, among others, by the Cheyenne, Cree and Chippewa was one in which George Copway told how "the majority of those who take part in this play are young damsels, although married women are not excluded[21]." Basically it was a field sport sharing many of the characteristics of other native stickball games, the difference being that two balls were attached to the ends of a cord of leather, a bit like the fluffy dice in Kevin and Sharon's Ford Escort, and the balls would be scooped up with a stick and even twiddled around in the air before being flung centrifugally around the field.

It was about sport, but it was also about flirting, and Copway's account suggests both male and female hormones must have been stirred into overdrive by the play. "Young women of the village decorate themselves for the day by painting their cheeks with vermilion and disrobe themselves of as much unnecessary clothing as possible, braiding their hair with colored feathers, which hang profusely down to their feet. At the same time the whole village assembles, and the young men … twist and turn to send shy glances at them, and they receive their bright smiles in return."

The men apparently found the whole thing very amusing, as would anybody wondering how much clothing a woman considers unnecessary, but the ladies took it very seriously, and in several Indian legends put their double-ball skills to good use to flee from peril, such as

---

[19] Another writer that failed to see the benefits of a short, snappy title and called his work *Voyages and Travels of an Indian Interpreter and Trader Describing the Manners and Customs of the North American Indians* (1790).

[20] Jonathan Craver *Travels Through the Interior Parts of North America* (1796).

[21] George Copway *Recollections of a forest life* or *The life and travels of Kah-ge-ga-gah-bowh* (1851). Copway was one of the earliest Native American writers, but used an English name because outsiders just couldn't quite get their tongues around his Mississauga name, Kah-ge-ga-gah-bowh, meaning 'He Who Stands Forever'.

the Wichita *Seven Brothers and the Woman*, in which the heroine escapes from said siblings by using the double ball as an improvised helicopter!

William Hoffman also described women playing the game, this time among the Dakota, whereby "when the women play against the men, five of the women are matched against one of the latter. A mixed game of this kind is very amusing", while Culin cites Bossu (1771) saying that among the Choctaw, the women's game usually followed after the men, when they "run against each other with extreme swiftness, pushing each other like the men, they having the same dress, except on those parts which modesty teaches them to cover[22]."

Aside from watching scantily clad ladies chasing each other around, another attraction of stickball was gambling. Albert James Pickett's 1851 description of the Creek in Alabama tells how huge crowds were willing to gamble everything they had on the outcome, while Colonel Willett writes that among the Muskogee in 1831, "it sometimes happens that the inhabitants of the town game away all their clothes, ornaments and horses."

Money is the root of all evil, and Hoffman believed "severe injuries only occurred when playing for high stakes." He also makes two other telling remarks. "The best players of either side gather at the centre of the ground. The poorer players arrange themselves around their respective goals." So the playground rules football tradition of sticking the crap players in defence was alive and well in North America. Also, "if too closely pursued, or if intercepted by an opponent, he throws the ball in the direction of one of his own side, who takes up the chase." That may seem an innocuous comment, but the passing game in rugby, or the 'combination' game as it came to be known in soccer, only really came about in the late 19th century as a development on what were previously highly individualistic tactics. But it seems a long time earlier, the Ojibwa had picked up on the idea that it sometimes paid to put the team before the individual and pass the ball to somebody else.

Lacrosse country

Like most sports, any theory about ancient origins is likely to be hogwash, and when it came to the great Indian game, there was no getting past Montreal dentist William George Beers, who wrote that "civilisation has not destroyed the Indian's love of hoaxing. Charlevoix, Catlin and a host of others were unmercifully hoodwinked and humbugged, and one need not travel far today to meet with the same." In Beer's search to find out where it all started "we had some charming and plausible legends invented for us impromptu, and the difficulty of centuries expeditiously unravelled in the rocky recesses of the Caughnawaga. If the soil of that settlement is not favourable for peaches, it unquestionably produces a spontaneous imaginative genius, not to be rivalled by anything red or white in Canada. We are satisfied, however, that the Indians of Canada know nothing whatever about the origin of

---

[22] Walter Hoffman *Remarks on Ojibwa Ball Play* in *American Anthropologist* (1890).

their native field game." And Beers was something of an authority on the matter. He wasn't called the 'father of modern lacrosse' for nothing.

The French, who generally occupied the areas further inland from the English settlements, had also been exposed to and impressed by the native game. Writing around 1640, and having observed the Huron and other tribes at play, Jesuit missionary Jean-de-Brébeuf, who was later killed by Indians, noted that the stick used to play the game looked curiously like a shepherd's crook, or crosier. He went on to explain the spiritual and even medicinal properties of the game, writing that "there is a poor sick man, fevered of body and almost dying, and a miserable sorcerer will order for him, as a cooling remedy, a game of *crosse*. Or the sick man himself, sometimes, will have dreamed that he must die unless the whole country shall play crosse for his health; and, no matter how little may be his credit, you will see them in a beautiful field, village contending against village, as to who will play *crosse* the better, and betting against one another beaver robes and porcelain collars, so as to excite greater interest[23]."

It is pretty obvious that the name 'lacrosse' is of French origin, coming from the word used to describe such games as *shouler a la crosse*, which as early as 1374 was said to be a custom that started "so long ago that no one remembers to the contrary." All the evidence of ancient French games points to something like field hockey, which would have been the same as the likes of *gugahawat*, *ohunistuts*, *kawasseti* and *oomastasha* that Oxendine catalogues separately from the usual Indian games as forms of 'shinny'. The Indian use of nets on the end of their sticks was probably a new concept for the French, but they still used the French word to describe it.

The two cultures, separated for millennia by the Atlantic Ocean, learned from and imitated elements of their respective stickball games. James Mooney wrote that "the French, whose light-hearted gaiety and ready adaptability so endeared them to the hearts of their wild allies, were quick to take up the Indian ball game as a relief from the dreary monotony of long weeks in the garrison." The Europeans adopted the Indian nets, while the mile-long fields and hundred-strong teams of the Indians became a thing of the past. The sporting cultures were merging, and the possibility arose of the settlers taking on the natives, quite literally, at their own game. German traveller Johann Georg Kohl, who felt that "nowhere in the world, excepting perhaps among the English and some of the Italian races, is the graceful and manly game of ball played so passionately and on so grand a scale," wrote that "on our island we made a vain attempt to get up a game" but although the Indians were well up for the challenge, "the chief American authorities forbade this innocent amusement[24]."

That game may not have happened, but others surely did. Lacrosse pioneer William George Beers apparently learned the Mohawk game of *tewaarathon* at the sprightly age of six. In his own book, he claims that "the game first met with popularity in Montreal about thirteen years

---

[23] Jean-de-Brébeuf *Relations des Jésuites en Nouvelle-France et autres documents affiliés* (1610- 1791).
[24] Johann Georg Kohl *Wanderings Round Lake Superior* (1860). He was describing the Ojibwa.

ago," which would have been 1856, "when the Iroquois Indians of Caughnawaga introduced it as a field sport." It is said that this was the year that Beers founded the Montreal Lacrosse Club when he was a sprog of just thirteen years. But this is clearly wrong, for in his own book he admits that the club was founded before he was even born, way back in 1839 when it played "several matches with the red-skins, only one of which it won … The Montreal Club did not flourish in its early history. For a long time it was dormant and practice was limited to a very small number."

1856 was when the club and the game were revived and taken more seriously, for "there had been no attempt made to reduce the game to rule. It was barren of laws and the goal-keeper was the only player with a definite name and position." Over the next decade or so there was going to be a craze for regulating sports all around the world, and Beers followed the trend in 1860 by producing a brochure that was later published "without any revision, during my absence from the city … I trust it will be regarded, by any who had the misfortune to buy it, as one of those productions of youth, which, in maturity, we would fain disown."

A game was even played before the visiting Prince of Wales that year, but it was not until 1867 that the first proper laws were framed, although Beers makes no claim that this was his doing. That same year saw the Upper Canada College lose 3-1 to the Toronto Cricket Club in the first modern game of lacrosse, and also saw the Canadians tour Britain, where early clubs were founded in their wake.

In Beers' writing, he makes it patently clear that lacrosse was based on the Indian game, and describes many of them, but they certainly imposed western ideals on it. And although he clearly respected the Indians, there are definite undertones that he considered his own people to be the superior race: "When civilization tamed the manners and habits of the Indian, it reflected its modifying influence upon his amusements, and thus was Lacrosse gradually divested of its radical rudeness … Only a savage people could, would or should play the old game; only such constitutions, such wind and endurance could stand its violence. The present game, improved and reduced to rule by the whites, employs the greatest combination of physical and mental activity white man can sustain in recreation and is as much superior to the original as civilization is to barbarism, base ball to its old English parent of rounders, or a pretty Canadian girl to any uncultivated squaw."

But although the whites appropriated the native game, none of this happened in isolation from its original creators. An Iroquois team even travelled on tour to Britain and remained the superior players, for there are reports of them fielding fewer players on a team when playing whites in order to even up the contest.

Lacrosse was expanding, perhaps never quite becoming a mainstream sport in Canada or the USA, but fairly widespread at high schools and colleges nonetheless, and the existence of lacrosse as an 'American' game was enough to ensure that hockey, at least on grass as opposed to the ice, never really made it to North America.

It even featured at the 1928 and 1932 Olympics, although it was not really until the late 20th century that it was exported to other countries, especially Great Britain and Australia, where despite its epic and very masculine origins, it has often been unfairly snubbed as a game for posh schoolgirls! International matches are now played. Fittingly, the Iroquois Nationals, representing the six nations of the Iroquois Confederacy, play as a country in their own right, making lacrosse the only sport in the world in which a Native American nation is internationally recognised as such.

Meanwhile, what are supposedly the historic Indian forms of playing the game are sometimes still played today. *Toli* is still common in the southeast of the USA, or perhaps better put has been revived from near extinction. The modern game has lost the epic nature of the near-battles of the past. Now much tamer, only the player in possession of the ball can be tackled and hitting other players with sticks (there are two in the Choctaw version) is illegal. Adapted to smaller pitches and more western influenced playing methods, the Mississippi Choctaw hold a tournament every July in which games are played on a 100 yard field and divided into four 15 minute quarters, which is the result of American football influencing *toli*, and not the other way round.

The Cherokee still enjoy their game, which uses just one stick, and does allow off-the-ball tackling and a certain use of the hands to control the ball. That is curiously out of keeping with an ancient Cherokee legend described by Oxendine that tells of the Cherokee's very own potential William Webb Ellis, who broke the rules by picking up the ball and throwing it at the opposing goal. But such blatant cheating didn't pay off, for the ball never made it to the other end of the field, but instead remained stuck to the sky. And there it has remained ever since, the moon being a now ignored reminder to the Cherokee that the use of the hands in the ball-game is illegal!

Arctic rolls

Before we leave the Americas, one of the last places you would expect an early football game to have been played is the Arctic, but the Eskimos[25] have their own traditional form of football. Most commonly known as *aqsaqtuk* or *aqijut*, it was certainly not invented specifically to honour the arrival in Greenland of English explorer John Davis, who first observed the game in 1586.

Certainly until the 19th century, Eskimo football was a big thing, and it is rumoured that around 1850, games at Point Hope in Alaska to celebrate the whale-hunt involved the whole community, women and all, and could often last for days, with goals up to ten miles apart! Culin seems to believe that of all the American people, "the game appears to be most popular

---

[25] The use of this racist and derogatory term will probably shock anybody who has been taught that the correct name for these people is Inuit. In Canada, that is generally true, but when we talk of all the Arctic peoples, such as the Yupik and arguably the Aleut too, there is no satisfactory alternative to the blanket term 'Eskimo', a name that, incidentally, is considered racist due to an unfounded belief propagated in the 1970s that it means "eaters of raw meat."

among the Eskimo, with whom in one instance it is complicated by the ball being whipped as well as kicked."

It was indeed whipped; one fine eyewitness report of the game in the 19th century comes courtesy of Lucien M Turner who observed that the Koksoagmiut of Labrador "are very fond of this game. All the people of every age, from the toddling infant to the aged female with bended back, love to urge the *aiuktouk*, as the ball is termed. They have not yet arrived at perfection in making a spherical form for the ball, but it is often an apple shape. It is made by taking a piece of buckskin or sealskin and cutting it into a circular form … This ball is very light and is driven either by a blow from the foot or else by a whip of peculiar construction … A lusty Eskimo will often send the ball over a hundred yards through the air with such force as to knock a person down … At Fort Chimon the game is played during the late winter afternoons when the temperature is 30 to 40 below zero. It is exciting and vigorous play where a large crowd joins in the game[26]."

It includes elements of interference in that you are legally allowed to shove your opponents over, or pull them over by their clothes, but it never appears to have been a particularly violent game. The snow would have cushioned the falls, and games often involved plenty of light-hearted singing along the way.

Naturalist and ethnologist Edward William Nelson described the unpronounceable *itigiimiuhlutfn* being played in Alaska: "The ball (*qfikak*) used in this game is made of leather, stuffed with deer hair or moss … I saw it played in various places from Bering Strait to the mouth of the Kuskokwim." The game starts with the familiar school playground 'pick teams' idea. "Two of the participants act as leaders, one on each side choosing a player alternately from among those gathered until they are equally divided[27]."

What he goes on to describe is as good as identical to what was mentioned in 1811 by Hans Egede, who felt the game was much like our football. "They mark out three barriers, at three or four hundred paces distance from the other … The ball being thrown upon the ground, they strive who shall get at it, and kick it with the foot, each party towards their own barrier[28]."

Nelson adds that "another football game is begun by the men standing in two close, parallel lines midway between the goals, their legs and bodies forming two walls. The ball is then thrown between them and driven back and forth by kicks and blows until it passes through one of the lines. As soon as this occurs all rush to drive it to one or the other of the goals."

They also had something like rugby where "the ball is thrown from one to another of the same side, who endeavour to keep it to themselves, while it is the aim of the other party to wrest it from them[29]."

---

[26] Lucien M. Turner *Ethnology of the Ungava District, Hudson Bay Territory* (Smithsonian Institute, 1882)

[27] Edward William Nelson *The Central Eskimo. Sixth Annual Report of the Bureau of Ethnology* (1888).

[28] Hans Egede *A description of Greenland* (1818).

[29] David Cranz *The history of Greenland, Volume One* (1820).

Nelson and Egede both conclude by noting the popular folk tale that is still told today. The former says "the northern lights (aurora) of winter are said by these people to be boys playing this game. Others say it is a game being played by shades using walrus skulls as balls." The latter had heard that "the deceased play foot ball in heaven, with the head of a moose, when it lightens, or the North-light appears, which they fancy to be the souls of the deceased."

Native origins of the gridiron?

And so to the theory that American football itself may have descended from the native games, or at least that elements of those sports were borrowed to shape way the football evolved when it was taken to North America. Could American football really have got its ideas from what early colonists observed among the Narragansett people of Rhode Island?

It's not very likely. American football was a direct development of rugby, and the way the game grew, and the new laws the Americans introduced, and others they chose to ignore, followed a logical, almost scientific pattern, and almost entirely within the insular world of the country's great colleges. The rugby the Americans imported from Britain was already a well-developed sport, and much as the native games were wonderful, rugby had little to learn from them. There is nothing to suggest that the introductions of the line of scrimmage, downs, the forward pass, touchbacks or special teams are things the Americans have the natives to thank for.

It's not an idea that serious sports historians are willing to waste time on. Benjamin Rader merely offers "neither the native Americans nor the imported black slaves greatly affected the pastimes of the main body of English settlers. The English colonists, unlike the Spanish and the French in the New World, assimilated little of the Native American culture." He doesn't bother to mention the subject again.

Gorn and Goldstein are not convinced either. Despite saying that "no doubt the English who colonized North America and the Indians whose land they took exchanged ideas about play," one paragraph later they totally contradict that statement by arguing that "Englishmen and Indians do not seem to have borrowed freely from each other. The wilderness was so frightening that they felt most comfortable and secure maintaining their own cultural practices … settlers did not just transport English pastimes to the New World; they also brought their ideas about the role of play – recreational ideologies we might call them – across the ocean."

The Christian settlers shared a deluded belief that they held the moral high ground, and felt they had something to teach the natives. But in many ways, it was really the other way round. It was rare for any European to admit to anything like that, but as we saw at the start of the chapter, when it came to football, a surprising number of writers conceded that native matches were far more civilised than their own. There were others. John Dunton, observing a game at Agawam in 1686, wrote of "a great game of football to be played with the feet, which I thought was very odd … neither were they so apt to trip at one another's heels and quarrel, as I have seen them in England[30]." It would be another 250 years before British football did likewise and outlawed hacking from the game.

Reuben Thwaites concluded that "a difference between the European and American style of sporting was readily emphasized by all observers. Sports and games were vigorous and violent affairs among the Indians as well as among the English. Nevertheless, English sports, not yet pervaded by the concept of fair play, were often rough and tumble pastimes in which a wide range of activities bordering on foul play were permitted. Contests of the Indians were conducted in an atmosphere of correctness and mutual respect. Cheating was almost unknown among them. One may compare the contemporary English and French sporting scene with the observation of Father Lalemant. In witnessing a Huron feast, the Jesuit wrote that, 'everything was done with such moderation and reserve that … one could never have thought that he was in the midst of an assemblage of Barbarians, so much respect did they pay to one another, even while contending for the victory'[31]."

In the 17th century, when the Europeans started populating the Americas, the contemporary evidence suggests that the settlers, who considered football a crude, unrefined game played by the common mob, observed sophistication in the game that they had never experienced before. European footballers had a lot to learn from the people of the New World, and maybe the Corinthian values that would later be applied to football were not devised within England's finest academic walls, but among the wigwams and totem poles of the great plains of North America.

---

[30] John Dunton *Letters from New England* (1686).
[31] In his 1896 translation and analysis of texts from 1610 to 1791 *Jesuit Relations and Allied Documents.*

6 WAY OFF THE MARK?
Ball games of pre-European Oceania

Marngrook

The first recorded European sighting of Australia was that by Dutch navigator Willem Janszoon in 1606. The discovery hardly kicked off an international frenzy. James Cook didn't arrive until 1770, and although the eastern coastline was mapped, it was not until 1788 that it was decided that, as there was no room left in the British jails, it would be a better idea just to ship pomegranate coloured Prisoners of Mother England down to the Port of Melbourne and dump them in penal colonies down under. They might have been inauspicious beginnings, but it wouldn't be long before those convicts were looking on the country their children were living in and thanking their lucky stars that they weren't stuck back in the misery of Industrial Revolution Britain.

There weren't many places as isolated from western civilisation as Australia. But among the possums, platypuses, eucalyptus and billabongs, damn it, if there weren't folk already living there. James Cook was the first person to spot them, when he wrote that his ship sailed "so near the shore as to distinguish several people upon the sea beach, they appear'd to be of a very dark or black colour but whether this was the real colour of their skins or the clothes they might have on I know not." If the sight was of interest to Cook, we can but imagine what the natives must have made of this great ship suddenly appearing over the horizon.

But not only were there people in Oz, but they were playing footy too! The sport of *marngrook* ('game ball') and other ball games of different names were played by several tribes of what is now Victoria, while other indigenous varieties of football were recorded as far up as the Northern Territory[1].

Like so many ancient games, we have no idea of the origins, but if the Aborigines were playing ball games, whose civilisation was nothing like as 'developed' as the Aztec or Chinese, surely that is all the proof we need that football-like games have been around for a lot longer than many historians give them credit. At a rough guess, *marngrook* has been given 40,000 years.

---

[1] These included the Gunditjmara, Djabwurrung, Wurundjeri and Jardwadjali. In 1889, anthropologist Alfred Howitt wrote that "this game of ball-playing was also practised among the Kurnai, the Wolgal (Tumut river people), the Wotjoballuk as well as by the Woiworung, and was probably known to most tribes of south-eastern Australia. The Kurnai made the ball from the scrotum of an 'old man kangaroo', the Woiworung made it of tightly rolled up pieces of opossum skin. It was called by them *mangurt*. In this tribe the two exogamous divisions, Bunjil and Waa, played on opposite sides. The Wotjoballuk also played this game, with Krokitch on one side and Gamutch on the other." Alfred W Howitt *Notes on Australian Message Sticks and Messengers* (Journal of the Anthropological Institute, London, 1889).

One of the best and earliest descriptions of Aboriginal ball play was offered by William Thomas, who was assistant protector and guardian of Aborigines[2] from 1839 to 1849. Most settlers simply dismissed the natives as savages and scant interest was shown in their language or culture, but Thomas was one of the few who felt a genuine fascination for them. Around 1841 he penned the following description of a form of football played by the Wurundjeri: "The men and boys joyfully assemble when this game is to be played. One makes a ball of possum skin, somewhat elastic, but firm and strong. The player of this game does not throw the ball as a white man might do, but drops it and at the same time kicks it with his foot. The tallest men have the best chances in this game. Some of them will leap as high as five feet from the ground to catch the ball. The person who secures the ball kicks it. This continues for hours and the natives never seem to tire of the exercise … It is truly a native game. The ball, I believe, is often made of twine formed of the twisted hair of the opossum. It is elastic and light, and well suited to be kicked from the instep, as the natives use it[3]."

We learn even more from a Scotsman named James Dawson[4]. A busy chap, he was a farmer, taxidermist, ethnographer, pastoralist and natural historian, and was appointed local guardian of Aborigines. He was a staunch defender of their cause, often to the annoyance of the local authorities. When he describes the games they played, he was in fact harking back to his childhood contact with the Gunditjmara tribe in the Western District in the mid 1840s. He tells us that "one of the favourite games is football, in which fifty, or as many as one hundred players, engage at a time. The ball is about the size of an orange and is made of opossum skin, with the fur side outwards. It is filled with pounded charcoal, which gives solidarity without much increase of weight, and is tied hard around with kangaroo tail sinews. The players are divided into two sides and arranged in opposing lines, which are always of a different 'class' – white cockatoo against black cockatoo, quail against snake, etc.

"Each side endeavours to keep possession of the ball, which is tossed a short distance by hand, and then kicked in any direction. The side which kicks it oftenest and furtherest gains the game. The person who sends it highest is considered the best player and has the honour of burying it in the ground till required next day. The sport is concluded with a shout of applause and the best player is complimented on his skill. This game, which is somewhat

---

[2] The role of the protector was part of the British government's concern for the welfare of the native peoples of the new colonies, and the protectors were expected to learn their language and act as mediators on issues such as encroachment onto their territory, and defending their rights against the cruelty, oppression and injustice to which they were so frequently subjected.

[3] In Robert Brough-Smyth *The Aborigines of Victoria* of 1878. Thomas had seen the game played in Coranderrk, a place in western Victoria that was in 1863 to become the site for a mission for indigenous Australians dispossessed by white settlements.

[4] In a chapter entitled *Amusements* of James Dawson's *Australian aborigines: the languages and customs of several tribes of aborigines in the western district of Victoria, Australia* (1881).

similar to the white man's game of football is very rough; but as the players are barefoot and naked, they do not hurt each other so much as the white people do; nor is the fact of an aborigine being a good football player considered to entitle him to assist in making laws for the tribe to which he belongs."

William Blandowski, up in Northern Victoria in 1857, spotted a children's game played by the Latjilatji people near present day Merbein, and even took the trouble to sketch it. The picture was not discovered until 2007 and on its reverse, the artist had scribbled a note saying that "the ball is made out of *typha* roots; it is not thrown or hit with a bat, but is kicked up in the air with the foot. Aim of the game: never let the ball hit the ground." That's basically the same idea as Japanese *kemari*.

Over the Victorian border in New South Wales they were playing ball too, as noted by Peter Beveridge who tells us that "ball playing is another game to which they are exceedingly partial. They make it much more boisterous and noisy than are the wrestling bouts, although it results in much fewer serious mishaps. The women participate in the game as well as the men. We have seen as many as two hundred (including both sexes) engaged in it at one time[5]."

Once again we have an opossum skin ball, and "before they begin to play they arrange sides, each side having a captain, whose place it is to guide his often times unruly squad. When all is in order, a *lyoore* starts off with the ball in her hand. She walks a little way out from her own side, and toward that of her opponents, drops the ball with seeming carelessness, but 'ere it has time to reach the ground, she gives a dexterous, and by no means gentle kick, which correctly aimed, sends the ball spinning high into the air. Thereupon the fun begins in downright earnest. Such screaming, jumping and frothing at the mouth, we are certain was never seen at any other game outside the walls of Bedlam; and then again such intermingling of bronze limbs, nude and glossy; or such outre grouping was never yet beheld under any circumstances other than those attendant on an Aboriginal ball match.

"They have not any goal to which the ball has to be driven, the whole of the play is merely to keep the ball in motion, and to prevent its coming to the ground; whilst the struggles of the game consist in which side can retain the ball longest in possession. Those holding the ball throw it from one to another, and it is during such flights that the opposing side vigorously run and jump with a view to its capture. As the eyes of the players are never by any chance bent on the ground, tumbles during a game are numerous, and in many cases indecorous enough, more especially when one goes down, and so becoming a stumbling block, over which a dozen or more come tumbling in a heap. These incidents, however, add mirth to the game, without creating the least ill temper.

"These games are frequently kept up from noon until dark, and even at that late hour they are given up with reluctance. The many laughable incidents which occur during these games

---

[5] In his posthumously published *The Aborigines Of Victoria And Riverina* (1889).

provide ample matter for consideration round the camp fire, besides affording abundant opportunity for boasting, to which they are addicted pretty much, old and young."

Where there's a Will

The Europeans naturally brought their own forms of football with them to Australia, and description of one such game in Adelaide in May 1862 tells us that "considerable amusement was created by the presence of a number of aboriginal natives who came from a camp close by and were permitted towards evening to take part in the sport."

From such situations, we could go on to wonder whether meetings like this produced any exchange of footballing ideas between the Aboriginals and the white settlers. It would be odd if they didn't. We know for a fact that the 19th century Aborigines played the far more 'white gentlemanly' game of cricket, a game they were often seen to approach as if it were a hunt, working in packs in pursuit of the ball, applying their tribal instincts in ways the whites had never contemplated. There is no reason to believe that they didn't do something similar with football. Coming from such a culturally different background, the Aborigines would have given a whole new ethos to the game.

At this point, we really should introduce Thomas Wentworth Wills. Born in August 1835, he grew up in Victoria's Western District, which at the time was like living on the very frontier of 'western civilisation', with the colonial world on one side, and the tribal homes of the aboriginal outback on the other. Relations between the two very different sets of people ranged from indifference to hostility, but were rarely comfortable. However, Wills was different. He and his family clearly despised the 'blacks' of Cullinlaringo that massacred 19 people including Wills' own father Horatio in 1861. But that was on a remote station in the Queensland outback, and Wills knew enough about the native tribes to differentiate between them and the people of the Djabwurrung clans near his native Melbourne. Surviving family letters reveal that not only did he befriend many local Aborigines, but learned their songs and dances, had an admirable grasp of their language and joined in with their children's games.

Having gone on to become a prized sportsman, Wills coached an Aboriginal cricket team that in 1866 left to tour England[6] but after doing the groundwork, he did not travel with them. He had been driven into depression, drink and ultimately suicide. But it was before that, in 1859, when Tom Wills had already done what he will always be remembered for in the land

---

[6] The story of the Aboriginal tour of 1868 is a fascinating one, and it's a shame that this book is not about cricket, because otherwise we could dedicate pages to it. The 20,000 people that packed Lord's for one of the games were there as much to see the cricket as they were there to catch a glimpse of this peculiar race of black people. Charles Darwin's *Origin of Species* was all the rage at the time, and the *Daily Telegraph* was impressed to observe that "although several of them are native bushmen, and all are as black as night, these Indian fellows are to all intents and purposes, clothed and in their right minds." *The Times*, meanwhile, opined that the sight of "the conquered natives of a convict colony" was nothing but a "travestie upon cricketing at Lord's." But the Aborigines could certainly wield a cricket bat, and played 47 matches throughout England, winning 14, losing 14 and drawing 19.

down under. His was the first of four names that signed the first set of official rules for any of the modern codes of football – what we know of today as Australian rules.

And from that comes the theory that Aussie Rules was not based on soccer, or rugby, or Gaelic football, or anything else. It was Wills' adaptation of British football to an ancient Aboriginal game he had played as a kid.

The fact that Wills might have played *marngrook* (we say 'might' because there is no textual evidence that he ever did), added to the fact that he seemed such a staunch supporter of the Aboriginal cause, makes it easy to understand where the theory may have come from.

One of the strongest propagators of the link is writer Jim Poulter[7], whose family has been associated to Aboriginal causes since the 1850s. He strongly advocates that we can't discard the idea purely because we have no direct evidence of it, and argues that if we look at the context of Wills and his relationship with the Aborigines, then the link is screamingly obvious.

Poulter's intentions are honourable, but his arguments are sometimes tenuous and the evidence is generally stacked against him. Describing the rapid spread of Australian rules, he asks "how this take-up rate across Australia could be so quick, if the groundwork had not already been laid by *marngrook*?" Probably quite easily. Football codes were catching on throughout the western world at a similar rate, and the Victorian rules were actually very slow to expand around the country, especially in Queensland and New South Wales, where rugby is still the dominant code. When Poulter states that "there is not a shred of documentary evidence linking the game to England" he is conveniently forgetting that there is plenty of very convincing evidence of that, and pointing out that Australian rules were codified before any of the British games is bending the truth, because although none of the FA, RFU or GAA yet existed in 1859, the seeds of all those games had already been sewn, it is just that no official governing body had been created to regulate the games on a national basis.

Making a mark

For added value, Poulter draws on the striking similarity between *marngrook* and the skill of marking, one of the most spectacular and distinctive aspects of footy played the Australian way. To take a mark, a player has to catch a kicked ball that has travelled at least 15 metres without touching the ground, whereupon the umpire blows to stop play, and the catcher is entitled to an unimpeded free kick.

Catching a ball in the air is hardly unique to Aussie Rules, but no other modern code has anything quite as dramatic as its long kicks and daredevil leaps to acrobatically beat your opponents to the ball in flight (what's called high marking). Not only is the manoeuvre a fundamental part of the game, but there is certainly something decidedly *marngrook*-esque about it!

---

[7] His thoughts were put into words in the form of *Marn-Grook's contextual link to Aussie Rules* (2007).

The possible link finds further support in Poulter's revelation that "the Aboriginal word for catch is *mumark*. And as soon as someone leapt on somebody's back to catch the ball … everyone would yell out the *mumark*[8]." Although this particular aspect of the ancient game seems to be more a product of Poulter's wishful thinking than anything else (he doesn't even tell us which Aboriginal language he's talking about), he goes on to back his argument up by pondering why the word 'mark' appears in inverted commas in the earliest edition of the rules for the Australian game, as if it had been imported from a foreign language. He thus concludes that "many explanations have been offered as to why in Australian rules we refer to a catch as a 'mark', but to me none of them wash."

Dr Poulter is again being selective with his choices, because the washing actually comes back dazzlingly clean when we note that the English word 'mark' makes perfect sense for describing the way the player physically marked the point on the field where he made the catch, as had been the practise in English football from at least the 1830s. The term 'mark' is also used in rugby union to this day to denote a fair catch within one's own 22, with very similar repercussions to what happens in Aussie Rules.

Even though Rob Pascoe reckons it is "not preposterous[9]" to say that high marking was a throwback to the Aboriginal game, the only real association seems to be that the natives had a game that involved jumping high to catch a ball, and this particular skill might have been transposed to Australian football, either by Aboriginals when they started playing the game, or by white men who had observed the natives playing *marngrook*.

Other arguments to support the *marngrook* theory rarely make any real sense. For example, the idea that the larger size of the Australian pitch is because they were playing a game 'out in the open' like the Aborigines is just silly and forgets that Aussie pitches are like that because they shared venues with cricket clubs. It has also been proposed that the huge 18-man teams are a replication of the large numbers that played *marngrook*, but the game developed at a time when most forms of football were still played with twenty or more people on a team. Revisionists can search all they like, but they will generally find that all of the elements of early Australian football were lifted in some way or other from the different football games being played in Britain and Ireland in the early 19th century. The fathers of Aussie Rules knew all about those games, and their influence is well-documented.

Poulter disagrees. He argues that in Wills' time "anything aboriginal was almost universally denigrated as 'primitive' or 'uncivilised' so it is easy to see compelling reasons why Wills should remain silent on any connection between the new game and *marngrook*" and that "surely it was much better to let the myth persist that it was derived from an upper-class English game, if this would ensure its support by the more affluent and influential sections of colonial society."

---

[8] Speaking to ABC television, 22/05/2008.
[9] Rob Pascoe *The Winter Game - Over 100 years of Australian football* (Text Pub Co, 1995).

It's hard to go along with that. Wills was only interested in a simple winter training exercise for cricketers, not in promoting it to 'more affluent and influential sections of colonial society'. And if he was so averse to any association between sport and Aboriginal links, we wonder what was he doing tutoring the first ever Aboriginal cricket team, even though it does appear he was in it more for the money than any particular desire to promote integration. But he was an outspoken, controversy-seeking character, and one imagines that if Aussie rules did have anything to do with native antipodean ballgames, then he would have been as proud as punch to point it out.

Fact versus fiction

We can attach much of the blame for the recent surge in interest in Tom Wills and *marngrook* to one book, Martin Flanagan's *The Call*[10]. In it, he describes the story of Wills growing up with the marginalized Aborigines, learning to play their game, and striving to create "a game of our own" for the Australian people that combined the best of both the indigenous and non-native cultures.

One of the few great pieces of fiction to use the origins of football codes as its theme is indeed a stirring read, but we must remember it is just that, fiction – what Flanagan calls in a note at the front of the book "an imagining of real events." As the author once wrote, "the great temptation in writing such a novel was to make Wills a romantic hero." In doing so, he takes the kind of liberties that Mel Gibson took with *Braveheart* as his main character is transformed into some kind of messiah for the Aboriginal cause, and the godfather of football at the same time. It's the kind of thing that people want to believe in, and it gives Australian football a 'myth-tory' that is so much more quixotic than the humdrum reality.

Too many people failed to realise that Flanagan's book was just a story. Ashley Mallet's *The Black Lords of Summer* refers to it as if it were a historically accurate record, as does a 1997 article in the *Herald Sun*, which categorically states that Tom Wills "returned to Victoria in 1856 and made his mark as a cricketer before returning to a variation of *marngrook*, the footy he had played with the Aboriginal children with whom he grew up." It is only speculation that Wills ever saw the game at all. Gillian Hibbins is one of the most respected football historians Australia knows[11], and following her extensive research, the closest indigenous community with any kind of ball playing tradition that Wills could feasibly have witnessed was at Port Fairy, about 150 km away. Based on that evidence, her conclusion is that although "some Aborigines were playing a form of foot-and-ball … they were living in different tribes, speaking different languages and dialects."

---

[10] Published by Allen & Unwin, 1998, and also turned into a stage play.

[11] This is the lady who told *The Australian* on March 22, 2008 that "understandably, the appealing idea that Australian football is a truly Australian native game recognising the indigenous people, rather than deriving solely from a colonial dependence upon the British background, has been uncritically embraced and accepted in some places. Sadly, this emotional belief lacks any intellectual credibility."

Gregory de Moore, a Sydney psychiatrist, has recently emerged as the greatest authority on the life of Tom Wills. He concludes his PhD on the man's life with words that are not only important for the potential link between Aussie rules and the natives of his country, but also for the common trend of rewriting the history books with political correctness more in mind than actual fact. "Poorly constructed arguments with distorted evidence are not without casualties" he writes. "The deliberate grooming of evidence to create a preferred past plants the seeds of a destructive debate. The onus is upon historians to reproduce the material as accurately as possible. To not do so, provides succour and licence for those who knowingly bend historical information to their own ends."

His excellent biography of Wills draws upon a staggering amount of letters and documents that have survived from his life to paint a far more historically accurate picture of the man. He is indeed a fascinating character, but we find little or even no evidence in Wills' life to support the Aboriginal theory. In something like 140 letters, articles and even books written by or about Tom Wills, never once is there even the remotest allusion to Aboriginal ball games, let alone the adoption of any of their elements.

Tom's upbringing on the colonial fringe would change dramatically in the 1850s when, aged just 14 years, he was packed off to England to get a quality education. And the place he went was none other than Rugby School. His wayward manner meant he would never live up to his academic potential, and it was on the games field that his passions were really let loose. Both at school and in later life he would excel at cricket, and the fact that he was once school captain would be an honour that would accompany him to his grave.

It was also while he was in England that he was introduced to Rugby's unique brand of football. Very unlike the modern incarnation, the 1850s game was anything but open or flowing. It was all about one swaying scrum of upward of a hundred bodies, which endorsed plenty of kicking of shins and all kinds of horrendously complex rules dealing with offside and other subtleties. It was hard for any one man to stand out above the rest, but Wills did. *Bell's Life in London* once described how "Wills, to the admiration of the spectators rose above the swarm of boys and displayed an eel-like agility which baffled all the efforts of his opponents to retain him in their grasp." He was also one of the finest kickers of the ball around, a skill he would take back to Australia, where ball kicking contests were all the rage. Wills could kick further than any other man in Victoria.

His involvement in the school's football matches were rarely mentioned in the letters he sent to his father, but they abound with accurate details of his first love, cricket. He played at county level and in England started honing his knack for sneaking a place in any team that would have him. He even turned out for Cambridge University, although he never studied there. Wherever he went, the local cricket eleven always seemed to be one player short. He would probably have gone on to play for England had he not returned to Australia after a seven-year absence, his obsession for the click of leather on willow having sidetracked him from any hope of realising his father's desire for him to go into law.

What he found on his return was a changed country. Melbourne was now the richest city in the British Empire, fuelled by the gold rush. The Aborigines were rapidly being dispossessed of their land, and living in disease-riddled squalor in the suburbs, while Wills was "the observed of all observers, with his Zingari stripe and somewhat flashy get up, fresh from Rugby and college, with the polish of the old country upon him. He was then a model of Muscular Christianity[12]."

Against this background, and five years after being introduced to football at Rugby, Wills would find himself sat at a table deliberating the first ever rules for the Melbourne Football Club. One of his co-founders, William Hammersley, with whom Wills would always struggle to see eye-to-eye, later said that "Tom Wills suggested the Rugby rules, but nobody understood them except himself."

Poulter feels we have made too many assumptions based on the fact that Wills was captain of the Rugby School football team, and he does seem correct in observing that Wills wasn't particularly fond of the rules used there. He certainly didn't make any major push for Rugby to be used as the basis for the Melbourne game, and later commented in a letter to his brother Horace that "Rugby was not a game for us, we wanted a winter pastime but men could be harmed if thrown on the ground so we thought differently." In fact, Wills' cousin Henry Colden Harrison contradicts Hammersley's story when he says that Tom "sensibly advised us not to take up Rugby although that had been his own game because he considered it as then played unsuitable for grown men, engaged in making a livelihood, but to work out a game of our own."

A game of their own

Until the recent boom in interest in Wills, HCA Harrison was the man most credited with fathering Australian football. Although Wills was one of the men that signed the first Melbourne rules, his was just a bit part in what was much more than a one-man show. He was a born wanderer, and for many of the formative years of Australian football, he was elsewhere, at the farmstead in Queensland or playing cricket in New South Wales and Tasmania.

Harrison's story does even less to support the Aboriginal theory. In his memoirs he wrote "of the Aborigines and their customs, so much has been written by experts that I am afraid I cannot add to the general information on the subject. Besides which, we were too young to take a scientific interest in their habits and history. We were so used to having them about, we took them very much for granted, as part of the ordinary scheme of things[13]." The founders of Australian football knew all about indigenous culture, but Harrison gives us no suggestion that they learned any footy tricks from them.

---

[12] Journalist William Josiah Sumner Hammersley (see next paragraph) describing Wills at a cricket game at the MCG in 1856 (*The Australasian*, May 8, 1869).

[13] Henry Colden Harrison *The Story of an Athlete: A Picture of the Past*, first published in 1923.

Robin Grow is as reputable a person as any to turn to for comment and his opinion is pretty clear. "I haven't been able to find any evidence that there was a lot of interaction, or any interaction, between those people developing the game and the Aboriginal tribes around, and I would very much doubt, given the way society was structured in those days, that there was a lot of interaction. I'd be delighted to find some evidence that the Aboriginals contributed to it, but as yet I haven't been able to[14]."

It is not difficult to understand the attractions of the indigenous theory. It's a lovely idea, and why knock something that is so obviously positive for relationships between the black Aborigines and the white Europeans and gives the game a distinct history to other football codes? Despite the academic scorn, in recent years, Aussie rules circles have made new moves to endorse the game as a descendant of *marngrook*.

The annual fixture between Sydney and Essendon is now dubbed the 'Marn Grook' match. Exhibitions of the game have been held before matches at the MCG and Melbourne based radio channel 3CR broadcasts a popular weekly AFL magazine focussing on indigenous players called the *Marn Grook Football Show*.

Alcoholism, petrol sniffing and similar problems are rife in Aboriginal communities, who for so long have been marginalized from white society, including sport, but the times are changing. Nowadays, only three per cent of Australians are Aboriginal in origin, yet they make up six per cent of AFL professionals. After enduring years of racism both on and off the footy field, they are finally being recognised for being the exceptionally skilful players they are. "It's just certain moves that you haven't seen before or that haven't been taught that show you they have a connection with the game," says former Essendon star Michael Long, who has developed a firm interest in *marngrook* and the indigenous desert games. "It was where they got their talent for high marking and the other uncanny things they can do." It's unlikely that modern-day Aboriginal footballers have ever played *marngrook* in their lives, but it's a nice image.

For them to have a reason to feel proud of their heritage and to feel that they are the rightful owners of Australia's national passion can only be a good thing. It goes a tiny way towards making up for so much injustice over the years, and so much denial of their role in shaping modern-day Australia.

Journalist Garrie Hutchinson summed up the spirit when he said "so it just seemed to me that if it was not true, then it ought to be true, that's my view of it, that there was an Aboriginal contribution to the Australian national game[15]." But unfortunately, when it comes to history, you can't make assertions just because you like the sound of them. You have to look for the truth, even though we can hear where Jim Poulter is coming from when he says "it is indeed almost ironic that Australian football represents probably the most potent, but

---

[14] Grow was speaking to *The Sports Factor* on Radio National in 1998.
[15] On *The Sports Factor* on Radio National in 1998, and who edited *100 years of Australian football, 1897-1996 Complete story of the AFL* (Viking, 1996).

still politically unrecognised force for reconciliation in our nation today, if only we have the sense and foresight to capitalise on it properly … Surely, with the 150th anniversary of the founding of our national game just around the corner, we should be doing all we can to recognise and celebrate the Aboriginal origins of our national game."

Noble sentiments, but was there really an Aboriginal origin? Probably not. Perhaps Greg de Moore provides the most sensible comment of all when he says "whether or not there is a link between the two games in some way for me is immaterial because it really highlights that games such as *marngrook* … were played by Aborigines and should be celebrated in their own right."

South Pacific

"They divide into equal parts, about twenty yards distant, and placing themselves in rows opposite to each other, a small green breadfruit is brought by means of a football[16]" wrote James Wilson in 1799, before going on to describe something that was part game, part dance, but involved kicking of the ball. *Marngrook* is by no means alone in Oceania's ancient sporting tradition. In fact, from the Philippines to New Zealand, evidence occurs of games that were being played long before the Europeans arrived.

In the Maluku Islands, now belonging to Indonesia, "they play at foot-ball, which is made of Spanish reeds. They that play make a ring, one standing in the center who tosses the ball to those about him, and they with a kick throw it so high that it is almost out of sight. If anyone misses it, they hiss, and hoot, to shame him for his unskilfulness[17]."

In Papua New Guinea, the New Hebrides and many surrounding islands, there are abundant local traditions of playing games with a coconut, breadfruit, a local variety of orange, or a hard fruit that sounds like a Dubliner being rude called *konts*. Almost all of these are played by teams and although there are not many rules, the basic idea is to kick the ball at some kind of goal or target.

There is another game found in the Torres Strait Islands, the New Hebrides, Tahiti and Fly River in New Guinea, most popularly played on the beaches, and which could be likened to hockey. The ball is made of wood, and hit with bamboo sticks. This game is unusual in that there does not seem to be any kind of goal or point-scoring, the winning team being the one in possession of the ball at the end of the match.

In Polynesia, "the *tuiraa*, or foot-ball, is also a frequent game, though perhaps it was followed more by the women than the men, yet whole districts engaged in this amusement. In the former, they only struck the ball with a stick; in this, they employed the foot, and each party endeavoured to send it beyond the opposite boundary line[18]."

---

[16] Captain James Wilson *A missionary voyage to the southern Pacific ocean, performed in the years 1796, 1797, 1798, in the ship Duff* (1799).
[17] Bartolomé Leonardo de Argensola *Conquista de Las Islas Malucas* (1708).
[18] William Ellis *Polynesian researches, during a residence of nearly six years in the South Sea Islands* (1829).

The same source also describes a game played only by women. This was "the *haru raa puu*, seizing of the ball … in which neither sticks nor feet were allowed to be applied … The boundary mark of each party was fixed by a stone on the beach … The ball was a large roll or bundle of the tough stalks of the plantain leaves … One party, seizing the ball, endeavoured to throw it over the boundary mark of the other … As the pastime was usually followed on the beach, the ball was often thrown into the sea; here it was fearlessly followed, and with all the noise and cheering of the different parties, forty or fifty women might sometimes be seen, up to their knees or their waists in the water, splashing and plunging amid the foam and spray." Nice.

Despite this veritable plethora of South Pacific ball play, none of these games have ever been the subject of particularly extensive anthropological research, and given the oral tradition of these cultures, it isn't hard to understand why. Although some of these games are remarkably similar to those that developed in Europe, the idea that their origins could be related in any way is generally greeted with an almighty scoff among academic circles. And that is something that has gone down particularly badly among the New Zealand Maori, where demand for retribution for their contribution to world sport has reached high politics. Many Maori are adamant that they created rugby.

Maori pride

It is all to do with *ki-o-rahi*, a term that was only coined in the early 20th century, but is used as the generic name for a number of ball games that were apparently played by the natives of Aotearoa, long before the land was discovered by Abel Janszoon Tasman in 1642 and renamed New Zealand by the European settlers.

20 year old student Mai claims that names for Maori ballgames pre-1940 included "*ki ora* (the *ki* being the traditional ball made from harakeke, light wood or raupo), simply *ki* or *kui*, *ponga* or *ki ponga*, *kiarahi* and others[19]" but there was never any standardised version of the game. In fact, when different tribes came together to play, part of the fun was the pre-match *tatu*, in which they would decide upon the rules for the day.

And those rules can be pretty hard to get your head around. Played with a flax ball on a circular pitch, *ki-o-rahi* combines different elements of ball-handling and passing with intricate teamwork and tactics. There is probably no other member of the footballing family that requires so much strategy, something that has been linked to the Maoris' extraordinarily well-developed intellectual capacity.

One website on New Zealand history[20] describes the rules as played by the Ngati Mahana. The pitch is marked out as a series of circles inside other circles, forming zones that each have their specific name and purpose. Around the outer circle called *te ao* are seven posts

---

[19] *Ki o Rahi Rocks!* at www.maori-in-oz.com.
[20] http://history-nz.org/kiorahi_rules.html.

called *pou*, and in the centre of the field there is the main goal, usually a large decorated rock, called the *tupu*. We are told there is a symbolic reason for all this, for the game is a re-enactment of an episode in the *Legend of Rahi*, where as part of his quest to rescue his abducted wife, Rahi-Tutaka-hina throws the large eggs of the extinct moa bird at a magical rock, which makes it turn green and thus provide our hero with much-needed rejuvenation.

In the game, teams take on different roles (a bit like one team batting and one team fielding in cricket or baseball), either playing as the *kioma* or the *taniwha*. There are four quarters to the game, and after each one, the teams switch roles. The basic aim of the *kioma* is to get the ball to the outer circle and touch one of the *pou*. Once they have managed this, they have to get the ball to the centre and score the equivalent of a try by touching the *tupu*. That gets one point, but this is where the fun starts. You can actually score as many as seven points for touching the *tupu*, it all depends on how many different *pou* you have managed to touch without the other team getting the ball.

What the *kioma* are trying to do is hit as many *pou* as they can, and make a strategic decision to dash for the centre when they think it makes most sense. To do this, they can use any part of their body, and can run with the ball, throw it, kick it or bounce it, although there are different restrictions. The *taniwha*, meanwhile, have to get the ball off the *kioma* and stop them from scoring, which generally involves rugby-like tackling and ripping the ball out of their hands.

The game also has its own system of penalties, with overzealous tackling and time-wasting being particularly frowned upon, and there are limitations on what players can and can't do in certain zones. There are usually seven or eight players per team, and one unique aspect is self-reffing, whereby each team nominates one referee to oversee the match.

Ki-o-rahi is clearly a game with pitch markings and complex rules, and despite being potentially rough, there are very strict laws to stop things getting out of hand. It is a far cry from the violent simplicity of most 'primitive' ball sports.

Rugby arrives

After New Zealand was settled by Europeans, and the ensuing wars that rattled the land, the native games had all but disappeared by around 1870. We are told that there were two main reasons for this. The first was that the early missionaries were anything but impressed by what they saw, and did all they could to stamp out games that were far too pagan and ritualistic for their liking. Just about all aspects of Maori culture, language and tradition were vehemently repressed until only very recently.

The other reason for the game's demise was the soaring popularity in New Zealand of rugby, which is said to have been introduced by Charles Monro when he returned from college in England and suggested the local Nelson Football Club should give it a go[21]. That

---

[21] 'British' football, if not necessarily rugby football, had been in New Zealand much longer than that, and can be traced to the first settlement of the Canterbury region in 1850. Among the 750 voyagers was Dublin-born

they did in an 18-a-side game against the local College in May 1870, and duly beat them 2-0 in what is considered the first 'proper' game of rugby on New Zealand soil[22].

Monro was in Wellington later that year, and came across a group of footballers playing some kind of amalgamation of the Victorian and Association rules. Rugby had arrived just in the nick of time, and Monro taught them the right way of doing things and arranged a game with his own team, the story going that the Nelson players traipsed about the city carrying two sets of rugby posts in search of a large enough area of grass that wasn't waterlogged.

Monro is thus heralded as the father of rugby in New Zealand. But that's not a mantle he felt he particularly deserved. Many years later, he insisted that "no credit is due to me in the matter. My introduction of Rugby to my native land was merely a coincidence of circumstances[23]."

The rest, of course, is history. The Kiwis loved the new game. In fact, they never really bothered with any of the other codes, which is part of the reason why they are so damned good at this one in particular. It spread like wildfire. By 1873, it was being played in Wanganui and Auckland and hit Hamilton a year later. By 1923, an article in the *Rugby Advertiser* described how "from the North Cape to the Bluff there is scarcely a spot worthy of that distinction in which the game is not played."

Right from the early days, the Maori took a particular interest, allegedly because the basic skills were almost identical to those of the ball games they had been playing for centuries, which they easily adapted to rugby, and to devastating effect.

The first New Zealand rugby team set off in 1888 for a tour of Britain, and although it did contain some 'colonists and half-castes', as they were described at the time, the vast majority were what were called the New Zealand Native Football Representatives. This was no early act of political correctness. The predominance of Maoris was for no other reason than the fact that they were the best players the islands had to offer.

Francis Marshall noted that "in the early matches the New Zealanders appeared on the field in their native hats and headdresses, and uttered their well-known cry of 'Ake, ake, kia,

---

Richard James Strachan Harman, who had been a noted footballer, cricketer and oarsman at Rugby School. He set up a number of sports clubs in the new colony, and for many years "Harman was the president of the Christchurch Football Club, and it is related that at the age of fifty he took part in a football match," as written in his obituary in *Star* (November 27, 1902). This is claimed as evidence of the oldest 'true' rugby club in the world, but a decade before the RFU was formed, it would be more accurate to say it was a hybrid game that Christ's College and the 'Gentlemen of Christchurch' played in August 1863. Meanwhile, at Nelson there were reports of two more Old Rugbeians, Robert Codrington and Henry Turton, introducing a game that was reported in the Nelson College records by somebody with the telling pen name of 'Scrum', and which involved kicking the ball over the bar.

[22] *The Colonist* reported on the game, and describes scrimmages, an oval ball and touching the ball down behind the posts.

[23] In a 1923 letter to *The Dominion*.

kaha'", so the iconic *Haka* was there from the start, although "later, when the real merit of their play was recognised, they discarded these advertising spectacles."

The story goes that the fast-flowing way in which these Maori players could run with the ball and pass it around was unlike anything that had been seen before in what was still a very young sport. It has even been said to have totally revolutionised the British approach to the game.

But did it really? In Marshall's same book, G Rowland Hill mentions that tour, saying the New Zealander's play "though unscientific at the start, showed great improvement before the tour was concluded. They made very good matches with several of the leading clubs." In the same book, RFU president Arthur Budd was hardly lavishing praise on the "completely outclassed" Maori, when more or less all he has to day about the game with England was that it "will be remembered for the rough play and extraordinary conduct of the Maoris, who during their visit to this country displayed a remarkable aptitude for disputing the decisions of the officials. The English umpire and the referee were anathematised and threatened, and at one period of the game, five of the Maori team left the field, but were induced to return by their manager."

Francis Marshall accepted that "undoubtedly they were a strong combination, and their wonderful physique was a great factor in their many victories, and in the successful manner in which they went through the most numerous list of matches ever undertaken by a single team" but judging by these eyewitness accounts, the Maori visit had less impact on the way the game was played in Britain than the romanticists have led us to believe.

As New Zealand became more and more Europeanised in all aspects, sport included, traditional ball games slipped out of public conscience. While not banned entirely, they certainly were not encouraged, and it was not until the 1970s, and the Maori cultural renaissance, that any major schemes were implanted for *ki-o-rahi* to be revived. The new version of the sport has been largely modified. Plastic *pou* and *tupu* are even commercially available. And it has even been exported, primarily to the United States, where so many schools now teach the game that there are more *ki-o-rahi* players there than there are in the sport's native country!

Seeking justice

In recent years the debate has moved up a notch or two. The claim now is that rugby itself was a Maori invention, and that the cover-up of its true identity is one of the greatest scams in sporting history!

The story goes that visitors to New Zealand around the 1840s were astounded by the athletic prowess of the Maori (who were generally a good ten centimetres taller than your average European) and the extraordinary amount of skill and thought that they applied to their ball games. *Ki-o-rahi* was such a refined sport that it made the barbaric forms of football played back home look embarrassingly primordial, with all the slow, clumsy scrummages and reckless hacking involved.

The Maori ethos was immediately applied to European football, taking all the ball skills and tackling from *ki-o-rahi*, and putting them into a context of getting the ball from one end of the pitch to the other, which was the way Europeans liked to play their sport. This was the origin of a game that would become popular at public schools as a way of forming honourably competitive gentlemen. It would eventually be named after one of those schools. Rugby.

The Maori conspiracy theory goes on to assert that no British gentleman would ever dream of admitting that this wonderful new creation was something they had learned from the primitive population of a far-flung archipelago, and instead came up with the story that the whole thing had been the doing of a schoolboy called William Webb Ellis when he picked up a football and started running with it. The Webb Ellis story, which we will be coming back to later, is almost certainly garbage, and in comparison, it has to be said that the *ki-o-rahi* theory stands up quite well.

However, a *ki-o-rahi* blog by a certain 'Ellison' is more of an example of the dangers of people now being able to publish whatever nonsense they like on the Internet than anything else. The whole world can read online that the connection dates back to the influential headmaster of Rugby School, Thomas Arnold, who was around just a few years before rugby started formalising itself into the code people know and love today.

According to the blog, Arnold "cleverly kept on the right side of parents and his school board with his ploy of injecting Maori ball game skills and physical requirements surreptitiously into the curriculum. He did this by walking the school yards and playing fields and 'suggesting' to his pupils how they might brighten up their staid plodding ball games with a bit of innovation … Arnold was smitten with the muscular vigour of Maori and attributed their superior physique to their physical games, such as their ball games, and their quick minds to their games' intelligence. Arnold was one of the main instigators who cleverly guided his pupils to create 'running rugby' after learning about the Maori ball game skills. He knew there would be a serious backlash if it was ever known publicly that he was teaching his pupils Maori education so he made it seem as if his pupils had come up with the ideas themselves[24]."

It's scintillating stuff, but sadly ludicrous for there is no historical evidence that Thomas Arnold ever did any of those things. We will be coming back to this remarkable man later, and will learn that he was indeed a revolutionary educator, but was unlikely to have ever taken much of an interest in the way football was played, and certainly wouldn't have instigated any rule changes.

In fact, there seems to be some confusion here between Thomas Arnold senior, the rugby headmaster, and his son, who went by the same name, and was also a renowned academic. It was Arnold 'the Younger' who, disillusioned with Britain, enjoyed a short but unsuccessful

---

[24] http://hubpages.com/hub/Ki-o-Rahi.

period of farming in New Zealand[25], but by that time, running with the ball was already an accepted feature of Rugby football.

The fact that another of Arnold's sons, William, was one of the three pupils who wrote the original rules of Rugby's game does add to the intrigue, but any connection between rugby and Maori games that may have come via the Arnold family still involves far too many fanciful assumptions to hold up well in the rugby court.

We get more luck with one of the key figures in early New Zealand rugby, who was a Maori called Thomas Ellison, and presumably the inspiration for our blogger's nick. Ellison wrote extensively on the game, most notably *The Art of Rugby Football* published in 1902, and often described how he adapted Maori ideas to it. It is said that he was the mastermind behind the wing forward system that served the All Blacks so well in their formative years and he employed plenty of Maori imagery in his creation of the All Black legend. The black shirts were based on the mythology of the (now extinct) black-feathered Haast eagle, while the silver fern is an ancient Maori reward for achievement.

Most of his accomplishments were tactics and skills based, but he was also a strong advocate of introducing the forward passing of *ki-o-rahi* to rugby. This was something he never achieved. However, it is also known that Walter Camp, regarded as the father of American football, was well-read in rugby, the game it is based on, and could quite conceivably have been familiar with Ellison's ideas. It is therefore at least remotely plausible that the introduction of forward passing to American football originated from Maori traditions. But 'remotely' is the key word here, and it should also be noted that forward passing was one of the few additions to rugby that Walter Camp did not support.

Nevertheless, some Maori are so convinced that they have been robbed of the credit for their contribution to world sport that the matter has led to intense political debate. It all boils down to the Maori Intellectual Knowledge Law and the reclamation of lost entitlements under the terms of the Treaty of Waitangi in 1840.

The claim is that the New Zealand Rugby Union should pay them compensation to the tune of several million dollars for the theft and destruction of their national sport and its re-branding as rugby.

And it's a big issue among the Maori. What Kiwis the call 'tagging' of rugby stadiums (i.e. writing protest graffiti along the lines of 'Ki-o-rahi Compo Now') has been rife, and it couldn't have been better for *ki-o-rahi* itself, with passion for reviving the game now at an all-time high.

And for many, NZRugby is just the start of it. Next, they could well be chasing other national unions and even the NFL has been targeted for a major cash payout. We wish them luck with that one. After all, although *ki-o-rahi* may have added a new philosophy to rugby,

---

[25] His enthusiasm for Maori culture is mentioned in the letters he wrote home (*New Zealand Letters of Thomas Arnold the Younger, with Further Letters from Van Diemen's Land and Letters of Arthur Hugh Clough*, 1847-1851).

surely the Maori can't claim to have invented the idea of running with a ball and passing it around, even if they were uncannily good at it. And most of the distinguishing elements of rugby (the scrum, the lineout, the H-shaped posts, drop goals, the rectangular pitch, the illegality of forward passing…) are only conspicuous by their absence in traditional Maori games. If the Maori can get away with this, then maybe it is time for the good people of Hamburg to start demanding a percentage cut from McDonalds.

Interesting as it is, it is still a very watery claim, and surely all we can realistically expect is for the rugby history books to be rewritten to admit that there is a chance that the Maori contribution to rugby as we know it today has been under-acknowledged.

Any kind of monetary compensation is opening up a very wriggly can of worms. For a start, there is the controversy that, if any money is to be paid at all, exactly who should receive it, and what should it be used for? The word is that the funds should go to those communities that are most actively playing *ki-o-rahi* today, although there is not a jot of evidence to show that these communities were the ones that developed the game centuries ago.

The whole *ki-o-rahi* thing has plenty of sceptics, and we could even question the authenticity of its claims to supposed antiquity. The game as it is played today seems to be a 20th century invention and the association between it and any game the Maori might have played of old is a very doubtful one indeed. As we have seen in previous chapters, the Europeans did describe the games played by the natives they encountered around the world, yet in the copious writing on Maori culture, next to nothing was ever written about their ball games, which seems extraordinary if we are to believe that this very game inspired the pupils of a school in Warwickshire to imitate it.

There is little indication of a football culture in New Zealand before the 1860s, and not until the 1870s was the game either widespread or rugby-like. By this time, the basic elements of British rugby had been in place for almost half a century. The time-scale doesn't fit.

There is increasingly more and more information about *ki-o-rahi* history appearing on the Internet, but hardly any of it is substantiated. Even the veracity of the *Legend of Rahi* has come into question and *ki-o-rahi* enthusiasts seem to be cooking up a pseudo-history for their game that is in dire need of a reality check. "We cannot track it in the traditional Maori world" said Maori language commissioner Patu Hohepa. "At this present time it is a mystery[26]." Might that be because *ki-o-rahi* never really existed? Is it really rugby that should be claiming money from *ki-o-rahi* for the theft of its game and its rebranding as a phoney Maori custom?

Although to the outsider the idea that the Maori should get any money may stink of opportunism, that would be because we struggle to understand just how strongly they feel about retribution for the holocaust of their people and culture for so many years. But to claim

---

[26] *McDonald's adopts obscure Maori ball game* (*New Zealand Herald,* Oct 8, 2005).

that anybody involved in rugby should have to hand over their money to modern-day *ki-o-rahi* players is frankly absurd.

If the Maori are to be paid off in recognition for their contribution to the sport, then who is to say that the Iranians, Indians, Egyptians, Greeks, Italians and so many others should not be given their slice of the cake too? Because they too could have played their part in the story…

7 STICKS AROUND
The ancient ball games of Southern Asia and the Middle East

Indian summers

In the 19th century, the British were everywhere. By 1813, the Empire held sway over about 458 million people, a quarter of the world's population. In terms of geographical expanse, it was the biggest Empire ever constructed, while the 'informal empire' meant the British influence was effectively much wider than that. As late as 1870, Britain was the only major industrialised power, producing 30% of the world's output, and was able to prosper in many places through trade alone, never having to resort to formal rule, often making the British government more influential than local rulers in countries that were never even part of the Empire.

And although popular history has tended to give Britannia and its wave-ruling a bad press, and in many cases rightly so, the world also had reason to thank the British for their expansionism, as they went about abolishing slavery, forbidding child marriages, supplying technology and medicine and, what interests us most here, teaching them to play ball games.

But while it was the football-like games that took off big time in most regions under British rule, in India, no variant of the sport has ever managed to catch on quite as much as it did elsewhere.

In fact, the Indians and their neighbours are to this day remarkably crap at football. You would expect a country with more than 1100 million people to be slightly better at soccer than it is, generally hovering around 140th in the FIFA rankings, while rugby is very much a minority sport in a country that by the early 19th century was directly or indirectly controlled in its entirety by the Brits.

The British did try to take the game there. The annual rugby fixture between England and Scotland has, since as long ago as 1879, been called the Calcutta Cup. This dates back to a game played on Christmas Day 1872 in that city between a team of Englishmen and another made up of members of the other home nations. It was a success, the Calcutta Football Club was founded, and rugby had arrived in India. The game was repeated the year after, but by now the players were realising that the only others going out into the midday sun were mad dogs. Interest was waning, and the club folded. Its funds (all in silver rupees) were melted down and turned into a small trophy that was presented to the Rugby Football Union in 1878, under provision that it be competed for annually.

And so it has done, although the trophy itself is generally kept away from the players. Which is just as well, because it was seriously damaged in 1988, when England number eight

Dean Richards and Scotland flanker John Jeffrey decided it would be fun to use it as a ball in Princes Street, Edinburgh. They were rightfully punished.

Rugby and soccer's failure in India can largely be put down to the weather. They were considered winter sports back home, but in a country where it is baking hot all year round, the cricket season never stopped. In a letter to *The Field* on the problems faced by Bombay FC, former Rugby School pupil William Paterson wrote that "I fear we shall not be able to get up any 'foreign' matches … I believe the game is being tried in Kurrachee, Scinde, where in winter the climate is cold enough to warrant it, but a three day's journey is rather too much to take for a game played on sand." And Admiral Alexander Arbuthnot noted in his autobiography that he scored two goals in a game of football played in Madras, India, but it was "rather too hot for that sort of fun[1]" and decided instead to form the Madras Cricket Club in 1846.

Rugby may have failed, but cricket was another matter entirely. The locals took to it in a huge way. The Indians and Pakistanis (who broke away to form an independent state in 1947) are among the most powerful nations in the sport, and Bangladesh (which in turn split from Pakistan in 1971), is also one of cricket's ten test nations.

Lapki dancing

But despite football's failure in India, even in this most unlikely corner of the world, we find clues to its ancient origins. *Dhada*[2] is played in a remote town called Awan, which not even Indians are likely to have heard of. It's in Rajasthan, about 150 km from Jaipur, if that helps, and their annual match is held on January 14th.

It's a men-only free-for-all that conjures up images of medieval mob football played by twelve local villages, with six teaming up together on each side to play in the town square, where goals are set up at either end. And they may have a case for having the bulkiest ball in footballdom, called the *dhadi* and weighing in at over 50 kg, although there is no standard weight and a new ball (not unlike a stuffed wicker basket) is made each year.

To be fair, we've given the 'symbolism' theorists a rough ride thus far, but not only do the people of Awan believe that their game's origins lie in a fertility rite, but many still believe that today. One of the goals symbolises prosperity and the other famine, so there's a lot riding on the result, while the ball itself symbolises one of the demon Ravana's ten heads, and getting to kick it just once is enough to bring plentiful luck.

Way over on the other side of the country, another football-like game springs out of nowhere. The game of *yubi lakpi* is popular to this day in the region of Manipur, which lies close to the border with Myanmar. *Yubi* refers to the coconut that is used as a ball and *lakpi* to the art of snatching it from your opponents in what is essentially a game like rugby with only one goal and all the complexities removed. Teams are all-male and although nowadays

---

[1] Sir Alexander J Arbuthnot *Memoirs of Rugby and India* (T Fisher Unwin, 1910).
[2] As featured in a short 1990 film *Dhada: An Ancient football game*, directed by Priti Chandriani.

it is generally established that it should be played seven-a-side, this was not always the case. To add to the fun, before the game, the players are doused in mustard oil, as is the coconut ball, which is then hurled into the midst of a mêlée of players. Kinky.

Although it's a team game, for the most part it is more about individuals vying for the coconut. The idea is to get the ball into a small area marked out as a box, and carry it over the far line, beyond which the 'King' (usually an important dignitary) is seated and waiting to be offered the ball.

The general skills of *yubi lakpi* share a lot in common in rugby, but we have no reason to doubt that the local game was played long before the British arrived. In fact, Emma Levine claims that in similar fashion to the Maori in the previous chapter, "most Manipuris are quite adamant that the modern world 'stole' the idea from them and made it into rugby[3]." It is highly unlikely that this really happened, but *yubi lakpi* may well have its place somewhere in football's complex evolutionary tree.

Other than cricket, another sport that has thrived in India is field hockey[4]. Modern hockey was introduced to India by British servicemen in the 1880s, mainly in and around Calcutta, and perhaps one of the reasons why the sport took off where soccer and rugby did not was because the Indians already had a long-standing history of stick-based field games of their own.

Given the British mentality of feeling the need to pass its supposedly superior values onto the peoples it conquered, the most likely scenario is that they observed the locals playing ball with sticks, admired their enthusiasm, and decided that the right thing would be to show them how to play hockey in a proper gentlemanly fashion. And that is why rather than teaching them soccer or rugby, they compromised, and it was hockey that took off in India instead.

This takes us back to the Manipur region, and a sport they call *khong kangjei*. We know very little about the ancient history of the game, except that it was played long before the British, French and Portuguese came along and started arguing over a patch of land that was never any of theirs in the first place. Local claims state it goes all the way back to the prehistoric Hayichak era, when it is said that a young member of the royal household was spotted playing the game, and thanks to his talents eventually became King of Manipur.

---

[3] Her excellent account of travels throughout Asia witnessing such exotic sports as buzkashi, horseback javelin and oil wrestling is titled *A Game Of Polo With A Headless Goat: And Other Bizarre Sports Discovered Across Asia* (Andre Deutsch, 2003).

[4] From 1928 to 1958 India was unbeaten in the Olympics and won the gold medal six years in a row. Pakistan also has a proud record, winning four of the first eight editions of the World Cup from 1971 to 1994. The fortunes of both nations have slumped in recent years, and that is mainly due to the shift to synthetic surfaces from the 1970s onwards, which has been tough on the poor Indians and Pakistanis, whose clubs often simply cannot afford to lay down plastic pitches. They have struggled to keep up with the wealthier European nations and (particularly in the women's game) Korea, Argentina and Australia.

Nowadays *khong kangjei* (*khong* being feet, *kang* being ball and *jei* being the stick) is played seven-a-side using sticks about a metre and a half long that look uncannily similar to regular field hockey sticks, and a ball made out of a bamboo root called a *kangdrum*.

The game offers a fascinating combination of different elements of 'western' field sports. Obviously, players can use their sticks to hit the ball, but they are by no means limited to doing that. There is nothing in the rules that says that players cannot also use their feet to kick it. Now, that's soccer!

It gets better. They can also pick the ball up and carry it. Any player holding the ball can then be challenged in the local style of *mukna* wrestling (the game is also known as *mukna kangjei*, or 'stickball wrestling'). Running with the ball and tackling? By Jove, if that doesn't sound like rugby!

The only compromise is that although you can throw and kick the ball as much as you like, goals can only scored by hitting the ball with the stick. That's Irish hurling!

The more one thinks about it, the more one is tempted to consider *khong kangjei* the finest all-round field sport ever invented. It effectively combines elements of hockey, soccer and rugby (or hurling, handball and American football, the list goes on), and players can opt for whichever is most to their liking – pick the ball up and you risk being wrestled, otherwise just kick it or use your stick.

Great sport as it is, *khong kangjei* received little recognition in the ancient texts. That was probably because the simple stick game that the plebeian masses played in the urine-infested streets was of minor consequence compared to *sagol kangjei*. *Sagol* means horse, so what we are talking about here is 'stickball on horses'. And that means polo.

People like polo

There is valid enough evidence that hockey was played on horseback thousands of years ago, but not enough for us to build up an accurate picture of how and where it developed. However, the common claim that 'polo is the oldest organised team sport in the world' is overstepping the mark somewhat. It is unlikely to be older than any of the sports played on foot. That would defy evolutionary logic.

Polo is more likely to be hockey on horses than hockey is to be polo on foot. In the evolutionary course of ball games, it was an adaptation of a new 'technology' (i.e. the domestication of the horse) to another sport, in much the same way that hockey was adapted to ice, roller skates, bicycles and even scuba diving shortly after the relevant equipment was invented. Even polo itself has moved on from horses in some parts of the world, and the game is popularly played on the backs of camels, elephants[5] and yaks[6].

---

[5] Elephant polo is played mostly in Nepal, Thailand, India and Sri Lanka, although the likes of Scotland, Ireland and Sweden also have international teams despite the lack of any native elephants in Northern Europe. Led by the Duke of Argyll, Scotland retained their unlikely world title in 2005.

[6] A new sport invented in Mongolia around the year 2000. It gets worse, they have also invented yak skiing, and how's about *aklagh tarteesh*, which translates as 'picking up sheep at a gallop'.

Polo was far better documented of old because, as a verse inscribed on a stone tablet beside a ground in Gilgit in the far north of Pakistan, proclaims: "Let other people play at other things. The King of Games is still the Game of Kings." History has revered the game and for centuries it has featured prominently in the art and literature of a wealth of Asian cultures.

As usual the Chinese, who generally beat the rest of the world when it came to documenting anything, have a strong claim. The oriental sport of *jiqiu* (or *gyoggu*, or however else you fancy transcribing Chinese characters) gets its first literary mention in a poem from the age of the Three Kingdoms (220–265 AD), in which some of the majesty of the prose is obviously lost in translation:

> "A lonely ball, a few riders after it,
> Led by their strength and agility,
> To the promise of success."

By the time of the Tang Dynasty (618–906), rules had been written and Liu Xu's *Jiu Tangshu* even describes a game, played in 709 AD between four players led by the future Emperor Vuanzong and ten players representing the Kingdom of Tibet in celebration of an important wedding. The poet Shen Chuan Chi described the game in 713 AD, and we know some kind of hockey on horseback called *dakyu* was played at the Imperial Palace during the Nara and Heian periods (710–1185).

Polo was also played in Japan, where it particularly thrived under the reign of Tokugawa Yoshimune, who ruled from 1716 until his abdication in 1745, and found it a useful method for training his horseback troops for warfare. In recent centuries, the sport has been more and more influenced by western ideas, but the Imperial Household Agency still organises games today played more or less akin to its ancient roots. The 'modern' game is played by teams of five riders on a pitch measuring 50m by 20m and one of its biggest curiosities is that both teams play into the same goal.

There are also very definite details of polo being played in Korea from 918 AD onwards. Saechong the Great (1418–1450) reckoned it was "not a mere game as thanks to its practice men can become superb warriors who are not only perfectly skilled horse riders but also experienced strategists." The Choson Dynasty certainly made it a part of military examinations, and sometimes top players reaped the kind of rewards reserved only for great military generals. But at other times, polo was banned, the Confucianists being particularly adverse to the negative effects that such pointless horseplay had on the people.

All this evidence in the Far East tends to conflict with the popular view of polo originating in the west of Asia, but we simply have no facts, for instance, to argue how long the game of *guj-bozi* has been played in what is now Tajikistan, played on the back of a small and particularly nimble breed of horse called the *pamir*.

The Indian subcontinent has some strong claims. Renowned Sanskrit scholar Pandit Sharma believes the game called *chaughan* (variations of the spelling include *chigan* and *tchaugan*) was played in the region as far back as 3100 BC. This was enough to convince the *Guinness*

Book of Records, but the claim seems a tad farfetched when we note that there is little or no evidence of humans on horseback at all from any earlier than about 1500 BC. Manipur's own game has a strong claim. The Imphal Polo Ground is said to be the oldest in the world and was mentioned in *Cheitharol Kumbaba*, which chronicled royal life from AD 33. The first Muslim Emperor in North India, Sultan Qutb-ud-din Aibak, died playing polo in 1210 when he fell off his horse and was impaled on his saddle.

The *Encyclopaedia Britannica* is happy to accept that Persian polo goes way back to the 6th century BC, but reliable historical evidence can go back no earlier than the times of Darius the Great (521–485 BC), but from then on what is now Iran has the richest polo history of all.

Polo had reached Turkey, or Byzantium as it was then known, by the 10th century, when Constantine Porphyrogenitus said it was an "established custom for kings and the sons of wealthy people to play ball on horseback." In 1170, contemporary writer Cinnamus wrote about how "they rush to meet one another at full gallop, each brandishing in the right hand a staff proportionally long, and ending abruptly in a broad curvature, the middle of which is divided out with gut-strings dried gradually and plaited into one another, net fashion. Each side now makes it a point of emulation to get ahead and transmit the ball to the other goal, which of course has been marked out for them from the first. For when the ball has been driven by the staves as to have arrived at either goal, the victory thereby falls to that side. Such is the character of the game, slippery in every way, and dangerous; leaning backward, and twisting from side to side, and wheeling his horse in a circle, and turning his horse in every direction, and to be jerked about in as many kinds of movement as the very ball itself may happen to be."

Spanish traveller Pedro Tafur was in Egypt in the mid 15th century when he noted that "the Sultan dined in the field, and afterward they played a game that is customary there, in this manner: they place a ball in the centre of the field, and some thousand horsemen, more or less, take up their position on one side … and each has a mallet in his hand … they all attack the ball at the same time, with intent, on the one side, to drive it across the line, while the others seek to do the same on their part, and those who succeed in driving the ball across the line are the victors." Tafur was lucky to be there for a particularly memorable match, in which "one of the players tried to hinder the Sultan's son, and he took out his sword, and tried to kill his opponent, and there was a great commotion until the Sultan came up and parted them[7]." But it is unlikely that the game had any ancient roots in the country. Polo probably caught on in Egypt during the Muslim Conquest (632–732), as the game appears in none of the art from the Pharaonic era.

Gradually, as the great eastern empires declined, particularly at the hands of the Mongol hordes in the Middle Ages, hockey on horses withered too, and survived only in more and more remote outposts. Manipur with its *sagol kangjei* was one of these, and there seems little

---

[7] Marcos Jiménez de la Espada *Pedro Tafur, Andanças e viajes de Pedro Tafur por diversas partes del mundo avido, 1435-1439* (1874).

reason not to believe the sources that claim that it was here that the British colonists made their first contact with the game. They played it locally, and the Calcutta Polo Club was set up as early as 1834, but the game was also taken home to Blighty, and also to South America, where the Argentinian *gauchos* as good as made it their own.

Tomb raiders

Only much later did anybody bother to record anything about the less glamorous form of the game in which the only mount was Shank's Pony. According to Lady Wentworth "there were two sorts of ball games, one called *savlajan*, played with a stick curved or hooked at the end, which was obviously the origin of polo, while *chaughan* was played with a shorter and stringed racket and must have been the origin of the French *chicane*, or *jeu de paume*, and the Greek game *tzganisterium*[8]."

That is a popular claim that the French learnt about hockey during the Crusades in Persia, where one of earliest and most prominent writers, Abu Ja'far Muhammad ibn Jarir al-Tabari, or just Tabari to you and me, wrote in the year 900, but about events 670 years earlier, of a trial in which "Ardashi ordered the boy to be groomed for presentation at court with a hundred, or according to others, with a thousand other boys of his age. These should all be led in at the same time, care being taken that no distinction be discernable in their dress, height or manner … No sooner did Ardashi look upon the boys than, without the slightest hint or suggestion, he delightedly recognised his son among them. He next commanded that they be led into the court of the palace. There they were given hooked staffs, and they played ball while the King watched them." No mention of horses there. That was Persian hockey.

There is more hockey in the astonishingly ancient evidence that has been found of the game of *pukku-mikku* on twelve ancient tablets that recount the tale of the great warrior king Gilgamesh, who ruled the Sumerian city of Uruk (modern day Iraq), and dated to around 2600 BC. *Pukku-mikku* was played with a long, curved stick and a hoop-shaped puck, and there is enough archaeological evidence to believe that this was the same sport that reappears in North Africa during the Middle Kingdom period (1975 BC–1640 BC), and may well have either influenced, or been influenced by, the *khong kangjei* they were playing over in Manipur.

The general assumption is that ball sports came to Europe via the Far East, the Middle East, Greece and then the Roman Empire. But if we look at the history of most things it seems they all came to Europe via the Far East, the Middle East, Greece and then the Roman Empire.

---

[8] Judith Anne Dorothea Blunt-Lytton, 16th Baroness Wentworth *Thoroughbred Racing Stock and Its Ancestors the Authentic Origin of Pure Blood* (George Allen & Unwin, 1938). At first glance the Greek word *tzganisterium* is nothing like the name of a medieval French game called *chicane*, a potential fore-cousin of both modern golf and hockey. But remove the *isterium* ending and replace the *tzy* sound with the more Gallic *chi* and it is one and the same thing.

That's partly because it might be true, and partly because in that order, these are the great civilisations from which the oldest evidence has survived to this day.

And if it's old evidence of ball games you want, then you won't find much that is older than what can be found in the archaeological heaven that is Egypt. Sticklers that they are, good historians only like to go by facts that can be backed up by solid evidence, and therefore conclude that the Egyptians invented the ball. But that is about as silly as singling out a single country as the one where dogs first learned to fetch sticks.

Nevertheless, in Egypt "many balls have been found in excavations, stuffed with palm or papyrus fibre, or straw, and covered in sewn leather or cloth[9]." Later, a ball stuffed with catgut was developed, which would have offered a bit more bounce.

To find clues about what the Egyptians actually did with these balls, we need look no further than the pictures found in the tombs at Beni Hassan in Menya, dating from around 2000 BC. They do most definitely show a group of scantily clad ladies playing a ball game, but whatever they are doing with them, it sure doesn't look much like football. What they are doing is throwing what look roughly like billiard balls up and down, and maybe to each other. There are actually more balls than ladies, which is what we call juggling. Not football. Not even slightly.

Pictures at the same site show similar girls playing what has been described as some kind of piggyback handball game. Maybe it is. But it looks a far more solid bet that it's just more juggling, only this time the ladies are really showing off and doing it on each other's backs. It's very clever, but once again, football it ain't.

We can bring Robert Henderson back into the fray here, the author who claimed this whole ballgame lark goes back to ancient Egyptian fertility rites, so this is definitely his territory. On these images he is up to his old trick of jumping to conclusions when he suggests that "since at a much later date we know of naked women engaging in ball games designed to encourage rainfall, it is probable that this ancient Egyptian ritual had a related purpose." Probable? Possibly maybe.

Ball tossing is actually the closest *The Holy Bible* ever comes to a footballing reference, in a verse in Isaiah 22:18, where it is said that "he will surely turn and toss thee like a ball into a large country; there shalt thou die." That's enough to tell us that there were balls in biblical times, and that said balls were tossed about, and that there was nothing particularly spiritual about doing it. In fact, quite the reverse.

Another example of Egyptian ball-play is depicted in a wall painting of around 1500 BC at Deir-el-Bahari temple. This game has been dubbed Hathor's Ball because that was the god in whose honour the temple was built. The image shows Pharaoh Thutmose III preparing to hit a ball with a large, curved stick (or maybe digging holes, raking, hoeing or anything else involving a long implement held in the hand) while two priests behind him are taking what look like basketball free throws. Not to say that Hathor's Ball is not some kind of early

---

[9] Zahi Hawass of Egypt's Supreme Council of Antiquities in *Al-Ahram Weekly* (December 2003).

hockey or baseball, but judging by the inscription under the picture warning that "all the foes shall perish", there is a good chance that this was no sport at all but some kind of ancient something or other that involved perishing foes. In Henderson's eyes, the inscription is a "nice figure of speech symbolising the defeat of the evil forces of the non-productive winter season." Of course it is, Robert.

In terms of real evidence, there is very, very little that Ancient Egypt *really* has to offer the football historian. All we can say is that they did play with balls, and if they had anything resembling our modern sports, then hockey would be a likely candidate. And they may well have even survived to this day, for you can still find children in some Egyptian villages playing a game they call *hocksha*, which may have descended from the game of old, although the name suggests a much more modern, and western, origin.

Out of Africa

In nearby Ethiopia, which at the time of the Pharaohs formed part of the Aksumite Empire that stretched right across the Red Sea and into modern-day Yemen, they have a game that is remarkably similar to hockey called *ganna*, which also happens to be the local word for Christmas. And that is no coincidence. Legend has it that the shepherds so rejoiced when Gabriel popped by with his joyous news of the birth of Christ that they started using their crooks to play a game. It's such a cracking theory that you just don't want to believe it isn't true. And why shouldn't it be? Who knows, maybe the wise men played polo on their camels? Just why it took the birth of the Messiah for their ancestors come up with the idea of hockey is not clear, but for that reason, Ethiopian families and friends traditionally play *ganna* on Christmas Day (which in Ethiopia is January 7th in accordance with the old Julian calendar).

And mighty pleased we are to get the chance to mention an African game. We know of football-like sports played all the way up through the Americas, and through Europe, Asia and down in Oceania, yet Africa has very little to offer us. The few examples include the game of *che* once played by the San people of what is now South Africa, who used a chunk of hippopotamus neck of all things, which could be hammered into the shape of a ball with a remarkably effective bounce. The idea was to slam it against a rock and battle to be the first to catch it. Not too unlike the Australian Aborigines and their *marngrook*.

Closer to hockey, Robert Henderson mentions the game of *koora*, noted by a traveller in 1925 to have been played in various parts of Algeria and apparently "of great antiquity … in one tribe, two or four naked women play a kind of hockey with large ladles, and in yet another place good old women play at ball when rain is desired. In one village something resembling a football match is played, after which a ewe is draped with a woman's shawl.

Again, at another village, it is custom for men and youths in spring to play at ball with sticks as a means of producing rain[10]."

Henderson's insistence on the Egyptian fertility origin of ball games has been given a rough ride on many of these pages, but it is hard to argue with him here. However, it's a bit of a chicken and the egg conundrum. After all, did the desire to make rain lead them to create hockey, or did the desire to play hockey lead them to use it as way of making rain? One suspects it was the latter.

Ireland's call

The potted examples of Mohammedan stick and ball games are probably quite rightly associated to the games of Ancient Egypt. And as the Moors moved north into Spain, they may have taken their games with them. William Baker writes how "the ball rites of Islam, practiced in the spring of each year, naturally blended with the Christian Easter festivals of the Spanish people. Especially in the countryside, illiterate peasants had difficulty keeping the rituals of the two religions separate. Firmly established in Spain, the customs of Islam spread into southern and western France."

Theories abound for where Middle Eastern games could have gone after that, some a little implausible, others more palpable, and the Society of North American Hockey Historians and Researchers[11] have some particularly fanciful theories. One of their finest tells how the ancient Middle Eastern stick games found their way as far as Ireland to eventually become modern day hurling. It's a tad farfetched, but worth documenting for curiosity's sake.

To vastly simplify several hundred years of very complex history, around 1000 years BC, there were two great powers in the Middle East: the Egyptians to the west and the Hittites to the east, while the area in between occupied by the Canaanite peoples in the general area of modern-day Syria, Israel and Lebanon was something of a power vacuum that would eventually grow into a powerful empire of its own, the Phoenicians.

As anybody who has played *Age of Empires* will be able to confirm, the Phoenicians were notable seafarers, and used their travelling and bargaining skills to trade with other peoples around the Mediterranean, Africa and some believe as far up the Atlantic coast as Ireland.

Lebor Gabála Érenn ('The Book of the Taking of Ireland') is one of the finest accounts ever written of Irish history from the creation onwards, although as it wasn't compiled until the 11th century its historic veracity is dubious. Rather like the Holy Scriptures, no doubt some element of historical truth is contained within, but it has all got so tangled up with

---

[10] *An Universal history, from the earliest account of time, Volume 39* (1760) in its section on the *History of Algiers* notes that the "ridiculous" customs of the Marabouts included not eating snails, not punishing children anywhere but on the soles of the feet and not striking "the ground with their foot when they play at foot- ball."

[11] *The History of Hockey* at www.sonahhr.com – we're talking ice hockey here.

legend, folklore and mythology that it is always going to be debatable which bits are fact and which are fiction, or at best, vastly embellished retellings of the truth[12].

The text tells of the arrival in Ireland of the *Tuatha de Danann,* who were intent on conquering the *Fir Bolg* that inhabited the island at the time. In 1272 BC, the rival leaders met several times to discuss terms for what would be the First Battle of Moytura, and at one point "twenty-seven of the sons of courageous Mil sped westwards to the end of Mag Nia to offer a hurling contest to the Tuatha De. An equal number came out to meet them. The match began. They dealt many a blow on legs and arms, till their bones were broken and bruised, and fell outstretched on the turf, and the match ended."

This text is popularly used in defence of hurling's antiquity, although more critical analysts might ask whether we should take the word of an anonymous chronicler of events over 2000 years earlier. And even so, the original Irish version never really describes any kind of stickball game. That was the work of the imaginative minds of later translators, and particularly John Fraser in 1915, who decided that two groups of people having it out with each other could justifiably be translated from the Old Irish as 'hurling'[13].

But the theory here is that the *Tuatha de Danann* were actually Phoenicians, maybe even of Canaanite descent and one of the lost tribes of Israel[14], and this tale tells us how they introduced Ireland to the Middle Eastern stickball game.

It's not the most solid of claims. After all, it was the Fir Bolg who issued the challenge, which would imply it was their game and not one brought by the invaders. We have no proof that the god-like *Tuatha de Danann* even existed, nor that the Phoenicians ever set foot in Ireland, and as the same text tells us that these particular invaders "came from the northern islands," it is highly unlikely that they were one and the same thing. That's not to say that hurling doesn't have a Phoenician origin, but this particular explanation of how that might have happened is as likely as Mary's trip to Bethlehem astride a donkey being the origin of horse racing.

Chile source

The idea that a stick-based field sport could have found its way from the Middle East to Ireland may sound a bit fanciful, but that is just the start of it when we start postulating about where the Phoenicians might have taken their games.

Around 100 BC, Sicilian historian Diodorus famously wrote of a remarkable Carthaginian discovery, claiming "over against Africa lies a very great island in the vast Ocean, many

---

[12] Although RA Stewart Macalister translated the text into English, he once said "there is not a single element of genuine historical detail, in the strict sense of the word, anywhere in the whole compilation." However, he later retracted those words as being a bit harsh.

[13] John Fraser *The First Battle of Moytura* (1915).

[14] Similar legend has it that Cessair, the granddaughter of Noah, arrived in Ireland forty days before the Great Flood.

days' sail from Libya westward. The soil there is very fruitful, a great deal whereof is mountainous, but much likewise a plain, which is the most sweet and pleasant part, for it is watered with several navigable rivers. The mountainous part of the country is clothed with very large woods, and all manner of fruit trees and springs of fresh water. There you may have game enough in hunting all sorts of wild beasts[15]."

If these claims are to be believed, then what they had found could not have been anything other than South America. The descriptions are uncannily accurate, and there are too many historical records of the Carthaginians, who dubbed themselves the 'masters of the western ocean', circumnavigating Africa for us to doubt their geographical skills and accuse them of confusing America with somewhere else instead. Diodorus really does appear to be describing the entrance to the Mar del Plata, the site of modern day Buenos Aires, and the Amazon jungle, the Great Plains and the Andean Mountains where the Pilcomayo and Paraguay rivers meet. It's all there. And this was the home of the Araucano Indians. Remember that name.

Diodorus could also be right when he said the original discovery was made by a West African merchant vessel being blown off course by a storm. Yachtie folk, who know about these things, can testify that the way storm currents work in the Mid-Atlantic there is every chance that a ship could be driven westwards to the Brazilian coast, and Carthaginian vessels were certainly able to make it that far. Their ships had keels, sails and rigging the likes of which would never be seen again until the 17th century. They could move 100 miles a day, and once transported an army of elephants across the Mediterranean (the ones Hannibal famously rode across the Alps). So the trip from the tip of West Africa to Brazil (a distance only about the same as travelling from Greece to Spain) was well within their means.

But rather than wallow in their discovery, it is said that the whole thing got the Carthaginians into a state of panic. Spanish historian Marianus de Orscelar wrote 1500 years later how "because the land was attractive and not crowded with inhabitants, many of the Carthaginians remained to settle there, the others returned with the fleet." The Senate did not rejoice at the news, but "put to death those that brought the news. They feared that the people, weary of the war that had lasted many years and desiring a change, would with a single mind move out of the city and go to live in such a good land."

All kinds of 'evidence' has been produced to show that there were Europeans in what is now Latin America long before 1492, but most of it is more the result of wild imaginations than anything else. Nobody is really sure what the Tree of Life on the cliffs of the Bay of Paracas in Peru ever symbolised, but its similarity to a Near Eastern symbol is probably coincidence. Associating trees to life is nothing new. The 'lotus blossoms' that have been spotted among the etchings in the ancient ballparks of Central America, despite the fact that this plant is not native to the New World, are about as convincing as some quack's idea that a stone carving at Copan in Honduras, dating back to 750 AD, is of an elephant whose trunk

---

[15] For a full account of the story, see Frederick J Pohl *Atlantic Crossings Before Columbus* (Norton, 1961).

has broken off, or that the slit-eyed bearded warrior at Veracruz, Mexico is a Chinaman. The inscribed stones found in Philadelphia in 1941 do have an uncannily Canaanite look to them, but even if they aren't a forgery, nothing can be proved.

Then there's the Araucano legend of the serpent of the sea, Cai Cai, wanting to rule the land and planning to make it rain so much that everybody would be killed by the floods. But the serpent of the land, Ten Ten, got wind of the plan, and warned everybody that it might be better if they all legged it to the mountaintops where they would be safer. Arguing that this is the same legend as that of Noah and the Great Flood is possibly pushing it a bit, especially given the conspicuous presence of snakes and absence of arks in the Araucano version.

But it's to the Araucano that we turn for our next revelation. They were a noble but fearsome lot, and one of the few peoples that were able to stand up to the all-conquering Incas. They gave the folk who fancied making South America an extension of the Iberian Peninsula a fair run for their money too.

Have a flick through Lonko Kilapan's *The Hellenic Origin of the Araucans of Chile* (1974), and it is astounding in the evidence it presents of the possible Greek connection. He claims that about 20% of the Arauca language is so similar to Greek that it is hard to laugh the theory off as coincidence, and even the Arauca calendar almost coincides with the Olympic calendar used in Ancient Greece, which dated from the first Olympiad held in 776 BC.

These were the people most likely to have run into the Phoenicians when they were in port, for they inhabited the lands around the Mar del Plata before the conquistadores forced them further and further west into modern-day Chile, where they live now. As they did so, the Spaniards also come across a sport called *palin* that reminded them so much of something they played back home that they named it after their own sport, *chueca*.

So, could this possibly be the same game that the Carthaginians had brought across the Atlantic hundreds of years before? Could it even have influenced the Mesoamerican ballgames, and the early forms of lacrosse played in North America?

The Araucano revered this game in much the same way as all Pre-Colombian societies revered their ball games. They accompanied it with feasting, religious rites and dancing, considered it a damn fine way of keeping fit and preparing people for battle, and like their cousins in the north, sometimes used it as a substitute for outright warfare.

Diego de Rosales provides the most brilliant description we have of the game before it was too heavily bastardised by others introduced by the Europeans to be of any anthropological value. "The most ordinary game is *chueca*" he wrote. "They hit a ball with some twisted sticks, which have a natural curve at one end and are used as mallets. They form two gangs to fight each other to get the ball, placed in the middle of a hole, to their own team until they take it out over a line, marked on both sides. They get a point when the ball goes over the line on their side. After four or six lines, the game is over, they can play a whole afternoon. After the game, they sit down to drink their *chicha* and get completely drunk. They sometimes come to agreements for uprising, because they call for other Indians from the whole Earth, and at night, they talk and agree on rebellions. Thus governors sometimes forbid this game and these meetings for the damages experienced. In order to be comfortable while running, they play the game naked, wearing only a loincloth to cover their indecency. Women sometimes play this game, but they wear cloth[16]."

None of this impressed Capitan General Don Martín de Mujica, who in Santiago in 1647 proclaimed "the prohibition of *chueca*, a game practised by the Araucano according to their tradition … Those who disobey will be punished with one hundred lashes and the others will be fined, because the vile *chueca* has been widely spread among Creole soldiers."

One thing that upset the conquistadores was the gambling associated with the game, while the church was most upset to view the promiscuity of a sport that men and women played together, the former not even wearing any clothes. And they can't have taken too kindly to all the very un-Catholic rites attached to the games, including the magical enchantment of sticks, pregnant women making a powder out of bird talons that could make the players stronger, the skulls of former champions being brandished as a sign of good fortune, and all kinds of songs and ceremonies led by shamans that simply weren't the done thing for people that would surely be much better off taking their orders from that man in Rome.

But as is so often the case with ball games, it prevailed regardless, and *palin* was still played extensively into the 19th century before it went into decline, just when its popularity was peaking, with the game spreading into Argentina and even having professional players. Like so many other traditional sports around the world, its downfall was the arrival of the different European sports, and especially soccer, to which the South Americans took a famous fancy.

The Mapuche of modern day Chile still dabble in the game today, but the impoverishment of this particular ethnic group has not helped matters at all. It is generally only played at Mapuche cultural events, where teams of anything between about 5 and 15 players try to get the ball to cross a short line and score what is known as a *tripal*. The sticks are similar enough to what would be used in hockey or hurling today. Although the standard method is just to thump the ball along the ground, it can also be played in the air, and the true art of a decent *palin* player is *malkokantun*, which is the skill of controlling the ball in the air as you run along. In hurling you call that soloing.

Purists now bemoan the way that what they call *winkapalin* (*palin* influenced by foreign *winkas*) has been bastardised, and how modern-day players lack the grace and skill of their forefathers. Rarely will these namby-pamby youngsters control the ball on their sticks and flick it back and forth between each other as they did of old, it's all just unsightly thumping of the ball long and hard along the ground. Pity.

---

[16] Diego de Rosales *General History of the Kingdom of Chile*, written approximately between 1652 and 1673.

Heading for the world

Our old friend Robert Henderson agrees that the American Indians were influenced by what he sees as an ancient Egyptian fertility rite. But his theory is not based on the Phoenicians, but on a very different route. He asserts that the games "travelled in an easterly direction through India, Assam, Borneo and the islands of the Pacific, in all probability reaching the west coast of South America, at what is now Peru, and from there spreading northwards through Central America to the North American plains." That's quite some theory to class as being 'in all probability', but he claimed to have the support of the archaeology community on that one. He reckoned the spread of football and hockey went in parallel with the spread of head-cults, the famous head statues of Easter Island being one of his most decisive pieces of evidence.

"When the trans-Pacific migrants, after many centuries, eventually reached the shores of South America, they imported their religious customs, one of which was their belief in fertilising the head of their ruler" he writes. "And just as this belief developed in the old world with a change to a ball as the head-like symbol of fertility, so we find it developed in the new world, as a series of fantastic myths and customs indicate." On the subject of fantastic myths, it is tempting to suggest Henderson was presenting one of his own.

He quotes Thomas Garn here, who claims "the whole probably represents the fertilisation of the earth by blood sacrifice to the earth god, and shows close connection between the ball game and the gods of fertility" and considers the legend of the Maya hero twins Hunahpu and Xbalanque, and also the decapitated heads being held aloft at the Chichen Itza ball court, to be comparable to similar legends involving Egyptian gods.

Henderson's is probably letting his imagination run a bit too far with his idea of the antediluvian head cults of the Middle East island-hopping around the South Pacific, but he is right to observe that there are some striking similarities between Ancient Egyptian and Mesoamerican traditions. The great Aztec pyramids and those in Egypt are prime examples, both of which were strikingly alike both in archaeology and purpose. Certainly, the civilisation that the Spanish discovered when they landed in the Americas was more or less at the same stage of technological development as the Middle East had been just a few hundred years earlier, and when we consider that the two continents had been almost completely isolated from each other since the Ice Age 20,000 years earlier, it does seem rather too great a coincidence to write off completely.

But when it comes to sports, hitting a ball with a stick is hardly the most complex of concepts, and whether or not the Phoenicians reached America, the argument presented by lacrosse pioneer William George Beers in 1869 is still the strongest. He had recently read the work of a writer "holding the identity of origin of the Indian and Irish races with the Phoenicians, and ingeniously attempting to show sufficient resemblance between lacrosse and *coman* to make a plausible argument for his theory … it seems rather far-fetched … were I inclined like the Irishman who traced his genealogy to the Ark, and the locality of Paradise to his potato patch, which he was irreverently offering for sale, I might enter into archaeological researches, and build up theories from hypothesis, but this would only lead astray ... unless some archaeologist can prove it was played by the extinct races of a cultivated and superior type of humanity said to have existed on this continent long before the advent of the Spaniards, it is only fair that [the Indians] should have the honour."

Personally, I'm inclined to agree.

8 FOOTBALL CLASSICS
Ball games in ancient Greece and Rome

Greece proof

Ancient Greece. The seminal culture and foundation of Western Civilization. Such was the extent of Hellenic innovation that it is almost as if before it, there was no language, no politics, no education, no science, no art, no philosophy, no sickly aniseed flavoured shots, and in fact a whole lot less of many things, yet by the time of its demise to the Roman Empire, Greece had set new standards for the world to follow.

Those standards were also applied to sport and its institutionalisation as part of society. The Ancient Olympic Games[1] were unprecedented in terms of major public athletic events and were, of course, the model and inspiration for Pierre de Coubertin's first Modern Olympic Games held in Athens in 1896, that quadrennial celebration of both the good and bad of international relations.

The most accurate date, though highly disputed among historians, of the first ever Games was 776 BC, and they were held every four years for well over a thousand years, until eventually being suppressed by either Theodosius I or II sometime around the start of the 4th century, mainly as part of the imposition of Christian values on Greek society. They were literally spoilsports.

The Ancient Olympics were not quite as all-encompassing as many believe. Only male athletes from the Greek-speaking city-states could enter, and there were other provisions, such as no slaves or former slaves, no former murderers, and nobody of illegitimate birth. Like the Egyptians, they did most of their running, jumping and throwing in the nude, although the more modest or less well-endowed had the option of what was called a *kynodesme* to cover up their pride and joy.

The earliest Olympic Games only included running races, and later additions included forms of boxing and wrestling, chariot racing and the pentathlon (running, long jump, discus, javelin and wrestling). As Harold Arthur Harris writes, "athletics and chariot racing were as fully organised in antiquity as modern football, and records were carefully kept. But nothing of the kind appears to have happened for ball games[2]."

The Olympics were all about individual rather than collective heroics, and balls were not needed for that. For a culture with such amazing powers of creation, coming up with a few

---

[1] Although the Olympic Games, held in honour of Zeus, were undoubtedly the biggest and most important of the great athletics meetings, they were by no means unique. There were also the Pythian Games, in honour of Apollo, the Nemean Games, also in honour of Zeus, the Isthmian Games, in honour of Poseidon, and Athens' own festival, the Panathenaic Games, to name but a few.

[2] Those people that are uncomfortable with the inclusion of the likes of football, handball and basketball will argue that those should be the ideals of the Modern Olympics too.

ideas for ball games would have been a cinch, and even if they were stuck for suggestions, they could always seek inspiration from the stick games of their neighbours in Phoenicia, with whom they vied for superiority in the eastern Mediterranean and eventually subdued.

But no ball games get anything more than brief passing references in the wealth of Greek literature that has survived, and that probably means they were either not particularly widespread, or considered to be of little cultural significance.

Nigel Crowther makes a very valid point here, saying "for the ancient Greeks … war was the team game … The ancients had no need to participate in games that served as a substitute for war, as most adult males in Greece engaged in the real thing[3]." However, that may be jumping to conclusions, for there are plenty of examples of warring nations over the years that did play team sports.

HA Harris considers sport to work on three levels. First, that of first class modern sports with their rulebooks, governing bodies and spectators. Second, there are the kind of games that a family might play with a ball on the beach, perhaps loosely based around 'real sports', but just played for fun and exercise and where any kind of score-keeping or serious competitiveness is largely an irrelevance. And third, there are the kind of games we have all played in school playgrounds, for which simple rules are passed on by word of mouth, but very little about them is ever recorded.

Harris is probably quite right in asserting that Greek ball games never made it any further than the second and third levels he describes. In a way this is odd, because the Greeks had a strong competitive spirit and took great enjoyment out of music and writing competitions and even male beauty pageants, yet the furthest they got with ball games was a bit of juggling and simple games of catch, despite all the modern-day attempts to distort the historical evidence and make it look like they also went in for something like rugby.

What we do have is evidence of games that went by a variety of names, including *keretizein*, *kpiskyros*, *kaininda*, *sphaeromachia* and *harpaston*, to name but five, but what little we really know about them is so vague that we cannot even be sure whether they were all different games or just umbrella terms for ball games in general, rather like the words 'football' and 'hockey' vary in time in space.

Sfaira play

The very earliest reference to ball-play in Ancient Greece appears in Homer's epic work, *Odyssey*, probably written around the 8th century BC, and which American football chronicler Parke Davis claimed was "familiar to all schoolboys." However, most 21st century readers are less groomed on the classics, and won't be quite as familiar with a delightful young damsel named Nausicaa, who 2nd century BC grammarian Agallis goes as far as to say was the very inventor of ball games. But by that kind of logic, thatching was invented by the first of the three little pigs.

---

[3] Nigel Crowther *Sport in Ancient Times* (Praeger, 2007).

In Homer's poem, Nausicaa and her friends went down to the river to do the laundry and to pass the time while it dried, threw off their veils and played with a ball. One of the greatest poets of the 18th century, Alexander Pope, took a few liberties with his translation in order to make it rhyme in English, but as the Latin original would be lost on most of us, it went like this:

> "O'er the green mead the sporting virgins play
> (Their shining veils unbound). Along the skies,
> Toss'd and retoss'd, the ball incessant flies.
> They sport, they feast; Nausicaa lifts her voice,
> And, warbling sweet, makes earth and heaven rejoice."

The game itself is of little importance to the story, it is just a plot device to lead to a shriek that wakes up Odysseus, who is sleeping nearby on his ten-year journey back to Ithaca after fighting in the Trojan Wars, and who would have a romantic fling with Nausicaa that eventually came to nothing.

> "Forth from her snowy hand Nausicaa threw
> The various ball; the ball erroneous flew
> And swam the stream; loud shrieks the virgin train."

It's a major quote in football histories, but it doesn't really tell us anything special. The only important point to be drawn is that Homer himself had seen little girls playing with balls[4] and mentioned the fact in what was probably pure fiction. There is no evidence that Odysseus or Nausicaa ever existed, or that the fall of Troy really happened.

Staying with *Odyssey*, Homer mentions ball-play again in *Book VIII*:

> "In dance unmatch'd! a wond'rous ball is brought,
> (The work of Polybus, divinely wrought)
> This youth with strength enormous bids it fly,
> And bending backward whirls it to the sky;
> His brother springing with an active bound
> At distance intercepts it from the ground."

This is not football, but Harris notes a whole series of references to what were probably similar activities. For instance, essayist Plutarch once said that "ball players have to learn how to catch the ball as well as how to throw it" to explain why students needed to be more active in lectures, while philosopher Epictetus, in an apology for his lack of debating skills, said that "in a game, even when I hold out my tunic to catch the ball, I miss it, but if I throw it, the expert catches it every time."

They were not speaking directly about ball games, and Plutarch and Epictetus would probably be amazed to know that 2000 years later, it would not be their opinions of the Greek education and debating systems that interested us even half as much as the innocent games they played in their spare time!

---

[4] That's if he could see at all, for it is popularly believed that Homer was blind, although there is no definite evidence of that.

Harris goes on to tell us that it was under Alexander the Great that ball-play moved up a notch in Greece. Fed up with athletics, because everybody kept letting him win, Alexander started focusing on ways of using balls to occupy his leisure time (Oliver Stone's movie suggests he found plenty of those). Kings, or in this case a *basileus*, are always great trend-setters, and it wasn't long before the *sfairisterion* became a common feature of the Greek urban environment, being flat ball courts covered in hard-beaten earth.

The term *sfaira* (from which we get the English 'sphere') means ball, and for the Greeks, these generally fell into two categories: either something small and hard, such as the *episkyros*, which means 'stone ball', and was used in a game that went by the same name, or the larger *follis*, a ball that was made in various ways, often using linen and hair stuffed with sand, flour, feathers or anything else that came to hand and then wrapped in string and sewn together. But the Greeks also knew about the ubiquitous pig's bladder. Claudius Galenus (130–200 AD), or Galen for short, described how children in Ionia (modern day Turkey) "take the bladders of pigs, fill them with air and rub them on the ashes near the fire … while they are rubbing, they chant certain words … to bid the bladder to increase in size[5]."

Any craftsman worth his due could knock up an *episkyros* to rival any modern day cricket or hockey ball, but even the very finest Greek *follis* would have offered little bounce and been liable to bursting or falling apart with the very first bit of rough treatment.

The small, hard and durable *episkyros* would have been better suited to a kind of hockey, and the Greeks did indeed play something they called *keretizein*, meaning 'to hit with horns', and which was considered important enough to appear in a bas-relief found in the Themistoclean Wall, Athens and now on display in the National Museum of Archaeology. It dates from around 500 BC, and shows six stark naked figures. The two in the middle look to be bullying off hockey-style for a ball about the size of an apple, while two other pairs of nude stick-wielders look on from either side, perhaps waiting their turn, which might even suggest a game like golf. That is about as much as we have to go on where that sport is concerned – but it does seem likely that it was related to the Egyptian stick-games.

The *Ball-player Relief* on a funerary monument dating from around the same period, and also on show in the National Museum of Archaeology shows what appears to be a naked man, the deceased, controlling a large ball on his upper thigh, presumably demonstrating a playing technique to a small boy. We can't be sure whether this is anything that even remotely resembled football, but it was enough to persuade UEFA to use the image on the European Champions Cup (now Champions League) trophy.

The same museum also houses what once formed the base of one of the famous Kouros statues, also from around 500 BC and not discovered until 1922. In what is clearly a tribute to the sports of the time, two of the sides depict people watching a cat and dog fighting, another shows a variety of different athletes, while another is blank, not because the artist didn't complete his work, but because the ornament was designed to stand against a wall. But

---

[5] Claudius Galenus *Exercising with a Small Ball* (2nd century AD).

the side that we are interested in shows two sets of three rather camp looking nudists on either side of what looks like a volleyball court without a net. One of the players is about to lob the ball in an action that fits one of the few surviving descriptions of *episkyros*, which appears in the *Dictionary Onomasticon*. This was written by something of a wannabe intellectual called Julius Pollux (150–200 AD), who originated from Egypt and has often been criticised for the disorganised and vague nature of his work, which is worth bearing in mind when we focus on his brief explanations of Greek ball games. But it is about the best we have to go on, and according to him, *episkyros* "was usually played by opposing teams of equal number. In the middle a line was drawn with a chip of stone they called a *styros*. They set the ball on this line and then drew another line behind each team. The team that got the ball first threw it over the opposition, who had to catch the ball as it was moving, and throw it back the other way until one team pushes the other over the line behind them."

It's hard to work out what he means, and it doesn't help not to know anything about the length of the court or weight of the ball. E Norman Gardiner feels that in *episkyros* "we really find anticipations of rugby football, at least in the arrangements of the ground[6]", but we don't really find anything of the sort, and *episkyros* might better be described as dodgeball with a rock.

Pollux also mentions *aporrhaxis*, which involved "bouncing the ball vigorously on the ground, and dribbling it again with the hand. The number of bounces is counted" and *ourania*, 'sky ball', which was "played with one player bending backward and throwing the ball to the sky, the others try to snatch the ball before it falls to the ground … when they dribble the ball against a wall, they count the number of bounces. The loser is called the donkey and has to do what he is told; the winner is called the king and gives the orders." Basically, this is the same kind of playground game we also enjoyed as children. At my school, we called it 'death throw'.

One of Pollux's contemporaries, and a fellow rhetorician and grammarian, Athenaeus, put together his *Deipnosophistai*, which is a haphazard selection of anecdotes and discussions on all walks of Greek society based on a rambling conversation between twenty-three learned men sat at a banquet in Rome. In it, he writes that a ball called a *folliculus* (which judging by the use of the diminutive was a small *follis*) "was invented by Atticus of Naples, trainer of Pompeius Magnus, as an aid in physical exercise."

Parts of the lines that follow are missing or illegible. Not helped by Athenaeus' lack of narrative continuity, scholars have struggled to translate them accurately, but the gist suggests a much more physical game than those we have met up until now. He tells how "great are the exertions and fatigue in contests of ball-playing, and violent twisting and turning of the neck. Hence Antiphanes[7] wrote 'Damn me, what a pain I've got in my neck!' He describes the game of *phaininda* thus 'He seized the ball and passed it with a laugh to

---

[6] E Norman Gardiner *Athletics in the Ancient World* (Clarendon Press, 1971).
[7] One of the most famous comic poets of the era, about 130 of his works have survived.

one, while the other player he dodged; from one he pushed it out of the way, while he raised another player to his feet amid resounding shouts of 'out of bounds', 'too far', 'right beside him', 'over his head', 'on the ground', 'up in the air', 'too short', 'pass it back in the scrimmage'. The game was called *phaininda* either from the players shooting the ball or because, according to Juba the Mauritanian[8], its inventor was the trainer Phainestius … Ball-players also paid attention to graceful movement. Damoxenus[9], at any rate, says 'A youngster, perhaps sixteen or seventeen years old, was once playing ball. He came from Cos. That island, it is plain, produces gods. Whenever he cast his eye upon us seated there, as he caught or threw the ball, we shouted together, 'What rhythm! What modesty of manner, what skill!' Whatever he said or did, gentlemen, he seemed a miracle of beauty. Never before have I heard of or seen such grace. Something would have happened to me if I had stayed longer. As it is, I feel that I am not quite well.' Even Ctesibius, the philosopher of Chalcis, liked to play ball, and many of King Antigonus' friends would strip for a game with him."

The original Ancient Greek text can, of course, be interpreted in many ways using modern English, so we should exercise caution before assuming that all that dodging and backwards passing in scrimmages equated to an ancient form of rugby. It sounds like it was closer to something resembling basketball without the baskets, or a piggy-in-the-middle type game. Athenaeus doesn't seem to go to any great length to describe the game as being violent, and the pain he describes is not a result of physical contact.

In another part of his book, Athenaeus explains that "Aristonicus of Carystus, Alexander's ball-player, was made a citizen by the Athenians because of his skill, and a statue was erected to him. For in later times the Greeks came to esteem vulgar skill of hand very highly, more than the ideas of the cultivated intellect. The people of Hestiaea, at any rate, and of Oreus, raised a bronze statue in the theatre of the juggler." Such tributes are hardly in keeping with the revisionist idea that ball games were of little importance to the Greeks, although his descriptions paint a picture more of individualistic gymnastics than full-contact footy.

For those that prefer to believe that football owes its roots to something altogether more wicked, violent and barbaric, the Spartans had a game with many of the clichéd rough and tumble elements we would expect of early rugby. The little evidence we have of it suggests it was a brutal affair, the idea being that teams of about fifteen gathered on a playing field surrounded by ditches, and had to push or throw the opposing team into the water. That involved plenty of fighting, eye-gouging, kicking and biting, and strict rules that players were flogged for disobeying. Excavations at Sparta have even unearthed inscriptions that seem to be records of the results of these matches, played to a knockout system. Probably some form

---

[8] A second century metric poet, none of whose works have survived.

[9] This was probably the same Damoxenus who famously boxed with Creugas. Their fight went on so long that the umpire decided that they would settle the bout with one punch each. After Creugas' hit barely caused Damoxenus to flinch, the latter lay a powerful blow to Creugas' ribs and then pulled out his entrails. But the umpire decided that this counted as two punches, and Creugas was declared the winner, although being dead, his celebrations were somewhat muted.

of military training, all that's missing for us to call this football is the ball. That the Spartans even played ball games is only theory, based on their word for a boy in his late teens, a *sphaereis*, which might be related to the fact that this was the age when they exercised with balls. It's a long shot. You'd imagine it's to do with the dropping of a very different kind of balls.

What with the Spartan game, rudimentary hockey, ball-throwing and all the formality of the different Olympic disciplines, it seems the Greeks had all the elements of football in place. It was just a simple matter of putting them together, but that does not seem to be something they ever did. Greece would have to wait until their shock 2004 win in the UEFA European Championship before they could claim to be at the forefront of European football.

Times Old Roman

Think Roman games, and the first thing that springs to our minds are gladiator fights. Bloody battles, often to the death, involving slaves, criminals, prisoners of war, wild animals, and sometimes volunteers desperate to find a way out, existed from at least as early as 264 BC and as late as about 450 AD. The immensely popular games also included such delights as executions and chariot racing in venues, such as the Coliseum (50,000 capacity) and Circus Maximus (250,000 capacity) in Rome, that set standards that would never be matched again until the great football stadiums of the 20th century.

It wasn't so much that Romans invented these games, they just took things one step further, as they would with so many other things they stumbled across on their conquests. And conquering was something they were very good at. Most of Western Europe fell to the Empire and Greece was no exception, becoming a Roman protectorate in 146 BC, and eventually being swallowed up as the province of Archaea in 27 BC. So, it doesn't take a genius to work out that the Romans learned the basics of their early ball games from the Greeks. The Greek origin of ball games is something several Roman authors allude to[10]. After all, they didn't even bother inventing a new name for *harpaston*; they just Latinized it into *harpastum*.

Other games included *expulsim ludere*, which seems very similar to the modern-day one-wall handball or the Basque *jai alai*, in which a ball is thrown squash-style against a gymnasium wall. Then there was *trigon* (think trigonometry and triangles), in which there was a three-sided court around which players threw a hard ball, although it is not clear whether the idea was to get other players to catch it, or to make it difficult for them. Whatever the case, it was certainly a bad thing to fail to make a catch, and skilful players were renowned for being able to catch the ball left handed. Martial once wished a friend luck

---

[10] Quintus Horatius Flaccus (65 BC–8 BC), for example, offered that "after hunting the hare, or being wearied by an unruly horse, or (if the Roman exercise fatigues you, accustomed to act the Greek) whether the swift ball, while eagerness softens and prevents your perceiving the severity of the game." Julius Pollux wrote that "the ball-game now called *harpastum* was formerly called *phaininda*, which is the kind I like best of all."

in a game by saying "when you are stripped and playing *trigon*, may the approving judgement of the ring of players looking on assign the palm to you, and not give higher praise to Polybus' left-handers", while in another of his bizarre one-liners[11] he says "if you know how to drive me swift left-handers, I am yours. You cannot? Then, rabbit, give up the game!"

One player, named Ursus, was no rabbit, for he was so good he played with a glass ball, but this was just showing off. Martial says that the *pila paganica* (which was not a reference to anything 'pagan', but meant 'rustic ball') "is full of easily-gathered feathers and is not as soft as a larger ball and less compact than a common ball."

That was strangely matter of fact for Martial, for most of his ballgame comments are more cryptic. On the *follis*, he offers: "Go for it boys! But I am of a conservative age. Balls are only for young and elderly people to play with." It's hard to work out what he meant by that, and as for *harpastos*, the satirist tells us that "these balls are rapidly robbed on the dust of Anteo, the bodybuilder that makes his neck big in a vain effort."

We find further mention of ball-play in a rare example of a Roman novel, the 1st century *Satyricon* by Petronius, which tells the tale of Encolpius and his promiscuous sixteen year old lover, Giton – homosexual paedophilia being quite acceptable in those times. Petronius' characters decide to check out what the local ball-players are up to. "Amongst these we all of a sudden catch sight of a bald-headed old man in a russet tunic, playing ball amid a troupe of long-haired boys." Such a sight was the kind of thing to start tickling their happy-hormones, but "it was not so much the boys, though these were well worth looking at, that drew us to the spot, as the master himself, who wore sandals and was playing with green balls. He never stooped for a ball that had touched ground, but an attendant stood by with a sackful, and supplied the players as they required them. We noticed other novelties too. For two eunuchs were stationed at opposite points of the circle, one holding a silver chamber-pot, while the other counted the balls, not those that were in play and flying from hand to hand, but such as fell on the floor … Trimalchio snapped his fingers, and at the signal the eunuch held out the chamber-pot for him, without his ever stopping play. After easing his bladder, he called for

---

[11] His full name was Marcus Valerius Martialis, and there are few finer sources than his epigrams published between AD 86 and 103, which are not unlike a modern day blog in the form of satirical snippets. He also offers some of the finest use of the Latin vernacular you could ever enjoy, and once issued the following warning to critics of his lewd style: "If you are likely to be the really pernickety type of reader, do you mind leaving now? Just head in the direction of absolutely anywhere else." So you have been warned, and if you are easily offended, then skip the rest of this footnote, as it is about to offer a couple of Martial's choicest cuts. One goes that "you sleep with well-endowed boys, Phoebus, and the thing which stands for them does not stand for you," and in another extract that we shall gratuitously include in a book about football, he offers that "you want to be fucked, Saufeia, but you don't want to have a bath with me. I suspect that there is something extremely dreadful: either your breasts hang down ragged from your chest, or you fear that when you are nude you might betray the furrows of your belly, or your mangled groin gapes open with an infinite chasm, or something sticks out from the mouth of your vagina. But, I trust, there's none of these things and you're very beautiful naked. If that's true, you have a worse blemish: you're a fool."

water, and having dipped his hands momentarily in the bowl, dried them on one of the lads' hair." It doesn't sound much like football, but it was worth including just so that modern day ball-boys realise how lucky they are.

Blood sport

A quote that has been taken horribly out of context over the years actually comes from the 6th century *Corpus Juris Civilis*, a Roman code of law, which ponders who the guilty party would be in the hypothetical situation whereby "several persons are playing at ball, one of whom gives the ball rather a hard stroke and so drives it against the hand of a barber, and thereby a slave whom the barber has in his hands has his throat cut, in consequence of the razor being knocked against it." This quote is often used as proof that the Romans played soccer, but nowhere does it does tell us how the theoretical ball was struck.

There is only really one contemporary text that sounds anything like football at all, and that was in Galen's treatise *On Exercising with a Small Ball*. The physician wholeheartedly recommends the activity, for it involved all parts of the body, offered a far better workout than wrestling or running, and what's more took less time and cost practically nothing for it needs "only a ball, and a small one at that."

Galen was arguably the most prominent medical researcher of the Roman period, having originally learned his art as a doctor for gladiators and ending up as personal physician to Marcus Aurelius and his son Commodus (the emperor that was so nasty to Russell Crowe in *Gladiator*). And this essay on ball-based exercise is the most extensive description we have of Greco-Roman ball games, but sadly for us, his interest lies in the medicinal benefits, and only here and there do his comments offer clues as to what the actual sport was like. But we do learn something when he says that "one can recognise that the eyes must get a workout, by noticing that if one does not make careful note of where the ball is thrown, he is certain to miss the catch. Sufficient strategy is required for this game not to throw the ball to the ground, or to hinder the man in the middle, or on the other hand, for him to snatch the ball … surely no other sport is capable of preparing a person in advance to guard what has been taken or to regain what has been captured, or to anticipate the enemy's plan."

It was good for the mind, but also good for the body, for Galen considers that "when people face one another and exert themselves in keeping the man in the middle from catching the ball, this is a very major activity and a very vigorous one, combining many neckholds and many wrestler's counterholds, the sides, chest and stomach with the feints of the face, the attacks, the defences, the stances, and the other wrestling holds … moreover, the attacks and sideward leaps also offer no small workout for the legs." It certainly sounds physical enough. Galen puts it on a par with wrestling, and Roman wrestling was no sissy thing. But though the writer scorns the perils of horse-riding and running, exercising with a small ball "entails no danger, it should appear to be of all activities the best suited for one's benefit."

122

It has nevertheless been concluded that Roman *harpastum* was an early form of football, or better put rugby, but the 'evidence' for that was written much later by people that had never seen the game played at all. Isidor of Seville writes how "they snatched the ball from one another, and threw it aloft, without letting it fall to the ground[12]" and Joseph Strutt offers that "the contending parties endeavoured to force the ball one from the other, and they who could retain it long enough to cast it beyond an appointed boundary were the conquerors[13]."

A barbaric Roman ballgame is certainly plausible, but despite the Romans' huge penchant for spectator events, *harpastum* never seems to have attracted much of an audience. The closest we get to one is the anonymous *Laus Pisonis*, where it is noted that "no less is your nimbleness, if mayhap it is your pleasure to return the flying ball or recover it when falling to the ground, and by a surprising movement get it within bounds again in its flight. To watch such play the populace remains stockstill, and the whole crowd, sweating with exertion, suddenly abandons its own games."

Then again, if the public had Christians being thrown to the lions to look forward to, a few people running around after a ball, however violent, might have looked a bit tame in comparison. Perhaps word got around that *harpastum* needed toughening up. Parke H Davis claims exactly that in suggesting the game was "too childish for Roman youths destined to be centurions and commanders of legions … The Emperor Augustus therefore selected a philosopher to effect the revision. This unknown philosopher … at last submitted his code of rules and they were approved by Augustus. Their introduction immediately divided the young athletes of Rome into two camps, each raging with debate and discussion, one for the new rules and the other for the old."

Caesar Augustus did play ball. "Immediately after the civil war he gave up exercise with horses and arms in the Campus Martius, at first turning to *pila* and the *follis* but soon confining himself to riding or taking a walk" wrote Roman historian Suetonius in *The Lives of the Caesars* but Davis seems to have plucked the rest of story out of his imagination. In fact much of what he writes on 'football in olden time' is quite frankly, fabricated nonsense.

Given the lengths promoters of Roman Games (i.e. the really juicy ones with the gladiators and all) went to come up with increasingly more ferocious beasts, gruesome deaths and spectacular bloodsheds in the amphitheatres, it is perfectly conceivable that they may have come up with a version of *harpastum* that did away with some of the finer points of the rules,

---

[12] Isidorus Hispalensis *Origines* or *Etymologiae* (7th century).

[13] Ah yes, the great Joseph Strutt and his ground-breaking *Sports and Pastimes of Rural England* (1801) to whom we'll be coming back to many times. Considering the time it was written, this is an absolutely astounding tome, made all the more fascinating now with two hundred years of hindsight. The first ever major attempt to produce an encyclopaedia of sports is gobsmackingly comprehensive, covering everything from falconry to board games, through bear baiting, jousting, tennis and a wealth of other games besides. All of this was achieved with very few comprehensive references, before the telephone or train, before television or photography, and long, long before you could Google anything you fancied off the Internet. What's even better, is the 'new, enlarged and much corrected' version edited by J Charles Cox in 1903. Almost a century later, Cox adds extensive footnotes to Strutt's text, which are often no less revealing.

such as no killing, and equipped players with the tools to ensure plenty of drama for the spectators. But this is pure speculation, and there is no record of this ever happening.

Word has it that Julius Caesar was a huge fan. He may even have enjoyed a game or two, and certainly advocated it as excellent exercise for his legions. One unsubstantiated story that's doing the rounds on the internet states that Caesar was once so horrified to learn that only 25 men had died in the morning's *harpastum* training that he threatened to decree it strictly a woman's game unless anything was done to up the death tally. Much to his delight, things had vastly improved the following day, with 47 soldiers meeting their fate on the *harpastum* court.

The idea of Caesar being so keen on having his own forces systematically slaughtered for the sake of a ball game makes too little sense to wash, and is about as likely to be true as the story that, on a visit to England, he inspired football by kicking a human skull over the River Brent. All told, the story of the Romans transforming a Greek game of ball skill into one of combat skill reeks of bogus 19th century textbooks and imaginative re-interpretations that have led people like Nicholas Mason to say that "there is very little difference between this and American football or rugby league." There probably was.

Britannia beckons

But the claim that *harpastum* had anything to do with the origins of modern football has one massive advantage over any of the others we have seen so far.

We have no idea what the Yamana of modern-day Chile played with the cracking balls they made by blowing up albatross feet and stuffing them with goose feathers. Neither is it clear how long the Igbo of Nigeria have been playing what they call *okpasa*, in which three players, one behind and two in front, have to avoid being hit by a ball. But what we do know is that neither these games nor *kemari*, *marngrook*, *pasuckuakohowog* or *ullamaliztli* were played anywhere near the shores of Old Blighty.

But the Romans, on their way to conquering most of Europe, made a point of checking out a place they decided to call Britannia. The future emperor Julius Caesar, then a general, led the first Roman expeditions in 55 and 54 BC. It was something of an offshoot to his plans to conquer the Gauls in northwest France and full-scale invasion did not occur until a century later under Aulus Plautius. Britain remained under Roman rule until the early 5th century, and when they weren't building sewage systems and straight roads, explaining that the metric system may not have been quaint but did make a whole lot more sense, and doing all the other things that they did for us, there was ample opportunity for the Romans to teach the locals something about their traditional ball games. But although this export of *harpastum* is firmly established in folklore, nobody has ever been able to come up with conclusive evidence to prove that was actually the case.

On British football's Roman origins, Stephen Glover explained in 1829 how "there exists a tradition that a cohort of Roman soldiers marching through the town of Derventio, or Little

Chester, were thrust out by the unarmed populace, and this mode of celebrating the occurrence has been continued to the present day. It is even added that the conflict occurred in the year 217 and that the Roman troops at Little Chester were slain by the Britons[14]."

The Roman settlement would not have lasted much later than the 4th century, and Little Chester is now better known as the Derby district of Chester Green. All that survive now are two Romans walls and an underground heating system that was discovered just up the road from Derby Rugby Club.

But the claim is almost certainly the stuff of legends, and if you don't fancy believing what 'they' say in Derbyshire, then you wouldn't be alone. We have to be very careful before we take as fact what Glover himself was cautious enough to call 'a tradition'. Even though he was writing almost two centuries ago, that was still 1610 years after these events supposedly occurred, with all manner of equally questionable feats by such folk heroes as King Arthur and Robin Hood going on in between.

An alternative version tells us that footy in Britain originated from matches not played in celebration of a victory in battle, but rather from early internationals actually played between the Romans and the Britons, with the home side always winning a comfortable victory. Again, there is no evidence to back the story up.

But there was a new twist in the tale in 2005, when what is believed to be a *harpastum* court was discovered at Caerleon in Wales, home to the only complete surviving amphitheatre anywhere in the UK. A spokesman from the local Roman Legionary Museum stated that "*harpastum* was brought to Britain by the Romans and it is very possible that it would have been practised here. Caerleon can now challenge Rugby, in Northamptonshire[15], for the title of rugby's birthplace[16]." It is not clear why the Welsh archaeologists are so convinced that this is a *harpastum* court, as nobody really knows what one would look like, and there are no claims to any in a more likely location, Italy.

In fact, we know a lot less about Greek and Roman football than we perhaps thought. As 16th century educator Richard Mulcaster wrote on their use of balls, they were "two nations, which either used the thinges most, and handled them best ... and when they had so done set them over unto us ... wherfore seeing they be so farre different from ours, and almost worne out of knowledge even to curious conjectures, which seeke to sift them out, I will neither trouble my selfe with studying to set downe their names[17]."

Mulcaster didn't really know anything about their games at all, and historians have not made much progress since. In 1892, Francis Marshall wrote that "the Romans may, or may not, have introduced the *harpastum* into Britain. There is no historical evidence to show that they actually did so; but only one conclusion can be arrived at ... that amongst the Romans

---

[14] Stephen Glover *The History Gazetteer and Directory of the County of Derby* (1829).

[15] We could point out that it's in Warwickshire, actually, but nobody likes a pedant.

[16] *Why we were all gladiators once* in the *Western Mail* (2005).

[17] Richard Mulcaster *Positions Wherein Those Primitive Circumstances Be Examined, Which Are Necessarie for the Training up of Children* (1581).

there was a game of ball strangely similar in its chief characteristics to the game now played under Rugby Union rules." Well, we can't even be sure of that, Francis. For all we know, *harpastum* was nothing like rugby, and was never played in England. But back home, in what is now Italy, it may never have gone away.

9 THE ITALIAN JOB
Ball games in medieval Italy

Out of the shadows

Historians have varying explanations for where it all went wrong for the Romans and what had once looked like an empire that would continue to expand until there was no more known world left to conquer. Ours is not to enter that argument here, suffice to say that it is generally agreed that the year 476 marked the end of the Western Roman Empire.

With that, Europe plunged into darkness. The Greeks had come up with all those different ologies, the Romans had used their technical prowess to perfect them, and then came hundreds of years in which human civilisation took an abrupt and mighty step backwards. Gone were the amphitheatres, the temples, the heating systems, the roads, the medicine, the poetry, the politics… everything. In their place, we had barbaric hordes, medieval plagues, grim castles, torture chambers, pagan superstition, dragon scares and only the occasional gallant knight to save the day by rescuing damsels in distress.

Revisionists argue that we have been a bit hard on this period. Such accurate records have survived from Ancient Greek and Roman times that we tended to consider the period directly after as lacking in culture and knowledge, simply because we had less evidence of it. As more and more is discovered about the so-called Dark Ages, we are learning that Europeans were a lot more developed between the time that the Romans declined and fell and the Enlightenment than the popular image has suggested.

Football explains this nicely. Though we have vague snippets of evidence that ball games existed in 'classical antiquity', we then have to wait roughly 600 years for anything else in Europe. There is no doubt the ball games were still there, but we know next to nothing about them.

In Italy's case, we need to take a massive leap forward to February 17, 1530, and by jingo, they might have been playing *harpastum* all along. Times had changed. The Rome of old was now in ruins, just a memory of its triumphant past. Even Latin had died out, with different dialects of Italian being the languages used in the streets. But by the early 16th century, Leonardo da Vinci had already been and gone, Michelangelo was busy sculpting away and Florence and its Duomo were standing proud at the heart of the Italian Renaissance, with literature, art and architecture flowing like never before, and much of it of damn fine quality too.

But despite the Bible still being top of the bestsellers list, one thing nobody had quite got the hang of was loving their neighbours and living in peace. Florence was under siege by the Medici and Charles V's imperial troops on that monumental mid-February day in 1530. The locals were not too happy about that, and decided that the best way to stick two fingers up at the oppressors outside the city gates was to go ahead regardless with their traditional carnival celebrations. The story goes that they got a band to play on the roof of the church to make sure the folk outside could see that the besieged were going to party whether or not there were cannonballs flying over their heads.

The most important part of the festivities, however, was the ball game in Piazza della Novere, played between the *bianchi* (whites) and *verdi* (greens). The result of that match is unknown, and given the circumstances, it probably didn't matter as much to the Florentines as the fact that it was played at all. Sadly for them, they weren't going to hold out much longer, and by the summer of the same year, Florence had surrendered.

Although the 1530 match stands out for its historical significance, the people of Florence did not spontaneously invent football that day to piss off the Medici. There are records of an earlier game, for instance, played on the frozen Arno River in January 1490. No, football was probably deeply rooted in local tradition, a tradition that had quite possibly been inherited in some way from the *harpastum* of old.

Its new name certainly bears no resemblance to what the Romans called it. It was now called *calcio*, which was a generic term for ball games in general and is the word that the Italians use to this day to describe soccer. To avoid confusion, Italians generally refer to the ancient version of the game as *calcio storico*, or 'historic football'.

It was rather like a combination of unarmed combat and rugby, and the ball could be played using any part of the body. You could throw it, kick it or run with it, while the other team did all they could to stop you, with almost no limitations on the way that was done other than those of human decency and etiquette (i.e. not breaking bones, at least not on purpose).

In 1580, and more than two and a half centuries before any of the rules of the modern day codes of football were written, Giovanni di Bardi published his *Discorso Sopra Il Giuoco Del Calcio[1]*, considered the world's oldest book on football, although rather than the laws of the game, Bardi concentrated on other issues of the Florentine tradition.

He was particularly concerned with keeping things proper, and "as every kind of man was not admitted to the Olympic Games, but only men of standing in their native cities and kingdoms, so in *calcio*, all kinds of rapscallions are not to be tolerated, neither artificers, servants or low-born fellows but honourable soldiers, gentlemen, lords and princes … gentlemen, from eighteen years of age to forty-five, beautiful and vigorous, of gallant bearing and of good report." He goes on to say that they were expected to wear "goodly raiment and seemly, well-fitting and handsome." It's a mentality that would still be alive and well in late 19th century England, when the rise of working class football struck fear into the hearts of the more privileged classes who had claimed the game as their own.

They even enjoyed a bit of *calcio* at the Vatican, with Popes Clement VII, Leo IX and Urban VIII all reportedly being keen players. But although the ceremonial games in livery were limited to high standing members of society, football was not limited to the higher

---

[1] There is a copy on display at the National Football Museum in Preston, England.

standing members of Tuscan society. Matches played by anything but the gentry get little coverage in the documentation we have of the period, but we know the common plebs in the rat-infested streets enjoyed similar kicking and rucking too. *Calcio* expert Luciano Artusi asserts that "the people considered it to be nothing other than their own game and it was played in all parts of the city. Walking around the streets of Florence, you can still see on palaces and near churches plates of marble or stone where the ruling powers placed warnings prohibiting unofficial games of *calcio* among the masses[2]."

For the next two centuries, *calcio* was widespread throughout the peninsula. In 1570, a game was played in Rome in honour of Cosimo I de Medici's investiture as Grand Duke. A group of Florentines went to France in 1575 to play a game in Lyon before King Henri III. In 1584, a crowd of 40,000 (surely a world record attendance for football at the time) watched a game in honour of Eleonora de Medici and Vincenzo I Gonzaga, the pre-match entertainment including a bullfight. There was more footy on the frozen Arno in 1605, while the Piattelli's victory in 1650 was described as one of the most epic ever, in a veritable on-field battle. This game, or something like it, was apparently played in Spain as well, for a dictionary entry in 1611 mentions "*calcio, as calce*. A kind of play used in Spaine and Italie like unto the play at *ballone*[3]."

The game clearly resembled rugby. Satirist Traiano Boccalini wrote in 1912 of a game in which a foreign courtier was unimpressed with the way the Florentines played and vowed that he could teach them "the true art how to take the ball, how to run with it, how to repulse the wrestlers dextrously, who would take it away, and other excellent master-like tricks." He was invited to take part, "and presently the ball was thrown up in the air by men appointed thereunto, which, which came no sooner to the ground, but that the nimble courtier ran towards it, and having taken it up, clapt it under his left arm, those of the contrary party ran to take it away from him, but he with great strength justled one and thrust away another, and whereas the Florentines, who were masters of the sport, thought to have thrown him down, they were thrown down themselves … and the courtier having overcome all that withstood him, threw the ball over the *Lists* and won the prize." The Florentines were so miffed that they decided that no courtiers would ever play the game against them, for they are "rather like Devils than men … in giving their adversaries such deadly squelches as they shall never rise again[4]."

Richard Lassels (1603–1668) was a Catholic priest whose account of his travels to Italy was published posthumously in 1670. In it he provides an excellent description of *Il Guioco di Calcio*, which he said was "played every night from Epiphany to Lent" and was "a thing particular to Florence … the two factions of the *calcio*, the Red and the Green, choose each a Prince, some young cavalier of a good purse. These princes being chosen, choose a world of

[2] Speaking on *History of Football: The Beautiful Game* (Fremantle Home Entertainment, 2004).
[3] John Florio's *Queen Anna's New World of Words* (1611), basically an Italian/English dictionary.
[4] Traiano Boccalini *I raggvagli di Parnasso* (1612, published in English as *Advertisements from Parnassus* (1656).

officers and lodge for the time in some great palace where they keep their courts, receive embassadors from one another, and give them publick audience in state, send post to one another, complain of one anothers subjects and take prisoners from one another, hear their councellors one after another, disswading from or perswading war, give order for settling their affairs at home, hear the complaints of their subjects, jeer their enemy princes in the embassies, and at last resolve to fight, with proclaiming war[5]."

All of this seems to have been a way of voicing grievances, partly in jest and partly serious, that would eventually be resolved on the football field. Pre-match build-ups in modern-day sports tabloids are much the same thing. "Having spun out thus the time till near *Carnavale*, or Shrovetide, the two Princes resolve on a Battle at *calcio*, to be fought in the Piazza of Santa Croce before the Great Duke and Court. Upon the day appointed, the two Princes of the *calcio* come to the place in a most stately *cavalcata*, with all the young noblemen and gentlemen of the town upon the best horses they can find, with scarffs red or green about their arms. Having made their several *cavalcataes* before the Great Duke's throne, they light from their horses and enter the *Lists* with trumpets sounding before them … This done, the ball, or *ballon*, is thrown up in the midst between them and to it they go with great nimbleness, sleight and discretion and sometimes they fall to it indeed and cuff handsomely, but upon pain of death no man must resent afterwards out of the *Lists* what happened here, but all animosities arising here, end here too. At last, the side which throws or strikes the *ballon* over the rails of the other side wins the day, and runs to the standards, which they carry away till night, at which time the conquering prince entertains them at a *Festino di Ballo* at court, made to some lady, and where all his chief officers and combatans dance alone with the ladies at the ball, none else being permitted to dance with them that night."

Football and the fascists

And for well over two centuries, the matches continued uninterrupted until the 18th century, when they seemed to go out of fashion, at least in terms of being included in official celebrations. The last of the games in Florence's Piazza Santa Croce was played in 1739, and although we know a game was played in honour of Leopoldo II's visit to Livorno in 1766, it was around this time that the sport died out as a public spectacle.

It may have been a big deal until the 18th century, but Italian football then took a nosedive. In the 19th century, while football was rampant on the playing fields of England, any kind of sport was actively discouraged in Italian academia. As David Goldblatt puts it "sport of all kinds was initially considered a baleful distraction from the rigours of prayer and study" and he also notes that as late as 1909 the socialist tabloid *Avant!* "was calling on supporters to throw nails on the road to sabotage bike races in an act of petulant class revenge and contempt for the ludicrous and illusory circus of organised sport."

---

[5] Richard Lassels *The Voyage of Italy; or A compleat journey through Italy* (1670).

Given the Italian antipathy for all things sporting, it was down to British and Swiss immigrants to popularise football in the country, with modern soccer appearing in Genoa and Turin in the 1890s. Getting actual Italians to show any interest proved surprisingly difficult in the early days, but when they finally did, they immediately set to work on squeezing out the non-Italian element, even banning foreigners outright for a while. As part of that Italianisation of soccer, in 1909, the *Federazione Italiana del Football* decided to adopt its present name, the *Federazione Italiana Gioco Calcio*, thus cementing the idea that soccer, rather than being an English import, was actually a natural descendant of their own ancient game. By the 1920s, rugby was also making inroads into the Italian sports calendar, and that too was re-branded *palla ovale* and marketed as a modern take on Roman *harpastum*.

That was not the end of it. By 1928, and with Benito Mussolini and his ultra-nationalistic fascists now in command, football and rugby were getting far too popular for the comfort of a government that had precious little time for English culture. The secretary of the Fascist Party, Augusto Turati, in a move not unlike the formation of the GAA in Ireland, decided the time had come to create a totally new sport to replace the British imports.

Unveiling his new product, called *volata* ('flow'), Turati announced that "we intend to re-educate the athletes in order for them to breathe some fresh air, to teach them to compete for pleasure. Football is an English sport … full of verminous mercenaries. *Volata* is a truly Italian sport. It allows harmony in the development of the body. It offers no money. By creating *volata* we revive the spirit of *calcio*, which had emigrated to the north and later returned under the exotic name of football. *Volata* is a superfascist sport for the Italians of tomorrow."

Volata was played on something resembling a normal football pitch, but eight-a-side, including a goalkeeper, although neither he nor two nominated defenders were allowed to cross the half-way line. The ball could be kicked, and also carried but for no longer than three seconds. Tackling was allowed above the waist, corner 'kicks' were taken with the hands, and goals had to be scored from outside of a marked goal area.

It must have been quite some sport, essentially combining soccer and rugby in an attempt to kill both codes with one stone, but despite all the mighty ideals, there is little reason to believe that the new sport was a direct descendant of ancient Italian games, but plenty to believe that it was all something Turati and his cronies simply made up on the spot.

Amid much ceremony, the first ever match was played in January 1929 at the Stadio del Partito di Roma, and the fascists saw to it that over 1000 clubs were formed up and down the country. When a national championship was held from 1930 onwards, Mussolini himself made a point of attending every final.

But the Italian public at large wasn't going to be fooled by any of it. Soccer and rugby continued to gain in popularity regardless, while *volata* was never much more than a political gimmick. In 1933, the fascists admitted defeat, and not only did they abandon the *volata* project, but all records of it were expunged from the party records as they attempted to hide all evidence of a thoroughly embarrassing episode.

One of the main reasons for cancelling the *volata* venture was the fact that in 1934 Italy was going to be holding the first FIFA World Cup on European soil, which Mussolini intended to make full use of as a means of promoting his fascist regime. With the help of some very dodgy refereeing, Italy would win the title, and won it again four years later in France. Mussolini milked these successes for all they were worth, despite the fact that only a few years earlier, he had tried to kill off a sport that has been one of Italy's finest passions ever since.

Back to the future

It was against this background of resurgent interest in Italy's historic footballing roots that, in 1930, on the fourth centenary of the siege of Florence, the locals decided it would be fun to recreate the events of one of the greatest days in the history of their proud city by bringing back the *calcio fiorentino* tradition that had been dead for the best part of two centuries.

The city decked itself out in period costume and played as accurate a copy as they could of the famous *calcio* match played to snub the oppression of the Holy Roman Emperor in 1530. This was just the kind of thing Mussolini loved, and although *volata* would prove to be a non-starter, the idea of staging period matches in Florence was a resounding success.

So successful was it, in fact, that they decided to make *calcio storico* an annual pageant, and it still forms part of the San Giovanni (Saint John the Baptist) celebrations, representing one of the finest living tributes to the long-lost past of the football we know and love today.

Three matches are played a year, in late June and early July, in Piazza Santa Croce. They are played by the same four teams that played in the olden days, the *Bianchi, Verdi, Rossi* and *Azzurri*, representing each of the four districts of the city - Santo Spirito, San Giovanni, Santa Maria Novella and Santa Croce. These sides meet on the first two Sundays in the play-offs for the right to appear in the grand final.

Calcio storico is not just about the game itself. The prelude to the match has nothing to envy of the Super Bowl, with no shortage of horses, trumpets, flags, oxen, pomp, ceremony and the odd yell of *Viva Firenze* before the players themselves have even appeared. No less than 530 people play different official roles in representation of different elements of the city's society of old and these participants parade through the city to the main square, all decked out in the period costumes of the nobility, military and laypeople of early 16th century Tuscany.

The *piazza* is covered in sand for the games, which last fifty minutes each. Luciano Artusi explains how the game works. "The players number 27 a team, split into four lines. The first line, numbering 15 players, are called *innanzi* or *corridori*, meaning runners. There were five *sconciatori*, which correspond to our midfielders, four *datori* in front, who would be our defenders and then three *datori* at the back, who would correspond to our goalkeepers. The field of play is a rectangle, whose sides are exactly twice its ends … The try, or *caccia*, was given when the ball was flung into the mouth of the net[6] of the opposing team. A half *caccia* was given … when the player throwing the ball towards the net made a mistake and the ball flew over the top of the net, over the fence."

The players are all volunteers, mostly in their twenties or thirties, and the only limitation on taking part is a recently added rule that nobody with a criminal record can play. The rules are overseen by a main referee, six linesmen, and a chap called the field master whose job is to sort out any major fisticuffs. In such a no-holds-barred game, one would imagine the field master has a busy time out there, but he actually gets involved very little, generally leaving the players to sort things out amongst themselves.

Calcio storico makes for a fast moving, dramatic affair, with one excellent rule being that the ball is never allowed to be still. Luciano Artusi claims this was also the rule in ancient times, when "Morticino degli Antinori did not pass the ball – he was holding it tight to his chest. So Dante the strongman picked up the player and the ball, which was still in motion even though it was not being passed around, and ran it into the opponent's net, throwing in the player still clutching the ball."

There is an American football-like element to the play in that it is not just the player with the ball who can be tackled, but absolutely anybody. So, while some players are directly playing for possession of the ball or trying to get it towards the other end of the pitch, others are taking out rivals, and not in the prettiest of fashions. Some would call it strategy; others would call it bare-knuckle fistfighting.

But despite the apparent violence, with the kind of Corinthian spirit you might associate with rugby, there is always an awful lot of mutual respect. Although very few players are lucky enough to finish the game without their clothes being ripped to shreds, there are remarkably few serious injuries, and once the game is over, there is rarely anything but joviality between the two teams that have just spent the best part of an hour beating the crap out of each other.

It is all now broadcast live to the nation on TV, and the two thousand or so spectators liven up the day with the same flares and smoke bombs that Italians seem incapable of enjoying soccer without. With every score, things go into frenetic overdrive. Cannons are fired and standard bearers run across the pitch waving the scoring team's colours. Surreal is the best word to describe it.

In the past, a white calf was butchered in the middle of the square as a prize for the winning team, but these days, to protect the squeamish and any veggie tourists from having to witness any bovine blood being spilt, the meat is readily provided in steak form and washed down with plenty of Chianti wine.

---

[6] This would seemingly be the first case of goal nets being used in football, but I know of no contemporary evidence to suggest that the Middle Ages *calcio* players ever played into nets.

Yes, the tourists. It seems at least half of the people in the crowd are 'not from these parts', and the cynics often scoff that the whole caboodle has denigrated into nothing more than a tacky little gimmick to keep the thousands of visitors that flock to Florence each year happy.

Others argue that *calcio storico* amounts to little more than an ugly mass brawl between local thugs. Some might call it legalised hooliganism. But condemning it thus is a bit harsh. *Calcio storico* may be anything but 'the beautiful game', but it is also a remarkably authentic replica of a tradition that was celebrated in the same square more than four centuries years ago.

Embryonic rugger?

So, to what extent is what the tourists enjoy on their summer vacations in Tuscany a precursor to our modern codes of football? We cannot really be sure, but there was enough to-ing and fro-ing between the British Isles and the Italian Peninsula for the idea of *calcio* influencing football to be perfectly viable.

Luciano Artusi certainly likes the idea that *calcio* is the missing link between *harpastum* and modern rugby and soccer. "*Calcio* was born on the banks of the River Arno" he says. "And only after centuries was it taken to those of the River Thames, where the English changed its name to football and gave it the precise rules by which football is recognised throughout the world. But this was only after the birth of football took place in Florence."

Stating this as fact is perhaps a bit adventurous, but it's certainly a strong claim. After all, until Henry XIII came along and broke from Rome, the Vatican held an awful lot of sway over what went on in England. And if Rome was able to dictate what the English church and nobility could and could not get away with, then transmitting ideas about a game played with a ball can't have been too tricky at all.

Calcio was often played in honour of visiting foreign dignitaries, and we know for a fact that a game played on occasion of the wedding of Pietro Leopoldo I was attended by the British Consul in 1766[7]." Football, by this time, was already widespread in England, so it would be preposterous to suggest that a few dignitaries seeing it in Italy was how the game was introduced to the islands. But it is fascinating that Richard Lassels, who provided that great description of the game in the 1660s, felt it was "a play something like our football, but that they play with the hands." Those 13 words lend massive support to the theory that there was an Italian influence behind the transformation of English 'soccer' into rugby. The way he said the violence on the pitch was strictly forgotten in the celebrations afterwards still rings true of the rugby spirit, and unlike the hideous ball-kicking of the English peasantry, Italian *calcio* was perceived as a noble art, which fits with rugby's more middle class image today. It was not until the year 2000 that the Five Nations became Six when Italy was

---

[7] Also, in a park in Rome in 1771 it was written that "the English are permitted by the Borghese family to … play at cricket and football. We women go sometimes and see the sport, as do the Roman ladies." *Letters from Rome* by 'an English woman' (Edward & Charles Dilly, 1776).

welcomed into the fold, but it is a country that has a very valid claim to be the true birthplace of the rugby game.

If *calcio* did influence English rugby, then we can't be sure exactly how that happened, but it is quite likely that the French acted as the middlemen...

10 FRANCE FOOTBALL
Ball games in medieval France

Vive le foot

Games resembling soccer and rugby existed in France centuries before the bicycle was invented and the locals started riding around the countryside in striped jerseys with chains of onions draped around their necks. In fact, they were probably kicking, throwing and catching roughly spherical objects around Gallic fields just as long ago, if not longer, than anybody on the other side of the English Channel. The development of the French game was so similar to what the Brits were doing that there is probably only one reason why the modern day codes of soccer and rugby were made official by the *rosbifs* rather than the frogs, and that's simply that the Brits got round to doing it first.

Just like anywhere else, there was never one single ball game that was played in an orderly, regulated and identical fashion from central Paris and outwards to the ever-moving borderlands. Just as there are countless varieties of French wines, smelly cheeses, and force-fed poultry, there were also different ball games, most of which tended to have more in common with modern-day rugby than soccer.

How it all started, we cannot be sure, as once again we are delving back into the uncharted depths of time, only this time we have to make sure we put all the accents in the right places too.

And we have a glorious reference that crops up in a letter written by the Bishop of Clermont in Gaul, Sidonius Apollinaris, around the year 470. In *Epistulae V*, he writes how "I was the first to call for a ball game, which, as you know, is as much my constant companion as are my books … I played for some time with a crowd of students, until my body felt refreshed from the sluggishness induced by my sedentary occupation. Among the onlookers was an older man, Philomatius, who had been a fine player in his youth; now with great courage he went to join the groups of players. While he stood watching, he was several times jostled by the middle runner. At last he joined in the game, but he could not intercept nor dodge the ball as it flew past or over him; he was often almost flat on his face when he ducked, and only just saved himself from a disastrous fall. So he was the first to withdraw from the violent action of the game, puffing furiously and hot all over."

The reference is extraordinarily ahead of its time, for a further five hundred years would pass before anywhere in the more northerly part of Europe, if we ignore what are really just myths and legends, do we find any precise and contemporary reference to a ball game. Scholars are puzzled by the fact that a member of the clergy was advocating ball-play, something the church would later be so averse to, but Apollinaris was clearly an exception, and it was not with the fellow clergy, but with local students, that he played.

The letter was originally penned in Latin, and it seems like some kind of piggy-in-the-middle or dodgeball game in which the 'middle runner' (*medius currens*) had to either catch the ball or avoid being hit by it. As any *Asterix* reader will know, the Romans took great pleasure out of conquering this part of the world (because away Gauls count double in Europe), so it's a very likely possibility that it was related to Roman *harpastum*.

Not that we should jump to that obvious conclusion. After all, the French have been credited with giving the world some damned fine inventions over the years (how's about the pencil, the bicycle, the battery, and the electric iron for starters...), so the idea of chucking a ball back and forwards can't have been too hard to think up without any outside help. In 1703, Paul-Yves Pezron was inclined to that way of thinking when he wrote that "I do not doubt that the round ball we call *la soule* was invented by the Ancient Gauls in honour of the sun, and for that reason it is thrown on high[1]." There is no real proof of that, although it's a fair point that the word *soule* could have been derived from the French word for 'sun', which the ball either symbolised or was at least roughly the same shape as. Other common spellings included *choule*, *seault* and *cholle*, while other games that were essentially the same idea played at different times and places included *savate*, *mellat* and *barrette*.

With rubber still unknown in Europe, *soule* balls were generally the good old animal bladder, stuffed with straw, bran, wood shavings, foam, compressed hay or, in later times, inflated inside a leather casing.

As early as the 12th century, we have evidence of what hot property the stuffed contents of a dead domesticated animal's intestines could be. In 1147, in the former southern province of Rouergue, a charter specifies that the local lord, the Seigneur de Trincavels, had the right to the feudal levy of seven large balls (*et VII maximos ballones*).

We can't be sure that these balls were used to play some form of football, and the chances are they weren't. They may have formed part of the bizarre ritual called *pilota* that was so common in French churches of the time, and was a "a liturgical game realized over an ecclesiastical labyrinth on Easter Monday and recorded as early as the 14th century. In the festive rite, members of the clergy engaged in a dance, enacted while tossing a ball back and forth, and singing the Easter sequence *Victimae paschali laudes* ... According to the monastic *Ordinatio de pila facienda* of April 18, 1396, upon entering the Auxerre monastery, incoming clerics were expected to supply a large ball[2]."

This *Ordinatio* has been called the oldest codification of any form of football. But it isn't really anything of the sort, it regulates a religious ceremony and the way wannabe monks had

---

[1] Paul-Yves Pezron *The Antiquities of Nations; More Particularly of the Celtce* (1703). Pezron was a 17th century priest from Brittany, but he is most remembered for his comparative study of the Welsh and the Bretons, in which he discussed the idea that their languages and cultures shared a common origin he called 'Celtick'. His work has often been criticised for lacking scientific grounds, and he was certainly no authority on football.

[2] Michael Eisenberg *Performing the Passion: Music, Ritual, and the Eastertide Labyrinth* in *Transcultural Music Review* (2009).

to donate a ball to the monastery before they could join. In fact, so eager were the younger monks to impress their seniors with the size of their balls (oh, do stop sniggering at the back), that they got so ridiculously large that a new rule was invented in 1412 that stated that a *soule* ball could never be so big that it could not be held in one hand.

In 1165, in the town of Poitiers, we find more evidence all ball-playing clergy, and Parisian theologian Jean Beleth was not overly impressed to learn of it. "There are some churches" he wrote with horror, "in which it is customary for bishops and archbishops to play in the monasteries with those under them, and even to stoop to the game of ball." He considered the game to be a "common festival after the collection of the harvest. Although great churches such as that at Rheims observe the custom, it is more praiseworthy not to play."

In 1286, the clergy had not mended their ways. William Durandus, Bishop of Mende, almost paraphrases Beleth when announcing how aggrieved he was that "in certain places in our country, prelates play games with their own clerics at Easter in the cloisters, or in the Episcopal palaces, even so far as to descend to the game of ball, or even singing and dancing." It has been assumed that these two critics were unhappy about the clergy playing football, but it is just as likely that they were referring to the strange ball rituals, and what seems to be the transposition of a pagan rite to the Catholic Church.

We can ask the same question of the string of examples provided by our Egyptian head cult fanatic Robert Henderson. "At Josselin the ball was presented at noon on the day of the Mardi Gras, before the Cross of Martray, between two dishes, with two loaves, two jugs of wine and two glasses: quite a formal occasion" he writes. "At Gué-de-l'Isle it was deposited on the seigniorial pew in the church after high mass. The same custom was observed in the Chatelain of Mereuil in Berry, where, *en secondes noces* after his marriage, each bridegroom had to present the seignior a bat of certain length and two new balls. In La Pommerale, in Normandy, the tenants had to supply the Seignior de Fleurs with a leather ball. There is on record at Vitre, as late as the year 1580, a custom which shows to what an amazing extent the Church had given significance to the use of the ball." Here, on the High Feast of St Stephen, at the most solemn moment of the High Mass, the proceedings stopped while the Seignior, in great dignity, marched up to the altar, and laid upon it a ball. At Rochefort in Pluherlin, as late as 1554, the last man married was obliged to carry a ball to the seignior, and then throw it over a purple oven, having one foot braced against the wall of the churchyard of Nôtre Dame de la Trouchaye. If he failed to accomplish that, he had to pay a fine.

An admiral under 16th century King François II, Philippe de Chabot, and whose tomb is still at the Louvre today, actually used images of a ball on his coat of arms. But Claudius Paradin writes how Chabot "alwais used for his armes, a round circle or globe like a ball (that I may so tearme it) swelling with wind[3]." By saying the symbol was 'like' a ball, and even mildly

---

[3] Claudius Paradin *The Heroical Devises of M. Claudius Paradin Canon of Bealeu* (1591).

apologising for the comparison, Paradin is not even telling us it was ball, but just something that looked like one, and in no way suggests that we were looking at an early Michel Platini.

Soule bothers

For something that is more football than ceremony, we can turn to an ancient chronicle of the founding of the town of Ardres near Calais that tells how "rustic men met to drink and play ball in a wide, flat field." It was written around 1200, but was describing events much earlier.

There are later records of similar goings-on in Rochay (where a black leather ball was softened with oil), Epinard (where the ball was decorated in different coloured quarters and covered in cross images), Beaufort in the Loire Valley (where newlyweds played against men who had already survived several years of marital bliss), Coriac (between married and single men), Cléville in Normandy (where two villages on either side of a river played each other for the delightful prize of a sheep), and also in Vermandois in what is now the Somme – more or less covering most of the geography of modern day France.

As time went by, *soule* balls became more and more elaborate, often decorated in the local province's colours. Touching the ball was adjudged to bring wonderfully good luck, and the last player to touch it in the game was often given the honour of taking it home as a keepsake. At some point, the tradition took root in many villages of the most recently married couple having to order and buy the ball from the local saddler.

Though it was mainly played in rural regions, it also made it to the streets of Saint-Eustace, in Paris, as a text of 1393 affirms. It was also played in the Dutch-speaking world, where there was almost identical sport called *sollen*, and we don't need the help of any etymologists to spot the similarity between the two names.

As the clergy were just about the only people who ever put quill to scroll in those days, our knowledge of historical society is always a tad biased towards the holy. But what's curious about the French church is that it was unusually encouraging of ball games in medieval times, often believing, unlike elsewhere, that just because an activity might appear pagan in origin, it did not necessarily have to be bad[4].

The church and the feudal barons may have tried to get involved in the games as a means of making sure they were controlled – if you can't beat them, join them, so to speak. And so balls, a churchyard, and even time in the form of Sundays and religious festivals were provided for what were considered healthy, strength building games, and which at least took the peasants' minds off revolutions for a while.

---

[4] As Saint Augustine influentially wrote: "Christians ought not to reject a good thing because it is pagan. God is the author of good things. To continue the good customs that have been practiced by idolaters, to preserve the objects and the buildings which they have used is not to borrow from them; on the contrary, it is taking from them what is not theirs and giving it to God the real owner."

There was even rare royal patronage from 16th century King Henri II (a dedicated sportsman even when it came to snowball fights), who actually played *soule*, according to a description of a game played on the gardens of Pré aux Clercs. We are told that they had different coloured kit, for the King's side played in red, and his opponents, Monsieur de Laval and his team, wore white. We also learn that the King himself refused to play unless the great poet, and presumably great footballer too, Ronsard, played on his team.

If we are right to assume that the Italian game of *calcio* was generally played on a specific court with defined boundaries, *soule* was more popularly played out in the open. Matches were usually contested between the people of different parishes, and the starting place was generally established as being an equidistant point between the two.

From there, the teams had to use pretty much any means at their disposal to get the ball back to a designated spot in their own parish (popular choices seem to have been the local church or village ponds). In some inverted versions, the idea was to get the ball into your rival's parish. It was a reckless, brutal, but rustically noble sport in which broken limbs were as common as decent medical care was not. Jean Jules Jusserand comments that "the quantity of 'letters of remission' in the fourteenth century, granting forgiveness to players who had, by error, split the head of a comrade instead of striking the ball, show that the games were played tough[5]."

Teams had to cope with whatever obstacles man or nature had put in the way – rivers, forests, walls, meadows, ditches, cemeteries and guillotines all added to the fun. Just like no two golf courses are the same, the varying landscapes meant that no one game between two parishes was like any other.

So, rules were generally localised, and most quibbles would have been more to do with whether or not you could cross a certain landowner's field or what happens if the ball gets lost in the duck pond than technicalities about which parts of the body you could use to hit the ball.

Whether he used his hands or not, it is unlikely that Thierry Henry's skills would have got him very far in this game. A stuffed bladder would have hit the ground with more of a thud than a boing, and it is easier to imagine one brawling mass of man-flesh fighting for possession of the ball, with the occasional breakaway by one of the players in an all-terrain charge to gain some ground.

In his invaluable journal of life and times in Nord-Cotentin (Normandy), Gilles de Gouberville offers us a description of a game of *soule* played in January 1554: "The *curé*, Robert Potet gave me a package … then he threw the ball which was contested until about one hour after noon by the sun and conveyed to the parish of Bretteville where Gratien

---

[5] The French ambassador to the United States during World War I, but who was also a Pullitzer winning author, writing on a variety of topics. The one we are interested in here is his *Le sport et les jeux d'exercice dans l'ancienne France* (1901).

Cabart took it and won the game … The same day, on the way home, Cantepie stayed to dine at Jacques Cabart's house because he had fallen into the sea and was soaked through."

He must have been quite a character that Cantepie, because a year later, in a game on Christmas Day 1555, we learn that "Cantepie ran into me so hard, his fist hitting my right breast and taking my breath away, leaving me speechless; it was with great difficulty that they managed to bring me back home. I thought I was going to lose consciousness on the way, and I was blind for half a quarter of an hour, which made me take to my bed." Poor Gilles spent the next three days housebound with "an extremely great pain in my chest."

The raw ingredients of rugby were all present in the medieval games of France. Running with the ball was widespread, but in Valognes, Normandy, it was particularly common for the feet to be used, where the game was dubbed *savate* (shoe) for possibly that very reason, while other versions of the game involved the use of some kind of stick. That's the sort Charles du Fresne mentioned in 1387, in which the "country folk of Vulguessin le Normand and the Forest de Lyons had the custom of assembling each year to play *soule* against each other against the door of the Abbey of Nôtre Dame de Mortemer[6]." These stick-games answer to such names as *bastonner à la soule*, *soule la crosse*, and later simply *crosserie*, which used curved sticks similar to a bishop's crosier, and provided the origin for the name of the modern game of lacrosse. *Crosserie* was still going strong in the 1780s, when we come across yet another curious association with the church in Mardi Gras matches in the town of Avranches in Normandy, where every score was marked by a chime of the cathedral bell.

The shared root with hurling, shinty and hockey is obvious, and Robert Browning[7] goes as far as to suggest that Scots helping the French fight the English at the Battle of Bauge (1421) would have witnessed the game of *soule la crosse* and that this ultimately led to the invention of golf. The birth of golf in Scotland does seem to have happened about then, and in 1424 James II of Scotland saw fit to ban both football and golf, so there could be some truth in the theory.

Soule fights the law

But although *soule* enjoyed some support from higher authorities, not everyone liked the way these brawls were wreaking their destructive force into the countryside, and concluded that the pastime was of no servitude to a country that had wars to prepare for.

Philippe V was the first King we know took objection, with his prohibition in 1319 of *ludos soularum*. Charles V came to the French throne in 1364, but a huge chunk of the country he was supposed to be ruling had gone missing. At the Treaty of Brétigny, part of Normandy and just about all the southwest quarter of modern day France had been signed over to

---

[6] Charles du Fresne *Glossarium Mediæ et Infimæ Latinitatis* (1678). Commonly known as Du Lange, the author was a distinguished French historian of his period, and was the provider of some great early research into the history of *soule.*
[7] Robert Browning *History of Golf* (1955 – and reprinted by A & C Black London, 1990).

Edward III, King of England, and Charles spent a good part of his reign fighting to get it back. It would not do to have his people wasting their time and energy playing with balls when they could be getting maimed on the battlefield, and he bemoaned "all the games that do nothing to teach the manly art of bearing arms" before issuing a writ in 1369 stating "that the *solles* cannot appear among the games which serve the exercise of the body." But as much notice was taken of his prohibition as was taken of Philippe V's attempt exactly half a century earlier, which was not very much notice at all.

In 1440, there was another attempt to ban the game. This time it was the Bishop of Tréguier, in the *Synodal Statutes of Raoul*, where "it is decreed that these dangerous and pernicious games be prohibited because of the ill-feeling, rancour and enmities, which in the guise of a recreative pleasure, accumulate in many hearts, and give baleful occasion for hatreds to arise. We have learned from the reports of dignitaries of the faith that in some parishes and other places under our jurisdiction, both on feast days and others, for long time past, of certain pernicious and dangerous games with a large ball, vulgarly called *mellat*. It has already resulted in many scandals, and it is manifest that it will produce others if a remedy is not found."

In 1781, a parliamentary decree decided to renew Philippe V's prohibition of almost half a millennium earlier and banned "all people from throwing any balls of leather on Christmas Day or any other day; or to run with the ball[8] under any pretext, which is to be fined fifty pounds."

One place where such orders fell on particularly deaf ears was Brittany, which kept its own tax and law system until as late as 1790, and was therefore largely unaffected by anything the Parisian legislators decreed. One description of a Breton game in 1799 goes that "the lord of the village threw a ball into the middle of a noisy crowd, and men of different cantons tried to grab it. Men sometimes followed the *soule* into the sea and drowned as they sought it … I once saw a man break his leg while jumping by a ventilator in a cellar to seize it. These games maintain strength and courage, but, I repeat, are dangerous[9]."

Brittany was also the setting for the following description of a game in 1825: "The *soule* was launched. The two teams choked together in a single melee. On the surface of this impenetrable chaos, thousands of heads were shaken, like the waves of a furious sea, and inarticulate and wild cries escaped from within. One of the champions found the strength to clear a passage through this compact mass and fled carrying the *soule* afar. Such was the intoxication of the combatants that at first nobody noticed! Then some of the more cool headed finally noticed that they were exhausting themselves in a futile effort, the immense single block of men broke, parted and divided. Everyone ran to this new battlefield, and

---

[8] The mention of running with the ball is particularly poignant; coming 42 years before William Webb Ellis supposedly 'invented' the idea at Rugby School in 1823.
[9] Jacques Cambry *Voyage dans le Finistère* (1799).

while running, they insulted, attacked and knocked each other over, and twenty different actions began around the main action[10]."

An 1824 description says that *chole* was "still present among some peasants in our provinces." It was "played on foot. On certain fête days, and generally on the festivals of the patrons of the villages, peasants invite their neighbours to a match. To play it they throw a large ball into a highroad between the confines of two villages." It sounds like soccer for "each party drives it with his foot till the strongest brings it home, and in this way carries off the victory.[11]"

By the mid 19th century, in the Breton department of Morbihan, the ball-playing custom was outlawed because it was getting too dangerous, although it was probably the mobilisation of young people to fight in the wars rather than the ban that really did the trick. Elsewhere in Brittany the game survived until later. In 1889, we learn of the fascinating idea of not two, but three, parishes (Locuon, Mellionnec and Plouray) taking part in a precursor of three-sided soccer[12].

Football also held on in Normandy, where in 1830 at Neufchâtel-en-Bray, Henderson finds they were still playing it "in the traditional manner, the game became so rough that a priest was struck in the face by one of the players, so as to call blood to flow. The players were threatened with expulsion from the game." To think that you could punch a priest in the face, and all you got was a warning!

A decade later, and still in Normandy, they were still defiantly playing *soule* on the beaches near Mont Saint Michel in 1840, the same year that in nearby Bellou-en-Houlme there are records of a game played by 800 players, with some 6000 spectators. Here we learn of a sneaky tactic employed by a struggling team – they cut the ball into pieces so that nobody could win! This bizarre problem was later alleviated by sheathing the ball in tin.

By 1891, France was only a decade away from fielding its first national rugby and soccer sides, but football was still being played the indigenous way in some parts of the country. Abbot Martin-Val said in 1891 that the ancient Mardi Gras game in his Picardy village was an annual event. He describes how "the ball is thrown about the houses, the hedges, the gardens; it lands in the midst of a group of curious girls who run away as fast as possible. People hustle about, shout insults, get kicked in the chest, have their hands crushed, one covered in blood, another with a black eye, another with a flattened nose for ever[13]." Charming. These games were played between the 'people of the mountain' and 'the people of the valley', and the game was won by the first team to get the ball into the other's pond, after which much dancing and merriment followed all night long.

---

[10] Alexandre Bouët *Breiz-Izel, ou vie des Bretons de l'Armorique* (1844).

[11] Claude Bernard Petitot *Collection des mémoires relatifs à l'histoire de France* (1824).

[12] A sport created by 20th century Danish situationist Asger Jorn to explain his notion of triolectics. But there are claims that a game was once played in the Breton town of Auray that included no fewer than sixteen parishes and more than 500 players.

[13] Abbé Martin-Val *Histoire de Boulogne-la-Grasse* (Compiègne, Mennecier, 1891).

English invasion

In some shape or form, *soule* was still played in France right up until the Second World War. One of the last recorded games was in 1930 between the villages of Saint-Léger-aux-Bois and Tracy-le-Mont, roughly 35 miles north of Paris. But this was the last hurrah for a game that might have survived to this day had it not been for the arrival of something that would prove to be its ultimate demise. The importation from England of both soccer and rugby in their newly codified and established forms meant that, almost overnight, *soule* was deemed antiquated, and was doomed to the record books.

The Penny Illustrated Paper carried a short report on December 26, 1863, of how "a number of English gentlemen living in Paris have lately organised a football club … The football contests take place in the Bois de Boulogne, by permission of the authorities, and surprise the French amazingly." It's curious to note that despite France's *soule* tradition, this article suggest the locals had never seen the likes before. *The Field* reported that the rules were "principally those from Rugby School," but there was no crossbar.

That report predates by a decade the formation in 1872 of what has traditionally been considered the earliest football club in France, Le Havre Athletic Club, who played both soccer and rugby, as well as a new version combining the two, and it was not until 1894 that they finally settled for soccer. The founders were obviously British and one tale goes of the English chaplain of the local college telling a strapping local lad who was on his way to the gym that he would be better off playing sport. 'But I am' replied the Frenchman, 'can't you see?' 'No, that's exercise' replies the chaplain. 'You should do sport, a real one, like football.'

Not everybody was stood on the beaches of Northern France welcoming the spread across the channel of *les sports Anglais*. They actually faced a very similar kind of resistance to that which Michael Cusack and his GAA would deploy against the English imports in Ireland. Leading the Anglophobe movement was political radical Paschal Grousset, who was engaged in a propaganda battle with the Anglophile Baron Pierre de Coubertin, the father of the Olympic Games. Grousset's *Ligue Nationale de l'Education Physique* promoted a bat and ball game called *theque* and a form of football called *barette*[14]. The world's sporting map could be very different today had that battle had a different outcome. As it turned out, Coubertin proved just too brilliant a man, while Grousset was elected to parliament and sidetracked by other issues, his ideas eventually coming to nothing.

Soccer took off big time in France. Although Britain loves to take the credit for inventing the game, the French deserve just as much thanks for teaching it to the world. It was the French who were largely responsible for founding soccer's international governing body, FIFA, in 1904. The FA in England unanimously rejected the invitation to get involved and the first FIFA president was a Frenchman, Robert Guérin. It was of course another

---

[14] Named after the game referenced in medieval texts.

Frenchman, Jules Rimet, who instigated the first World Cup in 1930. The British wanted nothing to do with it as they had no intention of playing against countries they had been at war with, and were unhappy about the increasing foreign influence on their game. The European soccer federation, UEFA was mainly the brainchild of another Frenchman, Henri Delaunay. Again, the English had no interest in taking part in the inaugural editions of either the European Champion Clubs Cup (now the Champions League) or the European Nations Cup (now the European Championship).

Rugby also flourished among the French, who were accepted as permanent members of rugby union's Five Nations in 1910 (it was the French, in fact, who coined the name, as well as the term 'Grand Slam'). The relationship was cagey, and France was banned from 1932 to 1939 for reasons both of their violent approach to the game and their increasing professionalism. It was during that time that the French set up instead the *Federation Internationale de Rugby Amateur* (FIRA), and started promoting the game in other European countries. The International Rugby Board had shown very little interest in doing anything similar, and so it was the French that gathered the founder members from Italy, Germany, Portugal, Sweden, Romania, Catalonia, Holland and Czechoslovakia. Once France rejoined the home nations after the Second World War, they went from strength to strength, and first won the championship outright in 1959. Since then, no other nation comes close to them in terms of titles won.

Soule searching

What this illustrates is how much the French embraced the sports of soccer and rugby, and against that backdrop, poor old *soule* was as good as forgotten. Although there have been several largely artificial attempts to revive the historic local variety of football, these have been surprisingly few considering the French people's devotion to sports and strong sense of nationalistic pride[15].

One place where the tradition is maintained is Tricot, a village in Somme, where a game is played on 'Soule Sunday', the first after Shrove Tuesday. Games are also played annually as part of the Normandy celebrations in Jersey and there was an attempt to revive the game in Vouillé, Vienne in 1994.

The drive to get the *soule* movement back on its feet on occasion of the France 1998 World Cup was a project best described a monumental flop. Considerably more success has been enjoyed by the *Association Interrégionale La Soule*, formed in 1997, and based in the southwest of the country involving around ten teams and 300 players. The Association has established modern rules for the game, which is played cross country, taking in different landmarks, including the essential ingredient of mass bundles in water features. Meanwhile, since 2003, the villages around Vendôme (near Le Mans) have been particularly enthusiastic,

---

[15] The game was even featured in Michel Sibra's unusual movie, *La Soule* (1989), in which a former officer in Napoleon's army uses a *soule* match to get his revenge on a soldier that betrayed him to the English.

and since 2006 have even been organising the *Traditionnel Championnat du Monde de la Soule du Vendômois'*. They find some suitable country terrain, and with modern players being more squeamish about using an animal bladder, teams of about 40 players fight it over a leather sack stuffed with straw.

It's is debatable how much these games are the direct descendants of the original games. They are more like modern revivals of a sport that was largely dormant for well over a century. But they share a lot in common with the British 'Uppies and Downies' games, and it's nice to see that there is mutual interest, and in recent years revivalists from both countries have made contact, swapped ideas and even participated in each other's games.

French connection?

Although the English wrote the modern day rules, through *soule* the French probably have as good a claim to the ancient origins of soccer and rugby. The most obvious clue to the French connection is the Norman Conquest. We're talking William the Conqueror, 1066 and all that. William was the Duke of Normandy, who conquered England at the Battle of Hastings, and established himself as King at the start of a royal lineage that has more or less continued unbroken to this day. Over the ensuing centuries, not only were there inter-royal marriages between the nations divided by the channel, but the French and English conquered sizeable tracts of their respective lands.

The Norman influence turned English culture on its head, even transforming the English language into something barely recognisable from the way it was spoken just a century or so earlier, so it is perfectly conceivable to imagine football-type games being introduced to the island around the same time. There is certainly very little evidence of anything similar to football being played in Britain before the Normans arrived, but then again, neither do we have much solid evidence of it being played in France.

However, there is some extraordinarily revealing evidence[16] in the Cornish plea rolls of 1283, when a certain Roger was accused of killing an opponent with a stone in game that was called *soule*.

It is also curious to note that the peculiar French tradition of donating balls on your wedding day was also present in England. One example from the *Inquisitions Miscellaneous* described how an argument in York in 1268 got rather excessively out of hand. "A certain stranger being new-married was taking his wife and others who were with her to one end of the town of Byrun, when William Selisaule asked for a ball, which it is the custom to give; and they having no ball gave him a pair of gloves for a pledge; afterwards other men of Byrun asked for a ball, and they said they would not give one, because they had already given a pledge for one, and the men of Byrun would not believe them, but still asked for the

---

[16] Leonard Elliott Elliott-Binns *Medieval Cornwall* (Methuen & Co, 1955).

said ball; and so there arose a dispute, and the wedding party, being slightly drunk, assaulted the men of Byrun with axes and bows and arrows, and wounded very many[17]."

The *American Mechanics Magazine* in 1827 reckoned "the game of football is but little played in England … and when played is … very inferior to that in the south of Europe, particularly in the southern provinces of France, where the villagers play it with a kind of madness, and where it holds the same rank as our cricket." Jean-Jules Jusserand felt "there is no unquestionable proof that this game was given to England by France or reciprocally. The most probable is the former assumption, because almost all that was play, recreation or relaxation in England was, in the Middle Ages, of Norman or Anjou origin. The idea of especially English characteristics to the game is very modern."

So why was it the English, rather than the French, that came up with the modern rules? The politics of the time had a lot to do with it. Great Britain was enjoying relative peace and establishing itself as the dominant world power at a time when France was engulfed in Revolutionary and Napoleonic Wars, even coining the phrase *levée en masse*, whereby the army could conscript as many young men as it needed from the civilian population. With so many young male peasants mobilised, and with the gentlemanly classes otherwise occupied, there was little time playing *soule*, and even less for structuring it as a codified national sport.

In 1815, at Waterloo, Napoleon did surrender. He spent the last six years of his life imprisoned on the island of Saint Helena pondering where it had all gone wrong for his plans of conquest. *Soule* was the least of his worries, but the shift in the balance of power in the early to mid 19th century seems to be the crux of the reason why the French missed out on the chance to claim any credit for something that would change the face of modern sporting culture.

---

[17] Also "in the north of England, among the colliers … it is customary money for a football, a claim that admitted of no refusal." Geeraert Brandt, Henry Ellis *Observations On Popular Antiquities: Chiefly Illustrating The Origin Of Our Vulgar Customs, Ceremonies And Superstitions* (1813). One Scottish claim (John Jamieson *An etymological dictionary of the Scottish language* (1808)) is that the ball was given by the happy couple to avoid their wedding being sabotaged by mischievous schoolboys, for "if this was withheld, the boys claimed a right to cut the bride's gown."

11 EUROSPORT
Other early forms of football in Europe

Germany

Modern soccer in Germany dates from 1874 when a Leipzig newspaper reported on the founding of Dresden FC, which in its first year had some 70 members, a mix of local Germans and Englishmen working in Saxony. They played in a meadow, more or less on the same site as the city's biggest stadium today, the Rudolf Harbig. According to contemporary reports, it all caused quite a stir, with hundreds of people turning up to watch their games, and the newspapers amused by the shorts that revealed their knees and the different coloured shirts worn to tell the teams apart. But Dresden must have been some side. When sports journalism became more of a regular thing in Germany in the 1890s, there are frequent references to this great DFC side that not only hadn't been beaten in twenty years, but hadn't even conceded a goal!

The same year that Dresden formed its club, there are stories of gymnastics instructor Konrad Koch at Braunschweig ordering a football from England for use at his school, although it is not clear whether he knew what he was supposed to with it, for what he called *königsbergerball*, and also the *raffballspiel* that was doing the rounds, involved carrying and kicking, and were more like gymnastics exercises than anything else. Koch could be excused, because the FA's laws for soccer would not be translated into German until 1891, something especially welcome for the players of FC Germania Berlin and Viktoria Berlin, which had already been formed, while the modern-day Hertha Berlin came into existence in 1892.

The real sporting craze in Germany at the time was *turnen* gymnasiums, and the arrival of football was not always well received. The terms *fussball ohne aufnahme* (football without picking up) and *fussball mit aufnahme* (football with picking up) for soccer and rugby were somewhat derisory, and in 1898 Otto Heinrich Jager published a major condemnation of what he called 'The English Disease'. Germany's relationship with the British was as bad as ever, and football was viewed as subversive and totally opposed to the German ethic of liking things to be orderly and purposeful.

In 1900, the *Deutscher Fussball-Bund* was founded in Leipzig, and one of its most immediate tasks was to translate all those nasty English sounding words into something more Germanic, so a 'goal' became a *tor* and so on. As David Goldblatt puts it, this was "to demonstrate a direct, if completely mythical, path from folk games in medieval Germany to the present day."

The problem was that there really wasn't an awful lot of evidence of football-like goings on in medieval Germany, and although the country went on to win more international honours than any other European country (to date, three World Cups and three European

Championships) there is very little to suggest that the game was in any way a historically German offering to the world.

What Germany can offer is *brautball* ('brideball'), which existed in such places as Tangermünde in the north-eastern part of Saxony-Anhalt on the banks of the Elbe.

The tradition went that at Easter women that wanted to get married would ask women that had already tied the matrimonial knot to make them a special cloth ball filled with a tarred fibre called oakum. They then took this into the nearby pine forests and played with it until it was torn to shreds. Just what kind of game it was that caused such destruction of the ball, we cannot tell, but it may have been football. Or it may have not.

The German towns of Schwedel and Camern, and quite probably several others, had a tradition by which the local folk would gather in a home and throw a ball back and forth among themselves and sing songs like the following:

"Green leaf, green leaf, the greatest prize! This summer, this summer,
All girls are full of life, we want to have the bride's ball,
And if she does not give the ball to us, we'll take away her man."

Similar customs pop up all over medieval Germany, such as one in early 19th century Arendse in Altmark[1] that involved balls being given out as wedding gifts, and another in Ellichsleben, whereby any newlywed couple that was having trouble producing their first sprog would get around the problem by throwing a ball covered in pins to a waiting crowd.

It sounds more like some kind of fertility rite, and it's all very cute, but throwing balls instead of bridal bouquets isn't really something we could consider a Teutonic claim to the origins of football. Neither is *fangballspiel* ('catch ball game'), as mentioned by celebrated medieval poet Walther von der Vogelweide (1170–1230). A translation of his poem *Uns hat der winter geschat uber al*[2] reads:

"But were I to see girls throwing their ball
In the street, the birdsong would soon be back."

There is not really any great revelation in the idea of children throwing balls around, but *fangballspiel* is often rather rashly cited as an early form of the modern Olympic sport of handball – to which we turn next.

---

[1] Wilhelm Mannhardt *Baumkultus der Germanen und ihrer Nachbarst* (1875).

[2] 'Winter has fallen over the world'. Von der Vogelweide is saying that children playing ball is a good sign that spring is coming. It is commonly noted that the poet called this the 'First Game of Spring', although he didn't really do anything of the sort.

Hand signals[3]

Football, and particularly soccer, may now be the king of sports almost anywhere you go in Europe, but in the late 19th century there were a number of pretenders to its throne. They were standardisations of old 'folk' and 'playground' games and many could have gone on to become the 'world's game' had the circumstances been different.

Chwytka was an old Polish word for 'ball' that was generically applied to a number of games that usually involved catching and throwing with the hands. Klementyna z Tańskich Hoffmanowa describes how 16th century "boys threw up a *chwytka* and then caught it skilfully[4]." This was the same kind of game we hear was enjoyed by Zygmunt III, the ruler of the Polish-Lithuanian Commonwealth from 1587 to 1632, and also the King of Sweden[5].

Łukasz Gołębiowski notes Zygmunt's partiality for ball sports in his invaluable *Gry i Zabawy Różnych Stanów* (1831), the Polish equivalent to Joseph Strutt's English masterpiece, where he notes references to different ball games cropping up all the way through four or five centuries of Polish history. We have, for instance, *ekstrameta*, a kind of dodgeball meets piggy-in-the-middle game that dates back at least to the 17th century. Or *lapa*, a two-player game played in 18th century schools where one player threw a ball at a wall and another tried to beat his opponent by catching it after it bounced back. *Meta* was a team game that existed by at least the 18th century, in which Gołębiowski tells us "once a ball was thrown, one of the players of the throwing team ran up to the centre line and returned to his team, while the receiving team tried to get the runner out by hitting him with the ball." He also mentions *podbijanka*, in which "the players stand in a circle. One tosses the ball up and the others try to hit it on the fly, but not catch it."

Moving south, we find the Slovak and Bohemian game of *hazena*, for which the earliest known rules were written by schoolteachers Vaclav Karas and Kristof Antonin around the turn of the century and were published in a Bernese journal in 1905. *Hazena* was similar in many ways to modern handball, with the curiosity that the court was divided into sections, and players were not allowed leave their delegated zone. It still exists today, with the game between Bohemia and Moravia being the highlight of the year, although it has largely been superseded by modern handball, which the Czechs and Slovaks also call *hazena*.

Similar games crop up all around Eastern Europe. In the Ukraine they were playing *gandbol*, and in Poland they had *jordanka*, named after Henryk Jordan, a pioneer of physical

---

[3] Note that this section examines the history of game now known in some parts as Olympic or Team handball. Although other games have been called handball over the years, in particular those that are similar to Eton fives and pall mall, these belong to an entirely different family, but just happen to have shared the same name.

[4] In her 1842 book *Jan Kochanowski in Czamolas*, in which she describes the 16th century childhood of the man considered the finest Polish poet to have ever lived.

[5] He was not the most distinguished of monarchs. His attempts to unite his two realms eventually had the opposite effect and led to them going to war, and it often said that his realm marked the beginning of the end of Poland's so-called Golden Era.

education, and particularly famous for his children's playgrounds. Industrious sports historian James Mangan notes that a 1937 textbook describing the sport contained no fewer than 64 pages of adverts, suggesting it was indeed a very popular game before the Second World War – and it was even able to hold a world championship that also included France, Czechoslovakia, Yugoslavia, Switzerland and Hungary.

Denmark has a few tenuous claims to a part in football history. The Danes shared the Teutonic fascination with associating betrothal to ball games – where the dancing ball players in a 14th century frieze in Ørslev were possibly up to similar zaniness, and the same picture of two players with crossed sticks that appears from Ancient Greece to Gloucester also appears in an altar set in the monastery of Soro. Meanwhile, nobody has quite worked out why there was set of mouldy old balls hidden under the tombstone of HM Storm in Aarhus, who died in 1659. The balls were not discovered until 1923, and we can only speculate as to whether they were placed there in honour of Storm, or whether the headstone merely provided a convenient place for the storage or hiding of balls by later generations.

It is many years later in the same country that we encounter Holger Louis Nielsen, who won medals in both shooting and fencing at the first ever Olympic Games at Athens in 1896. He came up with a game called *handbold*, and drew up the rules in 1898 for a seven-a-side game for use at Ollerup school. The story goes that the school doctor had decided to ban soccer due to all the injuries it was causing, and as a result, Nielsen and his pupils came up with a game that involved throwing rather kicking a standard soccer ball. An alternative version maintains that too many misplaced kicks were smashing the school's windows, and it was decided that if the kids used their hands rather than their feet, they would have better control over where the ball went. Whatever the reasoning, other schools seemed to think it was good, and *handbold* soon spread around the country and also caught on in Sweden.

Soon after, down in Germany in 1915, Hermann Bachmann was promoting something called *torball*, originally as a game for girls, although in 1919, Carl Schelenz, a teacher at the Berlin Physical Education College, decided it was suitable for boys as well, and it soon started spreading beyond the borders, with the first international played between Germany and Belgium in 1925, and Austria facing Germany five years later in the first ladies international.

Enough countries were playing handball games for it to be suggested for inclusion in the Olympic Games, but the obvious problem was that there was no international standard. So, the International Amateur Handball Federation was founded in Amsterdam in 1928 to lay down the laws and the many regional varieties were gradually phased out.

The newly codified game of handball was more like modern soccer than the handball played at the Olympics today. It was played 11-a-side on an outdoor field, and imitated most of the basic rules of the Association game, except that the ball was thrown rather than kicked. In fact, in many countries, the pioneering clubs were regular soccer clubs (such as AGF Aarhus in Denmark, Dukla Prague in Czechoslovakia, Steaua Bucharest in Romania and Atlético Madrid in Spain) and often used the same players, with handball considered a decent game to keep players in trim during the off-season. Field handball finally made its Olympic debut at Berlin 1936, reportedly at the behest of none other than Adolf Hitler, who would have naturally been keen to see a game with such a Germanic past included on the programme. Germany won the gold medal, but that was to be the outdoor version's only appearance at the Summer Games.

Handball developed in a curious direction. After the war, it was Scandinavia that led the way, where players discovered that the mechanics of the game were better suited to indoor play with smaller teams. Both the outdoor and indoor games lived on side by side, but perhaps due to its inability to compete with soccer, the world championship for outdoor handball was scrapped entirely in 1966, while by Munich 1972 indoor handball was on the Olympic programme to stay.

Georgia on the mind

Moving further afield, there was also some kind of football game played in Russia "particularly among the drivers of sledges and *drojekas* … A large ball, stuffed with feathers is kicked about and he who succeeds in catching it or picking it up with his hands, in spite of the kicks and cuffs of his playmates, carries off the prize of nuts or money[6]."

Further south, and we find the Georgian sport called *lelo burti* ('field ball')[7], which was played of old village against village using a heavy ball, "over a wide area sometimes stretching for several kilometres on very rough ground. The contestants would have to contend with spurs, hills, valleys, woods, cascading streams and marshes. Their task was to get a ball into a certain place, say, over the settlement boundary or to the foot of the mountain. Any means necessary could be employed to drive the ball forward – feet or hands. Sometimes they would play the game on horseback[8]."

The Georgians still use the word *lelo* for a 'try' in rugby, which shares much in common with the traditional game, although the latter allows forward passing and forbids carrying of the ball for longer than five seconds. French rugby clubs picked up on these similarities in the 1990s as they scoured the country for potential players, which led to a rugby boom in Georgia, and the team (nicknamed the *Lelos* in honour of their traditional game) is now a regular, and rapidly improving, participant at the Rugby World Cup.

Claiming that *lelo* had anything to do with the birth of rugby is a very long shot indeed, but it is curious to note that the handling code's rise to prominence in England happened around the same time as the Crimean War (1853–1856). We can at least speculate that British soldiers learned something of it while they were there. During and after the War, there were numerous troops stationed in Hampshire and the Isle of Wight, and with that a sudden

---

[6] Sir Richard Phillips *A general view of the manners, customs and curiosities of nations* (1810).
[7] In what at the time of writing was the self-declared but unofficially recognised independent state of Abkhazia, there is a similar game called *aimtskachara*.
[8] Yuri Lukashin (ed.) *National Folk Sports in the USSR* (Progress Publishing, 1980).

upsurge in the number of military-based football teams noted in the area, such as HMS Illustrious (1857), Parkhurst Barracks (1856) and the Winchester Garrison Officers (1859). The possible Georgian influence is at least worth a moment's reflection.

The golf war

When it comes to the stick games played around Europe, the main differentiating factor between the different forms was the amount of contention between players to play the ball. In some games, players battled to strike it, in others they took turns, and in the days before Astroturf pitches and immaculate fairways, the differences between what we know today as hockey and golf were considerably more blurred.

Tradition has it that golf is of quintessentially Scottish origin, but the truth is a lot less clear. We could start in Germany, and the hunting laws of Dreieichnear Frankfurt am Main in 1338, which state that shepherds were to determine the borders of their grazing grounds by hitting a stone with their crooks. But that is agriculture, not sport.

However, in the Netherlands, Steven Van Hengel[9] turned golfing history on its head with his revelation that the people of Loenen aan de Vecht played *spel metten colve* ('game with clubs') at Kronenburg Castle as early as 1297. Two teams of four struck balls over a 2.5 mile long course, the idea being to do so with as few strokes as possible. Van Hengel claims its golf, and the golf world was happy to agree for two decades before more scrupulous historians decided to examine his sources. Van Hengel was exposed as a hoax, but that's being a bit cruel. The Loenen story does appear in 19th century texts, which describe how the tradition had survived for 700 years, but there is no real evidence to support what probably amounts to little more than a folk legend.

Nevertheless, there are numerous references to a game that answered to such names as *het kolven, kofspel, colf* and *korf* that were played in that part of Europe. It was ordained in Brussels in 1360 that "whoever plays ball with a club, that is at 20 shillings or their upper garment." In other words, early players had to pay up or hand over an item of top clothing. This was a popular punishment, and in 1480 in Amsterdam things got tougher, when players were castigated by having to dress down to the nodder, a penalty so harsh that one has to assume that this was something more reckless than a simple golf-game. Orders like "the ball people with their balls shall post themselves along the canal from the bridge in front of the Master Arent Goes[10]" and "nobody strikes the ball on the streets with clubs with lead or iron heads[11]", or a sign in Harlem that states "here one makes clubs fine and noble, play *colf* with pleasure not brawls" make it clear enough the Dutch played stickball, but tell us nothing about whether it was more like golf or hockey.

---

[9] Steven JH Van Hengel, *Early Golf* (Drukkerij Tensinkl, 1982).
[10] *Magistrates of Bergen Op Zoom* (1461).
[11] *Ordinance of Zierikee* (1429).

The first time we hear of something with a distinctly golf-like feel to it is Johannes de Laet's Latin-Dutch phrasebook of 1552. It includes a dialogue between two *kolf* players, where the exchanges include "move back a bit while I drive", "step back a bit, you're in my light", "I'm not far from the target", "I'm playing first … You wait your turn" and "I want to stroke the ball in." This could well be the same stickball fun depicted as being enjoyed by Flemish children in the *Book of Hours*, published around 1498 and on show at the British museum[12].

From this period on we have a wealth of pictorial evidence of stick-and-ball games being played in Holland, often on ice around the time that our clog-wearing friends did not so much invent ice skating as turn it into a fine art[13], in more ways than one. Pieter Brueghel the Younger's *The Hunters in the Snow*[14] is one of his many paintings showing ice skaters, and one player does appear to be hitting something with a club. A few years later, the mute Hendrick Avercamp painted a number of early 17th century skaters, and his *A Scene on the Ice*[15] shows a group of gentlemen hitting balls around with sticks, as does an Adriaen van de Velde offering, *Golfers on the Ice near Haarlem*[16].

Medieval Dutch golf is not a theory that has gone down well in Scotland[17], where any suggestion that it wasn't their own creation is typically met with such responses as "golf bears about as much resemblance to *het kolven* as does haggis to hashish[18]." But rejecting *het kolven* as ice hockey fails to explain why a painting attributed to Simon Bening of around 1480 shows a player in Flanders clearly using a club to hit a ball into a hole. There is too much evidence from the Low Countries, where the village of Goile made almost its entire living from the manufacture of balls, including a consignment of 17,700 to Maastricht in 1731, to ignore the probable contribution that the region made to the game.

---

[12] *Les Heurs de Romme* is a kind of illustrated calendar, showing typical games and activities for each month of the year, including skittles, sledging, pretend jousting on hobby horses, bowling, walking on stilts, chasing butterflies, cock fighting and tug of war.

[13] Primitive skates dating back to 1000 BC were discovered at Bjoko in Sweden, while they are also believed to have been used in such places as ancient Siberia, Manchuria (China) and among Native Americans. It was probably the Vikings who introduced ice skating to most of Western Europe. Rudimentary iron skates were manufactured as early as the twelfth century in Holland, while the patron saint of Dutch skating, Lydwine Brugmann, took her fatal tumble in 1395, as depicted in a 1498 carving, Johannes Brugman's *Life of St Lidwina*, printed in Schiedam in 1498 and the oldest known image of ice skating. The *Catholic Encyclopedia* explains that "during the winter of the year of 1395, Lidwina went skating with her friends, one of whom caused her to fall upon some ice with such violence that she broke a rib in her right side. This was the beginning of her martyrdom. No medical skill availed to cure her … But God rewarded her with a wonderful gift of prayer and also with visions. Numerous miracles took place at her bed-side."

[14] On display at the Kunsthistorisches Museum, Vienna and painted around 1565.

[15] On display at the Teylers Museum, Haarlem, and painted around 1625.

[16] On display at the Louvre in Paris and painted around 1668.

[17] Nor has the idea of a Dutch origin for curling, to which both countries also have a disputed claim.

[18] As appears in an anonymous article at www.scottishgolf.com, titled *An End to Nonsense*.

Many Scottish clans are actually believed to be of Flemish origin[19] and the Dutch and Scots shared trade links for centuries, and so why not sporting links too? The opening verse to Johan Six van Chandelier's 1657 poem *Amsterdamsers Winter* is particularly telling in this respect, when it tells how the Dutch player "strikes his ash with lead weighted or his Scottish cleek of boxwood." Were the Scots exporting golf clubs or shinty sticks to Holland?

But Flannery believes France has older evidence than either of those two nations, and provides a wealth of details, beginning with the 13th century *paumiers* ('ballmakers') and *billardiers* ('stickmakers'), who produced the tools for *soule la crosse* and a less violent form that was rather like billiards played on the ground. The first description of something that really smells golf-like is a 1426 letter of remission that mentions *longue boule* where the idea was to hit the ball towards a neighbouring village "*avec le moins de cops de la boule de bois*[20]." Answering to such names as *pallemail*[21], there is copious pictorial and literary evidence of a game where the ball had to be struck towards a target while coping with natural obstacles along the way. Flannery notes that the game included the rough equivalents of "caddies, pros, clubhouses, penalties, handicapping, the cry *gare* that led to 'fore', the use of a tee for the initial drive, greenkeepers, and much more."

Of the game, an Englishman wrote in 1598 that "among all the exercises of France, I preferre none before the *palle-maille*, both because it is a gentleman-like sport, not violent, and yeelds good occasion and opportunity of discourse, as they walke from the one marke to the other. I marvell, among many more apish and foolish toyes, which wee have brought out of France, that wee have not brought this sport also into England[22]."

The *Regles Generales Du Jeu De Mail* were published in 1739, and explained that the idea was to strike the ball and then play it "from whatever stony or difficult place in which it is found, and one finishes the round by touching a tree or a marked stone which serves as the goal, or in passing through certain narrow *détroits*." At first they used a mallet, and later developed lofted clubs to give the ball the right lift. It sure sounds like golf.

The French speaking world also had *ball au pot* and *la truie*, which also involved smacking balls at targets with a stick, while there are 16th century references to a game called *argolla* played in Spain in which balls were aimed through rings in the ground (and which could be the game shown in a misericord in Barcelona Cathedral). In some way or other you will find something similar going on in just about every documented civilisation you could think of. To cite just a few more examples, there's Danish *bold i hul*, German *lochball*, Polish *czoromaj*, and Italian *budella*, all of which involved the same principles as golf, and only in the Italian game did you not use a stick.

---

[19] Beryl Platts (*Scottish Hazard*, 1985) lists twenty-nine, including Murray, Douglas, Sutherland, Fleming and Graham.

[20] In case you failed French at school, that's "with the fewest strokes of the wooden ball."

[21] The name was of Italian origin: *palla* (ball) and *mallaeus* (mallet).

[22] Sir Robert Dallington *A Method for Travell: shewed by taking the view of France as it stoode in the yeare of our Lord 1598.*

There is no definite point where the modern game suddenly appeared from the myriad of stick-sports played around Europe, and there is no evidence at all of golf in Scotland until relatively late in the day, and even then much of it is difficult to substantiate.

Take the famous first mention of the game in Caledonia, James II's decree in 1457 that "it is ordanyt and decreyt … at ye fut bawe and ye golf be utterly cryt done and not usyt[23]." James III and IV[24] also issued decrees against *golfe*, but although these quotes have Scottish historians leaping up and down with glee, we need to treat them with caution. As Michael Flannery writes, it probably "had nothing to do with golf but was, instead, directed at the violent hockey and football-like games that had raged on the continent since the thirteenth century." The accounts of folk being killed playing golf in the 16th and 17th century[25] suggest that the word was used to describe something very different in medieval Scotland.

Then there was the famous case of Mary Queen of Scots playing it in 1567, shortly after the death of her second husband Lord Darnley. Mary's half-brother James Stewart wrote how "staying at Holyroodhouse for a few days after the murder, she then went to Seton, taking exercise one day right openly in the fields with pall-mall and golf, and at night clearly dallying with Bothwell[26]." These were "sports that were clearly unsuitable to women" but the pall-mall reference is interesting, because Mary herself had not been raised in Scotland, but in the French court, where such games were played in all respectability by both genders.

At Elgin (1596), St Andrews (1598), Perth (1599) and Boharm (1658), there are church records of golfers being punished for playing the game on the Lord's Day, a letter from the Orkneys written in 1585 tells the reader to "remember to bring with you ane dossen of common golf ballis" and a letter written by the Marquis of Argyll while imprisoned for high treason in the Tower of London, where he was beheaded in 1661, writes that "tennis is not in use amongst us, but only in our capital city but in lieu of that, you have that excellent recreation of goff-ball than which truly I do not know a better."

From the 17th century onwards, we see Scottish golf gradually morphing into the game we know today. By 1627, multiple clubs were in existence, as revealed by a reference to a "bunker clubis, a irone club, and twa play clubis of my awin." But it is not clear how much this game was developing in isolation from European games. After all, when what would eventually be known as the Honourable Company of Edinburgh Golfers penned their historic *Thirteen Articles* in 1744, effectively the first official rules for the game of golf, these were little more than an adapted translation of the French rules for *jeu de mail* published five years earlier.

---

[23] *Anent Wapinshawing* ('of the practise of arms'). Act of Parliament number 338, Edinburgh, March 6, 1457.
[24] Somewhat hypocritically in the case of the latter, for in 1503 the royal accounts include an entry "for golf clubbes and balles to the King that he played with."
[25] Flannery records deaths at Breeching (1508), Sterling (1561) and Kelso (1632).
[26] *Articles before the Westminster Commissioners* (December 6, 1658).

As with so many sports, we can argue about this all night, and then suddenly the Chinese shut us all up by coming up with something older still. The *Dongxuan Records* written during the Song Dynasty (960–1279) describe a game called *chuiwan* that involved hitting mahogany balls with special sticks along the ground and into different holes marked with flags[27]. That sounds pretty golf-like, and this game is believed to have been the same thing as something called *buda* played under the Tang Dynasty several centuries earlier.

There are written records of the game played in the imperial courts, in the form of a set of rules reproduced by Gunson Ho[28], which even describe different strokes (among others, the 'standing still stroke', 'the squatting stroke' and the 'stepping forward stroke') and twenty-one different penalties. And there are also pictorial records, such as the early Ming (1368-1644) *Emperor Xuanzong of the Ming Dynasty is Playing* and Du Jin's 15th century *Beautiful Women Playing Chuiwan*[29].

The game mysteriously died out in the 17th century, with no further record of it, but Professor Ling Hongling of Lanzhou University has been making big claims of late that all this proves it was his Chinese who invented golf, reckoning that it was Mongol traders that would have taken it to Europe in the Middle Ages. But rather like *cuju*, the claim is probably more thanks to the fact that Chinese records generally go back much further and provide far more information than your average European chronicles do. The link is a tenuous one at best, and serves better as an example that golf is such a basic principle that anybody could have come up with it, and many did.

On hearing the Chinese claim, the Royal and Ancient Golf Club of St Andrews issued their official response that "stick and ball games have been around for many centuries, but golf as we know it today, played over 18 holes, clearly originated in Scotland." However, if one were to list the most defining features of golf, the fact that it is played over 18 holes would probably struggle to make the top ten. Although it is impossible to dispute their role in institutionalising modern golf, we have evidence that all the other basic concepts of the game were known elsewhere in Europe long before we can show they existed in Scotland.

---

[27] Also, a court record from Korea details a game where "the ball has to be driven with various sticks into holes surrounded with different obstacles."

[28] Gunson Ho *Physical Education in China* (1926).

[29] Both on show in Beijing's Palace Museum.

12 NORSE CODE
Ball games of the Vikings

Hornless warriors

The poor old Vikings have been given a bad press over the years. Misconceptions abound. So let's get one thing straight, and this might come as a bit of a shock, but, no, the Vikings did not wear horned helmets. Yes, there were many ancient civilisations, mainly in the north of Europe, which took to horny headgear in a big way, but judging by the total lack of such helmets in any archaeological, pictorial or written evidence to suggest otherwise, we can safely say that the Vikings were not among them. The whole idea seems to have originally been dreamed up by 19th century romanticists in Sweden, who confused the Viking warriors with the mythological Norse Gods and a Scandinavian culture of some 2000 years earlier, where horned helmets did crop up from time to time but even then were not omnipresent. Later still, it is probably such cartoons as *Hagar the Horrible* and even fancily dressed Minnesota Vikings supporters that have done more to perpetuate the misconception than anything else. Scandinavian soccer fans can wear horned helmets with pride, as long as they realise they are dressing up as ancient Norse Gods, and not Vikings.

And there's more. The Vikings were not unhygienic. The Anglo-Saxons were actually quite taken aback by this bizarre race that insisted on washing at least once a week (the word for 'Saturday' in most Scandinavian languages is descended from an ancient word meaning 'washday'). And no, the Vikings did not use human skulls as drinking vessels. And, to shatter yet another illusion, the Vikings were not hell-bent on raping, pillaging, murdering and generally wreaking uncivilised havoc wherever they shored their longboats. Well, no more than any other cultures of their time, which were pretty barbaric wherever you went. Scandinavia generally had a far more established and secure social and political system than most of Europe, and most of the seafaring Vikings were more intent on trading than the homicidal, plundering raids we associate them with nowadays.

And getting back to football, there is one thing we can certainly be sure of. The game was not invented by a group of Englishmen who, to celebrate an important victory against an invading company of Norsemen, decided to cut off the head of their leader and kick it around for fun. It's a popular story that has found its way into English and also Scottish folklore, but there are no historical records to back it up, and it is laughable to think that it was only after quashing a seaborne invasion that the locals suddenly came up with the simple concept of kicking a spherical object.

But the Vikings may have played a slightly less macabre role in the development of modern-day football codes, for it has been theorised that some form of the game could have been brought to Britain by our non-horned helmet wearing and actually sweet and cuddly Nordic friends. The time frame fits. Most of the earliest references to football in England and

France do roughly coincide with the period from the 8th to the 11th century BC, when the Vikings were at their most active in the west. The downside to the theory is that it's debatable that the Vikings played anything like football at all.

They sure had balls. The earliest, of which plenty have been recovered, were made of wood and were not unlike modern day cricket balls. And while the rest of the continent was struggling away with pig bladders, the Vikings had already developed, stuffed and sewn leather balls as early as the 11th century.

But what ball related exercises did they come up with to while away those chilly evenings long before Ikea came along with its flat-packed comforts? In the late 20th century, there was a resurgence of interest in Viking culture, and several attempts were made to recreate the ancient game, both in its native Iceland, and by batty Middle Englanders that like to toss aside their white collars and escape the tedium of the office week by dressing up as Vikings and re-enacting the different things they did. It has also gained in popularity on the American college scene, with the likes of Brandeis, Clark, Providence and Yale having fielded teams.

The obvious difficulty in doing this is the almost total lack of knowledge of what Viking football was. As a result, there has been a tendency for modern day enthusiasts to simply make up rules based on their own stereotypes of what Vikings were like. It's all great fun for those involved, but in terms of producing an accurate rendition of the ancient sport of the Norsemen, it is about as true to historical fact as a recreation of Roman chariot racing using a set of marbles and a Monopoly board.

The sagas

Most of what we know about Viking games comes from passing references in the great Icelandic sagas. Paul Du Chaillu did a grand job of summarising these in 1889, where he concludes that there were basically three different types of game: *knattleikr*, *soppleik* and *skofuleik*. As is so often the case when sport crops up in ancient mythologies, we are told plenty about the lordly folk that played the game, the disputes they had and the blood that was spilled, but very little is explained about what the game involved, which the reader is assumed to already know.

The descriptions suggest something like rugby, and there are so many references to ice and liquid landmarks that it is widely believed that it was mainly played on frozen ponds. But it seems hard to accept that the Vikings were so insistent on limiting their sport to such a daftly slippery surface. We are told that games were played in the summer too when even in Iceland it can get pretty warm, and playing fields are also mentioned in places where there are no bodies of water, so although they may have played on ice from time to time it seems likely that the game was more commonly played on solid ground.

As a taster for the kind of thing we're dealing with, here is an extract from *Gisla Saga*[1]: "Those brothers-in-law, Thorgrim and Gisli, were very often matched against each other, and

---

[1] Written between 1270-1320, and translated by George Webbe Dasent in 1866.

159

men could not make up their mind which was the stronger, but most thought Gisli had most strength. They were playing at the ball on the tarn called Sedge. On it there was ever a crowd. It fell one day when there was a great gathering that Gisli bade them share the sides as evenly as they could for a game … Now they began the game, and Thorgrim could not hold his own. Gisli threw him and bore away the ball. Again Gisli wished to catch the ball, but Thorgrim runs and holds him, and will not let him get near it. Then Gisli turned and threw Thorgrim for such a fall on the slippery ice that he could scarcely rise. The skin came off his knuckles, and the flesh off his knees, and the blood gushed from his nostrils. Thorgrim was very slow in rising. As he did so he looked to Vestein's house and chanted:

'Right through his ribs my spearpoint went crashing;
Why should I worry? 'Twas well worth this thrashing'

Gisli caught the ball on the bound, and hurled it between Thorgrim's shoulders, so that he tumbled forward, and threw his heels up in the air, and Gisli chanted:

'Bump on the back, my big ball went dashing;
Why should I worry? 'Twas I gave the thrashing'.

Thorkel jumps up and says 'Now we can see who is the strongest or the best player. Let us break off the game?' and so they did."

The sagas are always keen to describe the violence involved. *Herraud and Bosi's Saga*, written around 1300, tells of a game of *soppleik*, in which said Bosi "played roughly, and one of the king's men had his hand put out of joint. The next day he broke the thigh-bone of a man, and the third day two men attacked him, while many were harassing him. He knocked out the eye of one with the ball, and he knocked down another man and broke his neck."

Hord Grimkelson's Saga, written around the 10th century, described Yuletide games of *skouleikar* and *knattleikar* that were not for the feint hearted either. "Before dusk, six of the Strand players lay dead, though none on the Botn side", while the bad tempered Tord Blig played the game so violently that he was banned from playing altogether.

The texts often refer to the ball being struck with a bat (which often broke but was apparently quite easy to mend), but we cannot even be sure whether the bat was actually used as protection or even as a weapon. Take for example this extract from *Thorstein Vikingsson's Saga*: "Thorir threw down the ball so hard that it bounded over Olaf and fell a long way off. Olaf got angry and fetched the ball … Then Olaf struck at Thorir with the bat, and when Thorir saw it he ran under the bat, which hit his head and bruised it." Things are no clearer in *Göngu-Hrólf's Saga*, where a game that ended with a neck being broken featured the following series of actions: "Hrafn took the ball, and Krak the bat, and they played as they were wont. The Jarl sat on a chair and looked at the game, and when they had played it for a while Hrolf got hold of the ball. He snatched the bat from Krak and handed it to Stefnir. They then played for a long time, and the brothers did not get hold of the ball."

But was the game played by the common Viking in the street as violent as popular myth has led us to believe? After all, the sagas might tell us of all kinds of unspeakable acts going on, in a game where winding your opponents up with insults was part and parcel of the occasion (cricketers call it sledging), and where it was not unknown for somebody to produce a weapon and kill a particularly dastardly rival, but these were the sagas, which were not so much a reflection of Nordic society at the time, but were epic, romanticised tales of the heroic deeds of days that had long gone by, replete with exaggerations that are perhaps not be taken too literally. At the end of the day, the ancient legends are no more or less true than the story that Adam and Eve once had a rather embarrassing episode with an apple and a snake.

Atlantic crossing

If the Viking game was a kind of rugby with bats, then we can speculate about its relationship with modern stickball codes like hockey, hurling and lacrosse. The immediate reaction would be to eliminate the lacrosse connection from the outset, given the historic and geographic unfeasibility of a game we know to have its origins among the North American Indians being influenced by Norse culture. But this is where the story could have taken a particularly intriguing twist.

We have already pondered the theory that the Phoenicians took their stick games across the Atlantic. But if any ancient Greek presence in the Americas is regarded with sceptical eyes among the grey walls of academia, there is so much evidence that the continent was regularly visited by the Vikings that it is now considered historical fact.

It's only logical that they would have found their way there. They set forth from the Scandinavian Peninsula to settle *en masse* in Iceland and Greenland. There were about 50,000 of them in Iceland alone around 1000 AD and Greenland was settled for some 400 years before it was largely abandoned. It is simply preposterous to suggest that during all those years, in which the whole of Greenland was thoroughly explored, settled and exploited for what it was worth, nobody thought to make the two-day hop west to Baffin Island, and from there maybe on into Hudson Bay and mainland North America. But it was not until the discovery of a most definitely Viking site at L'Anse aux Meadows in Newfoundland that any conclusive physical evidence was ever found to prove it[2].

Plenty of descriptions of voyages to lands that were presumably parts of the Americas appeared in the Norse Sagas, and Bjarni Herjólfsson in the year 986 is generally heralded as being the first to make the trip. With resources being hard to come by in Greenland, he and later travellers were probably more interested in collecting fur, lumber and other vital commodities than any long-term settlement. Besides, it seems that the natives, or Skraelings as the Norsemen called them, were anything but welcoming hosts[3].

---

[2] There was also the controversial Kensington Runestone, which features carved writing in Old Swedish that details the events of a Norse expedition in the mid 14th century. It was discovered in Minnesota in 1898 by somebody who, by remarkable coincidence, happened to be a Swedish American. Historians are divided on whether the stone is genuine or a very convincing fake.

[3] Another reason that has been offered is that as so few women accompanied the men on these expeditions, it seems the trips inevitably ended in disaster with the Vikings fighting with each other over the ladies.

However, although the evidence is sparse, historians putting together the pieces of a very tricky jigsaw puzzle now tend to believe there was a lot more contact between the two worlds during the period of Viking expansion than was previously credited. So, perhaps it was not just a case of cutting down a few Canadian trees and battering their seal pups, but that the Norse left considerably more of their legacy in those parts than we once thought.

In fact, when Greenland was vacated by the Norsemen, historians are unsure as to where all those people went. Icelandic Bishop Gisli Oddson tells us that in 1342 "the inhabitants of Greenland voluntarily forsook the true faith and the Christian religion, after having abandoned all good morals and true virtues, and were converted to the peoples of America[4]." But he was writing almost three centuries after this supposedly happened, so his ideas may be just as speculative as those of modern-day historians. But explorations in later centuries would often come across strangely out-of-place tall, blue-eyed and blond-haired Inuit folk. These could well be the descendants of the ancient Norsemen that decided to move west, and would eventually lose contact with Europe altogether.

It was Norwegian historian Ebbe Hertzberg[5] who first suggested that the mingling of the two cultures may also have led to the mingling of their respective ball games. He noted such a wealth of similarities between *knattleikr* and Indian lacrosse that he was convinced that they were versions of the same game. But we know so little about the finer points of the Viking games that it is hard to make any definite claims that they was any more similar or different to cricket than they were to lacrosse, and Hertzberg's theories are not as conclusive as he might have thought. Most of the characteristics he mentioned are common to any team ball sport. The facts that both were played between two teams on a defined playing area, sanctioned extreme violence, were seen as tests of male strength and involved teams striving to get the ball to a certain point, or even the use of sticks to do so, hardly defined them as unique in the sporting world. Neither does the fact that they were played on both dry land and ice, as those geographic features are pretty much all you've got to choose from in any northern climate. And even if Ebbe was correct, we cannot tell whether the Vikings gave their games to North America, or whether that is the place they learned them.

Letter from America

Frederick Pohl[6] postulated that it wasn't just the Phoenicians and Vikings who may have got to North America before 1492, but also the Scots. The tribe at the heart of the theory is the Micmac, who inhabit what we now know as Nova Scotia (or 'New Scotland') in the southeast corner of modern-day Canada.

Although the claims that the Europeans encountered the Micmac in the 15th century and found that they knew the basics of several Old World languages, including Gaelic and

---

[4] Gísla Oddsson *De mirabilis Islandiae* (1638, reprinted by Cornell University Press, 1917).
[5] Ebbe Hertzberg *Nordboernes Gamle Boldspil* (published in Historiske Skrifter, 1904).
[6] Frederick J Pohl *Atlantic Crossings Before Columbus* (Norton, 1961).

Basque, may be pushing things a bit far, and it seems to be more speculation than fact that they already understood the basic notions of the Christian religion, there are too many freaky coincidences where these people are concerned to scoff too confidently at the idea of pre-Columbian contact.

For how on earth did a 14th century Venetian cannon come to be lying in Louisburg Harbour, Cape Breton? And why did they paint pictures of what look like New World cacti and Indian corn at Rosslyn Chapel in Scotland a few years before Christopher Columbus was even born?

And who exactly was this sword-bearing and white-skinned 'prince' called Glooscap, an important figure in Micmac legend, who apparently arrived from the sea in what the natives described as a village on a floating island covered with trees? Could it have been a ship with masts? Could it have been Henry Sinclair, Prince of Orkney and of Viking descent who led a westward expedition in 1398 (94 years before Columbus) and claimed to have discovered a new world? Well, it could have been, but so little is really known of Sinclair and his voyages that historians are sceptical on the issue, and many doubt he really went any further than Greenland.

Supporters of the theory turn to the controversial Zeno Brothers of Venice, who were apparently on the voyage too. In the 16th century, a series of maps and letters were published detailing their explorations of the North Atlantic under the captaincy of a mysterious character called Zichmni, whose name is apparently too similar to Sinclair to deny that he wasn't one and the same man.

Cynics consider the Zeno documents to have been a hoax, perhaps drafted as part of some zany scheme to claim that the Venetians had discovered America long before that Genoese imposter named Columbus. Pohl's theories have not always been taken too seriously.

Having drifted further off course than a seafaring Scotsman, we shall now get back to the point and reveal what the settlers that were busy founding Halifax around 1750 observed to be a popular pastime among the local Indian populace, who were a particularly friendly lot by all accounts. They were playing a form of stickball. There is nothing too unusual here; we already know that the precursors of modern-day lacrosse were being played in North America long before the Europeans arrived. But the unusual thing about the Micmac game is that rather than using elongated rackets, it was curiously similar to the traditional Scottish stick game called shinty.

It had been widely rumoured (by the Scots) that the people of the land Sinclair discovered had been taught, among other things during his half-year or so among them, such noble Scottish arts as dancing, fishing and games. Is that how the Micmac came to play something so similar to shinty? And maybe also the stick games on ice that they and the Montagnais of modern day Quebec, who call it *ice gugahawat* play? Does that mean the seeds of ice hockey were also sewn by this transatlantic contact? Or was it in America that the Scots first got the idea of shinty?

The idea that shinty, and by extension, hurling, were games imported from the North American Indians would soon be shouted down by fans of both those sports, who are very aware that their games date back much further than any of these supposed transatlantic crossings. But in the next chapter, we'll be asking how valid the claims to the antiquity of the Celtic stickball games really are.

13 CELTIC ART
Ball games of the ancient Celts

Camán feel the noise

The ancient ball courts of Central America are now just ruins. *Kemari* was merely performed as a folkloric sideshow when Japan hosted the 2002 FIFA World Cup. You will be lucky to see many natives playing stickball games on the North American plains these days. The revival of *la soule* in France has attracted next to nothing in terms of media interest, and if *marngrook* ever influenced Aussie Rules football, there can be no doubting which of the two games is the more influential now.

Ireland's contribution to the legacy of ball games is hurling. There are claims it could be as many as two thousand years old, taking us further back than recorded history can account for properly. But unlike most ancient sports, this is no small-scale revival by enthusiastic local heritage groups recreating the past in their *Frodo Lives* t-shirts before popping down to the most thatched pub with the realest ale they can find. No, hurling is a big deal in Ireland. It is a 'proper' sport.

Kilkenny beat Tipperary in the 2010 All Ireland Senior Hurling Final. It was played, as it is every year, at the third largest sports stadium in Europe, the state of the art Croke Park[1]. The crowd of 81,765 was larger than that for both Super Bowl XLIV and the UEFA Champions League Final played the same year.

It may not be the most internationally widespread of sports, and even in neighbouring Great Britain people often confuse it with curling in the same way continentals struggle to understand that cricket and croquet are not the same thing. Even the great Robert Henderson gets it embarrassingly wrong in his seminal *Bat, Ball and Bishop*, when he says "a modern variety of hurling in Ireland, instead of resembling hockey, as in former days, consists of a competition to hurl, or throw a heavy ball to a given point in the fewest number of throws … but the older forms of the game were all fiercely fought club-and-ball traditional games." It's hard to accept Henderson as an authority on the origin of anything when he didn't even know that, in fact, hurling was still alive and well in the year he was writing, 1947, when 60,000 people watched Kilkenny beat Cork the All Ireland Final of a game that involved no throwing of heavy balls to given points, but actually resembled 'club-and-ball traditional games' quite a lot.

Modern hurling and its sister sport, Gaelic football, share much in common. They both come under the auspices of the Gaelic Athletic Association (GAA), which was formed in 1884. They share the same stadiums and pitches, county teams in both sports wear identical kit, the structures of the respective competitions are organised in parallel to each other, and

---

[1] Only FC Barcelona's Camp Nou and Wembley Stadium in London have bigger capacities.

the scoring system, number of players, and many of the rules and terminologies are also the same.

That's not to say there isn't a certain rivalry between the two games. Hurlers in particular tend to shun football as less manly and less traditionally Irish. Although football is by far the most widely played of the two, hurling is traditionally strong in the south, particularly in the counties of Kilkenny, Wexford, Waterford, Tipperary, Limerick and Clare (as well as Antrim in the north). It's essentially the more rural of the two games. Dublin, despite being home to one sixth of the island's population, has not been All Ireland hurling champion since 1938.

Played 15-a-side, including a goalkeeper, it involves hitting the ball with an ash wood stick, called a hurley or *camán*, that is about a metre long and has a wider, flattened section at one end (for holding and hitting the ball). The ball, called the *sliotar*, is made of leather and is about the size of a baseball, the field is roughly the same size as a rugby or soccer one, and the goalposts are a peculiar combination of both those sports. Rugby's 'H' type posts are there in all their glory, but the area under the crossbar (which is a little lower down than in rugby) has a net like a soccer goal.

That's because there are two ways of scoring. Getting the ball through the posts scores one point (an 'over'), while scoring a goal in the 'soccer' net scores three. The Irish like to keep their audience thinking through a little mental arithmetic, for rather than doing the obvious and adding up all the ones and threes to get a round figure, they are recorded separately. So, a score of 3-14 actually means '3 goals and 14 points' for a total of 21.

The *sliotar* can be hit on the ground hockey-style, but the action tends to be more airborne (*a la* lacrosse), which can easily get the thing moving at speeds of up to 150 kph[2]. You don't want that in your face. That *sliotar* is one hard little thing. But hurlers are hard, too, and although helmets with protective masks have existed for some time, many players preferred to do without them until they were made compulsory in 2010.

One of the basic skills of hurling is what is called soloing, which is the art of moving around as you balance or bounce the ball on the *camán*. However, there is also the option of catching it in your hand. The ball cannot be moved from one hand to the other, but a player can advance a maximum of three steps while holding it, whereupon it must be released. The ball can be caught a second time, but no more than that during one possession.

The ball is propelled either by hitting it with the stick, or using the palm of the hand (the usual method for passing the *sliotar* to a team-mate). Straightforward throwing of the ball is illegal, and neither are you allowed to pick the ball up off the ground, you have to scoop it up with the *camán*.

---

[2] It's commonly said that it is the fastest ball sport in the world, but exactly on what criteria this is measured I can't be sure. We'll just have to assume that somebody did do the research and timed the speed of the ball in every game from *gugahawat* to *marngrook*. There are counter claims for the squash-like *jai alai* played in the Basque Country and also for golf. Although not strictly a ball sport, one game actually blows all three away. A badminton shuttlecock can reach a speed of 331 kph, twice as fast as a *sliotar*!

Setanta sport

"Hurling is indeed a game for the Gods. Hurling, which can claim to be the parent of every game played with a stick and ball, stands still unapproached as the greatest game ever devised for the diversion of men. Like the race that begot it, it is old, yet young, virile and fascinating, and though its origin dates away back in prehistoric eras, could Oisín come back again today from Tír na nóg, he would find in an all-too-changed world ... at least one familiar sight to gladden his heart[3]." That's quite some claim by Séamus Ó Ceallaigh, and as we are about to discover, probably misguided.

We learned earlier of the Battle of Moytura (*Magh Tuireadh* in Irish), which was allegedly preceded by a 27-a-side 'hurling match'. It was bloody, it was gory, and was fought "till their bones were broken and bruised and they fell outstretched on the turf and the match ended[4]," but as we saw in an earlier chapter, it belongs more on the mythology than the history shelf, and even so, the original text only speaks of a battle, and nothing even remotely like hurling.

Moytura is the first of many supposed references to ancient Irish games involving balls and sticks, but Gaelic sports historians have sometimes been a bit hasty in assuming that these were early forms of the modern game. The evidence is not always as conclusive as one might think. AB Gleason shows how "a critical examination of the terms and descriptions of early field games demonstrates there is no reason or justification to limit the discussion of the games to hurling or its precursor. The fact that this is largely the case in the established historiography is a reflection of modern sentiment rather than medieval reality[5]." She is particularly wary of the way texts have been translated fairly liberally into English to provide what she calls a "skewed report ... the medieval Irish sources describe manifold contests and games, providing detail as to who played the games, with what equipment and where. Unfortunately ... they remain rather silent on details a history of hurling needs to affirm an early existence."

We have seen in earlier chapters the dangers of assuming that expressions like *pilae ludus* refer to 'football[6]', and it is only fair for Old Irish to be treated with the same caution. But this has not been the case. The hurling historian's job has been to write the uniquely Irish history that hurling wants, the more ancient the better. Gleason explains how there was a major flurry from the late 19th century to use ancient texts to create a unique identity for

---

[3] Séamus Ó Ceallaigh *History of the Limerick GAA., Part 1 - 1884-1908* (*The Kerryman*, 1937), and cited in a lecture by Dr Paul Rouse in Dublin City Library and Archive on 11th September, 2010, which also provided useful, and probably more honest, information for this chapter.

[4] Grant Jarvie (ed.) *Sport in the making of Celtic cultures* (Leicester University Press, 1999).

[5] AB Gleason in *The Gaelic Athletic Association 1884-2009* (Irish Academic Press, 2009). Gleason earned her PhD at Trinity in Dublin and is currently a renowned expert on Medieval Ireland at Princeton in the USA.

[6] A similar example is how Irishman Charles Jarvas' translation of Don Quixote in 1742 caused much furore with its description of cricket being played in 15th century Spain. But all it really says in the Spanish original is that Basilius was a "*gran jugador de pelota*", or a 'great ball player', which was unlikely to have had anything to do with cricket at all.

Ireland, a movement the GAA exploited to promote its own ideas. "The atmosphere in which the texts were studied and translated necessarily prompted a heady blend of nostalgia and nationalism" she writes. "With few exceptions, translations rendered otherwise simple and often unaccompanied terms for ball, stick, game, goal or even hoop by the catch-all 'hurling'. This has inevitably led historians and fans alike to grant the sport of hurling an unassailable antiquity."

Two main sources for Irish mythology are *Lebor na hUidre* ('Book of the Dun Cow') and *Lebor Laignech* ('Book of Leinster'), although several pages of both have sadly been lost or damaged and are unlikely to ever be seen again. Both documents construct a 'myth-tory' for Irish culture on a par with Ancient Greek and Biblical texts. But although the surviving documents were scribed around the 12th century, there is enough evidence within them to suggest that certain sections were lifted from earlier texts dating back several centuries more.

Our main interest lies with that most esteemed hurler, Setanta[7], the nephew of the King of Ulster, a deistic folk hero whose story, to the best of our knowledge, was not written down anywhere until the bard Sechan Torpeist got around to it in the 7th century – and only a shameless cynic would doubt that he did so on the basis of very solid historical evidence.

Táin Bó Cúailnge[8] tells us how Setanta was an accomplished sportsman from a young age. Well, 'accomplished' is something of an understatement – this guy had the superhuman skills of a *Marvel Comics* hero. Still a wee bairn, "the boy went forth and took his playthings. He took his hurley-stick[9] of bronze and his silver ball. He took his little javelin for casting and his toy spear with its end sharpened by fire, and he began to shorten the journey by playing with them. He would strike his ball with the stick and drive it a long way from him. Then with a second stroke he would throw his stick so that he might drive it a distance no less than the first. He would throw his javelin and he would cast his spear and would make a playful rush after them. Then he would catch his hurley-stick and his ball and his javelin, and before the end of his spear had reached the ground he would catch its tip aloft in the air."

That, there can be no denying, was some neat trick, but such skill was just the start of it where this young lad was concerned. He once had the nerve to walk uninvited into the middle of a ball game involving 150 older boys "and caught the ball between his two legs

---

[7] It is in his honour that Setanta, Ireland's rapidly-expanding TV sports broadcaster, is named and it was a fine choice, for he was possibly the finest sportsman that (n)ever lived.

[8] In English, *The Cattle Raid of Cooley* from *the Book of Leinster*.

[9] 'Hurley-stick', of course, appears here as a translation. Gleason notes that the earliest version of this tale describes it as a *lorg áne*, or 'driving stick', and in a later version it becomes the modern *camán*, which in Gaelic is simply the word for a 'little bent stick' and needn't necessarily be the same thing that modern day hurlers use. Also, just because the ball is struck in the air should not be taken as immediate proof that this was hurling as opposed to hockey. We cannot be any surer that hurling was always played by striking the ball in the air as we can that hockey was always played with the ball on the ground. That distinction is unlikely to be any older than the late 19th century, when the respective sports decided on uniform rules and English hockey opted to outlaw any handling of the ball.

when they cast it … and he pressed it and held it close between his two legs, and not one of the youths managed to get a grasp or a stroke or a blow or a shot at it. And he carried the ball away from them over the goal."

Anybody who tried emulating that feat at Croke Park today would be met with some very strange looks. But impressive stunt as it was, Setanta was a long way from his peak. Follomain mac Conchobuir, who was running the show, ordered the players to attack the little imp "and let him meet death at my hands, for it is taboo for you that a youth should join your game without ensuring his protection from you. Attack him all together, for we know that he is the son of an Ulster chieftain, and let them not make it a habit to join your games without putting themselves under your protection and safeguard.

"Then they all attacked him together. They cast their thrice fifty hurley-sticks at the boy's head. He lifted up his single play-thing stick and warded off the thrice fifty sticks. Then they cast the thrice fifty balls at the little boy. He raised his arms and his wrists and his palms and warded off the thrice fifty balls. They threw at him the thrice fifty toy spears with sharpened butts. The boy lifted up his toy wooden shield and warded off the thrice fifty spears. Then he attacked them."

And so it went on, with our young hero annihilating the opposition, to the point that Conchobuir put a stop to whole thing and took the boy aside to ask "do you not know of the prohibition that the youths have, and that it is taboo for them that a boy should come to them from outside and not first claim their protection?" The kid said he did not, but by this point the battered youths were quite happy to offer him their protection regardless of the local traditions.

And so it was that the "little boy placed himself under the protection of the youths. Then they loosed hands from him but once more he attacked them. He threw fifty kings' sons to the ground beneath him. Their fathers thought that he had killed them but it was not so, he had merely terrified them with his many and violent blows. 'Nay' said Conchobuir. 'Why do you still attack them?' 'I swear by my gods that until they in their turn all come under my protection and guarantee as I have done with them, I shall not lift my hands from them until I bring them all low.' 'Well, little lad, take on you the protection of the youths.' 'I grant it' said the little boy. Then the youths placed themselves under his protection and guarantee."

It was epic stuff, and all true of course, but there is room for scepticism as to whether this really was early hurling being played. The original Irish term was *cluichi puill*, which means hole-game, and some have used the same passage to defend Ireland's claim as the birthplace of golf. Gleason refers to a couple of early law texts that support the idea that there was a game like this played in Medieval Ireland. Unfortunately, the texts are more concerned with the legalities regarding injuries caused by the game than describing the actual rules, but it does say at one point that "a ball is struck at a defended hole, from which a defender can strike the ball away, ideally towards a free dividing line." It may have been something like this that Setanta was said to be playing, which isn't really hurling at all.

In a later tale, Setanta's royal uncle was invited to a banquet at the house of a local blacksmith, Culain. Wee Setanta had also been invited to dine and help make small talk about hooves and the price of iron for the evening, but was going to get there late because he had a 'hurling' match to play first.

Forgetting the kid, and assuming the meal could start, the smith locked the doors and unleashed his vicious bloodhound to guard the grounds. This was no ordinary dog, but one that "when his dogchain is taken off no traveller or wayfarer dares come into the same canton as he … his strength is such that he can do the work of a hundred." So, when Setanta arrived, carrying just his *sliotar*, he was greeted by the gnashing of fangs. He calmly responded by casting the ball "and it went through the gaping mouth of the bloodhound and carried all his entrails out through the back way. And the boy then seized him by two legs and dashed him against the standing-stone so that he was scattered into pieces on the ground."

The diners were naturally alarmed by the rumpus, and ran outside expecting to find poor Setanta's face looking like a half-eaten bowl of Pedigree Chum. How wrong they were. Culain the blacksmith was obviously not quite so impressed at the loss of his prize pooch, but Setanta offered to make up for the canicide by taking the dog's place and guarding the Pass of Ulster in its stead, and from then on, he would be known as 'the hound of Culain' or Cuchulainn.

Cuchulainn gained such fame for his exploits that we are told the ladies regularly flashed their boobs at him whenever they saw him pass. But let that not be interpreted as encouragement to go about killing your neighbour's pet in the hope of improving your chances with the local ladies.

MacCool runnings

The *Book of the Dun Cow*, also scribed in the 12th century, tells of another legendary hurler of superhuman prowess, Fionn MacCumhail, commonly Anglicised as Finn MacCool. Names don't come much cooler than that.

A descendant of the Gods, which probably helped when it came to acquiring his remarkable skills with the *camán*, he led the mythical band of fighters called *Fianna Eireann*, and his various achievements included building the Giants' Causeway, the stepping stones that legend says once linked Ireland to Scotland. Meanwhile, on the hurling field his main accomplishment was to score the winning goal against a team of fifty, and thus win a kiss from King Cormac MacArt's daughter. Snogging royalty obviously appealed to him, for he'd end up marrying the girl.

Finn was an old man when he appears in *Tóraigheacht Dhiarmada agus Ghráinne*[10], where at one point in the tale we are told of "a great goaling match" in which "thou didst rise and

---

[10] Or *The Pursuit of Díarmait and Gráinne* in English. It's a love triangle story that was mentioned in the 12th century *Book of Leinster*, although there is no surviving version of the actual tale that dates back any earlier than the 17th century.

stand, and tookest his hurly-stick from the next man to thee, and didst throw him to the ground and to the earth, and thou wentest into the game, and didst win the goal three times upon Cairbre and upon the warriors of Tara."

But MacCool as they are, the anthropological value of stickball imagery in folk tales is questionable at best. Gleason notes how the same kind of thing went on with religious figures, showing how medieval translations of the lives of both Saint Gregory and Saint Columba added passing references to games involving a *camán* "to add national flavour to the tale." It was all about placing folk heroes in settings people could identify with. Nevertheless, if that was the kind of thing the Irish identified with in the Middle Ages, then it is still a remarkably early period in terms of evidence of ball games.

Hurling's antiquity is helped by the fact that there are few societies in Europe for which such a wealth of early medieval literature has survived as has in Ireland. Some of the best are the *Dlíthe na mBreithiún* (Brehon Laws), which were an elaborate pre-Christian attempt to regulate just about every aspect of Irish society, including property, marriage and language. The basic principles were passed on through oral tradition, but as early as the 3rd century, Ard Rí Cormac Mac Art busied himself by recording them in the *Book of Arcill*[11].

There were seven types of injury that could not be prosecuted. One of these, and the feminists will like this, was "blood shed by a jealous wife" and another was "blood shed by boys in games." You played at your own risk. The local ruler, the *rí*, could have a bronze hoop on his *camán*, while everybody else had to make do with copper. No child could be punished for the theft of a *camán* provided he returned it to its rightful owner, and in one game players were allowed to encroach on a landowner's property to retrieve a lost ball "if there be necessity and consent." These *Meallbreatha* ('judgements on games') may well have been referring to early forms of hurling, but the common assertion that hurling was mentioned in the Brehon Laws is jumping to conclusions.

Then we have the tale of Saint Féchin of Fore, a 7th century saint. In a highly disconcerting episode, "Féchin was in his cell at prayer when he was disturbed by children playing. 'I permit you' said Féchin 'to go and be drowned in the lake, and your souls will be free to ascend to heaven' whereupon the children went into the lake and were drowned[12]." This is supposedly telling us what a saintly gent he was, although modern paediatricians would beg to differ. The thing is, this text has since been modified to state that it was a hurling match that bothered Féchin, but the original text never said anything of the sort!

---

[11] What the Laws tell us is that the Ancient Irish were anything but the barbaric race they are misconceived to be. We are told, for example, that "if a pregnant woman craves a morsel of food and her husband withholds it through stinginess, meanness or neglect he must pay a fine." And the Laws were way ahead of their time when it came to animal rights, for "it is illegal to override a horse, force a weakened ox to do excessive work or threaten an animal with angry vehemence which breaks bones." But check this one out for sheer legal brilliance: "if a woman invites a man and screams during the act it is not considered rape, if she did not invite the man and screams it was rape."

[12] Nicol Óg *Betha Féchín Fabair*n (1328, but probably based on earlier texts that have not survived).

Neither can we be sure of the nature of the game described in the poem *Iománaithe Chill Cóirne* ('The Hurlers of Kilcorney'), written by Lochlainn Ó Dálaigh in 1565. It is set, appropriately enough, in Carron, County Clare, the same parish where the man who founded the GAA, Michael Cusack, would be born three centuries later. The verse referring to a game called *scuaibín* or *baithe boithe* goes thus:

> Did you hear about the Kiloughhrey family,
> Getting torn up and tearing up the ground all day?
> Canny was first on the scene and was better than five,
> He was a great help against the heroes.
> Diarmuid would hold back the goals, if he was helped.
> The men in black coats scattered before them on every side.
> Unless you trap them tightly by the turlough[13]
> They'll annihilate us all.

New angles

As ever, the best evidence of medieval sports tends to be produced when somebody decided to go about banning it. And there was going to be a lot of that once the Anglo-Norman invasion began in 1169 and ensured that relations between the two islands would be strained ever since.

It is simplifying matters to say the Brits simply stormed into Ireland and took it over. It was a long and complex process, with Ireland at the time really being a patchwork of kingdoms, with as much in-fighting going on between them as there was with outsiders, and England itself being a country that had only recently been conquered by the Normans from modern day France. But we have to blame somebody, and Henry II will do nicely, the great-grandson of William the Conqueror and the first English monarch to consider himself 'King of England' as opposed to 'King of the English', although his family were effectively still Frenchmen that had conquered England, and who, seeing the rising Leinster as a potentially dangerous rival, had now turned their eyes west. Henry was encouraged by the Pope (who handily enough happened to be the first and only English one, who was keen to convert Ireland to Roman Catholicism) to accept an invitation to help the dispossessed Diarmait Mac Murchada to regain his throne.

Ultimately, however, it was Henry who claimed the title 'Lord of Ireland', and by 1300 the Normans controlled practically the whole island. However, the people who settled there, rather than impose their own values on the Irish, did the reverse. They adopted the Irish language, customs and laws, and there was so much inter-marriage that they effectively became assimilated into the Irish population. In 1366, the *Statutes of Kilkenny* were passed to deal with the grave concern that "many English of the said land, forsaking the English

---

[13] A *turlough* is a kind of seasonal lake that is common in Ireland.

language, manners, mode of riding, laws and usages, live and govern themselves according to the manners, fashion, and language of the Irish enemies; and also have made divers marriages and alliances between themselves and the Irish enemies aforesaid." The solution was basically apartheid, and the two groups were even banned from attending church together and the authorities were particularly wary of Irish minstrels and storytellers spreading their propaganda among the settlers. The Statutes have often been wrongly interpreted as an attempt to "persuade or force the Irish to shed their racial distinctiveness" as Marcus de Búrca puts it. They were nothing of the sort. They were about stopping the settlers from embracing Irish culture for fear that they were becoming more supportive of their adopted homeland than they were of England[14]. And as it turned out, the actual enforcement of such regulations proved nigh on impossible.

One custom that gets a specific mention in the Statutes is hurling, in the first known genuinely solid and irrefutable contemporary reference to such a sport. It was announced that "whereas a land which is at war requires that every person do render himself able to defend himself, it is ordained and established that the commons of the said land of Ireland, who are in the different marches at war, do not, henceforth, use the plays which men call horlings, with great sticks and a ball upon the ground[15], from which great evils and maims have arisen, to the weakening, of the defence of the said land ... but that they do apply and accustom themselves to use and draw bows, and throw lances, and other gentlemanlike games." This is the first known use of any word resembling 'hurling[16]' to describe the game, and it is best not to dwell too long on the "upon the ground" bit for fear of upsetting the hurling traditionalists.

Later that century, in 1397, Archbishop Colton of Derry threatened excommunication for playing "the unlawful game of *galbarey* on Easter Monday and Tuesday because it leads to mortal sins, beatings and homicides[17]," which is assumed to be another reference to hurling.

The earliest physical souvenir we have of the game in Ireland is to be found on a grave slab dating back to the 15th century. It is at Inishowen, County Donegal and is dedicated to the memory of a Scottish gallowglass warrior with the tongue-twisting name of Manas Mac Mhoiresdean of Iona. It features the images of a claymore (the Scottish sword), and what are purportedly a *camán* and a *sliotar*, although at least from a modern point of view, the stick would look more at home in the hands of a hockey or even golf player.

Racial integration wasn't the plan behind the *Galway Statutes* of 1527. Anyone whose name began with O' or Mac was forbidden to be inside the walls of Galway after sunset. The

---

[14] It is also important to note that the Statutes were originally published in French, which was the language most of the settlers had brought with them. The Normans wanted to forcibly anglicise their people, rather than have them swayed by the more rebellious Irish way of thinking.

[15] The French original wrote of "*les jues que home appelle horlinges oue graunds bastons a pillor sur la terre.*"

[16] The word probably came from the Middle English *hurlen*, which was in turn probably inherited from the Lower German *hurreln* meaning to throw or to dash. In the Irish language, most names for the game are variants of either *camanachd* or *iomáint*, which you will still hear used in Gaelic today.

[17] *Acts of Archbishop Colton in his metropolitan visitation of the Diocese of Derry* (1397).

English were anything but impressed with this Irish stick game. It was "ordered, enacted and statuted" that an eight pence fine would be issued to any man "of what degree or condition so he be of" that, rather than practicing archery, was playing at quoits or stones, and dictated that men were "at no time to use ne occupy ye hurling of ye litill balle with the hookie sticks or staves, nor use no hand balle to play without the walls, but only the great foot balle."

It's a quote that has had many scholars scratching their heads. One would imagine that the 'hookie sticks' were hurleys, but if the prime motive behind the Statute was to get people practising their skills with the bow, then why this curious dispensation for football, which was surely no more useful than hurling for learning to direct arrows at your enemies?

The implication seems to be that "the great foot balle" was considered suitable because it was an 'English' game, which would be one of the first times in history that we know of a ball game being equated with nationality. AB Gleason comments that "the political and legal motivations ... are conventional for a coloniser, namely to prohibit behaviour that tends to unify or foster solidarity among the colonised." Indeed, Lord Chancellor William Gerrarde complained in 1587 that English settlers on the Munster Plantation were playing hurling and, perish the thought, some had even been heard communicating in the Irish language.

However, there were other reasons than nationalism for the dislike of the Irish tradition of playing with sticks. It was viewed more as a form of ritualised combat than a ball game. The Irish fighting-stick called the *shillelagh* was used in faction-fighting among Irish peasants, and the authorities would not have felt there was much of a divide between that and hurling.

However, the Kilkenny and Galway statutes may have been given too predominant a position in this story. They were highly localised decrees, we have no idea how effective they really were[18], and there is no evidence of any similar decrees being issued elsewhere. If hurling really was as violent as so many descriptions suggest, and considering the amount of banning of dangerous ball sports going on in Britain, then the English were surprisingly tolerant of it. It did take a knock when the 1695 *Sunday Observance Act* was decreed, but the problem there was respect for the Lord's Day, when not just hurling but most sports were banned, and the English imposed similar laws on themselves.

Golden years

There seems to have been a massive resurgence of hurling as it entered the 18th century and what is dubbed its 'golden age'. This probably came about mainly because the Anglo-Irish landowning gentry sought to get involved in promoting the game, but also, as is typical of all sports, an upsurge in printed matter meant a lot more about civilian society was recorded than ever before.

---

[18] But there was an incident at Phoenix Park in 1779, reported in the *Dublin Evening Post*, whereby Sherriff Worthington tried to put a stop to a game of hurling by referring to the 1527 *Statute of Galway*, which he reckoned had never been repealed. The report is somewhat sarcastic, and suggests Worthington was testing his luck.

As if to herald in that era, 1698 was when John Dunton provides an invaluable record of his travels around the island and at one point describes the sport of hurling played with a ball made out of cow's hair "which they strike with a stick called a *commaan* about three and a half foot long at the handle. At the lower end it is crooked and about three inches broad, and on this broad part you may sometimes see one of the gamesters carry the ball tossing it for 40 or 50 yards in spite of all the adverse players, and when he is like to lose it, he generally gives it a great stroke towards the goal. Sometimes if he miss his blow at the ball, he knocks one of his opponents down, at which no resentment is shown. They seldom come off without broken heads or shins. At this sport … they pick out ten, twelve or twenty players a side, and the prize is generally a barrel or two of ale, which is brought into the field and drunk by the victors on the spot, though the vanquished are not without a share of it too[19]."

Dunton also explains that parishes and baronies often played each other at games sometimes attended by as many as two thousand people, so we can assume hurling had become considerably formalised. It must have featured some kind of rules and 18th century games even got some press coverage. As early as 1708 there was an announcement in *The Flying Post* that St Swithin's Day would be celebrated with a 30-a-side hurling match between men from either side of the Liffey, with ale, pipes and tobacco provided to the players. But had they existed at the time, the staunchly amateur GAA would have taken a dim view of the idea that they would be competing for thirty shillings.

There are claims that tournaments and small leagues were formed, which may be jumping the gun a little, but there was certainly an inter-provincial game in 1748 at Crumlin Common in Dublin, where home side Leinster defeated Munster. *Faulkner's Dublin Journal*'s poetical match report went:

> "Munster powers, in vain, 'gainst East unites,
> The south is doomed to tread the Northern Flight,
> Gallea to Britain quits the glorious field,
> To Leinster, Munster ever forced to yield."

In 1759, *Pue's Occurrences* reported on a game between two teams from Clare and Galway, in which they marched to the game "preceded by a band of musick, a French horn, a running footman and a fellow in an antic or harlequin dress. None of the hurlers were in the least hurt, the greatest harmony having subsisted. The County Clare hurlers were elegantly entertained at Crushenahaire the following night."

In that game, "a hundred guineas was proposed to be hurled for" and there was yet more playing for money when Munster met Leinster ten years later. In 1769, the *Cork Evening Post* told of "a bet of 300 guineas, and a ball at night for the ladies, to be hurled for by 21 married men and 21 bachelors, on the Green of Ardfinnan in the county of Tipperary. None admitted to play but gentlemen of the baronies of Iffa and Offa." A year earlier, in 1768,

---

[19] John Dunton *Teague Land: or A Merry Ramble to the Wild Irish* (1698). Dunton also founded England's first populist newspaper, *The Athenian Mercury.*

Finn's Leinster Journal had written of the "grandest match that was ever hurled in Ireland" between the same two sides.

High society's appreciation of hurling was described by the *Hibernian Journal* in 1792. "A hurling match took place in the Phoenix Park, which was honored with the presence of Her Excellency, the Countess of Westmoreland, and several of the nobility and gentry, besides a vast concourse of spectators." Sadly, so large was said 'concourse' that the match was abandoned due to a pitch invasion. "Colonel Lennox, Mr Daly, and several other gentlemen, most obligingly used their endeavours to prevent any interruption to the players, but to no effect. This active contest ended without either side claiming triumph."

Hurling was to the Irish what cricket was to the English, and there doesn't seem to have been any team sport anywhere in the world that rivalled those two in the 18th century for popular interest and established structure. Arthur Young, who wrote of his travels to the country in the late 1770s, actually called hurling "a sort of cricket, but instead of throwing the ball in order to knock a wicket, the aim is to pass it through a bent stick, with ends stuck in the ground[20]," which suggests very different goalposts to the goals seen today in what he dubs "the cricket of savages." He may have had a point, for although the press reports are frequently full of praise for the athleticism of the players, as indeed was Young, who felt that "ought to evidence the food they live on to be far from deficient in nourishment," there was plenty of violence involved.

In 1755, two men were held on trial for the death of an opposing player in Laois, in Tipperary in 1786 one player accidentally killed his own brother, and a fight at a game in Kilkenny in 1768 led to Anthony Langford fracturing his skull, and the report in *Finn's Leinster Journal* didn't hold out much hope for the poor man's recovery.

As we shall see later, football in Britain was often viewed with suspicious eyes as a way of bringing the mob together for more political ends, and the situation with hurling was no different, and started sowing the seeds for hurling's image as being rebellious against British rule. As early as 1666, Roger Boyle, Earl of Orrery, wrote a letter expressing his concerns about Catholics getting together at Clanwilliam "under pretence of a match at hurling[21]" and in 1726 Owen Sweeney was suspicious that "a great assembly … was contrived on purpose to bring persons together in order to be enlisted[22]."

Freeman's Journal in 1766 believed that "hurling matches were the first beginnings of the deluded White Boys, who are now rising again in a neighbouring county … their wicked

---

[20] Arthur Young *A tour in Ireland: With general observations on the present state of that kingdom made in the years 1776, 1777, and 1778* (1780). Young obviously knew what he was talking about because he also said the Irish "talk without tiring until doomsday" and "are infinitely more cheerful and lively than anything we commonly see in England."

[21] Letters written by Lord Orrery cited in John Lynch *Cambrensis everus: the history of ancient Ireland vindicated* (1848-52).

[22] Which would have been to fight with the French or Spanish in support of James Stuart, the son of the deposed James II of England (James VII of Scotland) and pretender to the English throne.

combustans have already been the occasion of much blood spilt, of so many women bereft of their husbands and sons and so many helpless orphans."

The early 19th century conjured up the popular image of 'tithe hurlers', who allegedly gathered to play hurling, but instead used their sticks as tools to help them in their protest against the payment of tithes to the church. *Freeman's Journal* in 1825 reported that "a large mob who had gathered under the pretence of hurling" in Broadford, County Clare, ended up facing off not against each other but against the mounted police, who eventually fled under a hail of stones. In 1831, the *Clare Journal* reported on a soldier "injured by a hurling mob" on their way home after a game, and novelist John Banim once described how "at the village hurling match, the *hurlet*, or crooked stick with which they strike the ball, often changed its playful utility[23]."

When the GAA tried to promote a more controlled form of hurling after 1884, there was fear among many Irish that all the new association was really doing was encouraging the revival of infamous *scoobeen* matches that all too frequently degenerated into mass stick-fights. However, these reports are the exception rather than the norm, and most 'rebellious' associations to the game are more likely the result of later romanticism than actual fact. In the vast majority of cases, hurling was no more than a game, and political motivations were few.

The hurly burly's done?

The Golden Age would be short-lived. Ireland faced new problems, and matters other than ball games were on people's minds. There was increasing discontent with the landlords, who were more intent on producing food for export than feeding the local minions, and the gentry's association with the game also waned.

In 1800, the Act of Union was passed, and the entire British Isles became one single state, the United Kingdom of Great Britain and Ireland. Over the next century, rebellions against the British were largely unsuccessful, use of the Irish language declined at an extraordinary rate, and then came the potato famine of 1845-1849, which ripped an already troubled country to shreds. The suffering was unimaginable, and the British mishandling of a crisis in its own back yard has been described by many as genocide of holocaustic proportions. Others will point a finger at Irish over-dependence on potato crops and strict adherence to Catholic virtues leading to an uncontrollable population explosion, but the offshoot was around a million deaths while more than twice that figure fled, mainly to America, and over the second half of the 19th century, the Irish population was reduced by almost half.

The traditional game of hurling unquestionably faded while all this was going on, and the popular view that has emerged from this is that it was all the fault of the British. Their damned imperialism had throttled Ireland in every way, and devastated its culture. However, Eoin Kinsella concedes that "at no stage in Irish history does hurling appear to have been

---

[23] John Banim *The Peep O'day* (Original published by Duffy, 1865).

subjected to outright suppression[24]." The real reason for hurling's demise was the same as that of its hockey-like cousins on the other side of the water, be that water the Irish Sea or the Atlantic. People had invented decent footballs. The cumbersome blob of an inflated bladder was gradually replaced by regular shaped balls made of vulcanised rubber with leather-sewn cases. Footballs were now top of every teenagers Christmas present list, and hitting balls with sticks was *so* 18th century.

But hurling was still there, described, for instance, in a poem by Thomas Crocker in 1820 called *The Carrigaline Hurlers*, and which went:

> "Without exaggeration, our goalers take their station,
> For the highest approbation they have won their victory,
> 'Twas in no combination, or field association,
> But in rural relaxation on the plains of Ownabwee."

Hurling even made it to London. In 1801, Joseph Strutt claimed that "about the year 1775, the hurling to the goales was frequently played by parties of Irishmen, in the fields at the back of the British Museum … I have been greatly amused to see with what facility those who were skilful in the pastime would catch up the ball upon the bat, and often run with it for a considerable time, tossing it occasionally from the bat and recovering it again, till such time as they found a proper opportunity of driving it back amongst their companions, who generally followed and were ready to receive it."

Another fine reference to "the game of the peasantry of Ireland" was that penned in 1841 by Anna Maria Carter Hall, who told how "the great game in Kerry and throughout the south is hurley. It is a fine manly exercise with sufficient danger to produce excitement … the players, sometimes to the number of fifty or sixty, being chosen for each side, they are arranged (usually barefoot) in two opposing ranks, with their hurleys crossed, to await the tossing up of the ball, the wickets or goals being previously fixed at the extremities of the hurling-green … Then there are two men picked to keep the goal on each side, over whom the opposing party places equally tried men as a counterpoise … A person is chosen to throw up the ball, which is done as straight as possible, when the whole party, withdrawing their hurleys, stand with them elevated, to receive it and strike it on its descent; now comes the crash of mimic war … the men grapple, wrestle and toss each other with amazing agility, neither victor nor vanquished waiting to take breath, but following the course of the rolling and flying prize; the best runners watch each other, and keep almost shoulder to shoulder through the play, and the best wrestlers keep as close on them as possible, to arrest or impede their progress; and the tact and skill shown in taking it on the point of the hurley, and running

---

[24] *Football and Hurling in Early Modern Ireland* in Cronin, Mike et al *The Gaelic Athletic Association* 1884-2009 (Irish Academic Press, 2009)

with it half the length of the field, and when too closely pressed, striking it towards the goal, is a matter of astonishment to those who are but slightly acquainted with the play[25]."

Not everybody shared such fascination with the game. Reverend Michael Huleatt attempted to put a stop to a hurling encounter between natives of Kilbarron and Clonrush in September 1825. By the end of it the two teams had combined forces against Huleatt and his police force, who "were battered and wounded in every direction[26]." In 1808, Hely Dutton slammed it as "very injurious to the morals and industry of the younger classes[27]," but his main concern wasn't so much the matches as the debauchery that followed. "They too often adjourn to the whiskey-house, both men and women, and spend the night in dancing, singing, and drinking until perhaps morning, and too often quarrels and broken heads are the effects of this inebriety."

Double standards

It was in the mid 19th century that so many sports were standardised, so it was only natural for the Irish to do likewise with their hurling. The Ballinasloe club in Killimor published the first known set of rules in 1869, and a year later, the Dublin University Hurley Club printed rules of its own[28]. The surviving set from 1877 shows that the ball could only be struck with one side of the stick, had to be played on the ground, there was an offside rule and there was to be no kicking of the ball or 'crooking' of an opponent's stick. Hurley was identical in almost everything but name to English hockey[29].

Stickball games had been played for years not just in Ireland, but in England, Scotland and Wales too. They all had different sticks and balls, methods of striking and varying levels of violence, but they were all gradually being standardised as hockey for the sake of being able to enjoy playing against people from other places. It was this standardised version that the University took to other schools and clubs in the city, to the extent that the Irish Hurley

---

[25] In a series of articles titled *Ireland, Its Scenery, Character etc* (How & Parsons, 1841). Interestingly, the same book describes something different, the "game of shinny, as it is called by some, and *common* by others ... *Common* is derived from a Celtic word 'com', which signified 'crooked', as it is played with a stick bent at its lower extremity somewhat like a reaping hook. The ball, which is struck to and fro ... I called *nag*, or in Irish, *brig*. It resembles the game called *gold* in Edinburgh." At least judging by this, the *camán* may not have had anything to do with modern hurling at all, but was associated to an early form of golf, and which takes us back to the theory that Cuchulainn wasn't a hurler at all.

[26] Patrick Madden His*tory of Gaelic Games in Whitegate and Mountshannon from 1825 to 1984* (Whitegate Hurling Club, 1984).

[27] Hely Dutton *Statistical Survey of Co Clare* (1808).

[28] The club had been playing some form of hurley since the 1860s, but in 1870 their rules were published in *John Lawrence's Handbook of Cricket in Ireland*.

[29] One of the members of the Trinity Hurley Club was Edward Carson, later to become a prominent Unionist, so he was an unlikely choice for a GAA trophy to be named in his honour at Stormont in 2010, and endorsed by Gerry Adams, president of Sinn Fein. As Carson was a former hurler, Adams was happy to call him a 'Gael', and was left with egg on his face when historians pointed out the error.

Union was formed in 1882, which later became the Irish Hockey Union, and established links with hockey clubs in Britain.

Not everybody was so enthusiastic about deserting traditional hurling for the sake of globalisation. One of its defenders wrote in the *Irish Sportsman* in 1883 that the new game changed "the swiping game of the savage to a scientific recreation which may be indulged in by anyone without being in constant dread of having one's brains dashed out by an adversary's hurl." This new version seemed far too tame, and besides, it reeked of British cultural imperialism.

One of the chief opponents was Michael Cusack. There were few people more miffed than this man from County Clare about the replacement of a traditional Irish pastime, the "manliest game ever played by any branch of humankind," with new, imported standards from England. He was entranced by the mythological connotations of the old game that he himself had played as a child, in which "the size of the hurling field did not bother us. I played hurling in a room and I played it with the goalposts a mile apart. We made little of stone walls and roads and other obstacles. We played with sticks without bosses and we played with hurleys. We played when there were only two of us and we played when there were more than sixty of us locked in deadly combat."

He was one of those present at the College of Surgeons in December 1882 that met "for the purpose of taking steps to re-establish the national game of hurling." They resolved to form the Dublin Hurling Club, and devised rules more in accordance with Irish tradition. The club managed to play a few games among themselves, but the real idea was to forge good relations with the 'hurley' clubs in the city, though being careful not to be "antagonistic to any outdoor sports and athletics already in existence." Nevertheless, all they achieved was tension. The hurley clubs were quite happy playing the game their own way, and didn't quite understand why these zany and often violent rules were supposed to make them feel any more or less Irish than they did already.

The Dublin Hurling Club folded within weeks, but Cusack's emotions had been stirred. Starting with just four men playing in Phoenix Park, plus any passers-by he could persuade to "fall in and slash away" and using his column in *The Shamrock* to encourage readers to come along and join them, by December 1883 he had gathered enough bodies to found the Metropolitan Hurling Club, and also formed a team out of his own Civil Service Academy. Cusack was on a roll, and wrote of one of the first games that "the hurling became so fast and furious … that spectators expected to be called on after each charge to help the disabled to St Steven's Hospital."

A March 1884 report in the *Irish Sportsman* praised Michael Cusack, "to whom we are indebted for the revival of hurling in Ireland" and described the basics of a game in which "play begins with a lady on horseback, galloping across the field and tossing the ball in the centre amongst the players – a custom which seems to have been followed in all matches of which we have any authentic record." It would be interesting to know what authentic records he was referring to but, perhaps unfortunately, the horsey prelude didn't survive long.

The game Cusack himself had played in his youth was played cross-country by any number of players, using improvised goals, and plenty of violence. Although his modern version was created in defiance to English hockey, it was impossible for that to be done without borrowing heavily from it, with a regulated pitch and goals and defined regulations to control violent play.

On a fact-finding mission, Cusack took his Metropolitan team to Ballinasloe in Killimor, the place where the first known hurling rules had been drafted in 1869, where a strong Galway tradition for regulated hurling had emerged since, and even had umpires with the "power to order any hurler to cease playing, who in their opinion is under the influence of strong drink, who loses his temper or strikes any of his opponents intentionally."

The Galway papers promoted the arrival of "Dublin's champion club," and large crowds gathered in the hope of seeing the boys from the smoke put in their places. Rules were agreed, but without much success. Keeping the huge crowds off the field proved a problem, and the game was barely under way before Cusack, who wrote in the *Irish Times* that Killimor "slashed in a reckless and savage manner," put a stop to it and insisted that his Metropolitan players gave a demonstration of the way the game was supposed to be played. Ballinasloe then did the same, but although the *Western News* felt that "to the keenest judge no material difference could be detected in the style of either team", Cusack refused to restart the match, which was reason enough to spark off victory celebrations among the home supporters.

Despite the fiasco, Cusack was so pleased with what he had seen that he immediately wrote to the *Western News* with a plea for Galway's support in the revival of "a relic of a time that was the golden age of Ireland." Hockey was chewing away at hurling in the 1880s, but had yet to swallow. Now the seeds had been sown for Cusack to go on and found the GAA later that year. And from there, albeit in a modernised form along the lines of the newly codified English sports (Art o Maolfabhail even concedes that "many of the counties which have made progress in hurling under the Association have done so at the expense of their traditional *camanachd*[30]"), hurling held onto its separate identity, and went on to form part of both modern Irish society and also its folklore[31].

Highland games

Hurling is heralded as something uniquely Irish. However, similar stickball games were played all across western Europe, and there is one with which the GAA is quite willing to acknowledge its shared heritage. After all, it was, and still is, played by their fellow Celts, which makes it a whole lot more palpable. It's the Scottish game of shinty, or *camanachd* as

---

[30] Art o Maolfabhail *Camán: Two Thousand Years of Hurling in Ireland* (Dundalgan Press, 1973).
[31] Volume Two looks at Michael Cusack, the GAA and Irish sports in greater detail.

it is called in Scots Gaelic. The finer points of the rules differ considerably, but that is more the result of both sports being codified and modernised in different ways at the end of the 19th century than anything else.

Shinty is now played on a similar sized pitch as hurling, and is also a hockey-like game between two teams in which the ball can be played either on the ground or in the air. The most obvious difference is the goal. In shinty there are no rugby-like uprights as in hurling. The only way of scoring is by getting the ball into the goal, called a 'hail', which is best described as a square-shaped soccer goal. Although, like in Ireland, shinty players call their sticks a *camán*, and ash is also the most commonly used wood, they are not the same. Lacking the flattened end, shinty sticks are more similar to those used in the different codes of hockey. Another important difference is that the shinty goalkeeper is the only player who can touch the ball with any part of the body[32].

Apart from the technical differences, the games are miles apart in terms of social significance. Hurling is a mass media event, with something in the region of 200,000 players and large crowds at games. Shinty, however, isn't much more than a minority pursuit in Scotland. Despite being of relatively similar geographic and demographic proportions to Ireland, the country has just 2000 or so regular players. That's just one shinty player for every hundred hurlers.

Even the biggest shinty games attract crowds that would be a disappointment to your average Highland League soccer club. Television and newspaper coverage is as good as inexistent, with BBC Scotland only screening five or so matches a year, and that is more as a 'public service' than due to any massive demand. While hurlers are celebrities in their home towns, you would be lucky to find a Scotsman who could name just one important shinty player.

The sports are similar enough for cross-code games to be played, as first happened between Irish and Scots in London in 1896. A year later, Glasgow Cowal and Dublin Celtic played a challenge match at Celtic Park, won by the Scots, and attracting a fair amount of local interest at the time. A rematch was then played in front of next to nobody on a freezing afternoon in Dublin, and refereed by none other than Michael Cusack. The Scots struggled with the larger pitch yet narrowly scraped a two-goal win. There was the occasional contact over the next seventy or so years, but it was rare. The blame is put on the British unease with the Camanachd Association cooperating with the GAA, but lack of interest is likely to have been as much of a cause, as well as increasingly more different sets of rules.

The real inspiration to resume hurling-shinty matches was the international football series between Ireland and Australia, which the stick sports imitated by creating a composite game called *rialacha chomhréiteach sinteag-iomáint*, which includes hurling's 'rugby' posts, but

---

[32] Other technicalities include the fact that a shinty game, like soccer, is played over two 45 minutes halves (hurling is just 35 minutes each way), and shinty is played 12-a-side as opposed to the 15-a-side hurling.

disallows any use of the hands other than by the goalkeeper, and the feet can only be used to trap the ball, not to kick it.

A lot had happened in the interim, especially to hurling, but the Scots showed they still had what it takes. They won all four of the first matches played between 1993 and 1996, although this was followed by a period of Irish dominance. However, after a long drought, Scotland beat Ireland and shinty beat hurling at Inverness in 2005, and then claimed a historic victory on Irish soil a year later in a game that was played in front of the assembling 80,000 strong crowd to watch the Ireland v Australia international rules match afterwards.

Despite winning, the Scots were upset to see that they got none of the ceremonial treatment or national anthems that the footy enjoyed afterwards. But following the way the football match descended into little more than semi-organised thuggery, leading to calls to ban the series for good, one Irish paper even suggested that the far more dignified shinty/hurling match deserves to get top billing on future occasions. It won't, and although the Scots have continued to enjoy regular success over the Irish, this is mainly because the latter only field players from the second tier counties.

So, that's shinty today. But our main interest is in working out where the noble sport's origins lie, which means switching the fog-lights back on to see through the usual poppycock distorted by the mists of time.

Because there was generally more movement of people from Ireland to Scotland than vice versa during the Middle Ages, and because the known Irish references to hurling seem so much older than the Scottish ones to shinty, it is generally assumed that the game was introduced to the Scottish glens by the Irish. The ancient legends cited in the *Ulster Cycle* will have it that Cuchulainn himself "came to Scotland to complete his education as a fosterling with the Warrior Queen Sgathach to learn to battle and love. As a gift in return, he gave the game of shinty to Scotland." Mythology, as we know, is not the most precise of sciences, but that would put the arrival of shinty in Scotland at about 2000 years ago.

The 1881 *Book of the Club of True Highlanders*, published by the Highland Society, basically a bunch of homesick Scottish exiles living in London, is an incredible two-volume attempt to explain every imaginable aspect of Celtic and Highland culture. The authors were a little lenient when it came to verifying their sources, but they shared that faith in shinty's Irish origins when saying "the game is also called *cluich bhall*, shinnie, shinty, bandy, hurling, hockey, and at one time was a universal and favourite game of the whole of Keltland … The origin of this game is lost in the midst of ages ... indeed, it is said, and, no doubt, with great truth, that the game of *camanachd*, or club playing, was introduced into the Green Isle by the immediate descendants of Noah. On such authority we may rationally conclude that it was played by Noah himself; and if by Noah, in all probability by Adam and his sons."

Now, despite the noble text's claim that this is 'no doubt, with great truth', it might be time to get the fingertips reaching for the saltcellar here, considering we can't even be sure that there really was a Noah who built an ark and rounded up all the animals so their offspring could incestuously go forth and multiply. But to claim that he was also a shinty player, as had been none other than Adam before him, and that their descendants taught the game to the Irish, well, it's very tempting to at least dispute the 'in all probability' bit[33].

Hail, hail

The earliest known reference to the game is no older than 1589, as ever in an attempt to discourage rather than encourage the practice, when the *Kirk Session Records* of Glasgow state that "with respectt to the kirk-yeards[34], that ther be no playing at golf, carrict, shinnie[35]." However, although the game was quite possibly played "clan against clan, parish against parish and brae against strath" as the Camanachd Association's website puts it, it is not really until the early 19th century that we find much conclusive evidence of that.

It is feasible that shinty struggled against the background of the infamous Highland Clearances of the late 18th and early 19th centuries, one of the darkest periods of Scottish history, when landowners requiring more land for large-scale sheep farming not too politely asked the peasants living in Highland glens to vacate their homelands to make way for the operations[36]. But it was in the Highlands that shinty prevailed the strongest, where Alexander Campbell explained in 1804 that it was "a game performed with a wooden ball, and sticks or clubs crooked at one of the extremities, for the purpose of hitting the ball with more address and certainty[37]" and claimed it to be by far the most arduous and active of the different pastimes played by his people.

Shinnie was one of many names for Scottish stickball games. Others included *shinnack*, *shinnup*, *knotty*, the Gaelic *iomain* and the later *camanachd*, which is still used today in the

---

[33] The *Book of the Club of True Highlanders* is not the most reliable of sources at all, and eminent shinty historian Dr Hugh D MacLennan is scathing of what he describes as "the creation of a (largely, but not entirely bogus) set of criteria which would distinguish participants in its activities as being of a unique and superior race." Elsewhere he describes the text as "pseudo-scholarly balder-dash … based on research which the members claimed was, like the origin of shinty, lost in the midst of ages … their activities appear to have been no more than a vehicle for their own self-aggrandisement."

[34] Churchyards are called kirkyards to this day in many parts of Scotland.

[35] Nobody can be sure of the origin, but the most believable claim is that 'shinty' comes from the Gaelic *sinteag*, meaning jump. The idea that the name is a bastardisation of the expression "shin t' ye" (shin to you) that was commonly yelled during matches is over-imaginative rubbish. To this day 'shinny' survives as the name used in North America for informal pick-up ice hockey matches, while the *carrick* played in Fifeshire was probably something between shinty and cricket.

[36] These evictions were in many cases violent, and the former occupants of destroyed houses were forced to live in poverty elsewhere. The general idea was that the descendants of the former warrior clans of the north could do just as well on the barren lands nearer the coast, where they could make a decent living off fishing and seaweed harvesting. They didn't get much of a choice in this enforced change of career, and one that turned out to be anything but a move in the right direction. The rent was exorbitant, they practically lived as slaves, and besides, there simply weren't enough resources or markets. Similar processes occurred all over the UK, but the abruptness, brutality and scale of the Highland Clearances made them particularly notorious, and matters were not helped by an 1846 potato famine similar to that in Ireland.

[37] In a footnote to his epic poem *The Grampian's Desolate* (1804).

name of the sport's governing body, the Camanachd Association, and such terms as *hail-ba'*, *hand an' hail* or simply *hailes*. We can't be sure how similar or different these games were, and an 1804 poem by William Tarras doesn't do much to help. "The hails are set an' on they scud" he writes. "The hails is wun; they warsle hame, the best they can for fobbin." It's so much more charming not to have a clue what Tarras was going on about!

Hails was played with a bat called a *clacken*, which was sometimes used as the name of the game itself and looked roughly like a large, flat wooden spoon. *Blackwood's Magazine* referred to this in 1821 when stating that "the games among the children of Edinburgh have their periodic returns. At one time nothing is to be seen in the hands of boys but *cleckenbrods*."

By 1911, the happy sports ground in the sky had found a home for "the distinctively school game of clacken, now alas extinct! Less than thirty years ago no High School boy considered his equipment complete unless the wooden clacken hung to his wrist as he went and came[38]." The Edinburgh Academy did maintain *hails* as a junior activity into the 20th century, and it surged back into popularity following a game played between the 7th year and the Ephors as part of the school's 1924 centenary celebrations, and after that became a traditional end of year event that has survived to this day.

No proper rules were ever written, but that is all part of the fun, and for years the tradition was for the newest member of staff to referee the game. The fact that he hadn't the foggiest idea what the game involved was all part of the hilarity of the occasion. It's all taken in very light-hearted fashion, with the tomfoolery now including fancy dress and water pistols, and goals are never scored because nobody can remember what you have to do to score one!

Silliness prevails, and as a gem of a remark on the Academy's website tells us, "the point about traditions is that no-one can really remember how they started or what they are supposed to achieve." The site also bemoans the present day state of the game because "somehow along the way political correctness, health and safety or some other such nonsense took a hand and it became irresponsible for the limited number of Ephors to play all sixty or so leavers simultaneously. This clearly defeated the whole point of the exercise, which was a glorious opportunity to get your own back for all the real and imagined slights that you had suffered at their officious hands during the year … Will we never again witness heroic events such as the immortal MacSpraggon's (1898-1904) celebrated five points followed by public flogging awarded by the referee for hitting the rector as he observed from the balcony of the staff lodge? Well readers, you must decide. Let's be reasonable now. What's one child more or less? It is a tradition after all."

Hails at the Edinburgh Academy may be one of the wackiest traditional ball games around, and of very questionable historical accuracy, but there is something important sports historians can learn from it. Poring through the notes that have survived from ancient games, and trying to work out what influenced what and where the origins of certain rules and

---

[38] James J Trotter *The Royal High School, Edinburgh* (Sir Isaac Pitman & Sons, 1911).

traditions lie, we tend to forget the essence of what we are talking about. We are talking about a game, about something that is done entirely for fun. Early football was never a matter for academic debate, it was never a science. The point of *hails* lies precisely in its sheer pointlessness.

Shinty towns

In 1835, the Society for the Diffusion of Useful Knowledge, and what a top society that must have been, described shinty in *The Penny Magazine* as "played with a small hard ball, which is generally made of wood, and each player is furnished with a curved stick somewhat resembling that which is used by golf players. Large parties assemble during Christmas holidays, one parish sometimes making a match against another. In the struggles between the contending players many hard blows are given, and more frequently a shin is broken, or by rarer chance some more serious accident may occur." A broken shin didn't qualify as a 'serious accident' – those were tougher times indeed.

There was seemingly no limit on the number of players per side. People apparently joined in and dropped out when they felt like it, which meant matches could easily end up being day-long affairs. Local lords and gentry were often happy to lend their patronage, and that was despite the gambling that often formed part of the day's proceedings. A common reward for the winning team was the right to raid the opposition's crops, and this tradition was actually continued into the early 20th century, with legalised scrumping for the Halloween shinty champions.

It being Scotland, drinking was naturally part and parcel of the entertainment. An 1870 article in the *Oban Times* of Argyllshire describes games between districts which could involve up to 2000 players, with the prize being a hog's head of whisky. Now, the whisky sounds fine, but drinking it out of a porker's conk? In 1892, Sir Aeneas Mackintosh explained how the winning team "is rewarded by a share of a cask of whiskey, on which both parties get drunk. This game is often played upon the ice, by one parish against another, when they come to blows if intoxicated, the players' legs being frequently broke[39]."

Like most sports, shinty fell afoul of the administration on several occasions. In 1842, the Edinburgh police saw fit to do something about the "many complaints having been made of boys playing at shinty or football upon the public roads" and forty shillings was the fine in Oban in 1843 for "every person who shall fly any kite, or play at shinty, foot-ball, or other game, to the annoyance of passengers." Those pesky kite flyers. Although bitter Scots have claimed this was part of a bid to Anglicise Highland heritage, the fact that both these examples also mentioned football suggests any bans were fuelled by the desire to stamp out the unruly disturbances rather than any nationalistic motive.

---

[39] Aeneas Mackintosh *Notes descriptive and Historical, Principally relating to the Parish of Moy in Strathdearn* (1892).

Rather like the decline of hurling in Ireland, the main reason for shinty waning in Scotland was the arrival of codified soccer and rugby. But while a movement arose in Ireland to discourage 'foreign' games and promote the indigenous sport instead, there was no such negative reaction in Scotland. In fact, the Scots willingly embraced both codes and made several important contributions to their development.

The Edinburgh Academical Football Club was formed in 1857, and played their first game against Merchiston Castle School. When rugby and soccer split, the Academicals opted for rugby and are still playing it today, making them the oldest football club in Scotland. It was on their ground that Scotland won the first ever rugby international in 1871. The London FA was formed in 1863 to oversee soccer, and Scotland followed suit in 1873, a year after the first international match between Scotland and England was played in Glasgow.

With rugby booming out of Edinburgh and soccer doing likewise in Glasgow, by the 1870s, the only place shinty was still widely played was the remote Highlands, and any games played in the main cities from the 1870s onwards were probably organised by Highlanders that had moved south in search of work.

Some even took the game south of the border. The first shinty club in England is believed to have been the Cottonopolis Camanachd Club of Manchester, formed in 1875. Two years later they played the first of many games against their local rivals, the Manchester and Salford Caledonian Club. Of the 60 players on the field, only three did not speak Gaelic, a language that was only still in common usage in the Highlands.

The Manchester shinty boom failed to last much longer than a decade. These two sides last played each other, as far as we know, in 1881, by which time the Highlanders' original enthusiasm had presumably drifted towards other sports.

Shinty was still a rustic affair. The Aberdeen University Shinty Club published the first known written rules in 1861, the Glasgow Celtic Society came up with theirs in 1877 and instigated a cup competition two years later, and Captain Chisholm drew up *The Constitution, Rules and Regulations of the Strathglass Shinty Club* in 1880, but none of these managed to gain universal recognition. In fact, an anonymous 1893 article in the *Inverness Courier* commented that "it is, indeed, perhaps on the alien Scot more than on the native land that the survival of the game may depend in the future." Indeed, shinty can particularly thank the somewhat barmy crowd at the Highland Society in London, who despite their bogus histories worked wonders for the game. From 1873 right up until the First World War, it was regularly played at such locations as Wimbledon Common and Stamford Bridge, purportedly on the same site that is now home to soccer's Chelsea FC. Exposed to the structured way London's sports clubs went about doing their business, the expatriate Scots sensed the benefits of getting their brethren back home to do something similar with shinty, and the Camanachd Association was formed in 1893. The game finally had a governing body that was able to standardise rules nationally, which included playing 16 a side on a pitch that was 200 yards long and 150 broad[40].

But it was too late. Rugby had already taken centre stage on school Physical Education curricula, and stadiums around the country were packed to the rafters to watch soccer. The Celtic v Rangers Old Firm encounter was already steeping itself in legend. Poor old shinty just didn't stand a chance.

Further expansion was hardly encouraged by such rules as that of London Camanachd[41], formed in 1894, whose members were only to be Highlanders or those of Highland parentage, but Dr Hugh Dan MacLennan, whose noble efforts to seek out the past of his beloved sport seem to know no limits, has also tracked evidence of shinty making it even further around the world. Emigrant Scots took the game to North America, where it possibly played a role in the origins of ice hockey[42] and also went down under to Australia, where MacLennan has located potted evidence of late 19th century shinty matches adding to the melting pot of different ball games being introduced to the country.

We'll leave it to the venerable MacLennan to have the final word on a sport that has become synonymous with his life. "Shinty is also one of Scotland's truly national – indeed *international* – assets, which has an important, and hitherto largely undervalued pedigree and provenance world-wide. For too long now historians, and particularly sports historians, have at best under-valued, at worst ignored, shinty's rightful place and space in world sport." Hopefully, by dedicating a few pages to the sport here, I have done my little bit to help right that injustice.

Manx a lot

If shinty has been overlooked, a sport that has received even less attention is one whose name alone is enough to tell us that it formed part of the same family. That game is *cammag*, once the main team sport on the Isle of Man, the island that lies roughly half way between

---

[40] One year later, they would modify this to 12 players a side and a considerably smaller pitch, which shows just how little consensus there must have been among clubs regarding the rules.

[41] Finding funds to travel to Scotland for 'proper' matches was a constant headache, but this team soldiered on into the 20th century, when the World Wars put the final nail in its coffin, both metaphorically and sadly literally. But the great thing is that they were resurrected, although to be fair the connection with the modern incarnation is tenuous, given that when the club was reformed in 1982 it had been inactive for about sixty years. Things didn't start too badly. London made it to the quarter finals of the 1984 Camanachd Cup, losing to Skye, but the club folded again in 1992. Then in 2005, they were back again, and appeared in the first officially recognised shinty match outside of Scotland in 80 years in July 2006 against the Highlanders.

[42] Fast forward to this century, and Americans with a Scottish heritage are keen to have another go at promoting shinty in the USA, with a surprising number of clubs forming as a result. Northern California Camanachd Club was the first, formed in 2001, followed by Morro Bay Shinty Club (also in California, 2004), Houston Camanachd (2005), Dunedin Camanachd (Florida, 2006) and Washington Camanachd (2006).

northwest England and Northern Ireland[43]. Records of the ancient game are scarce, and by the early 20th century it was as good as gone, but in 1916, JJ Joughin reminisced about playing *cammag* as a child, saying it "was similar to the English hockey, but the number of players on a side was unlimited. The stick was called the *cammag* and the ball the *crick*. A gorse *cammag*, if of suitable size and shape, was a very much treasured possession. It appears to have been the national game of the Island, but it rapidly declined after the introduction of football. The *cammag* season usually began on Hunt the Wren Day[44], when matches would be played in every town and village in the Island, men of all ages playing … I have heard of a match being played between Ramsey and Peel a great many years ago, each town being its own goal. They started at Kirk Michael village, but I don't know now how the game ended, it is so long since I heard of it[45]."

In the early 21st century, there is now a movement to revive the game on the Isle of Man, though we once again have the sports revivalist problem of nobody really knowing what the original game was like.

There may be a case for the Isle of Man adopting the GAA hurling rules and even making a bid as a new county, but for now all they do is gather as they have done every Boxing Day since 2004 to play a game between north and south, with about 50 players on each side. But numbers are not necessarily equal, and the northerners are invariably outnumbered. Every year it's becoming a grander and grander occasion, but there are only very informal rules and no standard stick, so, if you really want to see hurling, shinty, *cammag*, *camanachd*, *iomáint*, call it what you will, being played in its true historical spirit then there is probably no better place to go than the Tynwald field near St John's on the Isle of Man on December 26.

Bando brothers

Gŵyl Mabsant was a form of Welsh folk fair cum Highland Games, first mentioned in writing in 1470, and described in 1803 as "a kind of circus for every sport and exercise[46]." The events involved a host of sports that it really is a shame never made it into the mainstream, including blindfolded wheelbarrow-driving, a women's race in a smock and petticoat, eating a hot pudding with a silver table spoon, and possibly the finest sporting event ever conceived: old women's grinning matches.

---

[43] The Isle of Man is something of a historical anomaly in that it never officially became part of the United Kingdom, but the Queen is still the head of state (the Lord of Mann to be precise) and the pound sterling is the currency. Most of us only know of it because of TT motorbikes, cyclist Mark Cavendish and cats with no tails, but it has a proud Norse-Celtic history and its own language, Manx, which is enjoying a resurgence in interest after its last native speaker died in 1974.

[44] December 26, where there is a Celtic tradition of hunting a fake wren, and putting it on top of a decorated pole.

[45] JJ Joughin was writing in Manx heritage magazine *Mannin* along with descriptions of other schoolyard favourites like Winchy my Donkey and Hop the Hat.

[46] Benjamin Malkin *The scenery, antiquities, and biography, of South Wales; from materials collected during two excursions in the year 1803* (1807).

There is no evidence that ball sports were ever part of *Gŵyl Mabsant*, but they might have been, and that's why we're mentioning it here. And who's complaining, if it gives us the chance to introduce old women's grinning matches to our explorations of the sporting pastimes of bygone years?

Wales did have its ancient stickball tradition, in this case a game called *bando*. It may tie in with hurling and shinty, but its name suggests a shared origin with East Anglian *bandy*. It was sometimes described using the English name, such as one quote from 1830 about "a peculiar proneness in the disposition of the Welsh towards all sorts of sports and diversion … the most popular of all the vale of Glamorgan is the important game of bandy[47]."

In keeping with Welsh stereotypes are claims that the game was played by coalminers who, in the absence of decent *camáns* like those of their Irish cousins, made do with the picks and shovels they brought up from the pits. That may have been the case, but the Welsh Folk Museum at St Fagans has a couple of *bando* sticks that look very similar to hurling's *camán*, and are even carved out of the same wood, ash. Meticulously adorned and varnished, with leather hand grips and even little hooks to hang them up by when not in use, they date back to 1845 and we are reliably informed that one of them belonged to somebody whose mother had not thought things through properly before baptising her son Thomas Thomas.

The *bando* ball was best made out of yew, although crab-apples, bundles of rags or old tins were often just as good for what at first were impromptu pick-up games at the end of a hard day's work, but which gradually evolved into one of the most seriously organised field sports of its time, with an established number of players and field of play, and teams decked out in their own particular colours.

Tommy Thomas was one of the Margam Bando Boys, who played on Aberavon Beach, and were famed for their red and white tops. Very much the team of the moment, they even had their own ditty, which reflects the moment the players joined the Margam Volunteer Rifle Corps in 1859, as most of the words are a dig at the French and Napoleon, as well as a pop at the other big team sport in Glamorgan:

> "Let cricket players blame,
> And seen to slight our game,
> Their bat and wicket never lick it,
> This ancient manly game."

We know little more about the actual game of *bando* as it was played in Wales than we do about the hockey-like games of England during the same period, other than they involved hitting a ball with a stick at a goal. But we also know *bando* presented an excellent opportunity for copious amounts of gambling and drinking, which would also seem fairly in keeping with the Welsh character, although that meant it was constantly at odds with the

---

[47] Heliwir Morganwg in *Sporting Magazine* (1830).

horribly dour and puritan Methodist ideology that was threatening to do away with anything that resembled fun in Wales.

If there had ever been any difference between the game as it was played on either side of Offa's Dyke, by the end of the 19th century the *bando* tradition had merged with English hockey. Like all stickball games, its popularity soon declined. The men of South Wales tossed aside their *bando* sticks as soon as they set their eyes on a rugby ball.

Caught cnapan

Wales is the land of Barry John, of JPR, of Gareth Edwards, the famous red shirt, the rousing choruses of *Hen Wlad fy Nhadau* and songs about big saucepans and small saucepans and the cat scratching little Johnny. Though it is hard to refute that rugby was born out of Rugby School in England, Wales still likes to feel it is its spiritual home. There are certainly few places where it is quite so ingrained in the local culture and there could be a reason for this. As well as the stickball game of *bando*, the country also had a football-like game called *cnapan*[48] that bore enough similarities to rugby to present a case for Wales being the veritable home of the carrying code.

It is in Cardiganshire and Pembrokeshire on the west coast that we find the earliest records, and if we turn to the somewhat eccentric Welsh historian George Owen we learn that "the game is thought to be of great antiquity[49]." He was saying that in 1603, so it's a fair assumption that it went back as far as the 1500s and probably before that too, because by the time he was writing, Owen could describe a calendar of matches that were played all year round, although the "great and main places, far exceeding any of the former in multitude of people" were those played by up to 2000 players at St Meigans[50].

Owen informs us that the ball was round, "prepared of a reasonable quantitie soe as a man may hold it in his hand and noe more, this bowle is of some massy wood as box, yew, crab or holly tree and should be boyled in tallowe to make it slippery and hard to hold." It wouldn't have been much fun to kick then, so think *cnapan*, think rugby, especially as the players went barefoot.

In fact, they hardly wore anything at all. They were "all first stripped bare saving a light pair of breeches, bare-headed, bare-bodied, bare legges and feete, their cloathes layd together in great heapes." Clothing was pointless for, as Owen points out, "if he leave but his shirt on his back in the furie of the game, it is most commonly torne to pieces and I have also seen some long-lock gallants, trimly trimmed at this game not by clipping but by pulling their hair and beards."

---

[48] Alternative spellings include *knapan* and *knappan*. The game could have been related to the 15th century English game of *camp-ball*, *camping* or *campan*, which sounds vaguely similar to the Welsh name.

[49] George Owen *Description of Pembrokeshire* (1603).

[50] In the historical administrative region, or *cantref* of Cemais in Pembrokeshire, where the Cemais men would play the Emlyn men on Ascension Day, and the men of Cardiganshire on Corpus Christi.

The game would start with the ball being "hurled bolt upright to the ayere, and at the falle, he that catcheth it hurleth it towards the countey he playeth for … for goal or appointed place there is none neither needeth any[51], for the play is not given over until the *knappan* be so far carried that there is no hope to returne it backe that night … the *knappan* being cast forth you shall see the same tossed backwarde and forwarde, by hurling throwes in straunge sorte, for in three or four throwes, you shall see the whole body of the game removed half a mile or more, and in this sort it is a strange sight to see 1000 or 1500 naked men to come near together in a cluster following the *knappan*."

It was cross country football at its finest, and "in the furie of the chase they respect neither hedge, ditch, pale or walle, hille, dale, bushes, river or rocke or any other passable impediment." But like so many of these medieval games, turbulent as it may have seemed "the gamesters return home from this play with broken heads, black faces, bruised bodies and lame legs. Yet they laugh and joke and tell stories about how they broke their heads, without grudge or hatred." Ah well, if you've broken your head, I guess you can always mend it.

The game certainly contained many elements of rugby. We can easily imagine the forwards and the backs when Owen says "there are, besides the corps or mayne body of the play, certaine scoutes or forerunners, whose charge is always to keepe before the knappan which way soever it passes, these always be of the adverse partie, between the other partie and home, least by surreption the *knappan* should be snatched by a borderer of the game, and so carried away by foote or by horse."

Horse? Too right there were horses, and carrying "monstrous codgells of three foot and a half long … and he that thinketh himself well horsed maketh means to his friends of the footmen to have the *knappan* delivered to him, which being gotten, he putteth spurres, and away as fast as the legges will carry. After him runneth the rest of the horsemen, and if they can overtake him, he summoneth a delivery of the *knappan*. If he hold the *knappan* it is lawful for the assailant to beat him with the codgell till he deliver it." But there were limitations to the amount of "annoyance" that the jockeys could cause, and if they overstepped the mark, the men on foot would chuck stones at them to chase them away. A quality sport it must have been, and you can't help but wonder whether, if it is possible for Australian and Gaelic football to come up with a composite code, that there might not also be some kind of opening here for rugby-polo at the Millennium Stadium.

As industry, agriculture and urbanisation crept as much across the Welsh landscape as it did everywhere else, *cnapan* would have changed with it, being forced into more enclosed spaces. The horses went out of fashion, and the cudgels and stone-throwing too, and the street football last heard of in Neath in 1884, and the cross-country *cnapan* last recorded as

---

[51] In saying there was no 'goal', Owen implies that he had witnessed ball games elsewhere that did have them, but in *cnapan* they didn't seem to feel there was the need.

being played across the eight miles between the churches of Llandysul and Llanwenog as late as 1922, were the final whimpers from a game that had seen its day[52].

But the *cnapan* tradition may well be the reason why the people of South Wales took so much more readily to rugby's handling code than the FA's kicking code when the sports spread west from England in the 19th century. Rugby, with so much more physical contact than soccer, was the kind of game they could identify with, and may well have even had an early hand in creating. As Jennifer Macrory so rightly points out, there is something about George Owen's description of ancient *cnapan* that brings to mind fifteen Welshmen dressed in red. Said Owen "they contend not for any wager or valuable thing, but … for the weaker number to save the glory of their country against the greater multitude." Which could just as easily be a beautiful tribute to the Welsh rugby union team before the modern era, when players that 'went north' to the professional world of rugby league were ranked somewhere just below the sewer rats in the social hierarchy.

As we start learning more about the sports played by our ancestors, there is an increasing desire to replicate them, and hence the movement to revive both *bando* and *cnapan* in the late 20th century. The greatest success was in *cnapan*'s homeland of Pembrokeshire, where the parishes of Newport and Nevern played on an annual basis from 1985-95. There was even a game played between Wales and England, won easily by the former because they accidentally on purpose forgot to mention some of the rules to their guests.

These matches were obviously far removed from the violent brawls of yesteryear, with much smaller teams and modified rules. Even so, injuries occurred, and one of the main reasons that the project has been put on hiatus is the problem with getting insurance to cover players of an unrecognised sport. Not that a minor problem like that would have got in the way of their broken-headed ancestors.

.

---

[52] A description was reprinted in the *Oswestry Observer* in 1877 of the Llanwenog game in which the ball "was thrown high in the air by a strong man, and when it fell [the players] scrambled for its possession and a quarter of an hour frequently elapsed before the ball was got out of the struggling heap … The whole parish was the field of operations and sometimes it would be dark before either party scored a victory … and sometimes a kick on the shins would lead the two men concerned to abandon the game until they had decided who was the better pugilist. There do not appear to have been any rules."

14 BANDY ON THE RUN
More on the origins of the hockey codes

Wrong end of the stick?

So, folk tales apart, there really is not much solid evidence that games like hurling and shinty have been around for any more than six hundred years or so, and although it is safe to assume that in some form or other both had really existed for much longer, the oft-heard claim that hurling is the oldest field sport of them all comes more down to tall stories than historical fact.

After all, remember those sticks pictured at Beni Hassan in Egypt, Greek *keritizin* and Roman *paganica*? Up and down the Americas they had everything from *palin* down south to the precursors of modern-day lacrosse in the north. Stick games existed all over Asia, such as the game played by the Li in China called *guoguipo*, played with a wooden ball and in which tradition dictated that the losing side had to carry the victors back to the village, and they even played stickball on horseback at the Imperial Courts. If you take the Dumbleyung Heritage Trail in Western Australia, you will learn that the area is said to be named after a game called *dumbung* that Noongar aborigines once played around the lake, in which bent sticks were used to hit a ball made of dried sap from a native pear tree. The Welsh had *bando*, the French had *soule la crosse*, the Spanish had *chueca* … the reality is that you would be hard pressed to find any nation anywhere in the world that does not have some kind of tradition of hitting balls with sticks.

England's own stick games could well be as ancient as any of them. A small clay mould found in Northampton in 1940 has been dated to the 2nd century AD, and shows a figure holding a curved stick and two round balls, with a third ball balanced on his knee. It's hard to discern whether this is really somebody playing a ball game at all, and neither is this conclusive evidence that the English inherited stickball from the Romans, but it was certainly an eye-opening discovery.

A myriad of stickball sports sprang up around England that sound like the kind of names on Bilbo Baggins' birthday party invitations list. These included baddins (in Cheshire), bandy (East Anglia), clubbes, clubby, crabsowl (in Lincolnshire, where they played with a barrel bung), doddorts, humney (which used a sheep's vertebra for a ball), jowling (in Yorkshire), not (in Gloucestershire, and apparently named after the knotty piece of wood that they used as a ball), scrush (in Dorset) and many more.

And then there were games called by names like chinnup, shinnup and shinney-law, all of which sound uncannily like shinty. Not to mention hurl-bat and hurley, which remind us of Irish hurling, as do cambuca, comocke and cammock, which were popular during the reign of Edward III (1312 – 1377), and show an obvious etymological link to such Celtic words as *camán*, *camogie* and *camanachd*.

Were these early forms of English hockey really any different from the 'Celtic' games? *Chambers' Information for the People* didn't seem to think so in 1842 when it noted that "shinty in Scotland, hockey in England, and hurling in Ireland appear to be very much the same out-of-door sport." Over in America, Benjamin Homer Hall didn't seem to be aware of any difference between the three games when he wrote in 1856 that "at Princeton College, the game of shinny, known also by the names of hawky and hurly, is as great a favorite with the students as is football at other colleges[1]."

Canterbury Cathedral, Kent, England. One of the most important Christian buildings in Britain, and famed, among many other things, for being the site of the shrine of Saint Thomas Becket, the destination of a curious bunch of farting and belching pilgrims described by Geoffrey Chaucer in his *Canterbury Tales*.

But the pilgrims were there late enough to have been able to check out, among the cathedral's prize collection of stained glass windows, a 13th century image of a young lad holding a stick, not unlike a hurley or golf club, in one hand, and a wee ball in the other. It is known as the *Puerilitia*, or *Childhood*, and is the earliest pictorial souvenir we have of ball sports in England[2], and could be the same game we see in a 14th century prayer book that includes an image of two hobbit-like chaps holding sticks that are curved at one end[3].

Artwork in another cathedral, Gloucester, appears in a stained glass window, showing a mid 14th century stickball player, who is missing his head thanks to the work of Cromwell and his image-bashing Roundheads. Head or no head, it is impossible to tell whether this was more like hockey, baseball or golf, but our friends at SONAHHR have a theory that the picture honours Wat Tyler and his 1381 Rebellion, because by fiddling around with history a bit, it can be claimed that the revolutionaries that made their enraged way into the capital were brandishing hurling sticks. One of Tyler's accomplices was Jack Straw, and that seems to be what SONAHHR are clutching at here.

Jolly hockey sticks

By the 19th century, the English language, like so many other aspects of society, was well on the road to being standardised. All the quaint regional names for stick sports fell by the wayside, and 'hockey' became the nationally accepted word. Just why that particular name triumphed is unclear. Although way back in 1527 the Galway Statutes had mentioned "hockie stickes," there seems to be no further record of the use of any name even remotely resembling 'hockey' until three centuries later.

---

[1] In his *Collection of College Words and Customs* (1856).

[2] Canterbury is right down in the southeast corner of England, which is just a short hop over the water from the Netherlands and their *het kolven*. It's curious to note that the Middle English used in Chaucer's Canterbury Tales is actually a lot easier for modern-day Dutch scholars to read than it is for the English. And what's easier to imitate; the complexities of an entire language, or hitting a ball with a stick?

[3] Shown in an illustration in Joseph Strutt's 1801 *Sports and Pastimes of the English People*, and apparently in possession at the time of a certain Mr Francis Douce.

In an 1822 children's book, a Mr White takes his son around London and tells him about all the different games they see being played. Hockey is the first, an amusement White is not too fond of, for "I cannot help thinking it a rather dangerous one … when I was a boy at school, it was put to a stop by a very melancholy accident … a boy who had not been long at the school … in striking the ball lost his aim and gave him so severe a blow as to occasion the loss of an eye[4]."

Mr White goes on to explain the rules, which feature all the right elements – teams battling to use their sticks to hit the ball though each other's goal. But despite his son's enthusiasm, his father advises him that "it is not a game which is now in very general use. The eagerness with which boys are too apt to play at it has been the occasion of many accidents, and it is, I believe, forbidden in many schools."

He was probably right about the schools. *Eton College Magazine* in 1832 considered itself "the only place in England where this ancient game is kept up." It was "never heard of across the channel and almost forgotten even in England," although they do concede that the Royal Military College at Sanhurst played it, but they hardly counted because they were so rubbish at it. Hockey was doomed at Eton too, where although it was written in 1872 that there had been a rule that "the foot of the stick was not to be raised above the level of the knee[5]" the same article also explains that the sport had not been played at the school for three decades.

However, in 1853, Lord Lytton wrote that "on the common some young men were playing at hockey. That old-fashioned game, now very uncommon in England, except at schools was still preserved in the primitive vicinity of Rood by the young yeomen and farmers[6]." In annoying fashion, this sentence is only quoted in sports histories as far as the 'except at schools bit', without letting Lytton finish his sentence and tell us that the game *was* in fact played by commoners.

One of his characters, Oliver, later gets into trouble for joining their games, and not doing too good a job of it. He is reminded how important it is that "in associating with his inferiors, a gentleman still knows how to maintain his dignity. There is no harm in playing with

---

[4] *Game at Hockey* in Marian S Carson T*he book of games, or, A history on juvenile sports practised at the Kingston Academy* (George Long, 1822). It also includes a picture of the game, and rather than a ball, they are hitting a disk-like object. This 'correctly' spelt reference is 16 years older than the one etymologists refer to in William Holloway's *General Dictionary of Provincialisms* (1838) to a West Sussex game called 'hawkey'. It has been claimed that that name was associated to the bird, the hawk, or that perhaps the way the ball circulated around the field was compared to the way a travelling salesman 'hawks' things. Clever theories, but neither is overly convincing. More likely, the word was derived from an Old French word for shepherd's crook, *hoquet*, or maybe the Middle Dutch *hokkie*, meaning shack or doghouse, or, more colloquially, goal.

[5] *The Graphic* (October 5, 1872).

[6] Edward Bulwer Lytton *My Novel or Varieties in English Life* (Serialised in *Blackwood's Magazine*, 1850-1853).

inferiors, but it is necessary to a gentleman to play so that he is not the laughing stock of clowns[7]."

At the village fairs in the former northern county of Cleveland "cricket, hockey, spell and knurr and every game of bat and ball are called into operation[8]" and there isn't much evidence that the public schools played a particularly prominent role in 19th century hockey at all[9].

But one that deserves a special mention is the posh Rossall School in Lancashire, where it is still played in its more or less traditional form today. A description in 1894 told how "'played on the sea-shore, which is as level as a billiard table, with the Irish Sea roaring at the verge of the sand and its salt spray often beating in the players' faces, Rossall hockey is as exhilarating as it is healthful[10]."

The earliest reference to the game being played at Rossall can be found in an 1867 edition of *The Rossallian*, although it is more than likely that it had been played at the school for many years before that. It was most probably influenced in some way by the soccer-like field game played at Eton, given that until 1900 it included the use of what were called 'rougeables' and still uses 'bullies' today, more or less for the same purposes as in Eton football.

To the best of our knowledge, Rossall had no written rules until 1873, two years before the school held its first house competition, and one of their game's defining features is the way the ball can never be passed forwards, which is also a common element of many traditional school football games including, of course, rugby[11].

Soccer was codified in 1863, but hockey was still far from being standardised. An 1867 entry in *Cassell's Popular Educator* tells how it consisted of "driving a ball from one point to another by means of a hooked stick. No precise rule is laid down as to the form this stick should take. It is simply a weapon with a bent knob or hook at the end, large or small, thick or thin, according to the option of the player" and adds that the game itself "in its principle bears a great resemblance to football and contains at least the germ of the Canadian la

---

[7] The danger of being shown up on the sports field by their 'inferiors' would be the source of the professionalism v amateur debate that would rock British sport a couple of decades later.

[8] *The Graphic* (April 15, 1871).

[9] Although *The Graphic*, no big fans of the sport, did say on January 30, 1886 that it "had long died out before the middle of the present century and like football only found a home at the public schools." Revisionists like Adrian Harvey have refuted the 'football only at public schools' idea of the late 19th century, and the same may be true of hockey, but there has been little in-depth research of the matter.

[10] J Heywood *The history of Rossall School* (John Frederick Rowbotham, 1894).

[11] The Rosall game is clear evidence of football and hockey interacting in a shared evolution. Indicating that things worked both ways, Kenneth Sheard and Eric Dunning, in their analysis of an early set of rugby rules muse that as "it was stipulated that players were to use only their persons for controlling and propelling the ball, this suggests that, prior to 1845 bats and sticks had sometimes been used."

crosse." A sports book in 1869 felt that hockey "must be played in pairs, though of course this does not prevent any number joining in at one time in the sport[12]."

The oldest claim to the formation of a hockey club is that of Blackheath in southeast London[13]. Although the oldest surviving document is the minutes of an 1861 meeting, it was written in 1899 that "this club was not formed later than the year 1840" and it is hard to argue with that because at that time of writing "members are still living who were playing at that date[14]." The game played in Blackheath was considerably more violent than the modern one, it was played on a much larger field (247m by 64m) and the rubber 'ball' was actually shaped like a cube.

Where most happened to mould the game into today's format was Middlesex, and if any town can be credited with the honour of being the birthplace of modern hockey, then that surely has to be Teddington. The story has it that in 1871 the members of Teddington Cricket Club were looking for something to play in the winter off-season, and felt a game using sticks and a cricket ball would be more appropriate than the usual solution of football.

When the Teddington boys drew up their first set of rules in 1874, these were largely based around those of football, hence the many similarities between the two sports. These included the same system of ten outfield players and a goalkeeper, and the same law for offside, something which remained part of field hockey until as late as 1998.

Teddington can also be accredited for introducing three of field hockey's most characteristic rules. First, the elimination of any use of the hands other than to wield the stick, which marked a break from hurling. Second, the prohibition of any hitting of the ball above shoulder height, which meant a split from shinty too. And third, the idea that goals could only be scored from inside the 'D'. The actual 'D' as a pitch marking did not come in until later, the so-called *Surbiton Rules* of 1874 merely stated that "no goals shall be allowed if the ball be hit from a distance of more than 15 yards from the nearest goalpost."

But with football enjoying such a boom, hockey was old hat. It was noted in *The Graphic* in 1874 that Teddington were playing "this somewhat old-fashioned game … hockey is all very well in its way, but with so many other games now in favour, it seems hardly worth the while to attempt to resuscitate it." Teddington persevered, and did try to set up an association in 1875 to spread their 'invention', but were largely unsuccessful, and the project folded seven years later. However, it's fascinating to follow *The Graphic*'s coverage of hockey's resurgence. In 1875, it reported on "the East Surrey Club being conspicuous in its attempt to revive what we are still inclined to think is but a poor game" but conceded a few issues later that it "seems to be weekly gaining fresh adherents." In 1881, hockey still showed "no signs

---

[12] Fr Warne and Co *The Boy's book of sports, games, exercises, and pursuits* (1869).

[13] A place that has quite a sporting legacy to it. It is widely believed that this was the place where golf was first played outside of Scotland in 1608, and the same Blackheath club also played a central role in the codification of both soccer and rugby.

[14] J Nicholson Smith and Philip A Robson (eds.) *Hockey, Historical and Practical* (London, 1899).

of becoming very popular," but by December of that same year, although "this old game seems unwilling to be expunged from the list of our outdoor pastimes ... it is well worth retention as now scientifically played. It is certainly a mistake to imagine that hockey is all furious 'swiping' as that football is all furious kicking." Hockey was slowly gaining favour, but in 1885 *The Graphic* still felt "the attempts of recent years to revive the old game of hockey ... have not been successful."

In 1886, Teddington had another go at forming a Hockey Association, and this time managed to convince seven clubs based around London plus Trinity College, Cambridge. Federated field hockey was finally born. Reporting on the event, *The Graphic* noted that the rules "which in most cases are those already in force among players ... remind one much of those of the Association game at football" and suggested that anyone who might "shrink from the roughness of football, to take the opportunity of witnessing a good game at hockey."

Blackheath reappear in the story at this point, for they too attended the first ever council of the Hockey Association, but rejected the offer to join because they were unhappy about some of the rules. They were still insisting that the game should be played with their rubber cube, while the Association had come to the logical conclusion that Teddington's cricket ball, being spherical, was a better idea. Being one of the pioneering rugby clubs, it is no surprise that Blackheath's version was more based on that sport than the essentially soccer-influenced hockey. Catching, marking and scrimmaging were all part of their game, and it must have provided quite a spectacle, but the Association were having none of it. Blackheath instead sulked off to form their own separate National Hockey Union. This was not the first time Blackheath had made a stand against tamer ball sports. 12 years earlier, the same club had refused to accept the Football Association's new rules for soccer, and would instead be instrumental in the foundation of the Rugby Football Union.

The Rugby Union may have flourished, but Blackheath had far less luck with their Hockey Union, which failed to win over many supporters and soon flittered away into nothing. Meanwhile the Association's game prevailed, although not without problems of its own, for disputes over the rules would lead to all kinds of disagreements and amendments throughout the ensuing years, but the general desire was to reduce the violence and make hockey safer.

The Hockey Association would not only influence its own game, but also those played elsewhere. Until this period, the different stick sports of Britain had coexisted in relative harmony. In 1880, Scotsman Colin Chisholm stated in an article in *The Highlander* magazine that shinty was known "both in England and in Ireland by the name of hockey and hurling." Until people began to insist on standard rules for everybody, it hardly mattered. But the formation of the Hockey Association, and its decisions to tame the game, led to touchiness among the different stickball communities, particularly when they sensed their national identities were in danger. Just over a decade later, an unnamed Scottish author bemoaned the fact that the English had created "an innocent, innocuous apology for *camanachd* in the game of hockey[15]."

Over in Ireland, hockey, hurley and hurling clubs had all been fairly happy to accept they were all more or less playing the same thing. All that changed in the 1880s when Michael Cusack and his Irish hurlers started murmuring their discontent at the influence of the soft English rules. They turned their backs on the hockey and hurley communities, and developed their own more physical set of rules – and out of that came the GAA.

Field hockey, meanwhile, went on to take a curious place in world sport. It is now one of the most global team sports of all, and yet with the possible exceptions of India and Pakistan, in every country where it is played there is at least one football code that has vastly more players, and even major international hockey tournaments struggle to attract crowds or television viewing figures. Very few people have managed to carve a living out of the game, and even in a country like Holland, which has more hockey clubs per members of the population than any other, the average man in the street would struggle to name one player in their national team. The football boom of the mid 19th century almost saw hockey off for good. Hockey bounced back but never made up the lost ground in the popularity stakes. But take the game onto ice, and it's a different story…

Bandying it about

One of the different names for stickball games in England is bandy[16], once widely used in Lincolnshire and Cambridgeshire, where it was played on ice. England is generally about as suited to ice-based sports as the Gobi Desert is to yachting, but the main exception is the Fens, a large expanse of wetland where the water is not particularly deep and freezes well in winter. There could be no standard bandy playing area, pitches were determined by the amount of playable ice available, while the goals were traditionally two willow branches frozen into the ice and bent over to meet in the middle.

---

[15] In an article titled *An English View of Shinty* published in the *Inverness Courier* in 1893

[16] One plausible explanation for the origin of the name is the Anglo-Saxon *bendan*, meaning 'to bend', in reference to the shape of the stick. But 'bandy' was and is also a generic expression for tossing things back and forth. If we are to take *Brewer's Dictionary of Phrase and Fable* (1898) at its word, then the sport came first and the alternative use after, for it claims that the verb 'to bandy' is a reference "to a game called bandy. The players have each a stick with a crook at the end to strike a wooden or other hard ball. The ball is bandied from side to side, each party trying to beat it home to the opposite goal." But if that's the case, what did Shakespeare mean in *Romeo and Juliet* (1592), when Romeo points out to Mercutio and Tybalt that "the prince expressly hath forbidden bandying in Verona streets." Fanatics often revere this mention of their game in The Bard's works, but sadly for them, Romeo is not making any reference to a game like hockey played in the streets of Renaissance Italy, he is telling them to stop their sword-fighting. Neither is there any indication that any sporting reference was intended when the word reappears in *King Lear* (1608) in the quote "do you bandy looks with me, you rascal?"

Although every bandy history by necessity opens by stating that there are 1813 records of the Bury-on-Fen team being unbeaten for the previous 100 years, there are actually no such records at all. What the game's great promoter, Charles Tebbutt, actually said was that "bandy matches have long been held in the fens. It is certain that during the last century the game was played … on Bury Fen, and the local tradition that the Bury Fenners had not been defeated for a century may not be an idle boast. But it was not until the great frost of 1813-14 that the tradition gives place to certainty[17]." It was just a rumour. Tebbutt concedes that "undoubtedly matches were held before this time … but we have no records." His report was mainly based on an interview with William Leeland, a bandy veteran who had died a year earlier, and who did have memories of such games as one played in 1827 for a leg of mutton. Although it is traditionally believed that the game was originally played on dry land before moving onto the ice, this is also idle speculation.

Poor old bandy was set to struggle against cricket and the growing popularity of football. But there was another problem. Bandy was played on ice, and although frost fairs could even be held on the frozen River Thames from 1607 to 1814, the so-called Little Ice Age was coming to an end. The warmer weather was welcomed all round by just about everybody apart from English ice skaters, because there was an increasing shortage of frozen ponds, lakes or rivers that were able to support any kind of athletic activity.

Artificial ice rinks were the solution. The first mechanically-refrigerated rink in the world was built in Chelsea in 1876, called the Glaciarium, to be followed shortly after by another at Charing Cross and one at Rusholme in Manchester (which proved a technical disaster and was closed down within a year).

Stickball games could be played on these rinks, and were, but in a far more reduced space and with fewer players than the large-scale outdoor bandy variety. What were being sown here were the seeds of what would eventually become ice hockey.

Bandy spread across the east of England, and even what would become Nottingham Forest soccer club was originally founded in 1865 to play the game. But it was not until 1891 that the National Bandy Association laid down official rules, which were very much inspired by soccer, and nowadays lie almost exactly midway between that game and ice hockey.

In his 17th century diaries, John Evelyn noted how the skaters on the London ice were doing so "after the manner of the Hollanders" and in 1891 an intrepid set of players from Cambridge University decided to follow that up by setting off for the Netherlands in search of better ice and potential opposition among the Dutch skating community. In a country where it was noted that you "must put on your own skates even if you are a lady[18]," they found what they wanted. After deciding that the English game was even more fun than drowning chips in mayonnaise, the Amsterdamsche Hockey and Bandy Club was formed in

---

[17] In Tebbutt's chapter on *Bandy* in *Skating and Figure Skating* by J M Heathcote et al (Longmans, Green and Co, 1892).
[18] In the *Badminton Library* series of sporting guides (1891)

January 1892, and a month later, they found opposition in the Bloemendaal Mussen Bandy Team.

Following the success of the Dutch venture, the spread of bandy around Europe was electrifying in the last decade of the 19th century, and much of that was thanks to the efforts of the sport's great missionary, Charles Tebbutt, the captain of the Bury Fen team who scoured the continent in search of suitable bandy terrain and converting the locals to his beloved sport.

Northern Europe was skating crazy at the time, and games like soccer were catching on in a big way, so the idea of combining the two was welcomed with open arms wherever it was taken. Tebbutt took bandy to Germany in 1891, although the first club to be formed there would not appear until 1901 in the form of Charlottenburger Eislaufverein. In Switzerland, St Moritz Bandy Club was formed in December 1893, Sporting Club d'Engheim were recorded as playing the game in France in 1899, and Tebbutt is also heralded as being the man who introduced bandy to Denmark in 1893, although there are no records of any games being played there until 1906, when Københavns Skøyteførening emerged as the dominant club.

The 1913 Bandy European Championships proved a milestone in the expansion of the game. Most of the major western European nations were represented, even Belgium and Italy put out sides, even though records of the game ever being played in those countries are virtually non-existent.

The tournament was won by England, but rather than marking the dawn of a great new era, it was more of a last hurrah not just for English bandy, but for that of most of the other nations too, with the 1913 championship being the final record of bandy being played in most of them. Many reasons can be given, but the biggest of all was the First World War, which put an end to so many of the beauties of Europe, and bandy was one of them.

When peace returned, bandy was forgotten by most of those who survived the slaughter, and even in England it disappeared. But it found a whole new market among Scandinavians, who as good as adopted the game as their own, and where the sport has never had to look back since.

A Swedish count, Clarence von Rosen, was responsible for establishing many modern sports in Sweden (including soccer and tennis), and he started getting his people interested in bandy from 1895, with Uppsala and Stockholm meeting in the first recorded game in 1901. It was originally played purely by the upper classes and it wasn't really until the 1930s that it caught on as the number one sport in some regions of the country for all classes. The national championship was born in 1907 and is still unquestionably the strongest in the world, with semi-professionalism attracting bandy players from other countries too.

Bandy also caught on in Norway, but it was the game's arrival in what was then Tsarist Russia and would eventually become the USSR that the game's history took on a new twist. It transpired that the whole development of bandy on the Bury Fens was a process that was being replicated at the same time in Russia. And when the Russians learned of Scandinavian bandy, they immediately scoffed that there was nothing new in that, for their own traditions included a number of different skating pastimes, with names like *jules*, *kotol* and *kumar*, that were very much the same thing. It is claimed that 'Russian hockey' dates back to at least the 1700s, and even Peter the Great played the game on Saint Petersburg's frozen Neva River. Certainly, by the 19th century, forms of hockey on ice were played all the way down Russian society.

Impressed by the way the Swedes had structured bandy into a federated sport, the Russians decided to do likewise. But rather than import bandy as it was, they rewrote their own rules at St Petersburg in 1898, with several minor differences to reflect their own traditions. The country was about to go into a pretty turbulent period. What with the Bolshevik Revolution, the fall of the Tsars, the transformation to communism, the establishment of the Soviet Union and Stalin's five-year plans there was plenty to be getting on with, so the country can be forgiven for being a bit tardy in setting up the first Soviet bandy championship, which was won by Dynamo Moscow in 1936. And just when things seemed to be straightening themselves out, the USSR was thrown headlong into the Second World War, suffering more casualties than any other nation and leading to the division of Europe into the capitalist west and the communist east.

So, it was not until 1955 that an International Federation was established for bandy, and the immediate problem was the fact that the two prime movers, Sweden and the USSR, did not share the same rules. Composite ones were agreed, which have since come to be the standard. What we are talking of here is essentially ice hockey, but it is played on a field the size of a football pitch, with eleven players on each side including a goalkeeper. Other similarities to soccer include almost exactly the same rules for offside, penalties and what happens when the ball goes out of play. And rather than ice hockey's puck, bandy is played with a solid ball, which is roughly the same size and colour as an orange.

With the rules sorted, a Bandy World Championship was held in 1957. Played every two years (and an annual event since 2003), the USSR won the first eleven editions, their dominance eventually being interrupted by Sweden in 1981. Since then the USSR (or Russia as it is now) and Sweden have been more or less evenly matched in terms of world titles.

Finland won its independence from Russia in 1919, and has bandy of its own, but here the game has particularly struggled against the immensely greater popularity of ice hockey. Having managed to break the Russian/Swedish duopoly of the sport on six occasions by making it into the world final (losing every time), Finland finally came good in 2004 and claimed a historic triumph. Norway have traditionally plodded along as the sport's fourth power, but the break-up of the Soviet Union has added a bit more variety to the international bandy scene, with Belarus, Estonia and most especially Kazakhstan able to field competitive teams.

Cutting no ice

Much as it is a well-established sport throughout Nordic Europe, there is not one nation where bandy is even half as popular or widespread as the scaled down variant, ice hockey. In Europe, Finland, Russia, Sweden and the Czech Republic are four of the six giants of global ice hockey, while particularly Slovakia, Switzerland, Norway, Germany and several former Soviet republics also have thriving scenes.

But the traditional home of ice hockey is, of course, Canada, where they don't even need to use the word 'ice' to clarify which type they are talking about. Yet although there can be no denying that the Canadians and the Stanley Cup popularised the modern game, it is far less clear that ice hockey was an entirely Canadian invention, or whether it was just a local take on an idea that takes us back through the centuries of frozen ponds in Holland, frozen bogs in Cambridgeshire, and frozen Viking dominions before that.

Tracking the origins of ice hockey is a big deal for Canadians, with copious literature and committees hotly debating the issue but coming up with remarkably little solid evidence for the origins of a relatively modern contribution to world sport. A lot of the discrepancy is the result of the shockingly partisan and self-interested claims put forward by Canadians on a wild goose chase to prove that the sport was their own invention and not something imported from Europe or even, perish the thought, the USA. The origins of ice hockey are not the issue – it's proving that they were Canadian and shunning all counter-evidence.

Despite the fact that it is a very similar game, bandy merits little more than a passing mention in ice hockey histories. It tends to be dismissed because it was not until the late 19th century that it was popularised beyond a very small corner of England, by which time ice hockey in America was already well established. But the theory that the 1885 Oxford v Cambridge Varsity Match was the first game of modern ice hockey played in Europe seems a little misguided. All evidence suggests that the students were actually playing bandy, and it wasn't until the start of the 20th century that they appeared to switch to the Canadian code.

The desire to shun any European origins is typified by the International Ice Hockey Federation's own website's claim that their sport's relationship with either shinty or hurling is debatable, given that neither of those sports includes goalkeepers. The argument falls a bit flat when we point out that both shinty and hurling *do* have goalkeepers. In fact, the very fact that ice hockey has goalkeepers (unlike Canadian football or basketball) rather than defining its uniqueness is more of an indication that it imported European ideas.

Another glaringly obvious connection between ice hockey and European sports is the word 'hockey', and yet there are even Canadian claims that the name was their invention too. One of the strongest campaigners for the right to be known as the birthplace of ice hockey is Windsor in Nova Scotia, where it is argued the surname Hockey is a common one, and even that a certain Colonel Hockey was one of its creators. It's absolute hockey-cock, because as we learned earlier, the Galway Statutes in Ireland made reference to 'hockie stickes' as far back as 1527.

The Nova Scotia claim[19] is mainly based on an 1844 quote from a Thomas Haliburton novel that makes reference to "the game at bass in the fields, or hurly on the long pond[20]" being played at King's College, Windsor, where the author was a pupil in the 1800s.

In 2002, the Society for International Hockey set up a committee to look into this one, and among their conclusions they note how the Nova Scotians "produce a single, seventeenth century Dutch painting of a non-hockey activity on the ice to purportedly show that hockey was not played in Europe prior to 1800. In fact, to the extent that the Avercamp, Beerstraten, and Bruegel works of documentary art show skaters with curved sticks, these pieces may be considered more credible as evidence of a hockey-like game than the Haliburton literary allusion[21]."

The committee defines ice hockey as "a game played on an ice rink in which two opposing teams of skaters, using curved sticks, try to drive a small disc, ball or block into or through the opposite goals" and argues that the Haliburton quote fails to mention any of these, and certainly doesn't merit the rewriting of the ice hockey books that it spawned. But although the committee is right to be sceptical, "hurly on the long pond" does sound very like a contender for early Canadian ice hockey.

Nova Scotia provides other clues. As most early evidence of sports comes in the form of decrees forbidding them, it is refreshing to find the Supreme Court of Nova Scotia issuing a decree in 1829 that tells the general public that they are free to play a sport as they please. Not everybody was glad to hear the news, as reflected by a report in the town of Pictou that bemoaned how "every idler who feels disposed to profane the Lord's day may now secure from any consequences turn out with skates on feet, hurly in hand, and play the delectable game of break-shins without any regard to laws[22]."

There's more Nova Scotian ice hockey in a poem written at Dartmouth[23] in 1823 to extol the many virtues of winter:

> "Now at ricket with hurlies some dozens of boys,
>
> Chase the ball o'er ice with a deafening noise[24]."

---

[19] Explained in depth by the Windsor Hockey Heritage Society at www.birthplaceofhockey.com. When talking about 'the Nova Scotians' in this section, it means this society.

[20] Thomas Chandler Haliburton *The Attaché* (Bentley, 1844).

[21] The *Research Sub-Committee Looking into the Claim that Windsor, Nova Scotia, is the Birthplace of Hockey* (2002).

[22] *The Colonial Patriot* (February 4, 1829). Pictou, 15km north of New Glasgow, incidentally, is dubbed 'The Birthplace of New Scotland', as this was the port of arrival of thousands of Scottish immigrants escaping the Highland Clearances around the start of the 19th century. 'Break-shins' does suggest some kind of shinty connection.

[23] Dartmouth was also the home of the Starr Manufacturing Company, the most important producers of commercially available ice skates, but despite rumours to the contrary, no evidence has ever been found to prove that this company ever produced a specific skate for playing hockey.

[24] In the January 1823 edition of a magazine called *The Arcadian*.

Here we can bring in an article in the *Boston Evening Gazette* called *Winter Sports in Nova Scotia* (November 5, 1859), which gives us the first reasonably complete description of anything resembling ice hockey to have ever been found. The article tells us of a game played on ice by teams hitting a ball with a hurley, and the idea was to score goals through a 'ricket', which was two stones set three or four feet apart. It even tells us that one player on each team had the specific job of stopping the ball from going through. That would be a goalie, and that, ladies and gentlemen, would also be ice hockey.

In 1863 and still in Dartmouth, a columnist answering to the name of Icicle told of a trip to Oathill Lake and made a distinction between that word 'ricket' as a game and another called hockey. He tells that "two well contested games of 'ricket' were being played … while the centre was occupied by a number of officers of the Garrison and Fleet, in a match game called hockey[25]." If Icicle's opinion is anything to go by, then the game was still highly rudimentary in form. The lack of defined boundaries seemed to cause no end of arguments as the "aristocratic hockey ball" and the "plebeian hurley" got in each other's way, and the matches displayed "very little science … the game as now played is dangerous to outsiders, especially to ladies, some of whom were rather roughly treated in the scrimmage after the ball." Icicle tells us that it was nigh on impossible to get a proper game going with so many people on the ice at the same time, and also comments on the potential hazard of falling into holes in the ice made by trout fishermen! But although this was 1863, it seems ice hockey was by no means new to the people of Nova Scotia. Icicle actually bemoans the way that the "old class of players seem to have died out, and their successors are not up in the science of leading off the ball, doubling and carrying it through."

Windsor and Dartmouth's claims for a Nova Scotian origin are countered by other Canadian locations, and especially Kingston, Ontario, which was hailed for many years as the birthplace of ice hockey. That was where British army officer Arthur Henry Freeling was stationed in 1843, when he tells in his diary how he "began to skate this year, improved quickly and had great fun at hockey on the ice." Shortly after in the same city, Edwin Horsey quotes from his father's diary of 1846–47 that "most of the soldier boys were quite at home on skates[26]," and that "shinny was their great delight," although we can't be sure that they necessarily did the two things together.

Or we could go right up north to the town of Deline on the chilly shores of the Great Bear Lake in Northwest Territories. A letter from explorer Sir John Franklin while on his second Arctic land expedition in 1825-1827 comments that "till the snow fell the game of hockey played on the ice was the morning's sport[27]," but this has been rejected because there is no

---

[25] *Skating Scribblings* from the *Halifax Evening Reporter* (1863).
[26] Edwin E Horsey *Kingston A Century Ago* (Kingston Historical Society, 1938).
[27] Letter from Franklin to Roderick Murchison (November 6, 1825) published in HD Traill *The Life of Sir John Franklin* (1896).

specific mention that they wore skates. As Franklin mentions skating at other points, it's highly likely that they did.

But who's to say ice hockey's origin is even to be found in Canada? The earliest and best reference is too frequently ignored on the obvious grounds that New York is not a place Canadians would like to situate it. But William Alexander Fuer's comment that he remembered the cold winter of 1783, in which "the icy surface was alive with skaters darting in every direction with the swiftness of the wind, or bearing down in a body in pursuit of the ball driven before them by their hurlies[28]" is older than anything Canada has to offer.

Or how about Niagara County, where it was written that in 1839 (and apologies for the very different racial views of time) "the skating on Chippewa Creek was excellent and added not a little to our amusement. Large parties contested games of hockey on ice, some forty or fifty being arranged on each side. A ludicrous scene, too, was afforded by the instruction of a black corps in skating: from the peculiar formation of a negro's foot, and the length of his heel, they were constantly falling forward; it was impossible to keep them on their skates[29]."

Describing Boston in the 1850s, James Lovett tells how "here also was the boys' paradise for ice hockey; the boys frequently lined up fifty or more strong on a side, and the constant 'mix-ups' that occurred, in which a hundred or more hockeys were flying about in reckless confusion, gave onlookers a decided impression that 'something was doing'. Surely those of us now living who took part in them will feel our pulses beat a trifle quicker as we recall these hard-fought contests on old Jamaica Pond[30]."

But are we sure ice hockey was even North American? It didn't appear out of nowhere, it gradually evolved, and its origins were almost certainly on the other side of the Atlantic. Here are a few more choice cuts.

Lieutenant-Colonel Sir John Dugdale Astley's memoirs contain a reference to his Oxford University days in the 1840s, where they played "an on-ice version of field hockey in which all players were required to shoot right-handed and offside rules varied[31]." Later the same writer refers to an incident at Windsor[32] in 1853 with royal involvement when the festive season produced "some first-rate ice, which gave me ample opportunity of playing my favourite game of hockey on the ice … it reached my ears that a match was to be played on the pond on the slopes below the Terrace of Windsor Castle and though I really had no business there, I felt very keen to show my powers before Royalty … At one end of the pond

---

[28] In an address to the St Nicholas Society of New York (December 1, 1848) in which he reminisced about the now non-existent Collect Pond freezing over.

[29] Capt RGA Levinge *The Echoes From the Backwood; Or Sketches Of Transatlantic Life* (Henry Colburn, 1846).

[30] James D'Wolf Lovett *Old Boston Boys and the Games they Played* (Riverside press, published in 1907 but in which he describing his childhood games of some fifty or so years before – the 1850s).

[31] Sir John Dugdale Astley *Fifty Years of My Life: in the world of sport at home and abroad* (1894).

[32] Not the one in Nova Scotia, but the one in Berkshire, England.

her Gracious Majesty[33] was seated, surrounded by several ladies of the court, watching the game with evident interest. The Prince Consort – who was a beautiful and graceful figure skater – kept goal for the opposite side."

In 1857, Montreal doctor W Lawrence wrote "in the winter of 1850, it appears, the patient was playing on the ice; while engaged in some game, the precise nature of which I do not understand, and termed 'hocky' – a game, as I learn (and you will correct me if I'm wrong) where there is hard hitting of a ball[34]." The thing is, the injury he was describing was sustained in London, England.

We have a description of ice hockey in England in 1863 being an unwelcome hazard to more leisurely skaters. The writer complained that "hockey is a noble game and deserving of every encouragement; but on ice it is in its wrong place and should be prohibited ... it is more than annoying to have the graceful evolutions of a charming quadrille broken up by the interruptions of a disorderly mob, armed with sticks and charging through the circle of skaters and spectators to the imminent danger of all. I should be truly glad to see the police interfere whenever hockey is commenced[35]."

And then in 1869, it was suggested that "we must absolutely forbid the use on the ice of the walking-stick, as it is utterly useless as an artificial support for the learner, and excessively dangerous to every one in his immediate vicinity. We cannot conceive how any skater can take delight in skating about with such a thing flying in all directions. It is only useful when hockey is in the case[36]."

If ice hockey was really such an ingrained part of Canadian culture, then why was hardly a word written about it in the early or mid 19th century? For every isolated example, we can usually find a British one to equal it – even Queen Victoria attended a game! As they went west, the English settlers took hockey with them, the Welsh took *bando*, the Irish took hurling and the Scots took shinty. The occasional game of those on the ice was nothing new to them, although in Canada they would find a country much better conditioned to the sport.

The ice age

And so we come to the monumental date in the history of ice hockey. Montreal, March 3, 1875 is heralded as the day when ice hockey was born, although a local skating judge, James Creighton, had apparently been playing games of shinny on the ice for at least two years before that. But this game was going to produce ice hockey's defining item.

Having announced it the day before, the *Montreal Gazette* then reported on the match between Captain Torrance's team and Captain Creighton's team, the former winning by two

---

[33] Queen Victoria, while the prince mentioned later would have been Prince Albert.
[34] *The Medical Chronicle* (May, 1857).
[35] *London Society – An Illustrated Magazine* (1863).
[36] HE Vandervell and T Maxwell *System of Figure-Skating - Being the Theory and Practice of the Art as Developed in England, With a Glance at Its Origin and History* (1869).

'games' to one. Of particular interest is the way we are told that ice hockey in Montreal was something of a 'novel' experience. The sport, though "much in vogue on the ice in New England and other parts of the United States, is not much known here, and in consequence the game of last evening was looked forward to with great interest." This comment comes as something of an embarrassment to those who defend the truly Canadian origins of ice hockey.

The *Montreal Gazette* describes ice hockey as similar to lacrosse, which suggests the people of Quebec would have been far more familiar with that sport than ice hockey, and feels obliged to explain that "the old country game of shinty gives the best idea of hockey."

But what makes the events of March 3, 1875 so particularly unique is that although the game was usually played with a ball, on that occasion "in order that no accident should happen, a flat block of wood was used, so that it should slide along the ice without rising, and thus going among the spectators to their discomfort."

Canada may have a claim to the invention of the puck[37], but probably had very little to do with the origins of ice hockey *per se*. A write-up of a game played between the Montreal based St James and Metropolitan clubs in 1877 includes the first known set of rules, although apart from one modification to include the word 'ice', they are a copy and paste of the rules of English field hockey at the time, including the use of the 'bully' method to get the game started. Ice hockey in Canada, like most sports, was just the final stage of a long evolutionary chain. As was football in the British Isles, to which we now finally turn…

---

[37] However, there was, for example, a traditional Turkish stickball game that used a small wooden wedge, called a *holani*, and for which it would be hard to find a better English translation than, well, puck. As for why we call it that in English, nobody is really sure, but the best suggestion can be found in *English as we Speak it in Ireland* by Patrick Weston Joyce (Longmans, Green, 1910). The word is reputedly derived from the Gaelic *poc* meaning to poke or punch, and according to Joyce was used to describe the "blow given by a hurler to the ball with his *caman* or hurley."

15 MIDDLE AGE RELICS
Medieval football in Great Britain

Certificates of origin

And it came to pass that something called football existed in the British Isles. And the time has finally come to track the origins in those islands of what would lead to the greatest sporting phenomenon to ever be created by the human race.

If football was imported from abroad, then we have seen several candidates. The Greeks and Romans had both ball games and contact with the islands. Leo Wiener argues that "the ball games were brought by the Arabs into Europe, where they became very popular and led to their introduction among the clergy and, in a rougher and simpler form, among all classes of people[1]." Footy could also have come through the Vikings, who had some kind of ball game and were active in the British Isles around the turn of the first millennium, and with the papacy governing much of what went on in the islands, it is also quite conceivable that ancient *calcio* spread from Italy to England. French games like *soule* could naturally have been brought into England any time after the Norman Conquest in 1066, but it is just as plausible that it was British football that led to the French variety.

The early Britons quite possibly had their own ballgame traditions all along. Perhaps these were modified as people from other cultures traipsed across their land or the British traipsed across theirs, but Richard Sanders may be quite right to say that by the time "the Chinese, the Mexicans and the Italians began to kick inflated balls round in the 20th century they were not playing their own ancient games, or even distant descendants of them. They were playing a game they had imported from Britain, and they knew it."

If it's solid fact you are after, the earliest known reference to anything resembling football being played in Blighty is a Welsh one to be found in Nennius' 9th century Latin chronicle that refers to a "party of boys that were playing with a ball and had fallen to quarrelling." It appeared in *Historia Britonum*, a hotchpotch of legends and other assorted texts described by archaeologist Leslie Alcock as "like a cairn of stones, uneven and ill-fitting … as an example of the historian's art it is atrocious." It was put together some time after 820 AD, some say much later. The ball reference comes in the story of Vortigern, a 5th century warlord who was building a fortress in Snowdonia. All kinds of mystic phenomena were disturbing the construction project, so he sought the advice of his wise men, who told him he "must find a child born without a father, put him to death, and sprinkle his blood on the ground on which the citadel is to be built, or you will never accomplish your purpose." Unfazed by paedocide not being the most morally correct solution for your real estate problems, off trotted Vortigern on his quest, and his travels led him to a gang of youth indulging in *pilae ludus*, as

---

[1] Leo Wiener *Africa and the Discovery of America* (Philadelphia, Innes, 1922).

the Latin original put it. There is certainly no indication in this text that playing with a ball was an unusual thing for young boys to do.

We may as well end the story. As luck would have it, Vortigern overheard one lad taunt the other by saying "boy without a father, no good will ever happen to you." He checked with his mom, and sure enough, she confirmed that "in what manner he was conceived I know not, for I have never had intercourse with any man." They had their boy.

When the lad got wind of why he had been captured, he was understandably none too pleased and asked to parley with the supposedly wise men of the court. He had a fairly valid question when he asked "by what means was it revealed to you that this citadel could not be built, unless the spot were previously sprinkled with my blood?" Following some rather embarrassed coughs and scratching of chins, the boy went on to prove himself to be a far wiser chap by half and explained how he was actually the son of a Roman consul called Ambrosius, and how they could never build a citadel on that spot because of dragons and the local Welsh folk's claim to the land. It's all great stuff, albeit the stuff of legends, but it does show that young boys were playing with balls (if not at football) in Britain long before we needed four digits to count the years.

The first description of ball games in anything other than fiction was penned by William Fitzstephen[2] around 1180. After informing us how young boys would get their cocks out at school ... let's rephrase that ... their roosters ... as part of the Carnival celebrations, Fitzstephen describes how "after lunch all the youth of the city go out into the fields to take part in a ball game. The students of each school have their own ball; the workers from each city craft are also carrying their balls. Older citizens, fathers, and wealthy citizens come on horseback to watch their juniors competing, and to relive their own youth vicariously. You can see their inner passions aroused as they watch the action and get caught up in the fun being had by the carefree adolescents[3]."

Unfortunately, like so many 'first ever reference' texts we have come across, we can't be sure just how explicitly similar the activity Fitzstephen describes is to football. After all, he

---

[2] Who wrote a brief description of 12th century London (*Descriptio Londoniae*) as a preface to the biography of his murdered master, the Archbishop of Canterbury Thomas Becket (*Vita Sancti Thomae*). The reference appears in the section on *Cockfighting and ball games*. This translation from the Latin original was the work of Henry Thomas Riley in 1860.

[3] It is important to realise that this and most other early football references are translations. The original Latin was written "*Post prandium, exit in campos omnis iuventus urbis ad iusum pila celebrem...*", and to illustrate the vagueness of translation, especially from a language that has been dead for the best part of two millennia, compare the text given above to Peabody Magoun's version, which reads "after the midday meal the entire youth of the city goes to the field for the famous game of ball. The students of several branches of study have their ball; the followers of the several trades of the city have a ball in their hands. The elders, the fathers, and the men of wealth come on horseback to view the contests of their juniors, and in their fashion sport with the young men; and there seems to be aroused in these elders a stirring of natural heat by viewing so much activity and by participation in the joys of unstrained youth." The gist is the same, but we can't too much into the 'subtleties' of translated language.

only tells us it is a 'ball game', which could just as easily have been an early form of baseball, tennis, golf, volleyball, skittles or anything involving a ball for that matter.

One contender in the vintage football stakes is a manuscript at Trinity College, Oxford describing the life of St Cuthbert, a 7th century monk from Northumberland who at the age of eight had "played at the ball with the other chyldren[4]." However, the anonymous author was writing in the 14th century, and wherever it was that he got the idea that Cuthbert had dabbled in ball games, it probably wasn't the most reliable of sources.

Another tenuous link to football appears in *Brut* around the year 1200, written by Worcestershire poet Layamon about King Arthur and his knights. We are told how "summe beo driuen balles wide yeond tha feldes", or that 'some drove balls over the fields', which is interesting in that it is the first use of the word 'ball' in English, not Latin. But again it does not necessarily mean this game was anything like football (at least in a modern day sense, it sounds more like golf).

There is also pictorial evidence, which appears on a misericord carved into the wood of the choir stalls in Gloucester Cathedral. It is one of 58 images depicting different medieval activities, including wrestling, hunting, bull baiting and gambling – an unusual set of images for a religious building to have on show, but Michael Flannery believes they were there as a reminder to the congregation of the different activities that the church did not tolerate. In the picture that interests us, it is hard to tell to what exactly is going on, but it does look like two players are engaged in some kind of rugby or handball game.

Whatever the case, records of football played in 13th century England are so conspicuous by their absence that we can assume that even if the game did exist in any shape or form, it was not particularly widespread. We can make that assumption on the basis of the argument that references to other sporting activities abound in the texts of the period. Researching 13th century lawsuits, John Marshall Carter[5] found 74 different incidents involving individuals from peasants to a knight in which sport was somehow involved. Those that led to crimes and deaths through accidents or related quarrels included archery, falconry, fishing, hunting, riding, boxing, swimming, water tilting[6], ice skating and even chess. It was the latter that got the knight, a chap called Bernard, involved. He was playing with a non-noble called William of Wendere, but an argument broke out that led the commoner to wound the knight, which just was not the done thing in those days. It seems odd that even a crime committed over a

---

[4] Not that this was a commendable action. The story continues that "sodeynly there stode amonge them a fayre younge chylde," who told Cuthbert off for his "vayne playes" and burst into tears when Cuthbert refused to obey. The children "left theyre playe and comforted hym and then sodeynly he vanished away. Then he knew verily that it was an angel and fro that forth he lefte all such vayne playes and never used them more."

[5] John Marshall Carter *Journal of Sport History* study of *Sports and Recreations in Thirteenth-Century England: The Evidence of the Eyre and Coroners' Roll* (1998).

[6] Trying to knock your opponent out of a boat using a small lance.

chess game can find its way into the records, but there is not one reference in Carter's findings to anything like football.

He may have had no luck, but for a similar period the *Calendar of Inquisitions*, a fascinating record of untimely deaths, suggests that there were 13th century football fatalities.

In Staffordshire in April 1266 "Alan the hayward of Hertil and William of Wyndhul were playing at ball and both running together, trying to get the ball first. Each caught the other on the shoulder and fell to the ground. Alan fell on Walter's knife, which was in its sheath, and received a wound between the shoulder and the elbow, by no fault of Walter's. They got up and went on playing, as Alan did not feel much hurt, and afterwards went to the tavern and drank new ale together, and afterwards went peacefully home. The next day the arm swelled up, and Alan, saying this was due to the new ale, asked Walter to send for a leech to heal his arm. Treatment was applied, but he died the following Saturday; and Walter, seeing that he had died of the wound, absconded and has not returned."

14 years later, in 1280, the *Inquisitions* mention a strikingly similar misfortune in Northumberland whereby "Henry, son of William de Ellington, while playing at ball[7] at Ulgham on Trinity Sunday with David le Keu and many others ran against David and received an accidental wound from David's knife of which he died on the following Friday. They were both running to the ball, and ran against each other, and the knife hanging from David's belt stuck out so that the point through the sheath struck against Henry's belly, and the handle against David's belly. Henry was wounded right through the sheath and died by misadventure."

Pilae cum pedibus

Lines from 14th century literature believed to be possible allusions to football include the way Geoffrey Chaucer's *Knight's Tale* of around 1380 tells how a horse "rolleth under foot as doth a ball." But explaining that a ball rolls is not really telling us anything we didn't know already. Then there is the line from *Sir Gawain and the Green Knight*, written in the same era and which describes the delightful scene in which Gawain relieves the Knight of the burden of having to carry a head on his shoulders, and "the handsome head flew from the neck to the ground, many kicked as it rolled past them." Unperturbed by any of this, the scene ends with the Knight picking up his battered head, placing it under his shoulder and walking off. A cooler reaction from an unfairly penalised footballer you will be hard pressed to find, but despite being a great story, it is questionable as a valid example of an early football quote.

Kicking things is nothing new, even if they are heads. And we get more of that in *The Ledger Book of Vale Royal Abbey*, where records from Darnhill, Cheshire in 1321 describe the death of "John de Boddeworth, the abbot's servant, killed by the Brethren of Oldynton … who are the malefactors and disturbers of our peace who villainously slew a certain servant

---

[7] Or *ludens ad pilum* in the Latin original.

of our well-beloved in Christ ... and afterwards cut off his head, and carried it away with them, and kicked that head with their feet like a ball and made their sport therewith[8]." And, much as it can't have been very nice for poor Boddeworth, it is refreshing, with so many 'head-kicking' tales floating around soccer folklore, to find an example that was probably true[9]!

There was another untimely death in 1321. The place was Shouldham, Norfolk, and we learn of it from none other than a dispensation issued by Pope John XXII to pardon an accidental killer named "William de Spalding, canon of Scoldham of the order of Sempringham. During the game at ball as he kicked the ball, a lay friend of his, also called William, ran against him and wounded himself on a sheathed knife carried by the canon, so severely that he died within six days. Dispensation is granted, as no blame is attached to William de Spalding, who, feeling deeply the death of his friend, and fearing what might be said by his enemies, has applied to the Pope." But apart from letting a very grateful William off the hook, what is unique about this little treasure is that it is the first text to irrefutably state that the ball was kicked[10], and hence the first recorded incidence, at least in Britain, that can be linked to modern day soccer without too much need for imaginative gap-filling.

Such frivolity infuriated Robert de Braybrooke, the Bishop of London, who wrote in 1395 that "there are also others – insolent, idle persons answering to no-one, troublemakers by nature, who would rather cause mischief than make themselves useful, who ... play ball-games inside and outside the church, and engage in other destructive games, breaking or seriously damaging the glass windows and the stone carvings in the church ... and also expose their souls to grave danger."

He was not alone in his concern. The first person on surviving record to issue a writ to prohibit football in England was King Edward II's Lord Mayor of London, Nicholas de Farndone, in 1314. Decrees in those days were still written in the language the Norman conquerors used, French, which probably wouldn't have helped get the message across to the laymen any better than it would have done in Latin, but the translation of that historic document proclaims that "forasmuch as there is great noise in the city caused by hustling over large foot balls[11] in the fields of the public from which many evils might arise which God forbid: we command and forbid on behalf of the king, on pain of imprisonment, such game to be used in the city in the future."

---

[8] Or, in the original "*as modum pilae cum pedibus suis conculcaverunt.*"

[9] In a similar example, "the said Peter or Patrick Inglis also killed one James White, struck off his head with an axe, brought it to Newmilns, and played at football with it. He killed him at Little Blackwood, the foresaid year 1685." Cited in John Henderson Thomson *A Cloud of witnesses for the royal prerogatives of Jesus Christ* (1714).

[10] The Latin original says he was playing *ad pilam* and struck the ball *cum pede* (with the foot).

[11] Or the far cooler sounding *rageries de grosses pelotes* in the original.

Edward II didn't have much success with his prohibition, or ruling in general as it happened, and after a particularly shoddy performance against the Scots at the Battle of Bannockburn, he was benched, and his son Edward III came on in his place.

Like father like son, Edward junior also attacked ball games in 1349, where an important distinction was made between games being played with the feet, with the hands, and with a stick when he declared that "moreover we ordain that you prohibit under penalty of imprisonment all and sundry from such stone, wood and iron throwing; handball, football, or hockey; coursing and cock-fighting, or other such idle games." He felt justified in doing so because unless folk used their spare time to practice using bows and arrows, his realm would "soon, it would appear, be void of archers[12]."

In fact, Edward III's declaration came just three years after his longbowmen had devastated the French at the Battle of Crecy, so it was probably his rival, King Charles V of France who had more reason to be worried. Indeed, Charles made a comment of his own to complain about the popularity of *jeu de paume* in his own nation, along with other games that "do nothing to teach the manly art of bearing arms."

Neither monarch had much success at outlawing these diversions. Throughout his fifty-year reign, Edward III continued with his crusade that every able-bodied man "shall in his sports use arrows or pellets and bolts", with further decrees against playing *ad pilam* in 1363 and 1365. He died of illness in 1376 and was succeeded by his ten-year-old grandson, Richard II, who in 1389 felt compelled to continue the royal campaign to stamp out footy when he decreed that "all playing at tennise, football, and other games called corts, dice, casting of the stone, kailes, and other such importune games" were henceforth illegal in his kingdom, apparently unaware that his predecessors had already been saying the same for years with limited success.

The ffooteballepleyers

Sussex in the south of England is our first port of call in the 14th century, where Magoun unearthed a document in which the locals recollected a series of unfortunate circumstances at local baptisms. On August 24, 1403, immediately after the christening of a certain William Selwyne in the village of Selmeston , a game resembling football was played, in which one of the unlucky number broke his leg. And if that wasn't bad enough, the very next year, Robert Tauk's baptism ended in remarkably similar tragedy, when John Coumbes from the nearby village of Chudham broke his leg in a game of ball.

And then, fanfare, fanfare, in 1409 we have what is officially regarded as the oldest known use of term 'football' in its English language form, and it had royal patronage by way of a

---

[12] I can't resist quoting Norman Giller, who suggests "there are those in the here and now who would like to see a similar proclamation made banning the playing of computer games, so that the youths of Britain can get back to learning how to control a ball with their feet rather than surrendering playing fields to foreign invaders."

proclamation issued by Henry IV to forbid "hokkyng on hokkedayes[13]," while money was to be levied for the practice of the games called "foteball" and "cokthresshyng[14]" on occasion of marriages.

And Henry IV meant it. On March 4 of that year, eight parishioners of St Dionis Backchurch in London were told that "none of them would in future collect money for a football" and that "they would not thrash any hen or capon or any other bird in the streets and lanes of the city, under penalty of £20." It would grieve the medieval animal rights activists to think that six centuries later the Spanish would still be getting away with bullfighting.

Banning football was as essential an ingredient of sitting on the English throne as organising wars with the Scots and French. Out went the House of Lancaster, and in came the House of York, and Edward IV made it clear that "no person shall practice any unlawful games, but that every strong and able-bodied person shall practice with bow for the reason that the national defence depends upon such bowmen." Edward IV was never defeated in battle, and perhaps it was his ban on football that did the trick.

Out went the House of York, and in came the House of Tudor. Henry VII placed a ban on football, and one of Henry VIII's statutes was not taken out of the books until 1845, although it is mere coincidence that that was also the year that the rules of the game were written at Rugby School.

These palatial decrees were supported by more local edicts. There was a 12d fine for playing football in Halifax in 1450. It wasn't quite so bad in Leicester, where the fine was just 4d in 1467. And in London in 1471, it was announced that "complaints have been made as to football being played … the council feel impelled to express their strong opinion that the game of football is quite unsuitable … and ought not to be encouraged."

These prohibitions of football may seem laughable to us now, but such medieval attitudes stayed with us much longer than one might be aware. That last London quote was not really made in 1471 at all, but 350 years later in 1921, and was issued by that fine bastion of gender equality, the Football Association. It actually referred, if we fill in the dotted spaces, to its objection to "football being played by women" due to it being "quite unsuitable for females."

It added that "the Council request the clubs belonging to the Association to refuse the use of their grounds for such matches." In deference of the ban, the English Ladies FA was formed nonetheless, and played its games on rugby pitches. There were around 200 clubs in England by the time the FA finally endorsed the women's game as late as 1973. They took their time.

---

[13] This had nothing to do with the game of hockey. Hocktide was a medieval festival in much of England. Henry IV outlawed it due to the disturbances it caused, and by the time Elizabeth I tried to re-establish the tradition in the 17th century, it was largely forgotten. It's possible that the game of hockey got its name from this festival, but there is no evidence to prove it.

[14] A most intellectually inspiring form of entertainment whereby a rooster was tied to a post and participants would throw stones to kill it.

Going back to the Middle Ages, and we find football was also being enjoyed north of the border, but James I was as adamant as his peers in England, who had held him prisoner for 19 years, to put a stop to the fun and made it patently clear in 1424 when he "forbiddis that na man play at the fute-ball, under the paine of fiftie schillings." That was quite a sum of money at the time.

James' son and namesake, James II, saw fit to proclaim a decree against football in 1457 and ordered that each man should instead "schutte sex schottes at the least", referring to archery rather than early porn flicks. There was a tuppence fine for anyone that failed to comply, the money being given "to them that cummis to the bowe-makers, to make them drink." What he was trying to say was that any man that did his duty by practicing a bit of archery had the right to make a claim for beer money from those that didn't. You can imagine the kind of arguments a system like that would have caused down the pub.

After James II came James III, and his son in turn, whose name there are no prizes for guessing, yup, James IV, continued the Stuart family tradition by issuing a largely unheeded statute in 1491 that "in na place of this realme ther be used futeball, golfe, or other sik unprofitable sportes."

James IV, however, may have been something of a hypocrite. The evidence against his name is found in the Doig family records, which tell us how a certain James Doig, who worked as his monarch's 'groom of wardrobe', was given a sum of money on April 11, 1497 " to by fut ballis to the King." We have no idea why James was ordering his servant to purchase a set of footballs, but it does lead us to suspect that in doing so, he was breaking one of his own laws.

An anonymous chronicler writing sometime towards the end of the 15th century described a game witnessed at Cawston in Nottinghamshire. Translated from the Latin, the text explains how a "game at which they had met for common recreation is called by some the foot-ball game. It is one in which young men, in country sport, propel a huge ball not by throwing it into the air but by striking it and rolling it along the ground, and that not with their hands but with their feet." This is the earliest reference to English soccer, as opposed to what might be considered rugby, in which the use of the hands is clearly illegal. Sadly, our unnamed scribe was not massively enchanted by a sport he considered "abominable enough, and, in my judgement at least, more common, undignified, and worthless than any other kind of game, rarely ending without some loss, accident or disadvantage to the players themselves."

Rather than being played cross-country or around the streets of some poor unsuspecting urban setting, the game was limited to a particular zone in which the "boundaries have been marked." Further evidence of more structured football appears in the *Crafts and Fraternities* section of the annual accounts of the Brewers' Company of London for the years 1421-1423. It turns out the guild was regularly hiring out their hall to the "ffooteballepleyers" for the princely sum of 20 pence a shot. It is not clear whether they used the hall to play football, or whether it was a kind of clubhouse, but the inclusion of these mysterious footballers under 'fraternities' has led to speculation that they belonged to the oldest club on record.

Further sanctioning of this supposedly outlawed sport was going on at Bicester, Oxfordshire, where the prior was providing sundry gifts of 4 dinar to the footballers on occasion of the St Katherine's Day celebrations, which may be the first occurrence of a prize or cash incentive being awarded in football. It certainly wouldn't be the last.

Camping it up

Over in East Anglia they were playing a football-like game known by a variety of names, including campball, campan and campyon[15]. It was first referenced by the poet John Lydgate around 1430 when he used the metaphor "lyck a large campynge balle" to describe the sensation of being thrown out into the void. The first ever Latin to English dictionary, the *Promptorium Parvulorum* of 1440, provides a definition of it as "campan, or playar at foott balle, pediluson; campyon, or champion" and one of the characters in the 1659 comedy *Blind Beggar of Bethnal Green* by John Day said "I am Tom Stroud of Hurling, I'll play a gole at camp-ball", which may mean he was the goalie, but seems more likely to be the first known reference to the action of scoring a goal.

In his 1466 *History of Hawstead*, John Cullum makes a brief reference to a "camping-fighte" and in his 1843 re-edition of the tome, Albert Way adds the footnote that "camping-land appropriated to this game occurs, in several instances, in authorities of the fifteenth century." We know of at least one example of this when in 1472, the rector of Swaffham, Norfolk was more than happy to allow a field next to his church to be used by the camp ball players. The 'camping-pightel' where the games were played over five hundred years ago, apparently as a traditional activity to follow the Sunday church service, is still there today. David Dymond[16] identifies no fewer than 105 such fields on old maps and documents all over the east of England, usually located close to inns or churches, and at Boxford in Suffolk, they had even erected a grandstand by 1750 and were charging a 6d entry fee and timing the game using a stopwatch and French horn – all of which was remarkably ahead of its time. The *Ipswich Journal* in October 1754 mentions a game played 10-a-side at Eye and there was a crowd of 6000 to watch a game in Newmarket that was reported in the *Norwich Mercury* in 1751.

It was not until 1823, and thanks to Major Edward Moor, that we have any extensive description of camp-ball, by which time it may have lost all resemblance to its medieval

---

[15] It has been claimed that 'camp' was an old word for 'kick'. Patricia Shaw Fairman observes how Thomas Drant's translation from the Latin of Horace's *Epistles* uses the expression "and campe you with theire feet." Another theory maintains that it was so called because it was played on army camps, while yet another plausible claim insists it derived from the Middle English word *campen*, meaning 'to contend'. The most likely argument is that 'camp ball' took its name from the Latin *campus* for field or the French *champ* of the same origin. In Joseph Strutt's section on football in 1801, he notes that "camp-ball, I conceive, is only another denomination for foot-ball, and is so called because it was played to the greatest advantage in an open country."
[16] In his 1990 article in *Rural History*, *A Lost Social Institution: The Camping Close.*

origins anyway. In the 19th century, it was played on an area roughly the size of a modern football pitch, and the goalposts were 15 yards wide and made by simply piling up the players' clothes! Teams of 10 to 15 players lined up in their respective halves, and the ball, likened to a cricket ball, was thrown in by "an indifferent spectator. The shock of the first onset to catch the falling ball is very great, and the player who seizes it speeds home pursued by his opponents, through whom he has to make his way, aided by the jostlings of his own side. If caught and held, he throws the ball (but must in no case give it) to a comrade, who, if it be not arrested in its course, or be jostled away by his eager foes, catches it and hurries home, winning the notch or snotch if he continues to carry (not throw) it between the goals[17]." That is basically rugby, and the fact that this text was written in 1823 is significant. This was the very year that, less than 100 miles away, William Webb Ellis supposedly invented a new sport at Rugby School.

Moor continues by saying that "a holder of the ball caught with it in his possession loses a snotch. At the loss of each of these the game recommences, after a breathing time. Seven or nine snotches are the game, and these it will sometimes take two or three hours to win. At times a large football was used, and the game was then called kicking camp." Moor is telling us that there were two different games, a rugby-like carrying game with a small ball and a soccer-like kicking game with a big ball, half a century before these two codes 'officially' split.

Moor adds that the game "if played with shoes on was termed savage camp ... the players were not disposed to treat one another gently." A few years later, in 1830, Robert Forby echoes the violent nature of the game by describing "black eyes and bloody noses, broken heads or shins[18]." But that was nothing compared to what appears in a re-edition of Forby's book a decade later, when the Rev WT Spurdens adds that "I have heard of old persons speak of a celebrated camping, Norfolk against Suffolk on Diss Common, with 300 on each side. The Suffolk men, after 14 hours, were victorious. Nine deaths were the result of the contest." Whether that really happened, or whether it was just a slightly exaggerated local tale, we cannot say, but it's tempting to go for the latter.

Camp-ball may have been booming in the 1830s, but the game would be yet another victim of the growing popularity of standardised football. Tamer sporting ideals led to the introduction of 'civil play', a softly-softly attitude that the camp-ball puritans shunned. Interest waned. It wasn't long before Norwich City and Ipswich Town came along, and camp-ball was forgotten forever.

---

[17] Edward Moor *Suffolk words and phrases; or, An attempt to collect the lingual localisms of that county* (Woodbridge, 1823).

[18] Robert Forby *The vocabulary of East Anglia; an attempt to record the vulgar tongue of the twin sister counties, Norfolk and Suffolk, as it existed in the last twenty years of the eighteenth century, and still exists; with proof of its antiquity from etymology and authority* (JB Nichols and Son, 1830).

Poet's corner

Renowned poet Alexander Barclay saw fit to put his feelings not just for football, but also for the actual ball into verse, and told posterity in his 1508 *Eclogues* how:

"They get the bladder and blowe it great and thin
With many beanes or peason put within
It ratleth, soundeth, and shineth clere and fayre
While it is throwen and caste up in the ayre
Ece one contendeth and hath a great delite
With foot and hande the bladder for to smite
If it fall to the grounde they lifte it up agayne
This wise to labour they count it for no paine
Renning and leaping the drive away the colde
The sturdy plowmen, lustie, stronge and bolde
Overcommeth the winter with driving the foote-ball
Forgetting labour and many a grievous fall."

And ain't it just cute to learn that peas were once called 'peasons'? Not long after, there was another attempt, this time anonymous, to blend football and prose, this time from north of the border:

"Brissit, brawnis and broken banis,
Stryf, discorde and waistie wanis,
Cruikit in eild syn halt withall,
Thir are the bewties of the fute ball."

As it's hard enough understanding a Glaswegian in this day and age, we'll tidy it up a bit to get 'bruised muscles and broken bones, strife, discord and futile blows, all crooked in old age withal, these are the beauties of football.'

Around the same time, another Scottish poet, Gavin Douglas, had the same strife and discord in mind when he wrote how:

"This broken shin that swells and will not be relieved,
Take it to him; he broke it at ball,
And tell him it will be his reward.
Take the whole of this bruised arm to him."

It may sound very manly, but as early as 1580 we get our first suggestion that women were playing football too. In a play written that year by Sir Philip Sidney called *A Dialogue Between Two Shepherds*, one of said duo of sheep herders comes up with a most unexpected quote.

"Tyme there is for all, my mother often sayes.
When she, with skirts tuckt very hy, with girles at football playes."

And one of the most fascinating literary references to football appears in the popular *The Ballad of Sir Hugh*[19], which opens:

"Four and twenty bony boys
Were playing at the ba'
And by it came sweet Sir Hugh
And he played o'er them a'
He kicked the ba' with his right foot
He catched it wi' his knee
And thro' the Jews' window
He gard the bony ba' flee."

The ball having landed in the Jew's house, young Hugh is then invited in to collect it and ends up being sacrificed. It's just one of many ghastly tales of the hideous crimes that Jews used to get up to in medieval times, all part of the anti-Semitic propaganda that was rife not just at the time but for further centuries to come.

Fout baule to football

By the 16th century, merchandising had already found its way into footy, for there were now specially designed boots to play it in. In 2004, clothes historian Maria Hayward discovered an order dated 1524 for a pair of handmade leather football boots worth four shillings and stitched to measure by a certain Cornelius Johnson. The finding made the international news. Because of all people, the order had been placed by the grand master of love you one day, chop your head off the next, Henry VIII. Though famed in later life for being an obese gluttonous pig with a putrid leg and an obsession with finding a vessel for his male heir, in his younger days Old Coppernose was an accomplished wrestler, hunter, fencer and tennis player. But to learn that his shopping list once included "45 velvet pairs and 1 leather pair for football" does come as something as a surprise, for it was anything but the kind of sport deemed fit for the gentry, especially when a quarter of a century later, in 1548, our Henry would add his name to the list of English leaders who lumped football in with dice, cards and other such evils as pastimes unsuitable for his realm, banning it on the premise that it was inciting riots.

Shoemakers didn't just make boots, but balls too, and sensed the marketing benefits of promoting football. Such was the case in Chester with its game played "always tyme out of mann's remembrance", where the custom detailed in a 1533 edict stated the shoemakers would "upon Goteddsday[20] at the crosse upon the Rood Dee, before the mayor of the cittie

---

[19] The precise origins of the song are unknown, but an extract from it appears in Latin in the 13th century works of poet Matthew Paris. Although the song probably originated in Lincoln, England, it was largely popularised in Scotland, and different versions of it managed to survive all the way through history, and received a new lease of life when Steeleye Span recorded it in 1975.
[20] Shrove Tuesday.

offer unto the company of Drapcrs an homage, a ball of lether, cauled a fout baule, of the value of 3s 4d, which was played for by the shoemakers and saddlers."

But the fun was over by 1540, when they were ordered to bring the ball "to the house of the Mayor or either of the Sherriffs. Much harm was done, some having their bodies bruised and crushed, some their armes, heads, legges broken, some otherwise maimed and in peril of their life."

The tradition of donating a ball was replaced by that of a silver bell, also valued and probably not by coincidence at 3s 4d, which would be presented "as a reward for the best runner that day upon the aforesaid Rodehee." By 'runner' they meant horse, and this is claimed to be the founding of the Chester Races, the oldest racing meet that still uses the same venue today[21].

The 16th century also brings our first surviving relic of medieval football outside of the printed word, and it is a ball, and a fine example it is too, being made of wonderfully preserved leather that once encased a pig's bladder. In an example of what would be a common problem in the urban sporting environment, the ball was kicked or thrown onto the roof of the Queen's Chamber at Stirling Castle in Scotland sometime between 1537 and 1542. We know this because it would end up lost behind a wall that was constructed by order of James V. It wasn't retrieved until quite a bit later, 1981, and now sits proudly in the Smith Gallery in Stirling.

Stirling is not the only castle with an intriguing 16th century footy story to tell. Mary Queen of Scots was imprisoned at Carlisle in 1568, where she famously embroidered the fact that her "end was her beginning" on her cloth of state. While she was there, a letter quilled by Francis Knollys describes how "20 of her retinue played at football before her for two hours very strongly, nimbly, and skilfully" something he put down to "the smalness of theyr balle", That's interesting, because the ball found at Stirling is also considerably smaller than historians had generally assumed early footballs to have been.

For further intrigue, old maps of Carlisle Castle clearly show an area of land in its vicinity called the 'Castle Soceries'. Is this mysterious name indicating that this was the place where the troops played soccer before the incarcerated sovereign and is hence associated to origins of the word 'soccer'? Unfortunately it's more a case of if you search history for long enough, you will probably be able to prove anything, as the explanation that the word 'soccer' is a late 19th century corruption of the word 'Association' is too convincing to debunk.

Mary may have found football entertaining, but 16th century scholar Sir Thomas Elyot did not. His much-quoted condemnation of football in his 1531 *Boke named The Governour* deemed it to "be utterly abiected of al noble men … wherin is nothinge but beastly furie and exstreme violence; wherof procedeth hurte, and consequently rancour and malice do remain with them that be wounded, wherfore it is to be put in perpetual silence." His text also

---

[21] York is actually an older meet, but has not always been raced on the same course.

includes fervent disapproval of seemingly all things physical, be they tennis, quoits or skittles. In fact, you would be tempted to write the guy off as a bigoted oaf it wasn't for the fact that he was also the author of the ground-breaking *In Defense of Good Women*, which argued for better education for ladies and did a lot to push the feminist movement in the right direction. Elyot also somewhat redeemed himself in football's eyes a few years later when he admitted in his *Castell of Helth* of 1534 that 'footeball' did at least provide "vehement exercise." Of course, in the interim, it may also have been pointed out to him that none other than his monarch was playing the game he had just written off as being "abject of all noble men", and with Henry VIII's reputation for sending folk to the chopping block, he had reassessed his judgement in order to, literally, save his neck.

Henry's daughter, Elizabeth I, reigned from 1558 to 1603, which may have done wonders for rural tourism by arranging public burnings of Catholics in country villages, but did little to help football's cause. Under Good Queen Bess, there were two proclamations made by the Corporation of the City of London (1572 and 1581) that "no foteballe play be used or suffered within the City of London and the liberties thereof upon pain of imprisonment" and the *Middlesex County Records* of 1566 detail a court hearing against a group of Woxbridge residents "with unknown malefactors to the number of one hundred" who had "assembled themselves unlawfully and playd a certain unlawful game called foote-ball, by means of which unlawful game there was amongst them a great affray likely to result in homicides and serious accidents." There was an obvious lack of synonyms for 'unlawful' in the Middlesex speech of the time.

Five years later, and a coroner's report from nearby Sowthemyms tells the story of a death by "playing with other persons at foote-ball in the field." It all took off when "Roger Ludford and a certain Simon Maltus, of the sd parish, yomen, came to the ground, and that Roger Ludford cried out, 'Cast hym over the hedge', indicating that he meant Nicholas Martyn, who replied, 'Come thou and do yt.' That thereupon Roger Ludforde ran towards the ball with the intention to kick it, whereupon Nicholas Martyn with the fore-part of his right arm and Richard Turvey with the fore-part of his left arm struck Roger Ludforde on the fore-part of the body under the breast, giving him a mortal blow and concussion of which he died within a quarter of an hour, and that Nicholas and Richard in this manner feloniously slew the said Roger."

There were two more mortal victims of ball play in Oxfordshire, where the parish registers for the village of North Moreton in May 1595 explain how "Gunter's son and ye Gregorys fell together by ye years at football. Old Gunter drew his dagger and both broke their heads, and they died both within a fortnight after." Those little devils were no better than an Essex man, Thomas Whistock, who in 1599 "with nyne other of his fellows … being the sabaothe did play at an unlawfull game called the fote bale whereon drew bludshedd contrary to her Majestis peace."

Condemnation and commendation

The footballers weren't helping matters, and were often fully deserving of the bad reputation they were gaining. And there was never a bunch of people keener to drive that point home than the Puritans, who were renowned for spreading anything but joy wherever they travelled[22].

In 1583, champion killjoy Philip Stubbes wrote *The Anatomie of Abuses*, a scathing attack on just about anything that might sound like fun, including the "reding of mery bookes." He pleaded "Lord, remove these exercises from the Sabbath. Any exercise which withdraweth from godliness, either upon the Sabaoth or any other day, is wicked and to be forbiden. Now who is so grosly blinde that seeth not that these aforesaid exercises not only withdraw us from godlinesse and virtue, but also haile and allure us to wickednesse and sin?"

Dancing around the maypole was certainly not on, something he felt was just a pretext for a sexual orgy. "Again May, Whitsunday, or other time all the young men and maids, old men and wives, run gadding over night to the woods, groves, hills, and mountains, where they spend all night in pleasant pastimes … The chiefest jewel they bring from thence is their Maypole, which they bring home with great veneration ... And thus being reared up with handkerchiefs and flags hovering on the top ... they fall to dance about it, like as the heathen people did at the dedication of the Idols ... Of forty, three-score, or a hundred maids going to the wood over-night, there have scarcely the third part of them returned home again undefiled[23]."

But his disgust for all things athletic went into overdrive when it came to "football playing", which he brilliantly considered "might rather be called a friendly kinde of fight than a play or a recreation; a bloody and murthering practise, than a felowly sporte or pastime. For dooth not every one lye in waight for his adversarie, seeking to overthrowe him, and to picke him on his nose, though it be upon hard stones? In ditch or dale, in valley or hil, or what place soever it be, hee careth not, so he can have him down … By this means, sometimes their necks are broken, sometimes their backs, sometime their legs, sometime their armes; sometime one part thrust out of joynt, sometime another; sometime the noses gush out with blood, sometime their eyes start out, and sometimes hurt in one place, sometimes in another. But whosoever scapeth away the best, goeth not scot free, but is either sore wounded, craised, and bruseed, so as he dyeth of it, or else scapeth very hardly. And no mervaile, for they have the sleights to meet one betwixt two, to dashe him against the hart with their elbowes, to hit him under the short ribbes with their griped fists and with their knees to catch him upon the hip, and to pick him on his neck, with a hundred such murdering devices; and hereof groweth envy, malice, rancour, choler, hatred, displeasure, enmite, and

---

[22] Although historians that blame the Puritans entirely for the anti-football movement are being a bit harsh. As we have seen, there had been footy bans before, and there would be many more after.

[23] With regard to maypoles, Stubbes may have been exaggerating things a tad, although some historians claim to have observed seasonal patterns in Elizabethan birth rates.

what not els: and sometimes fighting, brawling, contention, quarrel-picking, murther, homicide, and great effusion of blood. Is this murthering play, now, an exercise for the Sabath day? Is this a Christian dealing, for one brother to mayme and hurt another, and that upon prepensed malice or set purpose? Is this to do to another as we would wish another to doo to us? God make us more careful over the bodyes of our brethren!"

Somebody who would have agreed with many of Stubbes' words was Richard Mulcaster, a former Eton pupil who set new standards in the pedagogy of Latin, Greek and Hebrew and became high master of St Paul's School in London in 1596, where he also turned his mind to football.

Mulcaster has been called 'the greatest 16th century advocate of football', but in one of 45 chapters of a textbook on exercise, which also covered such terrific athletic pursuits as "loude and soft reading" and "holding the breath," he shunned "footeball play" as a game that "is now commonly used, with thronging of a rude multitude, with bursting of shinnes, and breaking of legges. It be neither civil, neither worthy the name of any traine to health[24]."

It was not football as it was, but football as it could be, that Mulcaster felt would make for a very fine game indeed. He was centuries ahead of his time when he remarked on the need for coaches and umpires, saying "wherin any man may evidently see the use of the trayning maister. For if one stand by, which can judge of the play, and is judge over the parties, and hath authoritie to commande in the place, all those inconveniences have bene, I know, and wilbe I am sure very lightly redressed, nay they will never entermedle in the matter, neither shall there be complaint, where ther is no cause." Of course, he was wrong and he was right. Having someone calling the shots would improve things no end, but the "neither shall there be complaint" bit, as we can now safely say with the benefit of considerable hindsight, was just a little bit over-optimistic.

His ideas get better, for why not play with "some smaller number with such overlooking, sorted into sides and standings, not meeting with their bodies so boisterously to trie their strength: nor shouldring or shuffing one another so barbarously." Limiting the number of players? Getting them to play in positions, or 'standings'? Rules to stop people from getting hurt? He was imagining what football would indeed one day become.

Unlike the evils most of his contemporaries associated to the game, Mulcaster felt it was positively oozing with potential benefits to the health, seeing "much good to the body, by the chiefe use of the armes. And being so used, the footeball strengtheneth and brawneth the whole body, and by provoking superfluities downeward it dischargeth the head, and upper parts, it is good for the bowels, and driveth downe the stone and gravel from both the bladder and the kidneys."

Mulcaster also makes a distinction between the aforementioned 'footeball' and the "kind I call the armeball, which was invented in the kingdom of Naples, not many yeares agoe, and

---

[24] Richard Mulcaster *Positions Wherein Those Primitive Circumstances Be Examined, Which Are Necessarie for the Training up of Children* (1581).

answereth most of the olde games." Was he saying that 'footeball' was so called because it involved kicking the ball and that 'armeball' was something more like rugby? And could the Naples reference have something to do with *calcio storico*?

Probably not. In Mulcaster's game, we are told the arm "is fensed with a wodden brace", so what he almost certainly meant is something like *pallone col bracciale*, forms of which are still played in Italy today, and which involve hitting a ball back and forth with a wooden cylinder, called a *bracciale*, worn over the forearm[25].

Nevertheless, the fact that Mulcaster has no reservations about accepting that a game played in England had been directly imported from Italy lends a lot of credence to those who suspect that *calcio storico*, which rose to prominence in the same century, may have had an influence on modern football.

---

[25] *Pallone* (for which there are rules dating back to 1555) and the similar Tuscan sport of *palla* (quite conceivably inherited from the Romans) are just part of a family of games played around Western Europe, which generally involve hitting a ball back and forth, with either the bare palm, bare knuckles or wearing or holding some kind of padding around the hand. *Jeu de paume* in France goes back to the 14th century, and like the Italian games, starting using simple rackets from around the 15th century and eventually developed into what we know today as tennis. The Frisian region of Holland has a similar game known locally as *kaatsen*, where the Permanent Committee tournament, which has been held annually since 1854, is claimed to be longest running ball sport competition in the world. You also have *parkspel*, which is played on the Swedish island of Gottland, and the Basque *esku-pilota*, the handball variety of *pelota*, in which a hard ball is rapped back and forth using the knuckles, a mad sport if ever there was one, which understandably leaves players with horribly swollen hands. The Valencian region has its own games, the oldest being *llargues*. Since 1993, the rules, tactics and equipment of all these different sports have been combined into the 'international game' for the sake of a world championship, with several Latin American countries participating too.

16 RUSTICAL DIVERSIONS
British football in the seventeenth and eighteenth centuries

God bless football

The fact that football managed to survive being the victim of its own particular medieval witch-hunt should come as no surprise. How on earth did they really think they could ban something that was as much a part of human nature as fishing, swimming or climbing trees? Balls had been invented and people were going to play with them, as observed by playwright William Davenant in London in 1634, where he writes on "one of your heroic games called football; which I conceive (under your favour) not very conveniently civil in the streets … Yet it argues your courage, much like your military pastime of throwing at cocks, since you have long allowed these two valiant exercises in the streets." Just what it is he finds valiant about chucking rocks at chooks is hard to understand, but judging by his tone, he was probably demonstrating that the art of sarcasm was alive and well in the 17th century.

As the 17th and 18th centuries went by, not only did many of the men in codpieces learn to tolerate football, but some even came to endorse it. James I became King in 1603, taking over from the childless Elizabeth. As it happened he was already King of Scotland, which would pave the way to the union of the two countries. He wasn't massively popular, and two years into his reign he came close to copping it when a certain Robert Catesby sent his pal Guy Fawkes to try to blow him up. For football's sake, it was a good thing the plot failed, as James was quite fond of the game.

John Aubrey claims that in 1615, when James I was visiting Cotefield in Wiltshire, the local minister, George Ferebe, "entertained his Majesty with a foot-ball match of his own parishioners. This parish in those dayes would have challenged all England for musique, foot-ball, and ringing." Far from being offended by what he saw, "for this entertainment his Majesty made him one of his chaplains[1]."

This was the same year of 1615 that the *Middlesex Sessions Rolls* were saying that "great disorders and tumults doe often arise and happen within the streetes and lanes neere adjoyninge to ye Cittye of London by playinge at the foote-ball" and that all constables "doe from tyme to tyme represse and restrayne all manner of footeball-playe in the lanes and streetes", and yet the King himself was well impressed by all sports, and was shocked on his first tour of England to learn of "the prohibiting and unlawful punishing of our good people for using their lawful recreations and honest exercises upon Sundays."

---

[1] John Aubrey *Memoires of Naturall Remarques in the County of Wilts* (1685).

That is the opening line to his 1618 *Book of Sports*, which wasn't really a book at all, but was an edict written as a backlash against mainly Puritan bans. James' reasons were that prohibiting games "cannot but breed a great discontentment in our people's hearts" and is just the kind of thing to fuel rebellion. And anyway, such exercises "make their bodies more able for war" rather than spending their time in "filthy tippling and drunkenness" which merely "breeds a number of idle and discontented speeches in their ale-houses." The paragraph concludes by asking "when shall the common people have leave to exercise, if not upon the Sundays and Holy-days, seeing they must apply their labor and win their living in all working days?" Never were wiser words uttered by a monarch.

As well as offering proof that the missing 'u' in words like valor, favor and here 'labor' was an English thing long before an American thing, the *Book of Sports* was a major boost for English leisure. James insisted that "after the end of divine service our good people not be disturbed, letted or discouraged from any lawful recreation, such as dancing, either men or women, archery for men, leaping, vaulting or any other such harmless recreation, nor from having any May-games, Whitsun Ales and Morris dances and the setting up of May-poles and other sports."

Funnily enough, football doesn't get a mention in the *Book of Sports*. But neither is it included in the list of sports that James I exempted, namely bear and bull-baitings (no complaints about that), interludes (bawdy comic sketches), and bowling (an odd inclusion, but that was because bowling was a strictly aristocratic game, and bizarrely forbidden for play by "the meaner sort of people"). There was a condition though – you could only play games if you had first done your duty and been to the divine service, for heathens that did not were "unworthy of any lawful recreation."

He may not have disapproved of football *per se*, but James I certainly didn't play it himself, or consider it the kind of thing any aspiring member of royalty should get up to. This we know because of his 1599 treatise *Basilikon Doron*, which is a detailed account of what a King should or should not do, written in the form of a letter to his oldest son and heir, Henry. He considered it "most requisite for a King to exercise his engine" but vehemently declared how "I debarre all rough and violent exercises, as the footeball; meeter for laming", suggesting instead "running, leaping, wrastling, fencing, dancing, and playing at the caitch or tennise, archerie, palle maille, and such like other faire and pleasant fieldgames", although the "honourablest and most commendable games that yee can use, are on horsebacks[2]."

Prince Henry never got to put what he learned from *Basilikon Doron* into practice, for he was outlived by his father, and the crown went to his younger brother, the eventual Charles II. The Merrie Monarch, as he was known, certainly had a jolly old life, happily admitting to have fathered 12 illegitimate children by various mistresses. He also demonstrated his

---

[2] Oxford University vicar Robert Burton echoes this in his 1621 *Anatomy of Melancholy* when he calls quoits, leaping, wrestling and football "common recreations of the country folk", while horse riding, hunting and shooting are for gentlemen.

approval not only of sport but also the gambling that went with it! Tennis, yachting, bowls and ice skating were all among his stately passions, although it was horse racing that he particularly went in for, which would have mightily pleased his father.

What most interests us, however, was 1681, when on the meadows near Windsor Castle he gathered together some men of the Royal Household and decked them out in red to take on the Duke of Albemarle's servants, wearing blue, at a wrestling match. Bets were laid, and the King's men were soundly beaten, and so they decided to get some fencing duels going instead. Once again, Albemarle's men came out tops and the monarch was further out of pocket, but not discouraged, he decided they should play football next. Yet more bets, and "the goals staked out, and the ball placed in the middle, the Duke held up an handkerchief over the ball, the letting fall of which was the signal to give the start[3]." There would be yet more humiliation for the King, but he didn't seem to mind in the slightest, and in fact "seemed highly pleased with that day's divertisement." Well, it's probably not so tough when it's the Privy Purse you're playing around with.

This was not the only case of the wealthier classes getting pleasure out of football. John Chamberlain in a 1600 invitation to a friend to visit his Knebworth estate said "you may do well, if you have any idle time, to play the goode fellow and come to see our matches at football, for that and bowling wilbe our best entertainment."

And Thomas Dekker's 1607 play *The Whore of Babylon* suggests it was even possible to see gentlemen taking on the lower classes. At one point, the excellently named Plain Dealing meets some lawyers, and "asked one of them if they were going to foot-ball. 'Yes' said he, 'doe you not see these countrey fellowes? We are against them.'"

Football wasn't all bad. In the Lake District, the *Boke off Kirkbie Kendall* of 1641 said nothing about forbidding football, but merely wanted to do something about the number of windows that were getting broken because of it. It seems reasonable enough to demand "that whosoever do play football in the street and break any windows shall forfeit … 3s 4d for every window."

In that football-friendly corner of England, James Walvin claims tolerance of football reached extraordinary heights from 1672, when the Reverend Thomas Robinson was appointed rector at Ousby. "It was his common practice, after Sunday afternoon prayers, to accompany the leading men of his parish to the adjoining alehouse, where each spent a penny and only a penny; that done, he set the younger sort to play at football (of which he was a great promoter) and other rustical diversions." That's the kind of vicar you want, one who follows his service by marching the congregation down to the pub and then gets them all playing footy.

---

[3] James Peller Malcolm *Anecdotes Of The Manners And Customs Of London From The Roman Invasion To The Year 1700* (1811).

Cornish pastime

Another big fan of sport, football included, was Oliver Cromwell, considered by many Brits to be one of the nation's greatest ever leaders and by most Irish as the perpetrator of genocide. James Heath, who studied with him at Cambridge in the 1610s, described him as "one of the chief matchmakers and players of football, cudgels, or any other boysterous sport or game[4]."

In 1654, Cromwell saw something that would certainly have tickled his fancy. An edition of *Moderate Intelligencer* tells of a game played in his honour in Hyde Park. Two fifty-strong teams of Cornishmen were playing a game called hurling, and the "ball they played withal was silver, and designed for that party which did win the goal." They even had different coloured caps, red and white, to tell the teams apart.

Hurling, as we know, is Ireland's historic stickball game, but there is no evidence that the Cornish variety (called *hurlian* in Old Cornish[5]) ever had an equivalent to the *camán*, which may be evidence that hurling was once a generic term for ball games played either with or without sticks.

Although Sicilian-Greek historian Diodorus Siculus's 1st century BC *Bibliotheca Historica* tells how geographer Pytheas, around 400 years earlier, had forged early links with Cornwall, that is hardly proof that hurling was of Phoenician origin. It is also safe to say that the legend behind the mysterious standing stones called 'The Hurlers' near Liskeard is not true. The story goes that St Cleer[6] was calling the locals to the service, but some preferred to go hurling instead. The punishment somewhat outweighing the crime, Cleer turned the truants to stone.

We know nothing specific about the game before 1584 and the work of the great topographer, John Norden, the first person to put together a complete series of English county histories and geographies. He tells us "the Cornish-men they are stronge, hardye and nymble, so are their exercises violent, two especially, wrastling and hurling, sharpe and seuere actiuties; and in neither of theis doth any Countrye exceede or equall them." He comments that there were two varieties of this "daungerous" game, namely "hurling to goales, and hurling to the countrye[7]."

---

[4] James Heath *Flagellum, or the Life and Death, Birth and Burial of Oliver Cromwell* (1628-29).
[5] Cornwall certainly has its historical connections to Ireland, being one of the oft-forgotten 'Celtic Nations'. Way out at the foot of Britannia's outstretched leg, the county has a culture all of its own, what with its pasties, its piskies and its mead. It even has its own language. Not enormously unlike Welsh, the two would be mutually understandable if it wasn't for the fact that Cornish died out of everyday usage around the beginning of the 20th century, meaning there is a decided lack of Cornish speakers to be mutually understood by anybody. However, with Cornwall's national identity coming back into fashion, the language has witnessed a revival in recent years, now having some 2000 students and 300 reasonably fluent speakers.
[6] Or Clarus, first Bishop of Nantes and allegedly a disciple of St Peter.
[7] John Norden *Speculi Britanniæ Pars: A Topographic and Historical Description of Cornwall with A Map of the County and each Hundred* (c.1590s).

A few years later, in 1602, a local historian called Richard Carew in his *Survey of Cornwall* elaborates somewhat further with the most detailed description of any code of football to date, for despite the name, that's what hurling was. Read it, and feel the saliva seep out of your mouth as you savour one of the most revealing pieces of text in sports history.

Says Carew "hurling taketh his denomination from throwing of the ball, and is of two sorts; in the east parts of Cornwall to goales, and in the west to the country. For hurling to goales there are fifteen, twenty, or thirty players, more or less, chosen out on each side, who strip themselves to their slightest apparell and then join hands in ranke one against another; out of these rankes they match themselves by payres, one embracing another, and so passe away, every of which couple are especially to watch one another during the play." The ultimate in man-marking.

"After this, they pitch two bushes in the ground, some eight or ten foote asunder; and directly against them, ten or twelue score off, other twayne in like distance, which they terme their Goales. One of these is appoynted by lots, to the one side, and the other to his aduerse party. There is assigned for their gard, a couple of their best stopping Hurlers." A coin-toss and goalkeepers. It is interesting that Carew feels the need to explain what a 'goal' is, as if non-Cornishmen would be unfamiliar with the term.

"Some indifferent person throweth up a ball, the which whosoeuer can catch, and cary through his aduersaries goale, hath wonne the game. But therein consisteth one of Hercules his labours: for he that is once possessed of the ball, hath his contrary mate waiting at inches, and assaying to lay hold vpon him. The other thrusteth him in the breast, with his closed fist, to keepe him off; which they call Butting, and place in weldoing the same, no small poynt of manhood.

"If hee escape the first, another taketh him in hand, and so a third, neyther is hee left, vntill … hee eyther touch the ground with some part of his bodie, in wrastling, or cry, Hold; which is the word of yeelding. Then must he cast the ball (named Dealing) to some one of his fellowes, who catching the same in his hand, maketh away withall as before." That's crying 'down' and passing, which some football historians insist were 19th century developmentd.

"The Hurlers are bound to the obseruation of many lawes, as, that they must hurle man to man, and not two set vpon one man at once: that the Hurler against the ball, must not but, nor hand-fast vnder girdle: that hee who hath the ball, must but onely in the others brest: that he must deale no Fore-ball, viz. he may not throw it to any of his mates, standing neerer the goale, then himselfe." That's offside, that is, and sounds extraordinarily like rugby. And this is 1602!

"Lastly, in dealing the ball, if any of the other part can catch it flying between, or e're the other haue it fast, he thereby winneth the same to his side, which straightway of defendant becommeth assailant, as the other, of assailant falls to be defendant." In America, it's called an interception. "The least breach of these lawes, the Hurlers take for a iust cause of going together by the eares, but with their fists onely; neither doth any among them seek reuenge for such wrongs or hurts, but at the like play againe. These hurling matches are mostly vsed at weddings, where commonly the ghests vndertake to encounter all commers."

Most descriptions of medieval football were provided by noblemen, clergy and intellectuals who viewed it in the most negative of lights. They make it sound like a disorderly brawl, but Carew tells us that there were in fact structured rules, and explains them.

Two conclusions immediately spring to mind. One is that the Cornish take on football was years ahead of its time. The other is that games played elsewhere in Britain were not as anarchic as we have been led to believe either, it's just that they lack any surviving texts of the quality of Carew's to redeem them.

To add to the dilemma, there was another slightly different version. 'Hurling to the country', played further west, was far more in keeping with the cross-country 'mob football' cliché. Carew describes a game that "is more diffuse and confuse, as bound to few of these orders: Some two or more Gentlemen doe commonly make this match, appointing … two, three, or more parishes … to hurle against so many other … Their goales are either those Gentlemens houses, or some townes or villages, three or foure miles asunder … When they meet, there is neyther comparing of numbers, nor matching of men: but a siluer ball is cast vp, and that company, which can catch, and cary it by force, or sleight, to their place assigned, gaineth the ball and victory … The Hurlers take their next way ouer hilles, dales, hedges, ditches; yea, and thorow bushes, briers, mires, plashes and riuers whatsoeuer; so as you shall sometimes see 20 or 30 lie tugging together in the water, scrambling and scratching for the ball. A play verily both rude & rough, and yet such, as is not destitute of policies, in some sort resembling the feats of warre: for you shall haue companies layd out before, on the one side, to encounter them that come with the ball, and of the other party to succor them, in maner of a fore-ward. Againe, other troups lye houering on the sides, like wings, to helpe or stop their escape: and where the ball it selfe goeth, it resembleth the ioyning of the two mayne battels: the slowest footed who come lagge, supply the showe of a rere-ward."

Though on a less epic scale, such positions have their equivalents on modern-day rugby and American football fields. However, the next bit he describes would look a little out of place in a match today.

"Yea, there are horsemen placed also on either party (as it were in ambush) and ready to ride away with the ball[8] … Sometimes a foote-man getting it by stealth, the better to scape vnespied, will carry the same quite backwards, and so, at last, get to the goale by a windlace: which once knowne to be wonne, all that side flocke thither with great iolity: and if the same bee a Gentlemans house, they giue him the ball for a Trophee, and the drinking out of his Beere to boote … I cannot well resolue, whether I should more commend this game for the manhood and exercise, or condemne it for the boysterousnes and harmes which it begetteth: for as on the one side it makes their bodies strong, hard, and nimble, and puts a courage into

---

[8] The presence of horsemen reminds us of something we heard about in the *cnapan* of Wales, and in fact, despite the different names, the two sports seem to be much of a muchness.

their hearts, to meet an enemie in the face: so on the other part, it is accompanied with many dangers, some of which do euer fall to the players share. For proofe whereof, when the hurling is ended, you shall see them retyring home, as from a pitched battaile, with bloody pates, bones broken, and out of ioynt, and such bruses as serue to shorten their daies; yet al is good play, and neuer Attourney nor Crowner troubled for the matter."

Carew's is not the only reference to Cornish hurling. Another was penned by naturalist John Ray in 1662, where the two versions are called "in-hurling and out-hurling[9]." His description of the tackling is highly reminiscent of rugby league's 'play-the-ball' rule, whereby when a player gets the balls he "endeavours to run with it to the furthermost goal. If he be stopped by one of the opposite side, he either saith I will stand and wrestles with him, letting the ball by him (which one the opposoite side must not take up, but one of his own) or else throws the ball to one of his own side ... When any one wrestles, one of his side takes up the ball and runs with it towards the goal, till he be stopped, and then as before he either wrestles or throws away the ball, so that there are commonly many pairs wrestling at once."

Ray reckons that out-hurling was played "in the same manner as in the other, only they make their churches their goals" and "they have not a set number on their side, but each have as many as they can procure. An hurler, to help him in running, may catch hold on an horseman's stirrup. No horsemen play."

Ray says the game was also played "Devonshire men against Cornish." Indeed, there is a record that in 1648 "the 2 Counties of Devon and Cornewall are on Munday next to meet at a hurling (a sport they haue with a ball)[10]." How much hurling actually got played we cannot be sure because "tis thought they haue an other designe, for they, but espetially theire neighbour countye, Dorsetshire, are very much discontented." This game may have just been used as a pretext for rebellion[11], but it reconfirms that Cornwall's neighbouring county, Devon, also had a hurling tradition, which was still alive in 1837, where it was described as "a rude country sport[12]" and as late as the 20th century, for *Devon and Cornwall Notes and Questions* says something called 'Out-hurling' was included in the 1922 Great Torrington Revel, where it was claimed it had been a regular sport in the region in which a small ball was thrown "over-hand" around a pitch approximately half a mile long.

Back in Cornwall, the game survived for even longer, a subject we shall be returning to in the next chapter.

---

[9] John Ray, William Derham, George Scott *Select remains of the learned John Ray: with his life* (1760, the text dates from 1662, and may have been published earlier).

[10] Samuel Rawson Gardiner (ed.) *The Hamilton Papers: Being selections from original letters in the possession of His Grace the Duke of Hamilton and Brandon, relating to the years 1638-1650* (Nichols & Sons, 1880-81).

[11] The issue led Nicholas Roope, a governor in Dartmouth, to write to the Secretary of State to express his concern about "the numerous meetings of people at football matches."

[12] James Frederick Palmer, Mary Palmer *A Dialogue in the Devonshire Dialect* (1837).

Poetry in motion

Having struggled our way through Carew's appalling spelling, it is good to know that there were big changes around the corner for the English language. This was particularly thanks to Samuel Johnson and his *Dictionary of the English Language* (1755), whereby English spelling started to be standardised. Until then, words were written more or less by ear, and letters were often added or taken away just to make them look nice. The Great Bard himself is a fine example. He was registered as Shakspere by Stratford church, while it says both Shakspeare and Shackspere on his will, yet he was never known to use the modern accepted form of Shakespeare at all.

So, it's curious that it was none other than Big Bill who is credited as the first person to write 'football' using today's spelling. The reference appears in *A Comedy of Errors* (Act II, Scene 1, written around 1594), where it is asked:

"Am I so round with you as you with me,
That like a football you do spurn me thus?
You spurn me hence, and he will spurn me hither.
If I last in this service, you must case me in leather."

Footy in Shaky is cool, although all that spurning doesn't provide an awful lot of insight into the formative years of Stratford upon Avon Rugby Club. Some ten years later, there is another reference to football in Shakespeare's tragedy *King Lear*, where in Act I, Scene IV, Oswald says "I'll not be struck, my lord", to which Kent replies "nor tripped neither, you base football player", whereupon he trips Oswald at the heels in an early example of football's now illegal art of 'hacking'. The extract suggests that football was not the classiest activity of the age.

A popular example of football in literature appears in a 1621 poem by Edmund Waller, where he uses the allegory: "As when a sort of lusty shepherds try

Their force at football, care of victory;
Makes them salute so rudely breast to breast,
That their encounter seems too rough for jest;
They ply their feet, and still the restless ball,
Toss'd to and fro, is urged by them al[13]."

Three things to consider here. First, Waller associated football to shepherds, second, it was a game with the feet, and third, in the dialect of his age, there was nothing wrong with rhyming 'try' and 'victory'.

A poetical account of a winter game was scribed in 1716 by the pen of John Gay:

"I spy the furies of the football war,
The prentice quits his shop to join the crew,
Increasing crowds the flying game pursue,

---

[13] Edmund Waller *Of the Danger His Majesty (being Prince) Escaped in the Road at St Andero* (1621).

Thus, as you roll the ball o'er snowy ground,
The gathering globe augments with ev'ry round
But whither shall I run? The throng draws nigh,
The ball now skims the street, now soars on high,
The dext'rous Glazier strong returns the Bound,
And gingling Sashes on the Pent-house sound[14]."

A similar sort of image is provided by an anonymous poem from *Gentleman's Monthly Intelligencer* in 1735: "It's then the swains defy their fellow swains,

To sport at foot-ball on the ample plains:
In form of battle drawn they issue forth,
And ev'ry one is proud to shew his worth;
With shouts the coward's courage they excite,
And warlike clangors call them out to fight,
The nimble foot-ball scours the fields of air;
They kick, they push and pushing loudly cry."

Richard Baxter's *The Saint's Everlasting Rest* (1650) also contains a football reference, albeit in allegorical form, with the sigh "alas, that I must stand by and see the Church, and Cause of Christ, like a Football in the midst of a crowd of Boys, tost about in contention from one to another."

And a personal favourite appears in the anonymous 1606 play *Sir Gyles Goosecap*, in which the knight explains to the lady Hippolyta why he fancied getting married. "Why, Madam" he says. "We have a great match at football towards, married men against batchellers, and the married men be all my friends, so I wood faine marry to take the married mens parts in truth." Hippolyta considers that "the best reason for marriage that ever I heard Sir Gyles." And so do we.

Great Scots

Like in England, Scottish football matches were used as pretext for greater mischief, and there was a notorious case of this in 1600 when a game at Mumbies was used by the Armstrong clan to plot the murder of an unpopular warden called Sir John Carmichael, and a few years after that, Robert Carey mentions in his memoirs "a great match made at football", although the real intention was to gather riders for an attack on the English.

In 1556 the hammermen (blacksmiths) of Perth issued a decree that servants and apprentices playing football would pay a "penalty of a pound of wax." In 1601 at Lochton, we hear of a football match that "fell in contentioun and controversie, ilk anie with otheris, and schot and dilaschit pistolettis and hacquebuttis." Getting around the language is a tad tricky, but basically what they're saying is that firearms came to be involved! In 1620, two parishioners of Abernethy were "accusit they on the Lord's day play at the football and keits

---

[14] John Gay *Trivia: Or, the Art of Walking the Streets of London. Book II* (1716).

in the said kirk, and yrby bringis in ane abuse in drawing peopill from godly exercise" and in Banff in 1682 it was ordained that "players of football on the streets to be fined 40s."

Where we have a wealth of football references is Elgin, where the church records first mention "passing tyme at the football" in 1598, where it and "all conucntioun of womenkynd" were forbidden on Sunday under pain of "publict repentans." In 1599, Elgin banned "futballing through the toun" but despite insisting that such sins as "snaw balling, singing of carrellis … and dancing" were forbidden in the churchyard, a curious exception was made for football, although this was no longer the case in 1620, when it was also forbidden for "wemen to be cled in mens apparrell nor men in womens apparel." This is in stark contrast to Glassford in the 1690s, where the minister actively encouraged his congregation to go out and enjoy football and dancing once the sermon was done.

In Aberdeen, the Puritans denounced the filthy acts of "drinking, playing football ... and roving from parish to parish" on the Sabbath in 1607, but this was also the place where a good man of the Granite City, David Wedderburn, and his 1633 Latin textbook *Vocabula*, sparked off a possibly misguided furore in 2006. One passage relates a fictional conversation between footballers, which students had to put into English, and the following attempt to do just that was made by the American historian Francis Peabody Magoun.

"Let us choose sides, pick your man first. Those on our side come here. How many are against us? Kick out the ball so that we may begin the game. Come, kick it here. You keep the goal. Snatch the ball from that fellow if you can. Come, throw yourself against him. Run at him. Kick the ball back. Well done. You aren't doing anything to make a goal. This is the first goal, this the second, this the third. Drive that man back. The opponents are, moreover, coming out on top. If you don't look out, he will make a goal. Unless we play better, we'll be done for. Ah, victory is in your hands. Ha, hurrah. He is a very skilled ball player. Had it not been for him, we should have brought back the victory. Come, help me. We still have the better chance."

Despite the fact that the text had been freely available on the Internet since 2000, and had appeared in two of the greatest football histories of the 20th century, this was heralded as an 'amazing discovery' in 2006. Richard McBrearty, curator of the Scottish Football Museum, told BBC Scotland that "the book is the first evidence we have of a passing game with goalkeepers and players passing the ball to score goals. Scotland has a fantastic claim to have developed the modern game."

It was a timely revelation by the Scots, seeing as they were currently being drowned by media coverage of England's participation at the 2006 World Cup in Germany, while their own team had not even qualified, but what is the text really telling us? The controversy lies in the translation. Another prominent football historian, Morris Marples, used the word 'pass' rather than 'kick' in his translation of *huc percute*. In fact, the term simply means something like 'strike it here' and *repercute pilam* means 'strike the ball again', so there is not necessarily any 'kicking' or 'passing' going on at all. If it was a kicking game, then this *praeripe illi pilam si possis agere* has a strong suggestion of the use of the hands. And is *tu tuere metum* really nominating a goalkeeper, or just ordering somebody to go to the goal?

Not only is the evidence considerably dodgy from the Latin scholar's viewpoint, but neither is it anything like the first evidence of any of these things, as we've already seen on the preceding pages.

And that's soccer!

Now we come to the great ornithologist and ichthyologist[15] Francis Willughby[16]. Famed for his naturalist ramblings, he was also fascinated by games and sports, and wrote the first known English language compendium dedicated to them, what he called his *Book of Plaies*. There are two great tragedies associated to this book. The first is that he died before it was properly complete. The second is that the only known copy sat unnoticed for years in the University of Nottingham library until somebody picked up on its potential in 2003 and it went back into print for the first time in five centuries. The title was changed to the *Book of Games*, to stop people assuming that Willughby was about to unleash his dramaturgy skills upon us. It was originally written around 1660, and mostly deals with card and board games, but football gets a mention too. It even includes the earliest known diagram of a football pitch.

Willughby explains that "they play in a long street, or a close that has a gate at either end. The gates are called Goals, say A B, and C D. The ball is thrown up in the middle between the goals, as about O." That's the bit shown in the diagram. A B and C D are the two sets of goalposts at either end of the pitch, and O is the centre spot.

"The players at A must kick the ball towards C D goal, those at C towards A B goal." Now that's not too hard to follow, but the revelation here is the use of the word 'kick'. If David Wedderburn had included the answers at the back of his *Vocabula* we may have had proof of this earlier, but Willughby makes it plentifully clear that football, in his mind, was a game that involved kicking the ball, and not using the hands. The players are "equally divided according to their strength and nimbleness … they that can strike the ball through their opponents' goal first win. They usually leave some of their best players to guard the goal while the rest follow the ball." There were clearly tactics and positions involved in team selection.

Here comes a good bit. "The players must at first all stand at their goals, the ball lying just in the middle between them, and they that can run best get the first kick." So, no drawing of lots, kick off was a question of the first to the ball, like in water polo today. "They often break one another's shins when two meet and strike both together against the ball, and

---

[15] The first is birds, the second, would you know it, is fish.

[16] Willughby was also a contemporary of the better known John Ray, the 'father of English natural history', and not only did they share a fascination for nature's wonders, but also a subsidiary interest in sports. Willughby joined Ray on the aforementioned 1662 expedition to observe Cornish hurling.

therefore there is a law that they must not strike higher than the ball. 'Tripping up of heels' is when one follows one of his opponents and (to prevent him from striking the ball) strikes that foot as he runs, that is from the ground, which (catching against the other foot) makes him fall.

"The trick is to hit that foot that is moving and just taken from the ground, and then a little touch makes him fall." This was all legal and part of the game. It is what would later be called 'hacking' and whether or not it should be allowed was just as controversial when the FA drew up its first soccer rules as the use or not of the hands.

And finally a bit of information about the ball. "They blow a strong bladder and tie the neck of it as fast as they can, and then put it into the skin of a bull's cod and sew it fast in. The harder the ball is blown, the better it flies. They used to put quicksilver into it sometimes to keep it from lying still." The bit about quicksilver may well be porkpies, it's certainly news to football historians, but what the complete text tells us is that by 1660, *fait accompli*. That's soccer pretty much in place already, and we've still got another two centuries to go before it was 'officially' created.

The discovery of this book has certainly caused historians to have a rethink of the origins of football in England. We could now revisit Francis Marshall's 1892 book, in which the editor starts by saying his aim is to prove rugby's "claim to be the most ancient of British sports" and show that "the Rugby game alone is the true issue … the game as at present played under the Rugby Union Code is the legitimate refinement of the rough and crude games of our ancestors. Nowhere can there be found any trace whatever of a game assimilating, however remotely, to the kicking game of the Association Code." The anti-soccer snobbery in his book is often so irritating that it is rather satisfying that thanks to Francis Willughby's book, found over a century later, Marshall can be proved so delightfully wrong!

Football for good

Is the popular image of medieval 'mob' football historically accurate, or is it something that we have created on the basis of our preconceptions of uncivilised medieval hordes? When Hugh Hornby, for example, asks on what evidence esteemed football historian James Walvin bases his claim that "sometimes quarrels spilled over into murder after the game", he is rightfully questioning the view that has seeped through to the history books, and it is a pity there were not more people like Carew and Willughby to tell us that it might not have been that bad at all.

Football was usually only noticed when it caused trouble. Rather like a modern-day darts league, nobody other than the players themselves cared about the games, but a stray arrow gouging somebody in the eye, or a pub brawl resulting from a controversy in the game… well, that might be a story worth covering. We know about the "young man killed by a fall while playing at football" in Aldeburgh in 1692, and also Richard Venable, a servant who died after colliding with two opponents in the parish of Great Ness, Shropshire in 1709, but we know much less about the scores of other games that passed off without incident.

Football could be good – it could even save lives. In East Looe in Cornwall, it was reported in 1722 that "during the usual time of the Divine Service, there happened such a violent hurricane that a great part of the steeple of the church was blown down; which would have done very considerable damage to the parishioners had they been at church; but they happened to be luckily at a foot-ball match, by which means their lives were probably saved."

In Scotland, it was even played by women. At Inveresk in 1795, the fishwives of the town "do the work of men, their manners are masculine ... on Shrove Tuesday there is a standing match at foot-ball, between the married and unmarried women, in which the former are always victorious[17]."

Neither was the infliction of any carnage mentioned in a letter sent by Sir Roger de Coverley to *The Spectator* in 1711. Describing a recent trip to find out what the country bumpkins got up to on their village greens, he commented how "I was diverted ... by a foot-ball match, which was on the other side of the green; where Tom Short behaved himself so well, that most people seemed to agree it was impossible that he should remain a batchelor till the next wake. Having played many a match myself, I could have looked longer on this sport, had I not observed a country girl, who was posted on an eminence at some distance from me, and was making so many odd grimaces, and writhing and distorting her whole body in so strange a manner, as made me very desirous to know the meaning of it." Any man in the same situation would have been tempted to do the same (she was watching a wrestling match as it happens).

The letters editor replies that there was "many a court lady who would be contented to exchange her crazy young husband for Tom Short." If only he had been born a few centuries later, young Tom could have given David Beckham a run for his money.

French writer Henri Misson also described the game in a positive light, and makes reference to the use of the feet in a description of how "in winter foot-ball is a useful and charming exercise. It is a leather ball about as big as one's head, filled with wind. This is kicked with the feet in the streets to whoever can trap it. There is no other science to it[18]." The way he writes implies that he had never seen anything similar in France, where *la soule* and similar games were supposedly living a parallel existence.

Football did not always have to wreak havoc around the town – it was sometimes designated specific fields. Malcolmson[19] notes cases of five different places having a 'football close' at different times between 1659 and 1775, plus a 17th century 'football garth' in Kirkleatham and a 'football field' mentioned in a 1668 will from Stock Harvard in Essex,

---

[17] In the *Statistical Account of Scotland* 1795.

[18] Henri Misson *Memoires et Observations faites par un Voyageur*, based on experiences around 1698.

[19] Robert W Malcolmson *Popular Recreations in English Society 1700-1850* (Cambridge University Press, 1973).

not to mention about a dozen 'camping closes' in East Anglia. In most games, such as the one between Billingborough and Osbournby in Lincolnshire, 1795, "several feats of agility were shewn[20]" and there is no indication that it bothered anybody in the slightest.

In 1737, James Howell gives us another example of the aristocracy indulging in a game with the locals – and getting injured in the process. He wrote how "many years ago my Lord Willoughby ... with so many of their servants ... play'd a match at foot-ball against such a number of Countrymen, where my Lord of Sunderland being busy about the ball, got a bruise in the breast which put him in a swoon for the present, but did not trouble him till three months after[21]." It is worth continuing the story if only to learn how much attitudes have changed over the years concerning the pros and cons of tobacco. "A qualm took him on a sudden, which made him retire to his bed-chamber. My Lord of Rutland following him, put a pipe full of tobacco in his mouth; he being not accustom'd to Tobacco, taking the smoak downwards, fell a casting and vomiting up divers little imposthumated bladders of congeald blood; which sav'd his life then, and brought him to have a better conceit of Tobacco ever after." So there you go, if anyone's feeling groggy, prescribe twenty Marlboro, and they'll soon be right as rain…

Football for bad

"For the players themselves, it was impossible to see a finer set of active and athletic young fellows than appeared on the field. But what we chiefly admired in their conduct was that, though several hundreds in number, exceedingly keen for their respective parties, and engaged in so rough and animated a contest, they maintained the most perfect good-humor, and showed how unnecessary it is to discourage manly and athletic exercises among the common people, under pretext of maintaining subordination and good order."

That is an extract from perhaps the first football match to ever get an extensive press report. The *Edinburgh Journal* described a game played on December 5, 1815 at Carterhaugh between the men of Selkirk and Yarrow, and preceded by the reading of a verse written especially for the occasion by Sir Walter Scott, sheriff of Selkirkshire[22]."

---

[20] *Sporting magazine* (vol 6, 1795).

[21] James Howell, the historiographer to Charles II in his *Epistolae Ho-Elianae: the familiar letters of James Howell* (1737).

[22] It goes on a bit, so we'll just print one stanza here:

> "Then strip, lads, and to it, though sharp be the weather,
> And if, by mischance, you should happen to fall,
> There are worse things in life than a tumble on heather.
> And life is itself but a game of football."

Scott was one of Scotland's most renowned writers, whose works included *Ivanhoe*, *Rob Roy*, and *The Heart of Midlothian*, and as a footballer himself, Scott would have been delighted to know that the name of the latter would later be adopted by an Edinburgh dance hall that, in turn, gave its name to a football club. In his *How the Councel of Safety sent the Gyant Husonius to kill the Christians for playing football* of 1812, the plot of which

It rings more of an ancient clan battle than a game, with Scott's own son carrying the Buccleuch banner bearing the ancient war cry of *'Bellendaine'*. Watched by some two thousand men, Selkirk won thanks to a goal *hailed* after an hour and a half by Selkirk mason Robert Hall. The second game was "still more severely contested ... after a close and stubborn struggle of more than three hours, with various fortune, and much display of strength and agility on both sides," Yarrow scored to tie the series, meaning a deciding game would be needed. But as light was dwindling, it had to be put off until sometime between Christmas and New Year. It had been agreed that the game would be played with 100 men on each team, and "all bets are to be paid by the losers to the poor of the winning parish."

But the rubber match was never played. Despite the stories told to the press about the excellent behaviour shown by the players, Scott would explain later that "the old feuds and local interests, and rivalries and animosities of the Scotch, still slept in their ashes, and might easily be roused; their hereditary feeling for names was still great; it was not always safe to have even the game of football between villages. The old clannish spirit was too apt to break out[23]."

They may be gobbling away at the prawn sandwiches in the director's box at Old Trafford these days, but in 1608 the civic authorities took a very different view on the issue, and the *Manchester Lete Roll* denounced the "greate disorder in our towne of Manchester we are told, and glasse windowes broken yearlye and spoyled by a companie of lewd and disordered persons using that unlawful exercise of playing with the ffotebale in ye streets of the said towne, breaking many men's windows and glasse at their pleasure and other great inormyties. Therefore wee of this Jurye doe order that no manner of persons hereafter shall play or use the footeball in any street within the said toune of Manchester." By 1618, there were even special 'football officers' whose duty was to see to it that the ban was upheld. It probably wasn't, because in 1655, the game was banned in Manchester again.

Frenchman César de Saussure, in a letter written in 1728, would be moved to describe how "in cold weather[24] you sometimes see a score of rascals in the streets kicking at a ball, and they will break panes of glass and smash the windows of coaches, and will also knock you down without the slightest compunction; on the contrary they will roar with laughter."

---

is pretty much given away by the title, said Christians "continued playing at foot-ball, not dreaming that their sport might have been offensive. But so it fell out that one of the Christians striking the ball right strenuous, by which his foot kick'd the ball full in the gyants face, so that his eye was in great danger. The gyant, who had but one eye, and being jealous that the Christians intended to put out that too, was sorely enraged ... killing six of the Christians at one blow ... and took up one of the dead Christians, and so sitting down upon the ridge of a house, in a moment devoured him raw, without either bread or salt." That taught 'em for playing football.

[23] Washington Irving *Abbotsford and Newstead Abbey* (1835).

[24] Interestingly, both De Saussure, and his aforementioned compatriot Henri Misson, comment that football was a cold-weather sport. It has generally been assumed that the traditional football season came about as an activity for 19th century public schools to play in the cricket off-season, hence its 'winter' status. But perhaps the association goes back further than that.

Little monkeys. Football had not fully redeemed itself yet. Any unauthorised gathering of the masses was something to be regarded with suspicion, and especially when it was to play this dangerously regimented game they called football. In 1653, four men were taken to court in Maidstone for "unlawfully playing at and exercising an unlawful, forbidden game called football," the same place where, three years later, a local apothecary was in trouble with the law for kicking a football "to the great disquiet and disturbance of the good[25]."

In 1743, Worcester's local bellman was rewarded with 2s 6d "for crying down football kicking." Commoners were gathering in what were not unlike small armies and going to battle with each other. If that energy were to be channelled in the wrong direction, all hell could break loose. We could compare this to the suspicious attitude of the British to the rise of the GAA in Ireland. The testosterone of the football playing hordes was frequently diverted to political causes. In 1647, the Puritans had the gall to ban Christmas, and ordered shops to remain open like they did on any normal working day. There were widespread riots around the country, including Canterbury, where the demonstrators forcibly closed all the shops, opened the local gaol and even hurled poop at the minister before getting stuck into a game of footy. The story has it that even some of the billeted soldiers deserted their posts and joined the game. You can't go taking Christmas away! Even the Grinch learned that.

In January 1660, thirteen footballers were arrested in Scarborough for playing football, and the town bailiff, in punishment for failing to do anything to stop the game, was publicly humiliated by being put in the stocks. Too right.

In York the same year, a football game ended with the windows of the local church being smashed and eleven players were prosecuted as a result. But this merely served to incense the football mob more, and they amassed whatever weapons they could find and stormed the Mayor's home. A major enquiry followed, and a hefty fine of £10 was slapped on the chief architect.

In 1740, we learn that "a mach of futtball was cried at Kettering of five hundred men of a side, but the design was to pull down Lady Betey Jesmaine's Mills." Football had been no more than a pretext to gather men together and fuel their minds with ideas of rebellion.

Not that far away, at West Hatton in Northamptonshire in 1765, an area of 2000 acres of communal land used by peasants was fenced off by a landowner, all part of the Enclosure Acts, which were designed to put an end to common grazing land and divide it into small plots. Your average villager was going to lose out big time, because their land would be reduced to less than an acre, and to rub salt into the wounds, their own taxes would foot the hefty bill. The locals naturally voiced their objections, but these came to nothing, and in retaliation they decided to invade the land *en masse* and play a game of football on it. But the game had barely started when the mob set about pulling down all of the newly erected

---

[25] There were similar arrests for the players that had the cheek to play while the divine service was in progress at Richmond, Yorkshire in 1668, and Colne, Lancashire in 1713, and it was nine yeomen from Burtersett, Yorkshire who were in trouble in 1669.

fences. The dragoons were called in from Northampton to calm things down, but before they could do anything, some £1500 worth of damage had already been done. Five men were jailed, but the authorities never managed to get their hands on the perpetrators.

All hell broke loose in Lincolnshire in July 1768 when work progressed on draining Holland Fen. This was not a project that the locals took to kindly, and James Walvin quotes a contemporary report of their reaction: "The insurgents, consisting of about two hundred men, threw up a football in the fen and played for about two hours, when a troop of dragoons, some gentlemen from Boston, and four constables, having seized four or five of the rioters, committed them to Spalding gaol. Dr Shaw of Wyberton set three women rioters at liberty, and the men were admitted to bail. On the 15th another ball was thrown up, and no person opposed them."

Resting in peace?

And so we arrive in the 19th century, when all of the major footballing codes came into 'official' being. By way of heralding in that era, 1801 was the year that Joseph Strutt unleashed his seminal *Sports and Pastimes of the People of England* upon us, where his football section explains that "when a match at football is made, two parties, each containing an equal number of competitors, take the field, and stand between two goals, placed at the distance of eighty or an hundred yards the one from the other. The goal is usually made with two sticks driven into the ground, about two or three feet apart[26]. The ball, which is commonly made of a blown bladder, and cased with leather, is delivered in the midst of the ground, and the object of each party is to drive it through the goal of their antagonists, which being achieved the game is won. The abilities of the performers are best displayed in attacking and defending the goals; and hence the pastime was more frequently called a goal at football than a game at football. When the exercise becomes exceeding violent, the players kick each other's shins without the least ceremony, and some of them are overthrown at the hazard of their limbs."

He also tells us that football "is so called because the ball is driven about with the feet instead of the hands." That's important. Like Willughby a century and half earlier, Strutt describes football as being a game that involved kicking the ball. The jury is out on Strutt though. Although it was played with the hands, the same man told us in the last chapter that the rugby-like camp-ball was "another denomination for foot-ball."

In the same period, married men and bachelors played the Shrove Tuesday match at Scone, Perth. "The game was this: he who at any time got the ball into his hands, run with it till overtaken by one of the opposite part; and then, if he could shake himself loose from those

---

[26] The pitch was roughly the same size as a standard football pitch is today, but the goals, just two or three feet apart, were considerably smaller.

on the opposite side who seized him, he run on; if not, he threw the ball from him, unless it was wrested from him by the other party, but no person was allowed to kick it[27]."

So it was hands and no feet in this game where the winning team got to keep the ball, but "if neither won, the ball was cut into equal parts at sunset." To be fair, the text never tells us that the Scone game was called 'football', the closest it comes to any kind of name is the comment that despite the "violence between the parties … all is fair at the ball of Scone." However, the same description resurfaces in William Hone's *Every-Day Book* of 1825-26, where it *is* called 'foot-ball', suggesting that at least to Hone, a ball sport played with the hands could quite conceivably be called football.

Judging from these inconsistencies, one conclusion could be that although 'football' was traditionally the name given to the kicking game, by the early 19th century the word was also being used to describe carrying games like hurling, camp-ball and cnappan[28].

But considering the amount of detail Strutt goes into when writing on other sports and games, it is remarkable how little space he devotes to football. In fact, the greatest eye-opener of all in his 1801 account is his comment that football "was formerly much in vogue among the common people of England, though of late years it seems to have fallen into disrepute, and is but little practised."

Strutt was writing just one year after *The Sporting Magazine* had offered that "football is fast going out and leap-frog is now the full sport of the day." Imagine, if history had taken a different course, Major League Leap-Frog could be topping today's TV ratings.

Like Decca's Dick Rowe commenting in 1962 that "guitar groups are on the way out, Mr Epstein" as he turned down the chance to sign up a mop-haired quartet called The Beatles, these people didn't appreciate the potential they were dealing with. Football was on the verge of becoming the biggest phenomenon since the Spanish came back from America with the potato, yet Strutt wrote it off as something doomed. How brilliantly wrong he was.

But Strutt did not have the benefit of hindsight. In March 1825, *The Circulator of Useful Knowledge*, a magazine offering a wealth of information on anything from science to entertainment, ran a cover feature on football and plagiarised Strutt word for word, suggesting football's fate had not changed too much for a quarter of a century. But the game was "played at some of our public schools, especially at the Royal Military Academy, where we have seen the young cadets amusing themselves with this harmless projectile."

That same year of 1825, Hone's *Every-Day Book* says football "was, and remains, a game on Shrove Tuesday, in various parts of England." His use of the past tense, with 'remains'

---

[27] Sir Frederick Morton Eden's contribution to the *Statistical account of Scotland* of 1791. Interestingly, Morton Eden also cites the local legend that the game originated when an Italian was in the area, and challenged the locals to a game wherever he went. Scone was the only village to take up the challenge, and duly beat the foreigner. The veracity of the legend is debatable, but it might be a locally adapted telling of how *calcio* was the true origin of rugby.

[28] It was also around this time that 'hockey' and 'golf' became the catch-alls for those types of games.

almost added as an afterthought also suggests football was in decline, and now only played once a year in a handful of places. A year earlier, in 1824, Thomas Dudley Fosbroke in his *Encyclopaedia of Antiquities* offers pages and pages of sporting info in the *Gymasticks* section, but all he can find for foot-ball are a measly four lines, and he makes conspicuous use of the past tense when he says "it was a favourite diversion even of noblemen." And a year before that it was said that "football is an exercise which has dwindled to nothing, compared to the estimation in which it was formerly held[29]." It was no better north of the border, where foot-ball was still "often played by the inhabitants of adjacent parishes" but "was anciently a very favourite sport all through Scotland[30]."

At Kennington Common in Surrey, matches for "small and large sums were played in the course of each year" up until 1789, when "twenty two gentlemen of Westmoreland were backed against twenty two gentlemen of Cumberland for one thousand guineas[31]." That was the last game played. In 1811, in Aberdeen, "in too many cases, cards and dice are substituted in the room of the more manly exercise ... of foot-ball[32]." By the time the London Gymnastic Society was founded in 1826, its founding chairman fondly reminisced that twenty years earlier "the fields to the north, south and west would be crowded every afternoon with cricket and football." Those days had gone.

In 1822, we are told the fictional tale of a football that was confiscated from some children in Kingston after it was kicked through a window. The ball finds its way into the hands of young George Benson, who is told he can play in a field "for it can do no mischief there[33]." But when asked by his chums if he knew how to play with it, he replies "Not I, indeed, but I think we may invent a game for ourselves." Children that don't know what you are supposed to do with a football? They end up playing a two-a-side game where they kick the ball to each other, and teams get a point every time somebody misses the ball. Football had sunk as low as that?

When we consider the wealth of prose that has survived from the first three decades of the 19th century, it is astounding how little mention football gets. Charles Dickens penned a wealth of chunky novels between 1836 and 1870, and unlike most of his contemporaries, he also described the lives of the lower classes and provides valuable insight into the everyday doings of the Victorian poor. He was no stranger to sport. Paul Schlicke reckons "he participated in bar-leaping, bowling and quoits, enjoyed cricket intensely as a spectator, and organized field sports for local villagers in a meadow at the back of Gad's Hill Place[34]." You'd imagine a man like that would mention football at some point, but he never did.

---

[29] W Litt *Wrestliana; or, An historical account of ancient and modern wrestling* (1823).

[30] James Mitchell *The Scotsman's library: being a collection of anecdotes and facts* (1825).

[31] *The Surrey Club* in *Bell's Life in London* (1849).

[32] George Skene Keith *A general view of the agriculture of Aberdeenshire* (1811).

[33] Marian S Carson T*he book of games, or, A history on juvenile sports practised at the Kingston Academy* (George Long, 1822).

[34] Paul Schlicke *Dickens and popular entertainment* (Taylor & Francis, 1985).

The people of Howarth "were in the habit of playing at foot-ball on Sunday, using stones for the purpose and giving and receiving challenges from other parishes[35]." Lord Sheffield's wedding in 1826 was celebrated with a football match. A large and aristocratic crowd was in attendance to see Penningham and Minnigaff play a game in 1816, a game in Cobham was stained by a fight and in Hertfordshire in 1822 it was even said that "foot-ball is now the most common sport, especially on Sunday afternoons[36]." But these examples are very much the exception rather than the norm.

The fact that Sunday was the only time most people could conceivably indulge in recreation did not help matters. One killjoy cleric wrote in 1835 that "nothing is to be done which is merely for amusement or for gain. To saunter in the public walks where the gay and worldly scene necessarily unfits the mind for devotion – to read the public journal, or other works which are not religious, to read and to write letters upon business, or any other common topics, to pay idle visits, to engage in frivolous conversation at home or elsewhere … must be contrary to the Christian's duty of the Lord's-day[37]."

In 1853, the journal *Household Words*, established by Charles Dickens, and comparing the abundance of French holidays to the abject lack of the same in England, bewailed the fact that "we have hardly a real holiday in England; executions and races make the nearest approach to one, but they are both too much in the way of business. A Sunday's holiday is looked upon as a heinous sin by so many worthy and respectable people, that it cannot be indulged with impunity."

Sporting superiors

But if football was going out of fashion for those reasons, how come other sports were getting so much attention? We may struggle to comprehend it now, but in the 18th century the average Briton got far more excited about playing, watching and gambling on other sports, some which already had elements of professionalism.

Betting on rowing was big business, especially on the Thames in London and the Tyne in Newcastle, but any navigable waterway would do. Doggett's Coat and Badge was first contested in 1715, and is still raced annually between London Bridge and Chelsea. One commonly cited piece of English sport-lore used to illustrate how rowing was once more popular than football is the fact that the 1873 FA Cup Final was moved to the morning so

---

[35] Elizabeth Cleghorn Gaskell *Life of Charlotte Brontë* (1857).

[36] *The Gentleman's magazine* (1822).

[37] Reverend Baptist Noel *The Sanctification of the Sabbath and the Blessing Attached to It* (1835). Not all the clergy would have agreed with him. At Kirkland, in Scotland, a former vicar "had a set of young men in his parish who often played the foot-ball all the way to church. When the congregation was dismissed, the vicar was wont to give the ball the first kick, in order to set them a playing home again." *Edinburgh medical and surgical journal* (1824).

that the players could watch the Oxford v Cambridge University Boat Race in the afternoon[38].

Boxing was also huge. It was fought bare-knuckle, and the first reference to an organised bout in England dates back to an article in the *London Protestant Mercury* in 1681. It was considerably fiercer than boxing as we know it today, and deaths were commonplace, which was one of the main reasons heavyweight champion Jack Broughton brought in the London Prize Ring rules in 1743. These included the one about not being able to hit below the belt, and the idea that there would be a 30 second count whenever a boxer was floored (and there would be no hitting him while he was down there). It is not surprising that the punters insisted on getting a few rules straight. Big money was exchanging hands, even with aristocratic support. In the late 18th century, both the Duke of York and the Prince of Wales had rings on their estates, and it is rumoured that they bet as much as £40,000 on fights.

The association between sport and betting was as strong then as it is now, and what was known as 'pedestrianism' (running races) was another focus of high stakes, and reportedly plenty of result-fixing too.

But the real love of the upper classes was, and continues to be, horse racing. In the 17th century, James I was instrumental in establishing Newmarket as the home of the sport, and ended up at loggerheads with his Parliament, who were concerned that he was spending too much of his time there. Charles I instigated the first Gold Cup as early as 1634, while in the next century Royal Ascot was the handiwork of Queen Anne. The popularity of the sport was getting so out of hand that in 1740, the same year the Jockey Club came into existence to establish a calendar and rules, Parliament passed a bill "to restrain and to prevent the excessive increase in horse racing", but the effort proved as fruitless as the many attempts to do away with football.

Bat and ball

All these sports were establishing fixture lists, official rules and a central federation to oversee the process. Football had nothing remotely like this until well into the 19th century, but when it did, it was clearly inspired by what had happened elsewhere. And if any one sport provided football with the greatest inspiration, then that sport was cricket, which most early footballers also played. For instance, although there is no direct evidence to prove it, it is likely that soccer is played 11-a-side because it was simply imitating the idea of naming an XI for a cricket team. And football is still considered a winter game in much of the world even though the real reason for that, to leave the summer free for cricket, hardly matters much nowadays.

---

[38] What most citations fail to point out, however, is that one of the teams playing in that final was Oxford University (who lost 2-0 to The Wanderers in what was only the second ever edition of the tournament), so it is no surprise that the players wanted to see their colleagues race, although the 3000 crowd for the FA Cup Final was considered poor and blamed on the Boat Race.

The immense popularity of the click of leather on willow would have been one of the main reasons for English football's possible decline in the early 1800s. The March 1825 edition of *The Circulator of Useful Knowledge* noted that "most of the ancient ball games have been superseded by the noble art of cricket, which is now frequently played in the vicinity of London … sometimes, a dozen parties at once." 'Ball games' had been standardised as cricket, and football was in danger of disappearing entirely.

Bat and ball games had been around for centuries in Britain. It's impossible to say exactly how long, but many of the ancient references to football, golf or hockey that we have already examined are so ambiguous that they could just as easily have meant early cricket.

Some date the game back to Edward I, or Longshanks as he is familiarly remembered, a king whose reign was most noted for expelling the Jews from the country and conquering most of Wales. Where cricket comes into the story are 14th century wardrobe records of what the then 15-year-old Prince Edward was using to play *creag* in Newenden in Kent. But the only real basis for the theory is that the word looks a bit like 'cricket'. In fact, it is more likely that the word *creag* was related to the Irish *craic*, meaning 'fun' and still used today, and that all Edward had in his wardrobe was a selection of typical adolescent toys[39].

The ambiguity continues regarding King Edward IV's decree of 1477 to ban certain games, one of which he called "handyn and handoute." Might have been cricket. Might not have been. Probably wasn't.

The first valid proof seems to be that offered by coroner John Derrick in 1597 whereby "being a scholler in the ffree schoole of Guldeford hee and diverse of his fellows did runne and play there at creckett and other plaies[40]."

But by the 17th century, cricket was everywhere. It was at odds with the authorities from time to time, as in the prosecution of several parishioners of Boxgrove in Sussex in 1622 for playing a game in a churchyard in which "a little childe had like to have her braines beaten out with a cricket batt" but such minor issues aside, even under the Puritans, opposition to cricket was nothing like as extreme as the hostility towards football.

Cricket boomed, and gamblers loved it. In 1660, the British parliament issued its Gambling Act, and limited bets to £100, which can't have caused too much outrage, as that was far more money than most people could dream of spending anyway. It was even getting press coverage, with the oldest known report dating back as far as the *Foreign Post*'s description in Sussex in 1697 of a "great match", played "eleven of a side … for fifty guineas apiece." Matches played between English counties were already in force by 1709, when Kent and Surrey played for a stake of £50, as advertised in *The Post Man* and from that year on, we

---

[39] Nobody really knows where the name 'cricket' came from, and you can take your pick from any of the French *criquet*, meaning a kind of pole, the Middle Dutch *krik*, meaning a bent staff used like a crutch, or the Old English *crice* for a stick used as a marker.

[40] In a court dispute over the Royal Grammar School in Guildford's rights to a certain plot of land.

have some kind of record of county cricket being played on an almost annual basis in England.

As it became more and more normal for villages, districts, schools and counties to play each other, there came with it a need to establish the first official *Laws of Cricket*, which were drafted in 1744, including the order that "the principals shall choose from amongst the gentlemen present two umpires who shall absolutely decide all disputes." The Marylebone Cricket Club was established in 1787 as the *de facto* governing body for the game, and pretty much remained so right up until 1993, when most of its responsibilities were turned over to the International Cricket Council (ICC).

Perhaps, as opposed to the wild and anarchic football, cricket by nature required a more structured approach. But the most likely reason for the lack of regulated football was that people simply weren't that bothered about it. From as early as 1736 the British broadsheets, while almost totally ignoring football, started providing more and more detailed reports of cricket matches to satisfy the nation's growing thirst for information about the game. When it was opened in London in 1787, crowds flocked to Lord's Cricket Ground, which in a somewhat modernised form still hosts test matches today.

Was football neglected as a working man's game as opposed to cricket being the game for the wealthier classes? We shouldn't assume that. An article published on January 18, 1862 in *The Field* commented that "one of the most encouraging features of the progress of cricket has been that it has brought out the spirit of order and discipline in the uneducated classes, and, like the volunteer movement, has infused self-control and orderly behaviour among the masses." Fact is, cricket mattered to a lot more people of all classes than football did.

First base

Cricket was also taken to America. Suffice to say that there is copious textual evidence to show that, but it eventually gave way to what would become baseball. There is an ongoing argument as to whether cricket spawned baseball, or whether that idea is ludicrous, and baseball is as American as the hamburger[41]. The 'proof' of the latter argument lies in the tale of a general named Abner Doubleday, who invented baseball in Cooperstown, New York, in 1839. Unfortunately, the claim is so flawed that it is a wonder it was ever taken seriously at all. It was the result of a 1908 enquiry called the *Mills Commission* to determine once and for all how baseball came about. This shockingly unscientific investigation revealed how Doubleday had written the rules, described the diamond and playing positions and even given the game its name.

The evidence to back any of this up is flimsy at best. In none of the many letters and papers that Doubleday left is there the remotest claim that he created baseball, or even played it, or

---

[41] Hamburgers are not of American origin. The name gives it away. Hamburg steaks were popular in the German city of the same name in the early 19th century, and as waves of Germans headed to the Americas, they took their culinary traditions with them.

went anywhere near Cooperstown in all his living days (which had conveniently ended 15 years before the report was made). In fact, the entire *Mills* report was based upon a single letter written by one elderly Abner Graves, who would have only been five in 1839, and who was later convicted for murdering his wife and wound up in a lunatic asylum. And even so, Graves never mentions anything about Doubleday writing any rules or describing the diamond – these were all things the *Mills Commission* invented to make their story sound better.

So why produce such an obviously fictitious tale in the first place? Why, to promote baseball as a local invention and cleanse it of any foreign stain. Doubleday was the perfect all-American hero, a veteran of many noble deeds in the Civil War, and plenty of other battles against nasty Indians and Mexicans besides. And Cooperstown was the ideal WASP rural town – they could not have wished for a place where the population was whiter or more Anglophonic.

But Doubleday was a lie. The truth is that any search to pin down the exact origin of baseball is futile. It wasn't born overnight. Long before there were any stars or stripes flying over America, what was basically the same game was being played in Europe. In the British Isles, the game of rounders (or in Irish *cluiche corr*) is basically the same thing, and was also called baseball a long time before the earliest known reference to it being played in the USA (a prohibition declared at Pittsfield, Massachusetts, in 1791). A children's book[42] published in England in 1744 used the name 'base-ball' to label a picture of some boys playing what looks very like, well, baseball, and the 1755 diary of Surrey teenager William Bray includes the entry: "After dinner, went to Miss Jeale's to play at Base Ball." If Doubleday invented baseball in 1839, how come English novelist Jane Austen in *Northanger Abbey* (1798) wrote how tomboy Catherine preferred "cricket, base-ball[43], riding on horseback, and running about the country at the age of fourteen, to books"? A German book on physical education written in 1796 dedicates no fewer than seven pages to the "English game of base-ball[44]", and although the rules are not exactly like American baseball, they're not far off. Abner Doubleday, my foot.

Baseball was no American invention, but it wasn't an English one either. It formed part of an extended family of bat and ball games that developed over the centuries, including the 'stoolball' that is mentioned in several early American texts and which can be dated back to at least 1672 in England. You'd struggle to pin down any European culture that didn't have

---

[42] John Newbery *A Little Pretty Pocket-Book, intended for the Amusement of Little Master Tommy and Pretty Miss Polly with Two Letters from Jack the Giant Killer* (1744). It was also published in Colonial America in 1762.
[43] She even makes the distinction of baseball being different to cricket!
[44] Johann Christoph Friedrich Guts Muths *Ball mit Freystäten (oder das englische Base-ball)* a chapter of *Spiele zur Uebung und Erholung des Korpers und Geistes fur die Jugend, ihre Erzieher und alle Freunde Unschuldiger Jugendfreuden* (1796).

some kind of game that could slip quite nicely into the evolutionary tree of baseball. The French had *la balle empoisonée*, the Finns had *poltopallo*, the Danes had *langbold*, the Poles had *palant*, the Germans had *schlagball*, the Russians had *lapta*, the Romanians had *oima*, the Turks had *chalita*, the Georgians had *gakvra-bukrti*, the Ukrainians had *miacz*... We could go on, but you probably get the message.

Let's just mention one, described by an Italian called Gaurinoni in Prague in 1610. He witnessed a Bohemian game in which "the players of one team spread out over the field standing 70, 80 and 100 steps from each other, prepared to catch the ball in the air. The players of the other team hit the ball in turns with a rounded stick thicker at the barrel end, three feet in length. The ball can be hit with great speed. The ball is pitched underhand to the batter by another player. The batter may hit the ball high and far away. If the ball is caught on the fly by a fielding player, the teams change sides. The batters become the catchers and the catchers become the batters ... The most skilful players come from Poland and Silesia, that is from the country of the game's origin, I presume[45]."

America developed the idea into a national phenomenon and a professional sport. England did likewise with cricket, and both sports shoved the rustic practice of football into the background. It would not be until 1895 that the great all-round athlete Charles Burgess Fry was moved to comment that "the great and widespread interest in football is a manifest fact. So much that nowadays it is frequently urged that cricket can no longer be regarded as our 'national game' in the true sense of the word[46]."

Against all the odds, football did survive. Let's find out how.

---

[45] Hippolytus Guarinoni *Titelblatt der Grewel der Verwüstung menschlichen Geschlechts von Hippolytus Guarinonius. Date. Ingolstadt* (1610).
[46] In *The Badminton magazine of sports and pastimes, Volume 1* (Longmans, Green and Co, 1895).

17 PLAY FOR TODAY
British Shrovetide football

Carnival games

Shrove Tuesday is often the traditional day for ball games, and that is not just in the British Isles[1]. There are many reasons for that. Some historians like to dwell on the pagan origins of a festival that honours the first full moon after the Vernal Equinox, and thus all the tales about lay-lines and fertility rites. But although the Bible has nothing to say about the date being a festival, and it is claimed the Christians hijacked a pagan feast day, neither is there any real evidence that Shrove Tuesday was ever celebrated for any other reason than it being the eve of first day of the Lent period of penance and austerity.

With forty days of abstention ahead, people did their damndest to make the most of the days before, and stuffed themselves with food and made merry in any way they could. Out of that, the carnival tradition was born, and Mardi Gras (Fat Tuesday), was the last chance to throw the rulebook out of the window and enjoy a day of wild excesses, revelry and even a bit of cross-dressing for those that are into that kind of thing.

The six day working week was the norm, and the only free day was Sunday, but it wasn't a day set aside for recreation. The church took a dim view of anything other than divine worship on the Sabbath. That is not to say that folk never got the chance to play games. In the days before television, record players or even books, they used their imaginations to find ways of keeping themselves amused in the little leisure time they had, and there would have been time for sport. But it was on feast days that the villagers could really get together and enjoy themselves, and with no religious obligations to get in their way, Shrove Tuesday was perfect[2].

This was a time for country fairs, where local farmers brought along their finest bulls, lambs, spuds and turnips and decided who had the best in the district. And they also competed at a whole variety of different games. Some of the typical Shrovetide activities have since disappeared (especially, and thankfully, those that involved the torture of animals), others like pancake races[3] still survive as folk traditions, while others still have gone on to become sports in the modern sense of the word.

---

[1] Shrovetide football was also common in France. Other nations that have or have had their own Mardi Gras sporting traditions include Sweden with its cracking *wädelöb* mixed relay races and Estonia with its luge races. Dutch painter Pieter Brueghel the Elder's classic *Fight Between Carnival and Lent* depicts a host of different Shrovetide games, while Denmark and Germany had their traditional Easter ball games.

[2] The other great day for community fun was New Year's Day, another secular holiday that gave the under-leisured commoners something to look forward to.

[3] Most modern British children would not know what a shrove was if it hit them in the face, but know exactly what Pancake Day is all about. It all started when dairy and egg products were forbidden for Lent, and there was a need to use them all up. Hence pancakes. The earliest reference to a pancake race dates back to Olney in

The latter was the fate of the football games that were so commonly associated to Shrovetide and New Year festivities. Yet in some parts of Britain, some of the feast day ball games managed to slip through the nets of both 19th century prohibition and codification and are still played in all their glory today. Hugh Hornby[4], the former curator of the National Football Museum in Preston, produced the most comprehensive study written to date in which he not only describes but often joins in with no fewer than fifteen different ball game festivals in Britain. So can they provide any clues to what pre-19th century ball play would have been like?

Kirkwall

We'll start from the top, and 'from the top' doesn't get much higher than Kirkwall, a harbour town in the Orkneys, an archipelago of 70 islands inhabited by some 20,000 people off the north coast of Scotland. Christmas and New Year (or Hogmanay, as they call it there) in Kirkwall are a time for barricading the fronts of homes and shops, while only a fool would leave his car on the streets near the town centre. That's because of a tradition known as the Kirkwall Ba Game, a form of street football that sends the town into an absolute frenzy for a day[5].

These islands were colonised by the Vikings around the year 1000 AD, which lends some credence to the theory that football could have come to Britain via games like *knattleikr*. There is a local legend that ties the game in with that heritage, which relates how a young Orcadian had gallantly dispatched a notoriously tyrannical Viking, who was named Tusker due to his protruding dentures. Our hero was carrying Tusker's severed head back home when one of his late victim's teeth scratched his leg. This caused an infection so bad that the poor lad dropped dead on arrival in Kirkwall. The villagers were so enraged that they started kicking the head around in anger[6].

Legends of goofy decapitations are great, but there is no solid evidence of ball play in Kirkwall until 1684 when the *Cathedral's Session Book* says "it was intimated that ther is non in toun and paroch that marries but shall pay a foot-ball to the scholars of the grammour school." It was originally played in the fields, known as the *Ba' Lea*, and it wasn't until sometime around 1800, when that land was enclosed, that it was brought into the streets, where it was not always a welcome addition to the local calendar. An 1826 edict decreed that

---

Buckinghamshire in 1445, the idea being to make a pancake, then run, frying pan in hand, to a certain point, and toss the pancake before running back.

[4] *Uppies and Downies: The Extraordinary Football Games of Britain* (English Heritage, 2008), to which this chapter is hugely indebted.

[5] Mainly thanks to the efforts of John Robertson (*The Kirkwall Ba', Between the Water and the Wall* Dunedin Academic Press Ltd, 2005), it is also one of the best researched folk games.

[6] Curiously, this is the same legend that appears in the Old Norse *Orkneyinga Saga*, with the protagonists reversed. In the Viking saga, it is Sigurd Eysteinsson who defeats his Scottish enemy, Maelbrigte Tusk, and who is infected by one his vile teeth.

"whereas sundry, idle and disorderly persons have occasionally disturbed the public peace … by playing at football through the streets … notice is hereby given that all and every persons are strictly prohibited and discharged from such practice in time coming." Fat chance, for another ban would go unheeded in 1841, and in 1845 plans to plant flowers and trees on the green in return for an end to the game were, not surprisingly, unsuccessful. Proposals to move the game back out of the town centre were met with a similar lack of support, and despite the *Orkney Herald* moaning in 1863 that "really it is high time that our citizens, young and middle aged, should bethink themselves of some more rational amusement" the Kirkwall Ba' Game continued regardless.

As it happened, by the 1870s, the game looked to be dying out of its own accord. Numbers were declining, and when in 1875 the Kirkwall Football Club held a rugby match on the same day as the Ba', there was widespread agreement that the new game was the way ahead. But the idea of limiting the number of players and moving to a nearby field actually had the reverse effect, seemingly reinvigorating the desire to maintain the old tradition as an annual alternative, and the Ba' has gained in strength and numbers ever since.

In medieval times, the land to the north of Kirkwall was governed by the bishops, and the land to the south by the local earl, creating a natural division in the community. The 'modern' Ba Game is traditionally played between the Up-the-gates and the Doon-the gates, which has nothing to do with any portals in the town, but is believed to be a corruption of the Old Norse term *gata*, meaning road.

Here we come back to the theory of football being associated to fertility, for it was once believed that winning would bring a good harvest to the Up-the-gates living inland or good fishing to those living Doon by the sea. An old rhyme reflects this:

"Up wi' the Ba' boys,
Up wi' the Ba'
An' ye'll get cheap meal
An' tatties an' a'."

The Orkney Jar[7] website goes on to say that "this belief seems to have survived through to the late 19th century, when, after a period of 29 years of Doonie New Year victories (1846-1875), the Uppies finally broke the Doonie domination and the ba' went up. After the game, an old spectator was recorded as saying that as it was 1846 (the first year of Doonie domination) that potato blight appeared in Orkney, 'we'll surely hae guid tatties this year, after the ba' has gaen up."

These days, with less defined family loyalties, the influx of 'ferryloupers' (outsiders) that weren't born above or below anything in Kirkwall at all, and the fact that most mothers now give birth at Balfour Hospital, which would make everybody in Kirkwall an Uppie, players are just as likely to represent one side or the other because that's the one their mates play for.

---

[7] *www.orkneyjar.com*, a website dedicated to the islands' heritage.

The Doonies also suffer from most of the new housing being in Uppie territory, which goes a long way to explaining why they only won one game between 1998 and 2007.

Although girls do appear in the junior Ba Game, this is really a game for men, although during the Second World War, and given the new role of women in society to cover for the soldiers who were away in battle, for a couple of years the women stepped in to play instead.

The Men's Ba kicks off with some local figure or former Ba Game great being nominated to throw the ball in at 13.00 at the Market Cross beside St Magnus Cathedral. What ensues from there is something little more aesthetically pleasing than a mass scrummage involving some 200 people, with the ball eventually breaking free for someone to make a run[8]. The aim is for the Doonies to get the ball into the water of Kirkwall Bay, while the Uppies have to touch it against a wall near the Catholic Church. But being the scorer of the winning goal is no major honour. What then happens is a bizarre ritual as the winning team fight amongst themselves for the ball, and the player who manages to raise it above his head is declared the champion – and is then obliged to hold a party for the rest of the players, which can be quite an expensive business!

The Orkney Jar writes that "there are no hard and fast rules. Although the game is fairly rough, tempers are usually held in check and foul play, or 'inappropriate behaviour', is not tolerated. Surprisingly, given the nature of the Ba', serious injuries to players are fairly rare. More often than not it is unfamiliar spectators who are hurt. When the pack breaks, there is often not much room to run! … A tight scrum forms around the leather trophy, while players on the outside brace themselves against any nearby buildings to prevent the opposition capturing ground. With the streets now their playing field, a heaving throng of men push and pull to try and gain a few metres nearer their goal … This struggle to gain ground means that a typical game can last for hours. Based on recent years, an average Men's Ba' lasts about five hours, but this could be anything up to eight hours, or more. Throughout the game, numerous tactics are used to achieve the goal. Very often, the majority of players have no idea where the ba' actually is. This leads to numerous attempts to smuggle the ba' out of the pack or create fake 'breaks' in the hope that the opposition will follow the wrong players."

Every now and again, games are won by cunning plans, all of which are accepted as long as they respect the spirit of the day. In 1901, an Uppie feigning injury in a doorway was actually hiding the ball, and eventually snuck away to score unchallenged, while in 1836, the Doonies managed to throw the ball out to a waiting boat, which they rowed around to the scoring point, much to the frustration of the exasperated Uppies on the land!

While many see it as an excuse for legalised thuggery, there has only ever been one recorded fatality, that of Captain William Cooper in 1903 due to a heart attack. Although there have been calls to end the festive games, the reason this has never happened was nicely

---

[8] Buckham Hugh Hossack (*Kirkwall in the Orkneys* (Harvard University, 1900)) remembered how some fifty years earlier "the ball was kicked or dribbled but never held." However, later in the century kicking was abandoned for the grappling and wrestling it involves so much of now, probably because once it moved into the city centre, a kicking game would not have been too window-friendly.

summed up by Councillor Mike Drever, who "wouldn't want to be the one that told the crowd on Christmas Day that they couldn't take part in the game[9]."

Although Kirkwall is the only one that has survived, similar games were once rife throughout the islands[10]. Stromness, the other major town in the Orkneys, also had its Ba', played by the Northenders and the Southenders, where games were played at weddings and the tradition was for the best man to supply the local boys with the ball. "Where the parties were stingy, the best man sometimes refused to pay the *ba' siller*, and in this case the wedding party was liable to attack from the youths[11]." The game was still going strong in 1910, when the locals took on a visiting group of trawlermen, and it was concern for the future of an expensive window installed in a café in Victoria Street that led to the game being banned for good in 1924. But a similar custom survived until 1936, which involved fighting it out not over a ball, but a tree trunk.

Further north, in the even more remote Shetlands, there was once ba' play too, in which "there are no goalposts, no scientific play, no attempt at combination by the players, each plays for himself, and tries to score with a long, terrific drive[12]." But by the mid 19th century, the games started including goalkeepers and a tripped player was given 'hailin' room' for a free kick on goal. It was turning into soccer.

Scottish Borders

The Borders region of Roxburghshire is so far at the other end of Scotland that it's almost in England. They bore the brunt of that of old. Whenever the Scots and English went to war, these poor folk would be caught up in the thick of it. That is often cited as the reason why the Borders people are such hardened souls, and hence created another ba' game hotbed. Jedburgh, Hobkirk, Denholm and Ancrum all still hold annual matches, as does nearby Duns in Berwickshire. Other traditional games no longer exist. Play was last recorded in Lanton in 1850, was successfully banned in Melrose in 1900, and lived on at Kirk Yetholm until as late as 1932. Hawick's game, which involved plenty of damp frolicking in the River Teviot, was reported with annual enthusiasm in the *Hawick Express*, but there was a forewarning of the game's demise in 1934, where it was noted that "at no time was the crowd anything like the dimensions of immediately preceding years ... the subject was debated and discussed among the onlookers, and the general feeling was that there was a marked lack of enthusiasm all over." The Second World War was on the way, and when it was over, the Hawick game was forgotten. Lilliesleaf and Selkirk both maintain the tradition of sorts, but at the former it's nothing more than a re-enactment by primary school children, and at the latter it's a bit of fun

---

[9] Quoted in *The Orcadian* in December 2001.
[10] In as many as 26 places, write Collins, Martin and Vamplew.
[11] Walter Traill Dennison *Orcadian Sketch-Book* (William Peace & Son, 1880).
[12] Ernest W Hardy *Life and Customs of the Shetland Isles* (1913).

for junior members of the local rugby team. Even so, throughout the region, the odd informal handba' game can still be seen played by adults, especially at weddings.

It all makes for an impressive concentration of Shrovetide games, and we even have pictorial testimony thanks to Scottish wig-maker turned artist Alexander Carse (1770–1843). His terrific 1830 oil on canvas, *The foot-ball play*, which sold for £266,250 at Bonhams in 2006, shows male villagers, apparently in Jedburgh, battling for a ball on the green as others stand by to watch. At least one of the players is most definitely trying to kick it, while there don't seem to be any attempts at handling going on. If anything, it's a very basic game of soccer, though there is nothing in the picture that, at least obviously, resembles goalposts. The same man painted *Doonies versus the Croonies on New Year's Day* some twenty years earlier, which shows a group of villagers vying to kick a surprisingly small looking ball on a plot of land near the sea. Once again, there is no sign of any goals.

The Jedburgh game is the biggest and most famous in the Borders. If the legend is to be believed, in ancient times, they used to play with the heads of English raiders. The tale recounts how, in 1548 and on recapturing Ferniehirst Castle from the English (who had committed unspeakable atrocities in the neighbourhood), the local Scots celebrated by kicking the severed head of an English officer who had raped a Scottish girl. It is also said that the streamers attached to the leather ball represent the hair of the deceased Englander. There is also a claim that James V rode from Melrose to Jedburgh to play in the game, but that wouldn't fit too well with the Ferniehirst Castle legend, as James died six years before that battle (leaving behind seven illegitimate children, including three conceived before his 20th birthday).

The tales are great, but all we know for sure is that Jedburgh has been playing ball for about three hundred years. It was in 1704 that the town council decided to "discharge the game now and all time coming … sometimes both old and young near lost their lives thereby." 'All time coming' was shorter than they hoped, for just two years later there was a report of a local youth being fined for "rastling at the football" and a century and a half later, in 1849, the authorities tried to use the excuse of a cholera epidemic to kill off the "eminently dangerous" activity that was "an obstruction to the business of the town." A judge from Edinburgh stepped in to see the ban overruled on a technically, adding that "I for one should hesitate to encourage the abolition of an old and customary game which from time immemorial has been enjoyed by the community."

The game has continued ever since, even through both World Wars. It has only once been cancelled, in 1901, out of respect for Queen Victoria's funeral on the same day, and not even the outbreak of foot and mouth disease, which put a hold on just about every rural festivity in 2001, from folk football to the Six Nations, was going to stop the people of Jedburgh, who defied a police barricade and played regardless. One thing that has changed is the day – for rather than Fastern's E'en, the game has been played since 1971 on a Thursday, because that's early closing day and makes more sense for everyone.

257

Like most Borders games, Jedburgh's seems to have undergone a transition from footba' to handba' over the years, involves play between the top and bottom of the town, in this case the Guppies and the Doonies, and the aim is to score a *hail*, that common Scots alternative for 'goal'.

It isn't always too thrilling to watch. Writing for the *Southern Reporter* in 2008, Sue Gyford called it a "15-minute stationary maul. It looked like a cross between a rugby scrum and the furtive, collaborative milking of a cow; only the occasional writhing of a Caterpillar boot or the twitch of a builder's buttock revealing the sneaky grasping for control taking place beneath." Sly ball-concealing tactics are not derided in the Borders game – they are part of the fun. What you often end up with is a bundle of twenty or so poker-faced lads scuffling about trying to work out who actually has the ball stuffed down their pants or hidden in a pocket. It's said that such furtive underhandedness dates back to the border conflicts with the English, where anything went when it came to dastardly methods for outwitting the enemy.

The earliest reference to the game in Duns comes just two years after the first mention of the Kirkwall game. That was in 1686, when John Bayne's complaint to the magistrate about unfair treatment in the Fasting's Even (Shrovetide) match was not upheld. In 1724, the town annals provide a tremendous account of an incident not so much related to the game itself, but to the drum that was used to herald the start of a game that "did always end and determine in the effusion of blood among the inhabitants." Local bailie, or magistrate, John Gray was under orders to "prevent riots and tumults" and confiscated the drum. The footballers went ahead with the game regardless, but the losing side to refused to accept defeat because when the "winners were then to shew the ball and proclaim their victory" the traditional drum was not there, meaning the result was invalid. "Whereupon they fell a fighting and beating and blooding of one another, but att length went into one common concert to goe in a body and seize by force the drum."

Off they went to John Gray's place, where they "broke down his windows and threw manie stones in at the said windows … and during this time they used manie execrable oaths that they would destroy the complainer and bereave him and those of his family of their lives." However, John Gray refused to give in, and members of the mob were held up for trial.

The game ultimately survived, being played as an annual event using three different balls, one coloured gold, the second silver, and the third spotted. It was played between the married men, who had to get the ball to the pulpit in the church, whereupon the bell would toll in celebration, and the bachelors, who had to get it to any of the grinding mills on the outskirts of the town. Any bachelor who scored was caked in flour but then rewarded with a meal of pork and dumplings by the miller. The game was last recorded in 1886, after which it was largely forgotten for more than half a century. The modern version is a revival, started in 1949 as part of the Reivers' Week summer festival, and does little justice to the game that so offended the drum-pinching John Gray. Though still played by teams of married men and bachelors, these rarely number more than ten or so a side, and there is nothing more inspiring to aim for than bins outside the Post Office and the White Swan hotel at either end of the market square.

The game in the small village of Ancrum is another revival, and for his efforts, local resident Iain Heard deserves as much hero status as any of the great and good to have been mentioned in this book. Back in 1837, it was written that "there is no species of amusement to which the parishioners are especially attached, with the exception of the game of 'ball' … the young men of one district being pitched against those of another[13]." The Ancrum game survived through to 1974, when lack of interest brought it to an end.

But Heard was determined not to let it die, and for each of the following 22 years, he trudged the distance between the two hailing points, even if it meant doing it on his own. That continued until 1997 when he finally managed to gather the support he needed. The sides are a bit of a mish-mash of locals and visitors from the other ba' playing towns, but the ba' is back in Ancrum, and all thanks to Iain Heard. With junior games now played as well, the tradition is being passed on to new generations.

Ancrum's game is now in a healthier state than another in a similarly tiny location, Hobkirk. It was once a grand occasion, with the death of a shepherd recorded in 1783 when he fell in the river and died of hyperthermia. It was leading to problems for local landowners in 1803 due to "the pernicious effects of a vast number of people assembling from this and other parishes for the idle purpose of playing the ball." Nowadays it's a low-key event that has lost its madcap cross-country roots, and just involves a group of twenty or so diehards who go out into the cold to battle over a ball in a stretch of country lane, stopping play now again to let a car pass by, the driver probably wondering what on earth is going on. Eventually the ball finds its way into the hands of a younger player, who no longer has any goal to aim for other than running so far away that none of the seniors have any chance of catching him, and a new ball is thrown up instead.

The other handba' village, Denholm, is also bravely maintaining its tradition, which starts on the huge village green, and has hailing points on the outskirts of the village. Also once played by married men against bachelors, teams these days are unlikely to have more than twenty players, with the people of Denholm playing as the Uppies, and visitors from the other handba' villages playing as Downies. There is no evidence for the age of the Denholm game, but it was very much part of the Borders circuit in the 19th century – 70 year old Mr Amos once defied his age to score in 1886, while an outsider by the name of Best was killed in one game when he was impaled on a set of railings. Ouch.

Cornwall

If we go right down to the other extreme of the British Isles, and St Columb Major in Cornwall, we find another Shrove Tuesday game that has survived down the centuries. But

---

[13] By the Rev John Pator in the *New Statistical Account of Scotland.*

here they call it hurling. It sounds too beautiful to be true, but the direct descendant of the sport so wonderfully described by Richard Carew in 1602 is still played today! So, let's go back and pick up the story where we left off.

Carew said it was a violent game, and it was. The 1705 parish register in Cambourne announced the burial of William Trevarthen after his "being disstroid to a hurling with Redruth men at the high dounes the 10th day of August." Some twenty years later, Daniel Defoe, he of Robinson Crusoe fame, was in the county as part of a remarkable journey documented in a series of letters. He wasn't too taken with hurling though. "The game called the Hurlers," he wrote, "is a thing the Cornish men value themselves much upon; I confess, I see nothing in it, but that it is a rude violent play among the boors, or country people; brutish and furious, and a sort of an evidence, that they were, once, a kind of barbarians[14]."

Defoe wasn't impressed, and neither were many Cornishmen, because from here on there was something of a lull in the game. By 1846, Richard Edmonds described something that had not been played since "about a century ago[15]" other than in the four places he goes on to describe for posterity.

At Germoe, near Penzance, he says the hurlers "instead of forming two parties, act independently, every individual striving to catch the ball for himself, and whoever succeeds in lodging it thrice at the goal wins the game." In Helston, the teams played into the same goal – the gate to the Guildhall.

The people of St Ives devised an inimitable way of sorting out the teams. Anyone called Tom, William or John played on one side, and everybody else played on the other. But Robert Hunt, writing in 1865, had noted that more imaginative trends in naming baby were starting to cause a bit of an imbalance, and it was not long after that the time-honoured division into Upalongs and Downalongs came into St Ives hurling.

Hunt claimed that although "formerly it was practised annually, from the many accidents that usually attended that game it is now scarcely ever practised[16]." Until recently, St Ives had played against the parishes of Lelant and Ludgvan, and "the struggle was to throw the ball into the parish church, the successful party keeping the ball, the unsuccessful buying a new one." What fate led to Ludgvan's loss of interest is not revealed, but Lelant pulled out because they were fed up with being outnumbered. With no opposition, St Ives started playing the game among themselves, where teams battled to touch the silver ball against a single pole staked into the beach. By the end of the century they were playing into separate goals at different ends of the sand, and this carried on until the Second World War, which brought an end the game.

Mayor Keith Slocombe decided hurling deserved a revival in 1972, but in all honesty, the new version does little justice to what was once Cornwall's finest sporting treasure. After

---

[14] Daniel Defoe *A tour thro' the whole island of Great Britain* (published between 1724 and 1727).
[15] Richard Edmonds *On Some Ancient Customs on the Western Extremity of Cornwall* (1846).
[16] Robert Hunt *Popular Romances of the West of England* (1865).

dabbling with basketball-style nets, hurling in St Ives today is a rather tame spectacle. It basically involves tossing the ball at 10.30 to a group of children assembled on the beach. The winner is the child that has the ball in their possession at noon, so you get one mad scramble that lasts but a few moments before one of the bigger kids inevitably gets hold of the ball and runs away to hide somewhere before reappearing at noon to collect their prize. Watching children play hide and seek may bring a moment of joy to the families of St Ives, but it no longer forms part of British footballing heritage[17].

In the 19th century, it was only at St Columb that there was still a form of hurling that seemed to do justice to the game's history, and that is still the case today. There, according to Richard Edmonds in 1846, "the shops being closed and businesses suspended, many hundreds of persons of all ranks from the town and country are assembled in the streets waiting for the hurling of the ball, the townsmen forming one party and the countrymen the other, each having its own goal – a low granite post with a concavity on top to receive the ball. The goals are about one mile and a half apart, having the town midway between them … St Columb is the only place where gentlemen now unite with the rest of the inhabitants in this diversion."

Nearby St Mawgan often provided opposition, and in fact their own 'low granite post with a concavity on top' is still in the churchyard. In 1858, St Columb's hurlers attended the regatta in nearby Newquay, now a bustling tourist resort. A triple-header was played, and Newquay won all three (against St Columb Major and Minor, and a 'County' team). The *Royal Cornwall Gazette* reported that it "could not but admire the good nature and temper with which the rude knocks and rough embraces were interchanged" and opined that this match "on the beach and therefore seen throughout, must have afforded the lovers of this athletic and thoroughly Cornish sport great delight."

The 1896 edition between St Columb Major and St Columb Minor was an altogether less jovial affair, as reported in *Newquay Visitors Notes and Directory*. "Two boys from Newquay" ruined the day's action by losing the silver ball in the sea. At a later meet, the "St Columb men acted in a vindictive spirit towards the Newquay Hurlers in consequence of the foolhardy action of a couple of Newquay Youths taking the ball to sea at the preliminary hurl, where it was lost and so bringing the match to an abrupt termination."

The games with Newquay lasted until the First World War, but only St Columb has maintained the tradition to this day, with games between Townsmen and Countrymen. Until the 1940s, the country folk were the majority, but St Columb has grown and agriculture has gone auto, so the balance has shifted, although the Countrymen do get to benefit from the help of outsiders too.

---

[17] There is a game played after the beating the bounds at Bodmin, which takes place roughly once every five years, at the time of writing for the last time in 2010. Players carry the ball from the 'Salting Pool' on the outskirts of the town, and the winning player is whoever has it in their possession when the play reaches the Turret Clock in Fore Street.

As in so many other towns, the town barricades its homes and establishments against the annual battle on Shrove Tuesday, and again the Saturday one week after. There are no written rules, and it can get pretty rough, but the players usually know what's traditionally right and wrong, so injuries are rare. The goals are still the old stone troughs on either side of the town, although the A39 bypass now causes something of an obstacle to the Townsmen's goal (an inconvenience that is compensated by the vast reduction in traffic in the town centre, which once led to chaotic scenes on hurling days). And a new concept crept in, nobody can be quite sure when, that goals can also be scored by crossing any point on the parish boundary with the ball. That, according to the *Guinness Book of Records*, makes St Columb the biggest sports ground in the world! It adds a cross-country flavour to the game in the mould of the ancient 'hurling to country', and sees the action commonly crossing private property or even entering buildings before it all ends with the famous silver ball being dipped in gallons of ale and 'called up' in honour of the winning goalscorer.

The majesty of hurling in St Columb is that whereas most ancient football games that 'have survived to today' are revivals rather than genuine continuations of a custom, there is enough evidence to show that hurling has been played in St Columb uninterrupted for over 500 years, aided by being played in an outpost of England where soccer and rugby cultures had far less influence in the 19th century. And long may it survive.

Derby

The game between All Saints and St Peters in the city of Derby is associated to the almost certain folk legend of the 3rd century win against the Romans and also a theory for the origin of the expression 'derby' for when two local rivals meet each other[18]. It is inevitably mentioned in any study of Shrovetide games, mainly because such a surprising amount of information has survived on it, and to add to the drama, the Derby game was successfully suppressed at its peak. Despite the public concern, it all sounds very quaint and olde worlde when he hear the 'Oranges and Lemons' rhyme that went

"Pancakes and fritters, say All Saints and St Peters;
When will the ball come? Say the bells of St Alkmun's;
At two they will throw, says St Werabo;
Oh! Very well, says little St Michael!"

But quaint it was anything but. It's questionable whether it goes all the way back to the Romans, but it was certainly around in 1731, when William Hutton describes how the local jailor, John Greatrex, was locked up in his own cells for playing football, a sport Mayor Isaac

---

[18] There are others. Most prefer the idea that it was inherited from the biggest horse race of the British flat season, the Derby, founded by the 12th Earl of Derby in 1780, and later applied to the biggest match in any sports team's season. As the *Widnes Weekly News* in March 1889 describes a game between the local rugby team and the touring Maori as a 'derby', we can assume it was only later that the term was strictly reserved for local rivalries.

Borrow, had decided to suppress. Greatrex vowed that he knew the local nick so well that it "should not hold him one night. He fulfilled his declaration, for he broke it, and fled before morning[19]." Fifteen years later, in 1746, another Mayor, Humphrey Booth, announced in the *Derby Mercury* that he had heard "there will be a public football playing" and ordered "that there be no riotous and tumultuous meeting of any persons … for the purpose aforesaid in said borough on pain of being rigorously prosecuted for the same as well as for the consequences of breaking windows and doing other mischiefs."

Whatever effect that ban had, Derby was still playing street football in 1791, when Hutton provided an excellent description of something between rugby and water polo. "I have seen this coarse sport carried to the barbarous height of an election-contest. Nay, I have seen a foot-ball hero chaired through the streets like a successful Member, although his utmost elevation of character was no more than that of a butcher's apprentice. Black eyes, bruised arms and broken shins are equally the marks of victory and defeat. I need not say that this is the delight of the lower ranks, and is attained at an early period. The very infant learns to kick, and then to walk. The professors of this athletic art think themselves bound to follow the ball wherever it flies; and as Derby is fenced in with rivers, it seldom flies far without flying into the water, and I have seen these amphibious practitioners of foot-ball-kicking jump into the river upon a Shrove Tuesday when the ground was covered with snow."

James Walvin claims that "in keeping with the unrestrained traditions of popular footballing violence, the Derby game claimed its share of victims," but Hugh Hornby feels the condemnations were exaggerated, pointing out that there is only evidence of one fatality[20]. John Snape, according to the *Derby Mercury* in 1796, "was unfortunately drowned in the presence of a great number of people who could not render any assistance."

That incident led to a serious reappraisal of what the Mayor felt "has no better recommendation than its antiquity for its further continuance … being full satisfied that many public and private evils have been occasioned by the custom of playing at football in this borough on Shrove Tuesday, we have unanimously resolved that such customs shall from henceforth be discontinued."

But it was yet another idle threat, because it was still around in 1829, being described as a game that "commences in the market place … about noon a large ball is tossed up in the midst of them … The struggle to obtain the ball, which is carried[21] in the arms of those who have possessed themselves of it, is then violent, and the motion of the human tide heaving to and fro without the least regard to consequences is tremendous. Broken shins, broken heads,

---

[19] William Hutton *The History Of Derby: From The Remote Ages Of Antiquity To The Year* (1791).

[20] Llewellynn Frederick William Jewitt in *The ballads & songs of Derbyshire* (1869) did write of "scores of people who were fortunate enough not to get killed or lamed" but it's unlikely he had any more first-hand evidence of this than we do.

[21] It is important that he mentions carrying. Glover also mentions that "a desperate game of football in which the ball is struck with the feet of the players is played at Ashover and other wakes", which suggests an early distinction between soccer and rugby type games.

torn coats, and lost hats are amongst the minor accidents of this fearful contest … A Frenchman passing through Derby remarked that if Englishmen called this playing, it would be impossible to say what they would call fighting. Still the crowd is encouraged by respectable persons attached to each party, who take a surprising interest in the result of the day's sport, urging on the players with shouts, and even handing to those who are exhausted oranges and other refreshment. The object of the St Peter's party is to get the ball into the water down the Morledge brook into the Derwent as soon as they can, while the All Saints party endeavor to prevent this and to urge the ball westward. The St Peters players are considered to be equal to the best water spaniels, and it is certainly curious to see two or three hundred men up to their chins in the Derwent continually ducking each other. The numbers engaged on both sides exceed a thousand, and the streets are crowded with lookers-on. The shops are closed, and the town presents the aspect of a place suddenly taken by storm[22]."

A letter from someone calling himself Pilarius[23] described the same goings-on a year later. He was writing in response to an article on the similar game at Kingston, a game he agreed was "properly called *foot*-ball" for in Derby, the ball "is taken up and hugged in the arms." Pilarius felt the game had been played in Derby "time out of mind", but makes no mention of the supposed Roman origin, instead speculating that it "originated from the regular game of *foot*-ball; and that the alteration in the mode of play was either caused by Magisterial interference, for as the line of road to either goal became more thickly studded by buildings, the danger of breaking windows, etc, dictated the adoption of the present method[24]." He also tells how the play would even move into the town sewers, which were populated by such pleasantries as decomposed cats and dogs. We even had early professionalism, for "some of the most opulent of the inhabitants have been known to hire men to play at five-shillings-a-head." The afternoon could involve twenty or thirty fights "but after this, goodwill and harmony are restablished and a fresh debtor and creditor account established for another year." He had heard of one attempt by the constables to put a stop to the game, but this had gone down in local history as ludicrous, having been thwarted by a lady smuggling the ball into the square under her petticoat, with "no farther obstruction having ever since been offered to this old and favorite recreation of my townsmen."

The future of the Derby game was not as bright as Pilarius thought. "It is not a trifling consideration that a suspension of business for nearly two days should be created for the inhabitants for the mere gratification of a sport at once so useless and barbarous" wrote the *Derby and Chesterfield Reporter* in 1832. *The Pioneer* denounced its "barbarous recklessness" in 1834, and also reported on how an alternative festival involving hymns and

---

[22] Stephen Glover, Thomas Noble *History and Gazetteer of the County of Derbyshire* (1829).

[23] In *Sporting Magazine* (June 4, 1830).

[24] This theory of football moving from kicking to handling to prevent damage from stray balls is a common one, and here is contemporary evidence to support it.

speeches was being organised by trade unionists[25]. There is no need to say what the footballers made of that.

In 1845, the Temperance Society decided to join the campaign to create a distraction for the Shrovetide footballers[26]. Shrove Tuesday and Ash Wednesday were instead to be celebrated with a sports day of jumping matches, blindfold foot races, sack races, a plum pudding and treacle eating match and races up a greasy pole to bring down a joint of meat, "to give a fair field for manly exercise and innocent relations free from all immorality and vicious excitement[27]." The sports days were all well and good, and the £10 prizes for each event even better, but some footballers didn't want compromise. They wanted footy, and the game took to the streets regardless. As punishment for being such naughty boys, all the other events were cancelled, treacle eating matches and all.

The following year, 1846, a more direct approach was adopted. The players were ordered to surrender the ball to the mayor, who put on a horse racing meet instead, and also promised to use his influence to arrange a holiday so the workers could enjoy the greatest thrill of the time – a ride on the new railway. But what were described as 'thousands' had no intention of giving in to such subornment, and descended upon the town centre to play no matter what. The police, assisted by the 5th Nottingham Dragoon Guards, were called in to put a stop to it, and the mayor himself was hit on the shoulder by a brick during the rioting that led to several arrests and fines. It was the last straw for too many, and a list of 178 influential names petitioned the mayor for even more drastic action. In the following years there would be further attempts to play games, but in Derby at least, Shrovetide football was doomed.

The bylaw that football is illegal in the streets of Derby still stands to this day, but that did not mean that football, or even Shrovetide football, had gone away entirely. In February 1856, the *Derbyshire Times and Chesterfield Herald* rather poignantly reported that "here and there might be seen a knot of lads outside the town keeping up the old custom of football, although this amusement has become by degrees beautifully less, till it has well nigh been discontinued." The authorities had won the battle, but not the war. Exactly forty years after football was banned in the city, Derby County FC was formed. There were few objections and the club is still going strong today. Treacle eating matches, to the best of our knowledge, are not.

---

[25] They may have taken their lead from the Methodists in such villages as Preston and Hedon in Yorkshire, who had also objected to the annual footy match and decided in 1820 to provide an alternative in the form of tea-drinking, prayer and hymn singing on a nearby hill. The rush of Yorkshire footballers chasing to be first to the hymn book was unlikely to have raised much alarm.

[26] Anthony Delves' 1981 report on *Popular recreation and social conflict in Derby, 1800–1850* provides a detailed investigation of the events.

[27] In the words of Mayor John Moss in the *Derby and Chesterfield Reporter.*

Ashbourne

Street footy may have been quashed in Derby, but just down the road in Ashbourne, what is known as Royal Shrovetide Football is still played today, and is the most celebrated game of its kind in England. Its 'royal' prefix is relatively new, but contrary to common belief, it had nothing to do with a visit from the future Edward VIII in 1928. It was granted when the organisers sent a ball as a gift for Princess Mary on occasion of her marriage to Henry Lascelles. Hopefully it cheered her up, as it was an arranged wedding to a man she allegedly detested.

The locals say their game goes back to the 12th century, which may be as much a folk legend as the claim that all records of its history were lost to a fire in the 1890s. Those flames handily removed any evidence to the contrary that the game originated when a severed head was thrown to the crowds following an execution, although it is speculated that poet and Derbyshire man Charles Cotton was referring to the game in his 1683 poem *Burlesque on the Great* that went:

"Two towns that long at war had waged,
Being at foot-ball now engaged,
For honour, as both sides pretended,
Left brave tryall to be ended,
Till the next thaw, for they were frozen,
On either part at leest a dozen,
With a good handsome space between 'em
Like Rollerich stones, if you've seen 'em
And could no more run, kick, or tripye
Than I can quaff off Aganippe,
Til ale, which crowns all such pretences,
Mull'd them again into their senses"

However, we can't be sure whether this poem is even about the Ashbourne game, and considering the Rollerich Stones are probably the Rollright Stones, a monolith more than 90 miles to the south, there's a good chance it is not.

As opposed to the Derby game that Stephen Glover believed could have been of Roman origin, the Ashbourne game was, in contrast "of modern date." The earliest surviving reference we have of it is an 1821 song performed not by the Rollerich Stones, but by an actor named John Fawcett at the Ashbourne theatre…

"Shrove Tuesday, you know, is always the day.
When the pancake's the prelude and the football's the play
Where upwards and downwards men ready for fun,
Like the French at the Battle of Waterloo run…
… The ball is turned up and the Bullring's the place,
And as fierce as a bulldog's is every man's face,
Whilst kicking and shouting and howling they run,

266

> Until every stitch of the ball comes undone,
> There's Faulkner and Smith, Bodge Hand and some more,
> Who hide it and hug it and kick it so sore,
> And deserve a good whopping at every man's door,
> In the neat little town of Ashbourne …
> … If they get to the park, the upwards men shout,
> And think all the downwards men put to the rout,
> But a right about face they soon have to learn,
> And the upwards men shout huzza in their turn.
> Then into Shaw Croft, where the bold and the brave,
> Get a ducking in trying the foot-ball to save,
> For 'tis well known they fear not a watery grave,
> In defence of the foot-ball at Ashbourne"

The game was as much a disturber of the peace as in Derby, and the 1835 Highways Act was used as the excuse to get it moved from the streets to the meadows, with £5 being offered to the goalscorer. The locals reacted badly, and refused to be taken in by what they saw as a bribe, obstinately declaring that "the old game of football will be played in the old way, the ball will be thrown up in the old place, and the old goals will be used."

By 1860, the town had its own fledgling police force, and one of its first projects was to do something about the ball game. Superintendent James Corbishley, in the *Derby Mercury*, explained that "I should not attempt to interfere with the play, but simply take the names of those who took active part in it." He did just that, with 54 people being summoned to court, and five of them receiving fines of 40 shillings each, plus damages. Amusingly, one of these was a lawyer who, after being found guilty, was then responsible for presenting the defence of one of his fellow accused!

The same thing happened in 1861, but in 1862, the authorities upped the ante and forced any prosecuted players to sign a pledge that they would no longer take part in future games and "severally use our best endeavours to discourage others from again offending as we have done." It's doubtful that many did that, but the players did agree to steer clear of the town centre. Matters proceeded with relative calm until 1878 when James Barker was drowned in the river. That was just the excuse the authorities needed to impose a ban, and the *Derby Mercury* came out with a scathing review of the events saying "it is gratifying for us to receive the assurance that this unmannerly custom … has been observed for the last time."

That's what the authorities thought, but the people had different ideas, and the 1879 game turned into a defiant confrontation with the police, with balls being confiscated only for new ones to appear in their stead. Landowner and magistrate Mr Frank, a Liverpudlian who had refused access to the 200 acres of land he owned in the town, came in for particular grief. A handbill was circulated inviting him "to leave Ashbourn, it will be no loss, but the old game will and shall be played."

Efforts to quash the game over the following decade were largely ignored, and in 1891 over 7000 people turned out to protest. Unlike at Derby, where local businesses supported the police, most of the good people of Ashbourne had no particular problems with the game, and the law's intervention probably stirred up more trouble than had they left well alone. The *Ashbourne News* was quite right to say in 1920 that "organised opposition had the effect of giving to the ancient game a new lease of life."

Players were unfazed by prosecution because it earned them a certain hero status in the community, and their fines were covered by well-supported fund raising events. The locals refused to be tamed, and with the policing and legal costs escalating, 1891 was the last year they bothered trying to suppress the game. It was a victory for the people, and the game is still played today.

Like so many Shrovetide games, it is played by the people from opposing sides of the town, here named the Up'Ards and the Down'Ards. The idea used to be to score goals by getting the cork-filled leather ball to one of two mills, and tapping it three times against the corresponding millstone. Neither of these mills exists any longer, and since 1995 the goals have been moved to the sides of the River Henmore to make the scoring more of a challenge, where special stone plinths have been erected.

As in most games like these, there are no team colours, and therefore no way of telling who plays for who among the messy 'hug' of bodies. The secretary of the committee, Jack Hawksworth, was most concerned about this in a letter to the *Ashbourne Telegraph* in 1934, urging players to keep "our traditions as of old … I mean 'football' not 'hugball' … let us see more of the ball … it does not require hugging like a child three weeks old. Give it plenty of boot." He didn't get his way. Nowadays, you will see very little kicking at Ashbourne.

Like many Shrovetide games, it has had to adapt to the times. In 1952 a motorbike was used, and in 1956 a car – leading the committee to decree the following year that "any form of mechanical propulsion" was illegal.

It can get pretty rough and claustrophobic out there, but the death of 51 year old David Johnson from a heart attack in 2007 was the first fatality since William Tunnicliffe perished due to hyperthermia in 1906.

Back-to-back games are held on Shrove Tuesday and Ash Wednesday, a tradition that goes back to the 19th century, although nowadays it is often said that the first game is for the benefit of the tourists, and the second is the real one. Although visitors are welcome to join in, they do have a habit of messing the whole thing up by not really knowing or caring which team they are playing for or where they are supposed to be taking the ball, and the action gets considerably more interesting after dark, when most of the outsiders have taken their photos and wondered off home.

They wouldn't have scored any goals. Goalscorers are traditionally predetermined – the idea being to get the ball to the designated person for them to score, and unlike most

Shrovetide games, the ladies have, to the best of anybody's knowledge, always taken part. As early as 1943 both Doris Mugglestone and Doris Sowter 'gaoled' on the same day.

Atherstone

Warwickshire was once riddled with Shrovetide ball games, but since Nuneaton's game was last played in 1881, the town of Atherstone has been on its own.

The claim it dates back to the early 13th century stems from a comment by Ralph Thompson in 1790 about a game played during the reign of King John for a bag of gold by groups of lads from Warwickshire and Leicestershire. "Atherstone being the nearest town to the place where they play'd it, it is and has been a custom to turn a Foot Ball up … every year since that time."

It's not clear how much veracity there was in Thompson's story, but Atherstone still celebrated its 800th edition in 1999, though that was actually the anniversary of King John's ascension to the throne, and not necessarily of the ancient match. All we really know is that by 1790, the game was already a long-lived custom, and like so many Shrovetide matches, fell afoul of the council and survived a particularly vicious attempt to see it abolished in 1901.

Since 1981, the ball, supplied by rugby union manufacturers Gilbert, has been thrown up from the balcony of Barclays Bank, usually by a celebrity guest. The game that follows is a curious one, as there are no teams and no goals. It is played for half an hour from 4.30 pm along a stretch of what was once the famous Roman road of Watling Street. The winner is simply whoever is holding the ball at five o'clock, rendering most of the play into one mass (and often drunken) bundle to hold on to the ball and ward off challengers trying to take it away.

The event's chairman Bill Dixon[28] once dauntingly claimed that "if a rugby team came here to get that ball in a scrummage, they'd never last. Not with the local chaps – some of them are deadly killers." It can all get pretty brutal, although since 1986, stewards have been strategically placed to at least try to make sure things don't get too out of hand.

Sedgefield

Sedgefield in County Durham was the hometown of Tony Blair, but far more importantly, it has Shrovetide football too. Claims stretch its history back to when the builders of the local church (constructed 1246–1256) challenged the local farmers. As always, there is no supporting evidence for the tale and not until 1802 is the game first recorded, in *The Sporting Magazine*. However, in 1827 the Shrove Tuesday game was old enough to be called "an

---

[28] A Scotsman cited in *The Birmingham Post* (March 2002).

ancient custom" after which the "victorious and the vanquished resort to the public houses, where they generally drink deep e'er they depart[29]."

Montagu Shearman refers to the following report he cut out of a local paper in 1887, at a time when the codified forms of soccer and rugby were already a quarter of a century old. "In pursuance of a custom which has been in vogue for centuries, the tradesmen and countrymen of the little town of Sedgefield, County Durham, held a week or two ago their annual football carnival on the old plan, the players being without limit and the field of play about half a mile long, the goals at one end a pond and at the other end a spring. At one o'clock the sexton put the ball through a bull ring and threw it into the air[30], and a scrimmage of four hundred persons ensued. After a series of 'moving incidents by flood and field' JB collared the ball and dropped it into the stream, dived for it, and gained the victory for the tradesmen, who carried him shoulder high."

Sedgefield's tournament used to be played between the Tradesmen and the Countrymen, but it is now just a free-for-all. It lacks the scale and violence of Kirkwall or Ashbourne, only being played by a handful of youngsters who rarely attract more than a handful of tourist onlookers. For much of the day, it is just one mad rush around the surrounding villages, motivated by a handy extra rule that the first person to get the ball into any local pub gets a free drink.

About three hours later, the ball is finally immersed in a stream near the church, and then the players return to the green for the only seriously competitive part of the game – the battle to become the day's champion by once again passing the ball three times through the bull ring. Like at Atherstone, this is an individual rather than team game, although the forming of alliances vastly improves your chances.

The winning player gets to keep the ball, which is inscribed with the game's traditional ditty, which goes:

> "When the pancakes are sated,
> Come to the ring and you'll be mated,
> There this ball will be upcast,
> May this game be better than the last."

Alnwick

Another annual football match is played in Alnwick, Northumberland, where it is known as 'Scoring the Hales[31]' and is contested by the parishes of St Michael and St Paul. But that division has only existed since the late 19th century, before which it was social and marital status that split the players. Alnwick has no particular pretence to ancient roots – the earliest

---

[29] William Parson, William White *History, directory, and gazetteer, of the counties of Durham and Northumberland* (1827).
[30] This is still done today, by the important personage of choice.
[31] A word that clearly suggests a Scottish connection, Alnwick not being far south of the border.

account is one that in 1788 "a foot-ball was thrown over the castle-walls to the populace[32]" and suggests that it was some kind of custom, and legend has it that the ball used to be a Scotsman's head, which is sweet revenge for the Jedburgh story! To this day, the action starts with the Duke of Northumberland tossing the ball from the second largest inhabited castle in England after Windsor, which is followed by a procession to the site of the game.

In the olden days that meant the streets, but given the problems this caused in the early 19th century, it was announced in 1828 that the Duke himself would still provide the traditional ball, but that the game would have to be played in the pastures "with a prize of five sovereigns for the winning side." Similar 'bribery' was met with hostility in other parts of Britain, but five sovereigns was a sum of money not to be sniffed at. The people of Alnwick were persuaded.

Arched goalposts decorated with greenery were erected some 650 metres apart for a game played along the same lines as the kind of football that would eventually become soccer. As a number of Pathé newsreel images show, the game was in good health in the 1920s, being played by teams of around 150 a side. It combines the goalscoring game (the first to two 'hales' unless time runs out) with a battle between the winning players to be the day's champion by getting the ball to the other side of the River Aln.

As the country picked itself up in the aftermath of the Second World War, Alnwick football was forgotten, and it was the latest Duke in 1952 who oversaw its revival. Even so, the game, played with a standard soccer ball, is hardly thriving these days, and usually involves sterling attempts by senior diehards to persuade 20 to 30 youngsters to get away from their PlayStations and maintain the tradition, many of which are the often female American students taking British Studies at a centre in the castle.

Workington

Further west, in Workington, there was a tradition of an annual face off between the two main working communities, the Downies that worked with the sea, including dockers and sailors, who had to get the ball home to the Merchants' Quay, and the Uppies living inland, mainly colliers, who strove to get it up to Workington Hall. The same goals are still used today, and stand about a mile apart.

All the local rag *Times and Star* can confer regarding its roots is that its "origins are shrouded in mystery and may well pre-date recorded history." We've heard that one before. The oldest hard evidence comes from the *Cumberland Pacquet* who reported on a game watched by 2000 people in 1775, yet even then it was described as "long contended[33]." But

---

[32] John Brand *Observations on popular antiquities, chiefly illustrating the origin of our vulgar customs, ceremonies and superstitions* (1813).

[33] Another Cumberland game was described by William Hutchinson in his *History of the County of Cumberland and Some places Adjacent from the Earliest Accounts to the Present Time* (1794), in which "the football was thrown down in the churchyard and the point then contended was which party should carry it to the house of his respective captain, to Dundraw perhaps or West Newton, a distance of two or three miles. The details of these

unusually, whereas most forms of folk football struggled to deal with the changing climate of the 19th century, the Workington game boomed. In 1873, it attracted a crowd of 10,000. If those figures were correct, that would have been over three times the number that turned out to watch the FA Cup Final. But that was only the start of it. Many British traditions were forgotten after the hiatus of the First World War, but no so Workington football. As Uruguay prepared to host the first World Cup in 1930, some 20,000 people turned out to watch a very different kind of football in Cumberland.

Part of the reason for Workington's success is that although not everybody was entirely approving of the game, it never really seems to have been at odds with the authorities or the general populace. This has a lot to do with what are known as the Cloffocks, which are to folk footballers what Augusta is to golfers. This expanse of fields, rivers, bridges and hillocks offers the perfect conditions for a great cross country game without worrying the local population too much. Even so, it is widely regarded that no game is complete without at least something of a foray into the town centre, which has led to attempts to blockade some of the more important roads from encroaching ball-chasers.

The real danger to Workington's game is that the Cloffocks are being encroached upon by the town. They are already home to a rugby league, a soccer and a cricket ground, as well as a bowling club and an expanding Tesco store, although Hugh Hornby doesn't see why that has to be a problem. "They already have to deal with rivers and mud, roads and railways" he writes. "A few trolleys and petrol pumps will surely not stop them now."

It was never the tamest of affairs, yet despite its roughness, 'only' four deaths have ever been recorded, all by drowning rather than violence. The latest was as recently as 1983 when 20-year-old Robert William Storey, who played rugby union for Workington Zebras, drowned near the harbour. Despite that tragedy, the locals are still proud of the fact that their game has never been troubled by such frivolities as rules, and as a result, is arguably the toughest of all the variants on the Shrovetide football theme.

Ball-maker Mark Rawlinson claims that "other games, like the Ashbourne game, have been 'tamed' into an official event. But the Workington game is still a game of raw football, and I think that's the way it will always be[34]." It may be violent, but at the same time it is caring. The 2006 edition raised £6000 for Cancer Research (and also featured the first ever 'hail' to be scored by a lady, 29 year old Catherine Malloy).

Where the Workington game is particularly unique is that the town is home to some 26,000 people, which makes it more than twice as big as the home of any other surviving Shrovetide games. It's the only exception to Hugh Hornby's observation that these traditions have only

---

matches were the general topics of conversation amongst the villagers, and were dwelt on with hardly less satisfaction than their ancestors enjoyed in relating their feats in the border wars." These villages are located close to the border with Scotland, but border wars had been a thing of the past for about a century, and judging by the use of the past tenses, football was also now long gone.

[34] *News and Star* (March 30, 2008).

survived in small-town communities, and that urbanisation was one of the main factors behind their disappearance. Even so, 26,000 hardly makes Workington a megalopolis, and it is certainly fair to say that there are no surviving Shrovetide games in any of Britain's major cities.

Highway patrol

What with the advent of so many new sports codes over the last century and a half, it is a wonder that any of these ancient customs survived. They have, but many others suffered the same fate as Derby's game. So little is known about so many lost traditions that it is safe to assume that there were hundreds more that simply vanished without record.

One that may still require a coroner's verdict to confirm it is clinically dead is the game played at Corfe Castle in Dorset. In 1553, it was deemed by the company of Purbeck Marblers, who quarried for a local variety of limestone, that "any man in our companie the Shrovtewsdaie after his marriage shall paie unto the wardings for the use and benefit of the companie twelve pence, and the last married man to brynge a footballe according to the custome of our companie." The custom, which brings back memories of the kind of thing that went on in France, was still in vogue when Monatgu Shearman was writing in 1888, but rather than a football match, it was more like an initiation ceremony in which, while balancing a pint of beer, a ball was dribbled along the road and then kicked off the quay, while other members did their best to make the inductee spill the drink. Some still struggle to maintain the tradition, and *Dorset Life* once reported that "in 1992 a young police constable, on temporary secondment from the North of England and ignorant of the 700-year-old Shrove Tuesday custom, confiscated the football which the company of Purbeck Marblers and Stone-cutters were kicking through the streets of Corfe Castle."

Joseph Lawson doesn't paint the prettiest of pictures of the game played back in the 1830s in Pudsey, Leeds. It involved "down-towners playing up-towners; in wet weather, bad roads and played through the village, breaking windows, striking bystanders, the ball driven into houses … it was quite common to see these up and down-towners kicking each other's shins when the ball was a hundred yards away. Of course, many received serious injuries[35]." It was time to get serious.

Playing ball in the street just wasn't what it used to be. The Highway Acts of 1830 are traditionally cited as the biggest cause for rural football's decline. With more and more stagecoaches on the roads of Britain, it became increasingly apparent that it was time to start devising what would develop into the modern-day Highway Code to cut down on accidents and improper usage of the nation's public highways, including the decision to get everybody driving on the same side of the road. They were not a call to stop people from having fun;

---

[35] Joseph Lawson *Letter to the Young on Progress in Pudsey during the Last Sixty Years* (1887). Lawson's description, like so many others, was actually written a long time after the game was really played, and he no doubt spiced things up with some poetic licence.

they were a call to stop people from having that fun in the middle of the road. The maximum fine for playing football on the street was 40 shillings – a good two month's wages for the ordinary labourer.

Royal decrees had largely failed to deal with the football issue for centuries, but the Highway Acts were boosted by a new shape to society. Robert Peel had come up with the idea of a police force. The 'Bobbies' or 'Peelers', as they are still called in some parts, were unleashed onto the streets of Britain, and by 1835 there were constabularies in all the major towns and cities in the country. This time when they said there was to be 'no playing ball in the street', they actually had the infrastructure in place to make sure people did what they were told.

As James Walvin puts it, "the days had gone when authorities stood by helplessly while their subjects took the law into their own hands with impunity; in the capital for instance, bands of footballers ceased to be able to create mayhem at will. Street football in the old cities was one of the victims of effective law enforcement."

Shrovetide football was once rife in London. A letter in 1815 provides the first mention of what is now the home of English rugby union, Twickenham, in a football sense: "I was not a little amused to see all the inhabitants securing the glass of all their front windows from the ground to the roof … at Twickenham, Bushy, and Hampton-wick and Kingston … at about 12 o'clock the ball is turned loose, and those who can, kick it. There were several balls in the town … I observed some persons of respectability following the ball: the game lasts about four hours, when the parties retire to the public-houses … I understand the corporation of Kingston attempted to put a stop to this practice, but the judges confirmed the right of the game, and it now legally continues, to the no small annoyance of some of the inhabitants. I was rather surprised that such a custom should have existed so near London, without my ever before knowing of it[36]."

He was quite right about the game being defended in court. It happened in 1790 when Baron Beoumount Hotham heard the defence that the devilish game of football was actually an invocation of an ancient tradition going back to Viking times when "the captain of the Danish forces having been slain, and his head kicked about by the people in derision, the custom of kicking a foot ball on the anniversary of that day has been observed ever since." They fell for the old Danish head excuse again[37]!

The game at Kingston was banned in 1799, but carried on regardless, to even appear in a drawing in the *Illustrated London News* in 1846. In 1852, it was written that "two rival companies of men collect about the Druid's Head Inn in the marketplace, and at eleven o'clock the ball is started. The sport continues with much spirit during the day; one party

---

[36] Cited ten years later in William Hone's *Every Day Book* (1825).

[37] However, some sixty years ago, the medieval Hocktide festival still existed in Kingston. This was said to be held in celebration of a massacre of Danish invaders, and most probably some kind of football was involved in the fun. It's feasible that lines got crossed here, and out of that, a fanciful legend was born.

endeavouring to kick the ball to the Great Bridge and the other party to Clattern Bridge; At five o'clock the game ceases and the parties adjourn to talk of their exertion, and to enter on business of another year with a firm determination to renew their riotous sport on the next anniversary of their forefather's prowess[38]."

In 1846, "some of the wealthiest inhabitants[39]" of Kingston were taking part in football games and local pubs would bribe players to kick the ball in the direction of their premises[40]! A petition was signed in 1858 by 132 local tradesmen in support of something they considered gave a boost to local business. Kingston's game may not have survived to this day, but its fate was similar to Alnwick's. By the 1860s the clash between the game and the developments in road transport meant there was a need for a rethink. In the wake of a particularly troublesome match in 1867, the game was moved to the more sensible venue of Fairfield Park.

In 1881, and for the last time, "the ancient custom of playing at football in the public streets was observed at Nuneaton on the afternoon of March 1st. During the morning a number of labourers canvassed the town for subscriptions and between one and two o'clock the ball was started, hundreds of roughs assembling and kicking it through the streets. The police attempted to stop the game, but were somewhat roughly handled. The football kicking was continued on Tuesday night, and led to great disorder, during which a number of police-officers who were on duty were badly knocked about while endeavouring to stop the game. Policemen's hats were knocked off and kicked about the streets, stones and other missiles were thrown, and the police were also pelted with mud[41]."

The rugby-esque game played between the east and the west of Dorking, Surrey enjoyed simply too much local support to be outlawed in 1839. In that game the idea was not to score a goal, but to have the ball on your side of the town at a certain time. An article penned by Charles Rose for the *West Surrey Times* in the 1870s considered the game to have been considerably sanitised since his own youth. "It was customary to make two bays in West Street, and into these were allowed to flow the blood and refuse from a neighbouring slaughterhouse. Into this disgusting fluid the ball was kicked, and the players would go, and the more the latter were bespattered and saturated, the better it was liked." How pleasant. Rose was also repulsed by the way the players would, in the middle of the game, apparently forget the ball and all run to the brook, where they would start ducking each other. Many of them caught colds, he remembered, and one or two even died. He was thankful to say that "this deplorable issue had a deterrent effect, and now the dangerous practice has, for many years, been wisely abandoned."

---

[38] William Downing Biden *The History and Antiquities of the Ancient and Royal Town of Kingston upon Thames* (1852), who also came up with the above Hocktide theory.
[39] *The Illustrated London News* (1846).
[40] George William Ayliffe *Old Kingston: Recollections of an Octogenarian from 1830 onwards* (1914).
[41] Evard Home Coleman in *The Antiquary: Volume 3* (1881).

Despite the clean-up, Dorking's game came in for more and more criticism, not so much from the locals but from Londoners, who thanks to the new railway, had moved into the suburbs and were commuting to work. Dorking Council seemed eager to defend the game, but in 1897, Surrey County Council stepped in by sending fifty or so police officers to quash the game for good.

If Shrove Tuesday football in Dorking was going out, it was going out with a bang, and what followed must have been one of the finest such games ever played. Some 2000 people gathered to play, but as the police set about trying to confiscate the ball, it effectively meant they had to join in the game, and a day of hilarity ensued as the people of Dorking kept producing more and more balls, and then enjoyed trying to keep them away from the law. In the aftermath, the matter went to court, where the usual claims about an ancient tradition were made, although in Dorking's case, nobody had any evidence that the game dated back any further than the 1830s. The police continued to make their annual assault on the game. By 1907, there were 20 policemen stood in the rain and not one Shrovetide footballer. The game was dead.

The Old Handsel Monday football match on the Roman Camp at Callander in Scotland, described in 1853 as a "custom of immemorial usage" is also no more, while Chester-le-Street in County Durham was the setting for 400-strong games between the Upstreeters and Downstreeters until 1932, when the game was stopped because it was causing such an annoyance to pedestrians. Barnes, Beverley, Cheam, Epsom, Ewell, Mortkale, Ripley, Weybridge, Molesey, Hampton Wick, Walton … these were all Shrovetide games that by the late 19th century were nothing but a distant memory. Roads were no longer football-friendly places.

Walvin quotes a Liverpudlian in 1831 who bemoaned the fact that "a spirit has lately arisen in the land that instigated the magistracy and other high and influential persons to curb, restrain and almost absolutely forbid the lowly, the humble of society from indulging in any pastimes whatsoever", a countryman in 1838 who felt "football seems to have almost gone out of use with the inclosure of wastes and commons, requiring a wide space for its exercise" and also *The Times* commenting in 1842 how "the poor have been deprived of their games, their amusements and their mirth."

But though there will always be somebody ready to write to the papers with a good moan, in a major historical survey published by Adrian Harvey in 2005, the author finds there were probably far fewer outright attacks on football in England than we might have been led to believe. The early 19th century was an enlightened enough period for there to be no attempt to stamp out the 'evils' of football for good, but there was a need to put a check on it wherever it went out of control.

The Principles of the Common Law of Scotland (1832) sum up the general view very nicely by stating that "assemblages for purposes no wise illegal, though sometimes contrary to morals, as foot-ball, racing, cock-fighting, etc, when the purposes of the meeting are not public disturbances or the accomplishment of any violent and illegal objects, do not fall under the offense of mobbing or rioting." Common sense prevailed.

The drastic moves to outlaw football games in places like Derby, Kingston and Dorking were probably more the exception than the norm. Games were more likely to be met with indifference, and in fact, there is widespread evidence that many walks of society, and in particular traders and publicans, often actively encouraged football because of the business it tended to generate.

The Alnwick game is a fine example of the dynamic. The local authorities had no problem with the game itself, the Duke of Northumberland was a fervent supporter who happily provided prizes and drinks, and even helped pay for some of the damages caused. It was just that the public highways were now needed for other purposes, and the game was moved to a field.

The same happened at Kingston, and also Twickenham, where the local judiciary successfully had the game taken off the streets, but had no intention of seeing it die out completely. As reported by *The Times* in 1840, they even donated a crown towards the expenses of relocating to Battersea Park, where hundreds met to play football in 1864 without the police batting an eyelid. Two years later, Battersea would be the venue for the first major representative match in soccer history, London versus Sheffield.

A new era was dawning. Even in the famous case of the outlawed game in Derby, we find that although the mayor was adamant in 1845 that the Shrovetide game was wrong, among the games he was happy to arrange with cash prizes as a less troublesome alternative was … football! Mass mayhem in the streets may have been unacceptable, but a nice controlled game in a field, well away from public thoroughfares, was fine.

Fair to say, there was some opposition to these moves, but rather like the reactions to smoking bans in our day and age, most people probably saw the sense of shifting to a recreation area purposefully set aside for the game.

Sometimes, in fact, it was the footballers themselves who wanted a more defined playing area. As early as 1769 it was written that "in these foot-ball conflicts, there are certain boundaries entitled goals … within which the parties are injoined to limit their contention, and when some extravagant and dissolute spirits have wantonly borne away the ball beyond the said bounds, we have seen both parties join in the pursuit of such vagrants, in order to bring back the ball to the regulated and appointed sphere of its activity[42]."

Once street football was moved into the nearby fields, it was played in relative anonymity and of little concern either to the authorities or journalists. Some games carried on regardless, but only in a few scattered towns and villages that were willing to give them special dispensation on public holidays, and that were later happy to promote them as a 'folk tradition'. Mob football in Ashbourne may be accepted today, but try doing the same thing

---

[42] Henry Brooke *The Fool of Quality: or The History of Henry, Earl of Moreland* (1969).

on the M1 motorway and you can expect a similar reaction from the police to that which most 19th century Shrovetide footballers faced.

Urban legends?

So, there may be a lot more asphalt on the ground, and vehicles and photo-happy tourists to dodge your way around, but in several corners of Britain, priceless souvenirs of medieval football can still be enjoyed today. Or can they? These festivals invariably claim to have 'ancient' or 'pagan' origins, but there is a lack of real facts to back them up. Harvey argues that only Corfe Castle (1551) and Ashbourne (1683) were 19th century Shrovetide games that could provide any substantial historical evidence that they were really any more than, at the very most, a hundred years old.

There was a tendency in the 19th century to make all kinds of outrageous claims to promote events, such as the travelling fairs with their fattest ladies and strongest men in the world, or to claim ancient rights that in all probability never really existed.

Given such vagueness, it's tempting to ask whether the Shrovetide games are just some fanciful invention of later years that in the here and now have degenerated into little more than excuses for 21st century adolescents in designer shirts to enjoy a mass scrap, for amateur history buffs to spout forth claptrap about keeping ancient traditions alive, and for otherwise insignificant rural townships to put themselves on the map.

In their defence, although most Shrovetide games make exaggerated claims to their antiquity, they very rarely assert that they are accurate re-enactments of that history. The players don't dress up in period medieval costume, they don't decorate the streets to make them look like scenes out of *Braveheart*, and there's no roast hog turning on the spit. The rules have even been adapted to the times. Medieval games never had to find solutions to deal with road traffic, but street sports do now, and in some of them players have been known to use motorbikes, cars and even busses to get the ball moving faster, and mobile phone technology has created a whole new field of tactical innovation. There may be some traditionalists that oppose all that, but in general the locals are aware that their games have always had to evolve with the times, and that they will inevitably continue to do so.

We also need to ask whether these games had anything to do with the origins of our modern day football codes, or whether they belong to a different category of ball game entirely. It seems to have always been assumed that the former begat the latter, but Hugh Hornby is not convinced. He prefers to refer to the games as 'Uppies and Downies' or 'Shrovetide' than early football. Adrian Harvey, meanwhile, opens his book with a chapter on Shrove-football titled *What football was not* and goes on to explain how he feels that "the Shrove-tide game has little to contribute to the evolution of the rules of football." His basic argument is that we have Francis Willughby's 1660 description to show that there was a form of football that very much resembled soccer before we have any evidence of Shrovetide games being played in Britain. He argues that "football is a much older game than the Shrove variety, and for at least 300 years matches have been occurring between equal numbers of players, often consisting of fewer than ten people on each side[43] ... such games attracted altogether less attention than the picturesque conflicts that occurred on Shrove Tuesday."

So did football begin as a relatively organised game played by small groups of people, only to later mushroom in some towns into a free-for-all event that involved the entire peasant throng as part of their Easter celebrations? It's a palpable theory. Small groups of people probably played some kind of football all year round, but the real excitement was reserved for when the whole town gathered for the feast. Bring in bigger teams, playing trade versus trade or village versus village, an element of 'us and them' as one social group played another, and the potential for chaos, damage, injury and general disturbance of the peace escalates. It was still the rustic game of football, but now on an epic enough scale to awaken the curiosity of the chroniclers of the time.

But the basic rules and traditions associated to the game would have essentially been the same no matter how many played, and it seems more likely that 'Shrovetide' football and what we could call 'Willughby' football were one and the same thing, and mutually influencing.

To deny that Shrovetide games form part of the evolutionary tree is going a bit too far. They are more like an 'extreme' form of the same game, and it is also worth pointing out that the game at Rugby School still had one hundred plus players on each side for much of the 19th century. Which conveniently leads us on to the next topic, the role the English public school system played in regimenting the old folk game of football.

---

[43] Take for example, the entry for September 18, 1683 in *The Diary of Jacob Bee of Durham:* "Seven bouchers should have play'd at foot-ball with seven glovers." But there didn't always have to be equal sides. *The World* in May 1789 has what seems too unbelievable a report to be true whereby in an "extraordinary match at Dunstable Downs – a young gentlemen took the hill for a wager of two hundred guineas against eleven of the best footballers in the county. He won after four and a half hours play."

18 HIGH SCHOOL BALLS
Early football at British public schools

Back to skool

Public schools. Some readers, and especially non-British ones, will need to know what the term means. Public schools in Britain, unlike the USA or Australia, for instance, aren't really public schools at all. They are those great definers of the class system that somebody pays for their kids to go to, thus ensuring that they get the pick of the crop when it comes to teaching staff and facilities, and don't have to rub shoulders with any lower class riff-raff.

Not that that has always been the case. In fact, most traditional public schools started out as charitable institutions providing an education to the poor, but taking on a few fee-paying pupils to help cover the costs. As time wore on, the charitable side gave way to the cost-covering side.

The schools were indeed public in the sense that the name distinguished between private lessons from a tutor at home and children going to learn in the same building. The former was still the 'proper' way of being educated until the late 18th century, when the rich started realising that it would be far better not only to get rid of their offspring for a few weeks, but also for them to learn something about the ways of the world and dealing with other people.

Over the years, a group of nine elite public schools popped their noses above the rest, and were regulated by the Public Schools Act of 1868. These are Charterhouse School, Eton College, Harrow School, Merchant Taylors School, St Paul's School, Westminster School, Winchester College, Rugby School and Shrewsbury School. Only the latter two were not located in or around London. Vying with them are other types, such as Grammar schools (like Repton and Uppingham) and Proprietary Schools (like Cheltenham, Marlborough and Clifton), which may differ in terms of purpose or prestige, but are basically the same thing.

British schools did it proper in the old days. There were none of the new-fangled nonsense subjects taught at modern day educational establishments. Perish the thought. No, back in the 16th century, the main ethos behind the public school system was to foster the gentlemen of the future, and the best way of doing that was to teach them grammar. But not the grammar of the language they lived and breathed, that would make far too much sense. No, they learned Latin grammar.

Although the times were changing, just about any text that was worth its while was written in Latin, so before any young Englander could even consider the study of science, medicine, history, geography, philosophy or even the other major element of the curriculum in the Middle Ages, religion, students were going to have to get their heads and quills around the complex matter of a language that had been dead in everyday conversation for centuries. And if you got the hang of that quickly enough, you might get a bit of the equally redundant Ancient Greek thrown in too.

This was all done in the most brilliant fashion. Resources were limited, but all you really needed was William Lily's *Short Introduction of Grammar*, Sir Thomas Elyot's Latin-English dictionary, a handful of well-thumbed classics and you were away. The methods were rudimentary. Repetition, repetition, repetition and more repetition, a clip round the ear if you forgot anything, a birch lashed across your arse if you were caught misbehaving (or dared utter a word of English in class) and lo and behold, either a dunce's hat was worn, or a true scholar was born. By the time you were fourteen and had reached the end of the education system, and if you had also managed to hold on to your sanity, you would now be able to attend a church sponsored institution or a university, where you would at last be able access and understand books that made all those parrot-fashion recitals of conjugations seem worthwhile after all.

Jolly good sport

Ah, yes, the dark, hallowed walls of academia, from whence some of the greatest ideas in human history were conceived. From catapults and conkers, all the way to Chinese burns and wedgies … and it was also here that we are told that these enlightened thinkers transformed football from mob disorder to the regimented delight we know today.

The first direct association between public schools and football was in an early Latin textbook written in 1519 by the former headmaster at Eton and Winchester, William Horman. In his lovely sounding *Vulgaria*, one of the seemingly infinite list of sentences he believed children should know how to rewrite in Latin was "we wyll playe with a ball full of wynde." Such balls were clearly something Horman approved of, for elsewhere he suggests that "there muste be a measure in gyuynge of remedies or sportynge to chyldren, leste they be wery of goynge to theyr boke if they haue none." In words other than 'gyuynge', by which he means 'giving', kids should play sport, otherwise they won't have the energy to study.

Another 16th century advocate of ball sports for pupils was Christopher Johnson, headmaster at Winchester in the 1560s, who remembers how he himself had "cared much more for balls, quoits and tops" than he did for books and school, although public school sports specialist Steven Bailey observes that in "over 400 Latin themes Johnson consistently supports the need for recreation, but often chastises his pupils for preferring their sport to their work" so it's hard to know what tree he was barking up.

Harrow School gets the prize for the first direct description of ball games being played at a public school. It was in 1591 that pupils were declared free to play games "upon Thursday only sometimes when the weather is fine, and upon Saturday, or half-holidays after evening prayer. And their play shall be to drive a top, to toss a handball, to run, or to shoot[1], and none other[2]."

Robert Matthew was a pupil at Winchester in the 1640s, and later remembered how they would "play quoits, or hand-ball, or bat-and-ball, or football; these games are innocent and lawful[3]" and records from Christ's Hospital (despite the name, a school) in 1725 say that greater control was needed over the boy's practices of "throwing of snowballs; playing of football; throwing at cocks or bricks, or other things sett up in imitation of cocks; trapp ball or crickett; castle topps; throwing balls or sticks at one another[4]." Still, if football was no worse than snowball fights, it can't have been that bad.

Football and similar games were a part of life at many schools by at least the 18th century. At Eton, fields were purchased way back in 1443, and it is hard to fathom for what other purpose it might have needed those grounds if it wasn't for playing games, although the first evidence of them being used as 'football fields' only dates to 1766. The records of just about every other public school include the acquisition of similar plots of land over the next centuries.

The games they played were far too culturally insignificant to warrant any kind of scientific analysis that found its ways into the books of lore, be they Latin or English, but we can be sure that the football played at each school varied enormously both in time and space. The level of violence permitted was limited by what they could get away with. The ball would have been whatever they could get hold of. The game had to be conditioned to whatever playing field the school possessed, including the quality of the playing surface at different times of year and rules were devised to deal with such obstacles as trees, walls and gates. As the games were played on the same field for decades, even centuries, and passed on from one year to the next, in a small community with a lot of time on their hands, school traditions would develop. Especially once these boys were introduced to the regimented rules of cricket, there is no doubt that they would have turned their scheming minds to the more savage alternative they played once the bats had been put away for winter. Cricket was the game for demonstrating your skills in the institutionalised world. Football was the game for reckless subversives.

---

[1] It seems somewhat worrying that 'shooting' was on the 'accepted' list, but we assume he meant archery practice. Spinning tops may also strike us as fairly odd, but they were all the rage in the Middle Ages, no less at the cutting edge of home entertainment than the latest generation videogame consoles are now.

[2] John Lyon *Orders, Statutes and Rules* (1591).

[3] Cited in AK Cook *About Winchester College* (Macmillan, 1917). The 'innocent' and 'lawful' bits are especially curious. Can this really be the same football that was causing havoc, even deaths, on the streets of England? How can something be 'lawful' if the authorities spent so much time trying to outlaw it? What Matthew might be telling us is that football in schools was a tamed down affair. This type certainly fits a whole lot better with former public schoolboy Francis Willughby's description in 1660.

[4] Ernest Harold Pearce *Annals of Christ's Hospital* (1901).

Children love to use their imaginations to dream up all kinds of different games and the football traditions that emerged from these adolescents' efforts would play an important role in the development of the modern codes. Those codes have now become so established that rather than being encouraged to use their imaginations to invent games of their own, today's children receive adult instruction in learning to play football 'properly'. Times have changed.

The 'civilised' middle class

Public schoolboys were no softies, that's for sure. Once they'd grown out of spinning tops, they set their minds to far more wicked affairs than putting itching powder under Sir's mortarboard. As David Goldblatt writes, "mere indiscipline was often succeeded by openly seditious rebellions and occupations. The army was called into Rugby in 1797 to put down a pupil's revolt, while the militia was summoned to Winchester in 1818 with fixed bayonets." Throwing stones at cocks was just the start of it, for "no dog could live on Harrow Hill" and "ponies frequently lost their eyes if they had to pull their owner's carts near the school[5]."

Discipline was one of the biggest problems at Georgian schools. Cooping all those boys up in the same place was asking for trouble, especially when, to take Charterhouse in the early 19th century as an example, you had just seven resident masters trying to control over five hundred young rascals. Bullying was rife, there being no end of stories of the monstrosities the bigger pupils would commit on the more defenceless. At Eton, boys were tossed in blankets at the ceiling, at Rugby they were forced to drink filth-ridden water or held close to the fire to near-roasting point, at Charterhouse there were tales of kids being shut in chests of sawdust and almost suffocated to death and at Marlborough "boring the ears of small boys with pins and even with pocket-knives was another form of pastime[6]."

The public school status quo was maintained by the fagging system. The 'fags' were the junior pupils, who the older boys would use as servants, bossing and bullying them into doing all manner of menial chores from carrying their bags to doing the tearing up for paper chases and fielding for them as they practiced their cricket strokes. Those were the nicer 'fag masters'. Others subjected their inferiors to routine torture and humiliation, such as the famous case of a boy called Rolles at Eton, who would get his fag down on all fours and ride him like a horse, digging his spurs deep onto the poor lad's haunches.

It was not unlike the fag culture that still exists in prisons today. The term is derived from the same root, and yes, in a world where young ladies were nowhere to be seen, the homosexual connotations were often very present indeed, especially when many boys shared not just dorms but beds too[7]. Harrow was "an adolescent boy's jungle; a jungle where lust and brute strength raged completely unrestrained[8]." The school had a common practice of the

---

[5] Which Goldblatt quotes from John Chandos *Boys together: English public schools, 1800-1864* (1984).

[6] Arthur Granville Bradley et al *A history of Marlborough college during fifty years: from its foundation to the present time* (1893).

[7] Although today it's in American rather than British English where 'fag' still survives as a synonym for gay.

[8] Jonathan Gathorne-Hardy *The Public School Phenomenon* (Hodder and Stoughton, 1977).

more effeminate fags being given girl's names and forced to be the 'bitches' of older students and to perform all kinds of obscene acts

The greatest evil of all was masturbation. Enter Edward Thring, headmaster at Uppingham Grammar and whose son would be instrumental in the foundation of the Football Association. Blessed with one of the most forward thinking minds in education history, he opened the first ever gymnasium at an English school and, as Uppingham's own website tells us, felt "every pupil must receive full and equal attention; as much time should be spent in class on an ordinary as on a brilliant pupil; those not intellectually gifted should have opportunities to succeed in other occupations." He was also keen on introducing subjects like French, German, Science, History, Art, Carpentry and Music to schools, rather than the tired old format of classic and maths *ad nausea*. But when it came to stroking the satin-headed serpent, there was nothing that disgusted him more.

Thring saw football as "a way of installing order and discipline and also providing a healthy activity for adolescent boys, distracting them from possibly more antisocial or even disgusting personal activities[9]." By that, he meant the horrors of the five-knuckle shuffle. In one of his sermons he warned how "all of a sudden, you know not how, all that you have learnt to love through years of baseness will drop off." Yep, we knew that a quick spank of the bishop, or "the worm-life of foul earthly desires" as Thring put it, could put a bit of a strain on the eyesight, but now we're told that it could make your trouser-snake snap off entirely!

It gets worse. "Boys who indulge in these wrong acts invariably become weak and sickly, and unfit for playing games. They often die young or go mad or become idiotic" claimed the booklet *Schoolboy Morality* published by the Social Purity Alliance. It's laughable now, but at the time there was genuine scientific concern about the dangers of a quick rub of the nether regions.

Something had to be done to keep this overflow of testosterone in check, and also prevent severe penile-loss among the upper crust's offspring. Corporal punishment was a favourite solution, and the cruel and often arbitrary nature of the gruesome floggings in English public schools of the 19th century is legendary. One of the champions in this department was Dr John Keate, headmaster of Eton from 1809 to 1834, and perhaps not surprisingly, a clergyman as well. In 1832, he was up all night whipping away at a succession of eighty boys that had been involved in a protest about the expulsion of a pupil who had refused to be flogged. At Marlborough, "a master lost control over himself in his efforts to wring some note of pain from a peculiarly heroic victim. The former gave up exhausted, but the latter had to be consigned to the sick-room, where strips of his shirt were extracted from his lacerated

---

[9] In the words of Hunter Davies, who presents a whole new angle to the argument regarding the use of the hands in Victorian public schools in *Boots, Balls and Haircuts* (Cassell Illustrated, 2003).

back by the tender hands of Dr Fergus[10]." The case of Eastbourne master Thomas Hopley, who beat 15-year-old Reginald Cancellor to his death and was jailed for manslaughter, was one of the stories of the year in the newspapers of 1860.

Social reformers had been questioning the practice at least since Roger Ascham in the 16th century[11]. Violence will ultimately only breed further violence. It became more and more apparent that simply force-feeding Latin classics down people's throats and whipping the living daylights out of non-conformists was hardly the way to prepare them for a changing world in which science, technology and industry were now the way forward.

Education needed to reinvent itself, and a popular remedy was the idea that "a daily proper portion of bodily fatigue is the antidote to all wandering of the thoughts and dwelling on improper objects[12]." Sport was seen as a new way of channelling all that adrenalin into something more controlled and positive. The boom of football in public schools was about to commence.

Such modelling of a new kind of gentleman wasn't an entirely new idea, for they had been hardening up young princes for imperial rule through archery, fencing, hunting and horsemanship for time immemorial, and Swiss philosopher Jean-Jacques Rousseau suggested much the same thing in his famous treatise of 1762, *Émile: or, On Education*. That book was received with public burnings, but by the Victorian era, the same ideas were extensively researched and the biological and psychological values of a healthy diet and physical exercise were to be institutionalised all the way down society. The ideas would lead to what was called Muscular Christianity[13].

From previously being shunned, football was now all the rage. At Shrewsbury, headmaster Samuel Butler from 1798 to 1836 had described the game as "only fit for butcher boys " and "more fit for farm boys and labourers than for young gentlemen." His colleague, the Reverend Arthur Willis, would patrol the grounds on his pony in search of any illicit ball

---

[10] Arthur Granville Bradley et al *A history of Marlborough college during fifty years: from its foundation to the present time* (1893).

[11] Who wrote the influential *The Scholemaster* (1570) based on his concerns that "divers scholars of Eaton be run away from the schole for fear of beating."

[12] *Of the Discipline of Large Boarding Schools* (in *The Quarterly Journal of Education*, 1835).

[13] In response to comments in *Saturday Review* (1857) on his novel *Two Years Ago*, Charles Kingsley called the expression Muscular Christianity "painful, if not offensive." But he happily used it later in life and went on to be known as the godfather of the movement. It was he who put it in a nutshell in *Health and Education* (1874): "in the playing field boys acquire virtues which no books can give them; not merely daring and endurance, but, better still temper, self-restraint, fairness, honor, unenvious approbation of another's success, and all that 'give and take' of life which stand a man in good stead when he goes forth into the world, and without which, indeed, his success is always maimed and partial." But historians are probably wrong to say that football was born out of Muscular Christianity. The game was already well developed by the time that movement was in full swing. It might be more accurate to say that the football was one of the tools that Muscular Christianity adopted and promoted.

games[14]. Under Butler's successor, Benjamin Kennedy, football was not only legal in the 1840s, but in a dramatic turn of events, it was now the school that was forcing the pupils to play football three times a week whether they liked it or not, and only a bona-fide medical report could get them out of it.

Football's masculine nature coupled with the unified spirit of a team working towards a common goal soon made it vogue thing for character-building in public schools, but there was one major stumbling block to overcome. Unlike the regimented game of cricket, Victorian football had no standard set of regulations.

Each school went it alone, devising their own rules which allowed varying degrees of use of the hands or feet, condoned different levels of violence, and used a diversity of balls, goalposts and fields for the purpose. New and more complex rules were constantly added, which developed into proudly observed school traditions. Although people in the outside world would eventually devise standardised football codes, by that time many public schools were so attached to their own games that they were appalled by the very suggestion that they should change them just to appease a bunch of bigwig upstarts from the city.

It took some time to convince the schools. Three of them, Eton, Winchester and Harrow, were so steadfast that their pre-codification football games are still being played today.

Eton

Eton College, Windsor is arguably the poshest, most exclusive and most famous school in the world. Its former scholars include no fewer than nineteen British Prime Ministers, not to mention James Bond and Captain Hook. Being a bastion of the proudest British tradition, it maintains no fewer than three of its very own ball games, the Field Game, the Wall Game and Eton Fives[15].

It was said that "the battle of Waterloo was won on the playing fields of Eton[16]" in reference not only to the discipline, ethics and athleticism of Eton football, but probably also

---

[14] It is commonly stated that Butler banned the game, but "Old Salopians now living remember how, when they had carefully selected a field in which they might play football without much fear of interruption, Mr Willis would occasionally ride up on his dark chestnut pony and put a stop to the game. Now, much as Dr Butler hated football, there is no doubt that he would regard interference of this sort by a master as showing want of tact Mr Willis." Cited in George William Fisher, John Spencer Hill *Annals of Shrewsbury School* (1899).

[15] A member of squash-without-a-racket family of handball games. Thankfully the hunting and butchering of a ram was outlawed in 1747, while the school's records mention other games from bygone days, and we can only guess what was ever involved in 'puss in the corner', 'hurtlecap', 'conquering lobs', 'headers' and 'cloyster and glyer gigs'.

[16] The comment has been attributed to former Eton pupil Arthur Wesley, the Duke of Wellington. Charles Montalembert originally quoted this in his 1855 *De l'Avenir politique de l'Angleterre*, three years after the death of the Iron Duke. However, it's unlikely Wellington ever said such a thing at all, for he was notably averse to any form of team sport.

to the need to keep fighting while also having to use an awful lot of grey matter. Eton's games are not the easiest to get your head around.

In the 1860s, when the editor of *The Field* was discussing the different public school rules, he dismissed the Eton game as "unintelligible" and a century and a half later, little has changed. The extraordinarily complicated rules, called 'legion', would take a chapter all of their own to explain in full, and even then most mere mortals would be none the wiser.

Remembering his Eton days of the mid 1820s, when he played football and "seldom saw much of the ball but frequently saw and felt the nailed shoes of my adversaries[17]," George William Lyttelton felt football was a simple concept that any man could grasp, but "made more intricate at Eton than it ever entered into the head of any other football players to conceive. The interminable multiplicity of rules about sneaking, picking up, throwing, rolling in straight … would probably be to many of our readers as perfect Hebrew as they are to us." What he considers Eton 'football' was played in "a space not more than five or six yards wide, bounded on one side by a wall" and whose virtues far exceeded "that played in the minor clubs of Eton, and in all other places, viz, that which takes place in an open field." For him, it was all basically football, but without Eton's iconic wall, it was nothing.

Turning to its origins, the Wall Game can't be any older than 1717, as that's the year the wall was built. Eton College's own website claims the earliest record of the game was in 1766, although *Ode on a Distant Prospect of Eton College* (1747), Thomas Gray's nostalgic yearnings for his childhood days, may well have had football in mind when asking:

"What idle Progeny succeed,
To chase the rolling Circle's speed,
Or urge the flying Ball?"

The Etonian made the bold claim in 1884 that the Wall Game "was the author of every sort and condition of football now played throughout the United Kingdom." That's quite some assertion, and not one to be taken too seriously. Influential as the Wall Game might have been, there was football in England long before Eton College even existed, let alone its famous wall or the game that goes with it.

Unlike the Field Game, which has since been taken on by the masters and is part of the curriculum, and is still the main sport played in Lent Term, the Wall Game is still the domain of the children, who traditionally oversee the whole affair. Although there are a few lesser matches, the only one that really matters is the St Andrew's day clash, which dates back, it is believed, to 1844, and is played between the Collegers (scholarship holders, of which there can only be 70 at any time by order of Henry VI) and the Oppidans (everybody else). The Oppidans may seem to be at a huge advantage, considering they have about 15 times more

---

[17] *Eton College Magazine* in (1832). Lyttelton was the 4th Baron Lyttelton and a Conservative politician. His son Edward Lyttelton was not only a first-class cricketer and FA Cup finalist, but was later headmaster at Eton (1905-1916). It was he who made a most invaluable contribution to the future of both football and the English education system when he said that cricket was becoming "comparatively worthless" as the new pitches had reduced the chance of injury.

pupils to choose from, but traditionally the wall was in a Colleger section of the grounds that the Oppidans were never allowed to enter, meaning they never got to practice. Although that's not really the case anymore, the game still begins with the Oppidans storming the wall as they symbolically break into Colleger territory.

Described by a former player as "the world's dullest game" in *The Economist* in 2003, even if they do understand what all the complex rules for 'heads', 'furking', 'sneaking' and so on are all about, spectators can rarely tell what's going on or even see the ball under the huddle of bodies. Teams of ten players form what look like rugby scrums, called 'bullies', and it all develops into a marathon battle to push the pack and the ball down to one of the 'calx' zones at either end. It's a pretty brutal affair, with players generally ending up squashed against the wall and watching each other's skin get scraped to the bone. The ball can never be handled or played backwards, so one of main tactics to get nearer to 'calx' is to use strength to force what is called a 'phalanx', a kind of human tunnel through which the ball can be kicked.

If and when the ball ever comes out of the mêlée, the best option is to kick it forwards and out of play, where there's the curious rule that the game restarts from wherever the ball comes to rest.

Should the ball ever get to the calx zone, the rules change, and a different type of Bully called a Count's Bully occurs, where the ball can be passed back. To score, the attacking team has to get the ball up against the wall, apply a hand to it, and yell "Got it!" If this happens, it's a 'shy', which is worth one point, although the hour-long matches commonly end without either side doing that once.

Scoring a shy brings a chance to go for goal, which is like a conversion and increases the value of the shy to a whopping ten points. This means throwing the ball at your corresponding target, which are a garden door at one end of the field and a tree at the other[18]. This is as good as impossible to do, and at the annual St Andrew's Day match, no goal has been scored since 1909! You can also score five points for kicking a goal in open play, which is also extremely rare.

It is not until 1841 that we find any particular kind of sanctioning of the game by the school authorities, when an article in *Bell's Life* mentions how the masters found it handy because of the way it "contributed to keeping the students within bounds." In *Bell's Life* in November 1842, headmaster Edward Craven Hawtrey, who had previously been unimpressed by the craze for sports at schools, showed a complete turn of direction when he claimed the suggestions that football was the reason for a recent outbreak of scarlet fever were nonsensical, saying "I have received no intimation from any person capable of forming an opinion that it was any other than beneficial to the health of the scholars."

It is not clear whether the Wall Game led to the Field Game or vice versa, but it may have had something to with a ten-year ban on the former following a particularly raucous game in

---

[18] Sadly, the original oak recently died, and the remaining stump was destroyed by vandals, so the target is now a young sapling.

1827. The first recorded set of rules for the Field Game, written in 1847 and signed by HH Tremayne and AR Thompson (*See Appendix One*), are highly revealing. The idea that the Eton Field Game could have influenced soccer may seem unlikely judging by the way the game is played today, but back in 1847 it was a relatively straightforward soccer-like game. Most of Eton's modern-day complexities came much later, probably imported from the Wall Game.

The basic idea in 1847 was to kick the ball between seven-foot goalposts. Players were allowed to catch the ball, but it "must not be carried, thrown or struck by the hand," which may sound odd, but such catching was also permitted in the first soccer rules drafted by the Football Association in 1863. The offside rule that "a player is considered to be sneaking when only three, or less than three, of the opposite side are before him and may not kick the ball" was the same in soccer until three became two in 1925.

However, the rules often refer to a 'bully' being used to restart play, the same term used in the Wall Game for the rough equivalent to a rugby scrum. And also present is something called a 'rouge', which happened when the ball was kicked over the goal-line but not between the goal sticks. If that happened, then the first player to touch it with their hand earned the right to a free kick one yard in front of goal, which for the attacking side was basically the same as scoring a try in rugby and following it up with a conversion. Rouges were only counted in the case of a tie, and this same system was often used in early soccer, while rugby eventually made such touchdowns an integral part of the scoring[19].

However, an account that appeared in *Baily's magazine of sports and pastimes* (1868) but describing a game called Eton Against The World in 1815, and played, of all places, on an Easter vacation to Geneva, Switzerland, tells us that the term 'rouge' was originally used to describe something similar to a rudimentary rugby scrum. "Broadhead has the ball at the first bound; attempting a run which in so narrow space, with a wall on each side, can only be brief, down it goes and the 'rouge' begins[20]. Shoulder to shoulder, legs going, one firmly supporting the body, whilst the other is brandishing and kicking at something – it may be the ball – but who can see it amidst such a confusion of limbs long and short? A deep thud or two gives notice of a damaged shin, without a murmur or sign of flinching, although the skin may be peeled off for many an inch. Gradually the ball is squeezed up by pressure as high as the knees of the players in the ruck: a short lunge brings it out. Burke … catches it, and coming out of the throng with a lusty kick sends it flying away towards the Eton goal."

Like all football codes, the Eton Field Game has evolved considerably in over a century and a half, and as well as introducing some of the most convoluted rules ever to appear in a ball sport. Played today, it is best described as rugby played with the feet. The ball is round like a

---

[19] As did other codes. The Australian 'behind' and the Irish 'over' originate from the same idea, and the 'single' in Canadian football is, of course, also known as a 'rouge'.

[20] It does sound like Broadhead was running with the ball here. In fact, there is strong indication in this text that the running and scrummaging game created at Rugby School in the 1820s was actually something they had learned from Eton.

soccer ball and can only be kicked, and it is so hard to make a pass without breaking some rule or other that ball-hogging is often the only viable option. But dribblers rarely get far without being hacked down and much of the game is an interminable 'bully', the scrum-like formation in which only one team crouches down as they would in rugby (called 'heads') and the penalised lot have to stand up, which means they are at an immediate disadvantage due to instability and the inability to exert pressure (but they do have the advantage of being in a handy position for kneeing their opponents in the face). Heeling the ball backwards out of the bully is as illegal as it was in rugby football until the late 19th century. That's 'furking'. No, in a bully the ball has to be kicked forward, and getting it out into open play without either of the two umpires spotting that you have broken one of an unfathomable number of rules is nigh on impossible. And the players in the bully have to stay together smelling each other's armpits as a unit for the whole game – leaving the bully is called 'cornering' and that's illegal.

The aim is to score into what look like soccer goals, although there are no goalkeepers, which earns three points. But there is also the 'rouge', which is basically the same thing as it was in 1847, only rather than being used as a tie-breaker, it now nets five points and is similar, at least in principle, to a try or touchdown. A ball becomes 'rougeable' (i.e. you get a rouge if you touch it) whenever it rebounds off a defender and over his own goal-line, whereupon the players race to see who can touch it first.

A rouge is followed by a conversion (for two extra points), which has nothing to do with the rugby equivalent, but is a case of three men binding together to form a human battering ram that runs headlong into the defence in what looks like an attempt to see who can break their neck first.

Then there's 'sneaking', which is not unlike offside in most codes of football, but especially rugby. Again, the rules are so tortuously complex that it's hard to imagine how a player can ever be onside, and basically leads to futile sprints up and down the pitch. Then there's a three-yard area marked in front of the goal-line, and when attackers are in that area, the ball can never be still, and must be kept moving in what becomes a tactical battle to either score a goal or get the ball rougeable.

And then there's… OK, let's just say that that's the simplified rulebook, and there is no shame in admitting that you got lost somewhere. Learning all the rules of the Field Game is often a far tougher challenge for the Eton schoolboy than anything he ever has to tackle in the classroom. This is because Eton football has only ever been restricted to a highly exclusive and closely-knit community. The only place anybody really cares about the Eton game is Eton itself. Making the game more accessible to a wider market was never an issue.

Harrow

Harrow School, founded in 1572 by order of Elizabeth I, has had its fair share of high brass alumni too, including Winston Churchill and the first Indian Prime Minister, Jawaharlal

Nehru. Its 'footer', like Eton's, has that weird 'alternative reality' about it. The school claims it originated from a 17th century game they called 'fug football', which was more of a playground kickabout than any kind of structured sport. From 1803 to 1850, it shared the same field as the cricket ground, but as football started gaining in popularity it was given a field of its own, and proper rules were developed. Like at Eton, the realisation of the benefits of healthy exercise led the masters to start taking an interest in what had previously been a pupil-only domain. This was especially so after the posting in 1844 of Dr Charles John Vaughan as headmaster, a protégé of the great Thomas Arnold at Rugby School, and a major supporter of the games ethic. Under his office, the Philathletic Club was set up to regulate games at the school from 1853, and also the annual house competitions that were run from the 1840s onwards[21]. Although Edward Bowen has been credited for first writing down the rules of Harrow football in 1865, this is nonsense. Graham Curry provides one set that was some seven years older than that, and even then didn't claim to be the first (*see Appendix Two*).

Writing in 1888, Shearman notes that "until quite recently all boys … with the exception of those who had been in the school for three years and those excused by medical certificates, were compelled by the school rules to play football at least twice a week … Harrow football is essentially a game for boys and those who love hard exercise. It has simple rules, is fast and manly, and has no penalties or ceremonies which waste time. It probably takes more out of a player who goes in to win heart and soul than any other form of the game."

Most of the action is centred on kicking and dribbling with the feet, but other bits would look more at home on a rugby pitch, and a very wet and muddy one at that. All that's missing, other than most of the pitch markings, is the crossbar. That's because there is no limit on the height of goals, or 'bases'. Like in Aussie rules, you can score as high as you like.

The best way to describe the game is to start with soccer and then explain the bits that aren't. Any number of players is on a team as long as they are equal, although eleven-a-side is the standard for competitive matches, with no goalkeepers. The basic idea is to kick the ball up the field and score a 'base'. But the ball is not round. Or even oval. It's made by taking two circular pieces of leather and sewing their entire circumferences to the longer edges of a rectangular section. With a rubber bladder stuffed inside, this is probably the simplest way to make a kickable 'spheroid', and uses the same method as that used for the 'oldest football ever' found at Stirling Castle. Looking more like an oversized porkpie, it rolls about reasonably well, and skids along the mud like an inflatable ice hockey puck. It's big and hefty, and if it gets wet (and it will) it can get extremely heavy. As Harrow's own

---

[21] It was a grand job Vaughan was doing until he unexpectedly resigned in 1859. According to evidence that was not made public until the 1970s, he left when his homosexual relationship with an eleven year old pupil came to light. "Vaughan's penchant for personally thrashing boys across the bare buttocks until he drew blood … ought to have set the alarm bells ringing" writes Richard Sanders. He allegedly destroyed all documents bearing his name before departing to eventually become a bishop. Say no more.

website says, it "is only headed by the more foolhardy player – and then only once." Rather than heading, the players have developed the alternative of controlling the ball with their shoulders, which despite being legal, is called 'fouling', such are the zany nuances of public school football terminology.

In short, getting a Harrow football from A to B is a fair bit harder than doing the same thing in soccer. Normal soccer tactics go out of the window due to a rugby-like offside rule, whereby you can never stand in front of the ball. All direct passing has to be backwards, or otherwise the giant porkpie is kicked forwards for somebody to run on to. In fact, this rule cuts out most passing altogether, and players are as likely to opt to go it alone and try to dribble the ball as far up the pitch as they can (as was the case with early soccer).

If the ball goes out of touch, it is returned by a throw-in, although it can be thrown any way the player likes (an underarm bowling motion is the norm). Corners are also thrown, for which the teams form something similar to a rugby lineout.

The Harrow game is a lot more forgiving when it comes to physicality. As long as it's not in the back, shoulder barging is completely legal, and the victim of said barging does not even have to be in possession of the ball. You've got players bumping around like dodgems and the referee doesn't bat an eyelid. It's what Americans call interference.

Where Harrow was ahead of the rest of the field was that rather than impose some kind of penalty for improper play, offenders were simply ejected from the field – although Montgu Shearman noted in 1888 that the "power of sending a 'rule-breaker' off the field" was in practice "very seldom to be exercised" because players respected the rules and penalties were rarely an issue.

Another oddity is the concept of 'yards'. This happens when a player catches a kicked ball before it touches the ground, which wins the right to a free unimpeded kick on the same spot. The way a Harrow football match generally pans out is for players to attempt to dribble the ball as far up the pitch as they can without being tackled or barged off the ball, and then either kick at goal, or turn around and 'give yards' to a team-mate. Despite the strict offside, no Australian football fan could possibly watch this without noticing a host of familiarities.

Harrow is built on clay. That makes for a tough, solid surface for summer cricket, but little more than gooey slush when the rain, and football season, come around, as described in the school song: "Forgotten cheers are in our ears, again we play our matches,
And memory swells, with magic spells, our boyish scores and catches,
Again we rush across the slush, a pack of breathless faces,
And charge and fall, and see the ball, fly whizzing through the bases[22]."

It was the dreadful pitch that was to thank for Harrow football's survival in the face of competition from the codified forms of soccer and rugby. It was noted that "in 1883 there was some considerable correspondence in *Harrow Notes* on the advisability of altering the

---

[22] Attributed to Harrovian poet Edmund Whytehead Howson on occasion of an 1891 dinner, but it appeared previously in a slightly different form in Horace Annesley Vachell's *The hill, a romance of friendship* (1861).

ball and the rules so as to bring Harrow football into closer conformity with the Association game. On that occasion the conservatives appear to have triumphed, and the proposed changes were not adopted[23]." As Schoolmaster CH Byre wrote in 1913, "Soccer[24] and Rugger in the Easter term call for little comment. The ground is ill-adapted for either game and the interest is practically limited to the players themselves. The fixtures are inclined to be dull and moderate."

Rugby was eventually introduced in 1925 at the behest of a huge advocate Dr Cyril Norwood when he became headmaster, and Harrow now thrives on the game. But despite being relegated to the spring term, the school's unique form of football was able to survive thanks to their pitch being so inappropriate for soccer. However, an improved drainage system means the pitch is now more playable than ever, and coupled with new plastic balls, soccer can be, and is, played at Harrow.

They have been able to deny Harrovian pupils soccer for well over a century, but now they're running out of excuses. Besides, proper Harrow footballs are getting harder to come by, and the game played with newfangled balls just isn't the same. The majesty of the Harrow game is how hard it is to work the ball forwards, while with a soccer ball it's just a simple matter of hoofing it up the pitch and watch that Nike swooshed thing fly.

Nevertheless the sight of it still being played today would probably bring a tear to the eye of our Old Harrovian friend from 1892, who wrote that "we hold that the present game is the best for the school … we can yet wish that younger generations should do so in our place, and learn the same lessons of daring, endurance, and unselfishness, as their predecessors did, when they formerly 'drank delight of battle with their peers' on the fields beneath Harrow Hill." Harrow football is still around, but in 2003 it was relegated to what they call 'minor game status'. Time could be running out for one of football's finest anecdotes. No matter what your opinion of the public school system and all that it stands for, that does seem a crying shame.

Winchester

Founded in 1382, Winchester College in Hampshire has the longest unbroken history of any school in England. And there too they have managed to maintain their own brand of football[25], known to Wykehamists[26] by the familiar names of 'Winkies', or 'WinCoFo' (short for Winchester College Football).

---

[23] An Old Harrovian contributing to Francis Marshall's book.

[24] Sceptics of the English origins of the term 'soccer' should take careful note.

[25] Winchester in the 1880s, is also said to have been the birthplace of 'lawn football', a sport that is basically a combination of soccer and tennis. In 1886, official rules were written and an English association was formed, and although it never came to much, perhaps Winchester can be thanked for coming up with an idea that now forms a common part of soccer skills training.

[26] As the pupils call themselves, in honour of the school's founder, William of Wykeham (1320–1404).

It is claimed that Winkies dates back to the 16th century. There is no evidence to back this up, but there are enough reports to show that football, albeit rugged and badly organised, was a common practice at Winchester as early as 1825 but probably much, much earlier. There are occasional references to the game in the college records, called *The Notions*, which give us a reasonable idea of what was going on, but no full rules that we know of were written until 1863, probably by request of outsiders as they worked to create a common code for the nation.

Winkies threatens to even make Eton's game sound blandly straightforward. International cricketer Budge Firth warned that "it would take a parliamentary council to draft it intelligibly … it is not, as is sometimes loosely said, a mixture of soccer and rugger. With soccer it has really nothing whatever to do[27]." He may have felt that, but the game is still largely based on kicking the ball, despite adding plenty of its own peculiarities. For a start, there are no goalposts. The idea is simply to kick the ball into the end zone, called 'worms', to score three points, with no need for the ball to be touched down. This may sound astonishingly easy to do, and generally is, for although games are never longer than thirty minutes each way, scores of fifty-plus are commonplace.

The ball can be passed backwards, but the player following up is then limited to kicking the ball below head height[28], a system that can be used to get out of a tight spot, as it often is, but that limits the power of the actual kick. The ball can be caught with the hands, but only by the full-backs, or 'kicks', and only before it bounces. That gives these players the chance to punt the ball out of their hands (with a maximum three steps in the run-up).

But it ain't quite that simple. The main reason is that Winkies includes its defining rule that teams take turns to kick the ball. If a player kicks the ball twice in a row, that's 'dribbling', and if he kicks it before the other team has had its turn, that's 'tagging'. With dribbling and tagging out, the concept of a passing game is basically destroyed.

19th century public school football was obsessed beyond proportion with offside rules, and Winkies is no exception, calling the offence 'behind your side'. Like in rugby, players must always position themselves behind the ball. What you end up with is a game in which teams take turns to hoof the ball upfield, and the defending teams do their damndest to get in the way. The height of bravado in the Winchester Game is what they call 'raising a plant', which is throwing your body in front of the ball to block it. It's the kind of thing a defensive 'wall' does in soccer, but taken to the next level, and although Winkies is now played with a standard soccer ball, a hit from one of those chunky Victorian lumps of leather was not something to be taken lightly.

---

[27] John D'Ewes Firth *Winchester* (1936). He was also a Wykehamist chaplain.

[28] This 'below head height' rule is one that has survived in many forms of indoor football in Britain, sometimes to protect the surrounding infrastructure, but often for what seems to be no logical reason other than to respect a rule that is just the 'done thing'.

Eton has its bullies, and Winchester has its 'hots', which work along similar lines to scrums, and are the normal method for restarting the game when the ball goes out of play or after minor fouls. Like at Eton, the ball cannot be hooked back out of the scrum, the players have to force their way over it, whereupon the 'hotwatch' (what rugby calls a scrum half) takes the ball into open play.

One of the biggest annoyances in any code of football is the way the ball has a habit of flying out of bounds. Winchester found a solution, as explained in 1842, whereby "about forty boys stand outside the ropes, on both sides, at equal distances from each other, and when the ball is kicked outside the ropes, it is their duty to put it inside the ropes again, at the same place as it came out[29]." The 'ropes' were what marked the boundary of the pitch, and this may have been the earliest use of ball-boys, known as 'kickers in' at the time, a bunch of probably very gloomy, shivering fags gathered along the touchline, and 'learning the ropes' so to speak.

The juniors got something of a reprieve from such child labour in the 1850s when a huge canvas was attached to posts along each of the touchlines, acting as a screen to trap the ball, hence the origin of the name 'canvas' to describe the Winchester football field. The canvas itself proved a dumb idea because it blocked the view for onlookers, but that problem was averted when somebody provided a huge net instead. Even so, it was only semi-efficient at doing its job because an 1860 order for juniors to "stand outside canvass to put in balls" reveals that fag ball-boys were still needed. They were actually reintroduced a few decades ago, though they're now dubbed 'watchers out'.

These ropes, canvasses or nets also came to play a fundamental role in the game, for they are held in place by nine posts, which divide the field in an American football kind of way into eight zones, logically enough called 'posts'. Certain penalties demand that a team retreats a certain number of posts, and if they have to go right back over their goal-line, they concede a 'behind', for a single point.

That's not the only way a team can score a 'behind'. In Winkies, a goal that crosses the opposition's goal-line, but hits a defender or goes through the ropes zone on the way, only counts as a 'behind' and scores one point. It's not quite the same as a 'behind' in Australian football, but it may not be coincidence that AFL and Winkies use the same term for a 'bonus point'.

But at Winchester, there is a chance to take a conversion and turn that one into three. Simplifying matters, that involves a defender hoofing the ball up the field, and one of the converters then has to kick the ball back into worms (the end zone) in a kind of 'let's see who can kick the ball the furthest' contest.

There has never been a universal law for the number of players on a side. In 1866, matches were "usually only played with six only on each side; and in this respect the Winchester game differs entirely from the exciting scene of the Rugby matches, where a hundred players

---

[29] William Tuckwell *The Ancient Ways: Winchester Fifty Years Ago* (Macmillan, 1893).

… may be seen[30]." It seems that in the 1850s they even dabbled in goalposts, something that was dropped soon after, and hacking, one of the most controversial issues of the era, was fine in 1863, but strictly forbidden at Winchester by 1876.

Winkies would soon be facing stiff competition. "Football is played in the afternoon" wrote Arthur Leach in 1899, but "not Winchester football, the glories of which are reserved for Short Half, but the modern mixture, Association game, commonly called soccer[31]." Most public schools eventually gave up on their own rules altogether, but Winchester, like Eton and Harrow, has managed to maintain the tradition to this day.

Football relics?

Although for some observers, the Eton, Harrow and Winchester games provide us with a fascinating living history of football in the days before codification, others have written them off as irrelevant anecdotes and reject these "ritual offerings to an unknown god[32]."

Steven Bailey puts it well in his book, when he says that there is a widespread belief that Eton, Harrow and Winchester only play their alternative football games "to colour the image of these schools' peculiar and traditional nature" and that "even the sports historian could come to the conclusion that these displays are quaint attempts to pay tribute to one of the aspects of 19th century life that sets them apart from other schools."

He then goes on to explain that this is a cynical view. These games have a long history at each of these schools, and all of them had written their own rules long before the modern soccer and rugby codes were created. They were reluctant to adopt the FA or RFU's rulebooks when they first came out, and had every right to feel that way, for there was little incentive to change until an inter-school football culture developed, whereupon they were quite willing to embrace soccer and rugby for the sake of 'foreign' matches. Those two codes are now a far bigger deal among the pupils at Eton, Harrow and Winchester, but they should not be criticised for maintaining their own traditions, which is something no less commendable than the survival of games like Cornish hurling and the Kirkwall ba' game.

Like Uppies and Downies contacting each other by cellphone, rather than sticking in the mud (in the literal sense at Harrow), the public school games have developed with the times. In the early 21st century, a number of minor and not-so-minor modifications were made to the Winchester game to deal with some of its more flawed aspects and loopholes. All three games have incorporated new sporting trends and technology, which is testimony that they are living, rather than archaic, sports.

The great 19th century chroniclers of football history generally concurred that the Football Association drew on public school games as inspiration for modern soccer. There is plenty of contemporary evidence to support that, and the Eton game in particular had very similar rules

---

[30] Henry Barnard (ed.) *The American journal of education, Volume 16* (1866).
[31] Arthur Francis Leach *A history of Winchester College* (Duckworth, 1899).
[32] Percy Young *A History of British Football* (Stanley Paul, 1968).

to those that the FA would draft in 1863. But soccer ultimately became a working class phenomenon, and for later revisionists, there seems to be something about the public school games that gets their goat. We like the tales of peasants kicking around the heads of vanquished landowners. We like the tales of the medieval horde wreaking havoc in the streets. We don't even mind if they were Scottish medieval hordes. And we love the fact that this is the great working man's game. But the idea that football as we know it was the result of the refinery of the game by the privileged few at the poshest schools in England, well, it's one a lot of people would rather disprove than prove. The role of football outside of the elite institutions certainly merits the increasing consideration it is getting in recent research, but that should not be at the total expense of what the public schools achieved.

Charterhouse

Eton, Winchester and Harrow have been given priority treatment here because their games still exist today. But there was nothing particularly unique about those games back in the 19th century. Most other schools had their own rules too, and although all of these were dropped somewhere along the line in favour of the standardised codes, at the time some of them were just as influential as the three that survived.

Charterhouse School, founded in Surrey in 1611 (and according to Forbes the second most expensive school in Britain after Eton), had a game that dated back to at least 1794, when the following ditty was first recorded, one that unquestionably has some kind of soccer game in mind:

> "I challenge all the men alive,
> To say they e'er were gladder,
> Than boys all striving who should kick,
> Most wind out of the bladder."

In 1895, two Old Carthusians provided a priceless record of what they remembered of the game in their youth. "Football was of two kinds at Charterhouse. On dry days the game was played in Under Green under Association rules; on wet days, in Cloisters … The cloister, a species of tunnel paved with smooth flagstones, but roughly constructed with sharp, jagged flint at its sides, was about 70 yards long, 9 feet wide, and 12 feet high … On Wednesday afternoons a written notice, 'All Fags to be in Cloisters at 2.30', used to be posted up on the principal archway … At the appointed time the Fags would assemble, and take up their position twenty strong at each end of Cloisters … The boys of the higher forms would then range themselves … the ball very soon got into one of the buttresses, when a terrific squash would be the result, some fifty or sixty boys huddled together, vigorously rouging[33], kicking, and shoving to extricate the ball. A skilful player, feeling that he had the ball in front of his legs, would patiently bide his time, until, perceiving an opportunity, he would dexterously work out the ball and rush wildly with it down Cloisters towards the coveted goal. The

---

[33] The use of 'rouge' here suggests that in 19th century public school slang, it was used as verb for some kind of footballing action, probably fighting to touch the ball with a hand.

squash would then dissolve and go in pursuit. Now was the time for the pluck and judgment of the Fags to be tried … The Fags would strive their utmost to prevent the ball being driven through, and hammer away with fists and hands grasping the corners of the wall to obtain a better purchase for shoving. One of these scrimmages sometimes lasted three-quarters of an hour. Shins would be kicked black and blue; jackets and other articles of clothing almost torn into shreds; and Fags trampled under foot[34]."

It sounds very like the 'football rushes' at US colleges, and much as there is a common belief that the public schools refined 'mob football', these descriptions hardly suggest their game was any more or less 'civilized' than anything you might have seen on the streets of Ashbourne or Kirkwall.

What they called The Green was "full of holes and quite unfit for the playing of games[35]" until 1821, when it was renovated into a reasonably decent playing field, where they could now play football outdoors, although in bad weather they would still retreat to the good old cloisters. The field game was called 'ledges' and rules of sorts were written in 1862 for what primarily seems to have been a kicking game, although there was no shortage of roughness and ball-handling too.

It was in the 1850s that we start seeing how the Charterhouse game started exerting its influence on, or maybe being influenced by, other forms of football. While Eton, Harrow and Winchester were surprisingly insular and rarely took any interest in playing anyone other than themselves, there are scores of reports of Charterhouse playing 'foreign' matches. The earliest on record was a visit from St Bartholomew's Hospital in 1856, and they went on to play the Dingly Dell Club, Tonbridge Wells School, the Civil Service and Crusaders. Charterhouse would also be the only public school to send a representative to the first ever meeting of the FA in 1863, but such interest in football contact with the outside world was the exception rather than the norm among Victorian public schools.

Westminster

Westminster School, next to the abbey of the same name in central London, has a reference to football being played on their green as early as 1710, and there is no reason to doubt that the practice continued uninterrupted until the 1840s, when there are better details. An account of the game around 1848 tells us that "the width between the two goals was the whole length of the Green, and the goals were imaginary lines at either end, a few yards in advance of the railings – lines recognised, but as truly imaginary as the equator … There were an indefinite number of goalkeepers, perhaps eight or ten, for as the distance between goals was short, and the breadth of the goals comparatively great, a 'goal' would otherwise be too easily obtained. The rules were very simple. Sides were chosen from all the boys on

---

[34] Wilmot and Streatfield Eardley *Charterhouse: Old And New* (1895).
[35] Gerald Davies *Charterhouse in London* (1821).

the Green. Holding and throwing were not allowed, but the scrummages were sufficiently hot, and a 'rally' by the iron railings become sometimes agonising if not dangerous[36]."

A description written a few years later informs us that "when I first came, running with the ball was allowed, and 'fist-punting' when you had the ball in hand[37]." But these elements that remind us of rugby and Gaelic football were later abandoned. "When running ... the enemy tripped, shinned, charged with the shoulder, got down and sat upon you – in fact did anything short of murder to get the ball from you. I think that this running and fist-punting was stopped in 1851 or 1852."

The writer also reveals that putting crap players in goal is anything but a new invention. Back then "the small boys, the duffers and the funk-sticks were the goalkeepers ... if any fellow who was playing out showed any sign of 'funk', he was packed off into goals ... not only for that day but as a lasting degradation." Remembering that these games were generally played in the freezing English winter "the boys in goal had a cold time of it ... jackets on, but no caps, and hands deep in pockets." It was not a fun place to be, but any goalkeeper who "made a good save ... was called for immediately to play out ... The ball was thrown in between the lines; then there was a general shinning match till it worked out ... You might not pick a ball up from the ground, or after the first bound was over, but you might catch it before or after first bound fairly in the air." Then, as long as you could avoid being "knocked head-over-heels" you were free to try something like a rugby drop-kick, described here as "a half-volley kick off the hand. You might not 'punt' it from the hand – this is, kick it full volley – or drive it with your fist."

There seems to have been nothing about offside rules or outlawing forward passing, but a game where "shinning was allowed and many a hack was got" was no game for funk-sticks. Generally it seems a far simpler game than the convoluted monstrosities of some of the other public schools.

There certainly seems to have been a shift in football trends at Westminster in the 1850s, and the elimination of handling may have been because the school started flirting with the idea of progressing from rudimentary teams like the tall versus the short to accepting challenges from other institutions, something for which their enthusiasm was only truly shared among public school circles by Charterhouse. A historic attempt to get a game going between past and present Westminster and Harrow pupils in 1859 was reported by *Bell's Life* as something of a disaster because "the game of each is so different," but Westminster did manage to get up games against Dingly Dell and Haileybury.

Shrewsbury

The Shrewsbury game that was first despised by the masters was later enforced on the pupils by a system called 'douling', after a Greek word for 'slave', which was also what they

---

[36] Frederic Hale Forshall *Westminster School Past and Present* (1884).
[37] Francis Markham *Recollections Of A Town Boy At Westminster, 1849-1855* (1903).

called their own particular fagging system. "All boarders who were not specially exempted on medical grounds were expected to take part."

The earliest rules were written in 1855, and of all the school codes, it's probably the most similar to what would eventually become soccer. "The most distinctive features of the game, as formerly played at Shrewsbury, were these: there was no crossbar between the goal posts, and a ball kicked between the posts counted as a goal, however high it went; the offside rule was strict, and no loitering was allowed between the ball and the opponents' goal; and a free punt or drop kick was allowed to any player who fairly caught the ball in his arms or hands after it had been kicked by one of his opponents and before it touched the ground[38]."

Catching the ball, no crossbar and no moving ahead of the ball? It may not sound particularly soccer-like to the modern-day player, but all of these ideas formed part of the earliest rules drafted by the Football Association. Considering the similarities between their games, it should be no surprise that unlike other public schools, Shrewsbury were well impressed by the FA. They enrolled as members almost immediately, and went on to feature among the key promoters of the earliest official rules of soccer.

So similar in fact is douling to early soccer that it's tempting to hypothesise that Shrewsbury was far more influential on modern soccer than any other school. It was written that "between 1854 and 1860 there were few better players at Cambridge than Shrewsbury men. Some of them shared with Etonians and Carthusians the credit due to expert dribbling, and many of them were vigorous forward players. No eleven would have been considered representative of Cambridge football in those days without a sprinkling of Shrewsbury men … One year Shrewsbury men up at Cambridge managed to get together fifteen players for a match against a Rugby twenty-five, and the match ended in a draw, neither side kicking a goal."

After all, it was two Old Salopians, Henry de Winton and John Charles Thring, who called a meeting at Cambridge University to draw up a common set of football rules in 1848. The earliest surviving copy of those rules was found in the Shrewsbury School library, a modified version of which was almost entirely copied by the FA's first rulemaking committee in 1863.

Marlborough

Marlborough College in Wiltshire, founded in 1843, would eventually import rugby football and be one of the important popularisers of that code. But in its infancy, as three Old Marlburians explain, "it would be difficult perhaps to recognise in the elaborate system of 'screwing' or 'wheeling', 'roking' and 'passing', which is now called Football, the same game as it was played at Marlborough in the forties … Piles of coats supplied the first goal-posts, between which was stationed some shivering small boy who suffered dire physical woe for any unhappy dereliction in duty. The ball – for the School boasted but a solitary

---

[38] Cited in George William Fisher, John Spencer Hill *Annals of Shrewsbury School* (1899).

specimen – was a small round one. The rules, such as they were, and there were none in particular, were somewhat similar to those of the present Association game; for no handling of the ball was permitted, except in the case of a fair catch, which gave the right to a free kick off the ground. 'Off side' was unknown. Indeed, the whole game was played in a senseless, unscientific manner, and attracted but few supporters.

"Anybody who cared to put in an appearance was welcome to play, but it was seldom that more than thirty or forty out of the whole School availed themselves of the doubtful privilege. The hour first chosen for play was between twelve and one o'clock, and there was a general rush to the pump for a 'wash and brush up' when the bell rang for dinner. However, the game lived, and little by little developed an influence, till it became considered worthy of a place in the afternoon's programme of amusements, and to a certain degree a recognised institution[39]."

"It was not till the advent of Cotton as master in 1852, bringing with him the traditions of the Rugby 'Big Side' that football was placed on any substantial basis … The whole system was changed; the Rugby shape of ball was introduced, Rugby goalposts were erected, and the Rugby rules … practically adopted. The principles of 'off side' were inculcated. The art of 'drop kicking' was taught…"

"It must not, however, be supposed that the game became universally fashionable all at once. For a long time it was an open question whether a boy who had slain a squirrel fairly with a 'squaler' was not to be considered a greater hero than he who had received promotion into the Twenty." That was the utmost distinction on the football field, where games were also played by the 'Forty', 'Sixty' and even 'Hundred'.

Marlborough soon swayed from the Rugby tradition and invented its own ideas. Their scrum was called a 'squash', and the maul-like thing they called a 'grovel' "presented a most grotesque spectacle, formed as it was of wriggling, writhing figures, with interlacing legs and arms, for all the world like a mass of mammoth worms, who struggled to prevent, or secure, a touchdown or 'try' and who only dropped off one by one as they lost touch of the ball." An extra point was scored for what they called a 'rogue', which "arose when either side was driven to touch the ball down in self-defence behind its own goal", basically the same thing as an American safety.

Other school games

By the 1850s, the pros of football in schools vastly outweighed the cons of the potential havoc it raised, and the odd broken limb was just the outcome of a gentle kick in the right direction towards manhood. Any school worth its salt was playing football. Rossall, Brighton, Cheltenham, Haileybury, Uppingham… they were all at it. Whereas the schools with the longer standing traditions had largely come up with their own games, the newer

---

[39] Arthur Granville Bradley, Arthur Charles Champneys, John Ward Baines *A history of Marlborough college during fifty years: from its foundation to the present time* (1893).

schools often imported ideas from others and adapted them to whatever ball or field they could find.

Radley College in Oxfordshire had a game that survived until 1882 and borrowed heavily from the Harrow rules. Played fifteen-a-side using soccer goals without crossbars, the ball could be carried 3 yards as long as it was received from another player and not picked up off the ground. Where it was unusual was that to score a goal, the ball had to be kicked so that it bounced before going through the posts, and it had a goalkeeper who was not allowed to catch the ball on the fly.

At Tonbridge in 1858 football was already beginning to rival cricket's position as the number one sport, and the citation James Walvin offers is a great indication of its coming of age. "Hitherto, as has already been said, 'the ambition of the school has been monopolised by the cricket field'. But we cannot play cricket all year round; and second to, if not equal with cricket, comes football. At the beginning of the football season there is a good deal of spirit in the game but after a month or so interest lags, and games are waning in spirit. Now this occurs to much less extent in other schools; and the reason I take it, is this; at other schools there are divisions in football, corresponding to our 'elevens' at cricket and, consequently, the players feel a noble desire to be one of the 'twenty', or whatever the number may be. They have also uniforms at football as well as cricket, and far more gorgeous caps in the former."

This chapter has illustrated the confusion any hope of standardisation faced in the mid 19th century. There was still this generic thing called 'football', but it was more of an umbrella term like 'motor sport' is today. Forming some kind of association for all these schools to play each other was going to a very, very difficult process. The idea was often discussed, games were even attempted, but usually to little avail. Eventually it was in the adult world, though often through involvement of public school old boys, that a standard game was created. And that game was such a huge success, and affected British society on so many levels, that the old school games were slowly forgotten.

Stonyhurst in Lancashire's game was maintained for most of the 19th century. It was described in 1904 as "one of the red-letter days of the year ... The opposing sides were known as English and French, during the match great enthusiasm always prevailed, flags were flying and cannons firing ... Stonyhurst football is now, alas! being superseded by the more up-to-date Association Rules and the 'grand matches' at Stonyhurst are a thing of the past[40]."

Mangan cites one schoolboy's sadness to see the Stonyhurst game superseded by the modern codes: "Avaunt your soccer's mincing grace, your rugger's rigid common place,

> Line out my splendid Stonyhurst, line out there for the game."

---

[40] William White *Notes and queries: Volume 109* (1904).

Only the Eton, Winchester and Harrow games have stood their own against the forces of adversity. No other old school game exists any more. Well, apart from one, although now it only shares a historic relation with the school that created it. It is now played from Canada to Argentina, from Scotland to Namibia, and from Japan to New Zealand. But its spiritual home will always be Rugby School in Warwickshire...

19 ALL ELLIS BREAKING LOOSE
Rugby School and the origins of rugby

Big sides

Lawrence Sheriff, a gentleman who made his fortune selling groceries to the great and good of the nation, including royalty, died in 1567. Having no children of his own, he left all of his considerable estate to found Rugby School. It went on to become one of the oldest and finest schools in England, but what it's famous for around the world is the game its pupils invented.

The earliest record of football being played in the town of Rugby is an entry in the Constable's books for New Year's Eve 1743, which notes "Pd Baxter for crying no football play in ye street, 2d."

That's about all we know about football in Rugby, inside or out of the school grounds, before the 1800s, and it is not a quote that gives us an awful lot to work with. Letters from Rugby schoolboys have survived to this day, but despite plenty of mentions of swimming, cricket, fishing and running, we find not one mention of football before the 19th century. If it was played at all, it can't have been very important.

The common public school practice of making life a misery for the local fauna was far more entertaining. Cock-fighting, badger baiting and poaching poultry from the local farms were all the rage, and they even had a pack of hounds for hunting. The pupils once even tried to set the town's Guy Fawkes bonfire alight ahead of time. Now who would think of doing such a wicked thing as that? While the schoolboys would do anything they could to get out of the school, the local boys got their thrills from breaking in, and plenty of argy-bargy between the two groups, from snowball fights to worse, would provide endless pleasure.

The rugby game is unlikely to date back any further than 1748, because until then they had nowhere to play it. That was the year the trustees wrote to parliament saying they were "in a place too much confined, and without any ground or enclosure adjoining for the recreation of the youth." The playing fields were purchased, and the masters must have been delighted with a place where the pupils could catch a bit a fresh air in a reasonably enclosed space and not keep straying off the grounds to make life hell for the local people and animals alike.

When football was introduced to those fields, the pupils must have taken at least some of their inspiration from some kind of street football they had seen either in the town of Rugby, or back home. The teachers themselves took surprisingly little interest in what the brood got up to in their free time, and the unique brand of football played at Rugby was entirely the children's own invention.

One of its extraordinary aspects was that the entire school played at once. There are some great early paintings of the Rugby game showing over a hundred players on each side. But there was regimentation, which ensured that only the seniors saw any real action. The fag culture was brought into football, and the juniors would gather around the goal-line as the last line of defence, generally just getting bored and cold as they learned the basics before eventually being considered senior enough to get involved in the game proper. Their main responsibility was to touch down any loose balls before any opposing player got to do likewise, and sometimes to push the scrummage from the back.

The role of the fags would later be the subject of much controversy, but a man who had been there and done it, Arthur Guillemard, wrote in 1892 that "truth to tell, standing in goal for a couple of hours on three afternoons during the season was no very great hardship; there was always some grand football to be watched, and in a gathering of four hundred and fifty boys there are enough lively ones to create plenty of fun, the more mischievous of the crowd snatching a fearful joy from attempts to attach lighted crackers to the coat-tails of unpopular praepostors[1]."

There being no strictly codified rules to play by, the teams would just make them up as suited them best, and the rudiments would be passed from the seniors to the fags, who would then become seniors themselves, and pass the game on to their own fags, and so the game progressed as a school institution.

The best description we have of what the game was like in the early 19th century was penned in an 1880 letter by Matthew Holbeche Bloxam, where he tells us how he himself had "played at Rugby in my time, 1813–1820. The last time I played at Bigside[2] in the close was just 60 years ago … all had assembled in the close, two of the best players in the School commenced choosing in one for each side[3] … After choosing in about a score on each side, a somewhat rude division was made of the remaining fags, half of whom were sent to keep goal on the one side, the other half of whom were sent to keep goal for the same purpose. Any fag, though not specially chosen in, might follow up on that side to the goal of which he was attached. Some of these were ready enough to mingle in the fray, others judiciously kept half back, watching their opportunity for a casual kick, which was not unfrequently awarded to them. Few and simple were the rules of the game: touch on the sides of the ground was marked out, and no one was allowed to run with the ball in his grasp towards the opposite goal. It was football and not handball, plenty of hacking, but little struggling … All were scratch matches, one boarding house was never pitted against another … There were no Rugbeian matches; railways had not commenced to pervade the land, and Rugby was a good twelve hours' journey from London. With Oxford there was no direct communication[4] …

---

[1] A 'praepostor' was the Rugby School equivalent of a prefect.

[2] Bigside was the nickname given to the main field where the football matches were played at Rugby.

[3] That's picking teams one-by-one by the time-honoured method still used in playgrounds around the world today.

[4] Here he is referring to the fundamental reason why football developed in so many different ways at different schools. There was very little interaction between them, and they never played each other, so there was no more reason to formalise rules for football than there is now for British Bulldogs (or Red Rover, Cock-a-Rooster, Pile-ons, Cocky Laura, call it what you will…).

after the games of the day were concluded, however vigorously they may have been contended, all further remembrance of the game was consigned to the limbo of oblivion, our tasks to be learned at night were sufficiently onerous to allow leisure for discussion, and there was no *Meteor* in which the incidents of each game could be recorded[5]."

It was just a playground kickaround. No wonder so little was ever written about it. It was as significant to society at large as pass the parcel at Junior's birthday party is today.

A fine disregard for the rules

The game Bloxam describes was more like soccer. But he hasn't finished. He then goes on to make a statement that has puzzled rugby historians ever since, and created one of the most iconic figures in world sport. He explains how, in 1823, one of the young lads picked up the ball and started running with it. His name was William Webb Ellis.

A plaque was hung on the walls of Rugby School in 1900. It says: "This stone commemorates the exploit of William Webb Ellis who with a fine disregard for the rules of Football as played in his time first took the ball in his arms and ran with it thus originating the distinctive feature of the Rugby game. AD 1823."

The Webb Ellis story is now deeply ingrained in rugby culture, and his name was forever associated to it in 1987 when the first Rugby World Cup was played and the prize was the William Webb Ellis Trophy.

Ten years later, England outside centre Jeremy Guscott unveiled an extortionately overpriced £40,000 bronze statue of Webb Ellis running with a ball on the corner of Lawrence Sheriff Street in Rugby, opposite the school. For rugby fans all over the world, the school has become a pilgrimage site to rival Mecca, Lourdes and Santiago de Compostela, although they should probably not get too excited by the statue. It's not really of Webb Ellis at all, but is modelled on sculptor Graham Ibbeson's son.

In the entire history of the different football codes, there is probably no person who performed any action of such singular magnitude as the great William Webb Ellis. As Rudolph Brasch writes, "there is nothing obscure about the origin of Rugby or, as university slang came to call it, rugger. It is known who started it and where and when he did so … Rugby began quite accidentally. One afternoon in 1823, William Webb Ellis, a student at the college, was participating in an interclass football match, then played according to traditional soccer rules, which permitted only kicking and bouncing. He became bored with the tedium of the game and on the spur of the moment, picked up the ball, and ran like mad, carrying it down the field. The move was so unexpected and contrary to the rules that some spectators imagined the boy only wanted to steal the ball. His action caused much consternation. His captain, deeply embarrassed, apologized for the lad's unsportsmanlike act and breach of the rules. Ellis was sharply criticised but there is no evidence that he was ever punished. Reports

---

[5] *The Meteor*, the Rugby School paper (December 22, 1880).

of his escapade spread beyond the boundaries of Rugby and became the topic of much discussion at other schools. Some players began to speculate that running with the ball would give the game new verve and improve its appeal[6]."

Brasch is making stuff up. In reality, there is very little evidence that Webb Ellis had anything at all to do with the invention of rugby. The story did not even come to light until eight years after his death, and only then in remarkably ambiguous circumstances. Neither of the great 19th century chroniclers of rugby history, Montagu Shearman and Frank Marshall, even mention William Webb Ellis, so, where on earth does this story about his "fine disregard for the rules" come from?

It was Matthew Bloxam, of course, and the letter he wrote to *The Meteor* in 1880. He continues by saying "in the latter half of 1823, some 57 years ago, originated, though without premeditation, that change in one of the rules, which more than any other has since distinguished the Rugby School game from the Association Rules. A boy of the name of Ellis, William Webb Ellis, a town boy and a foundationer, who at the age of nine entered the school after the midsummer holidays in 1816, who in the second half year of 1823, was, I believe, a praeposter, whilst playing Bigside at football in that half year, caught the ball in his arms. This being so, according to the then rules, he ought to have retired back as far as he pleased, without parting with the ball, for the combatants on the opposite side could only advance to the spot where he had caught the ball, and were unable to rush forward till he had either punted it or had placed it for someone else to kick, for it was by means of these placed kicks that most of the goals were in those days kicked, but the moment the ball touched the ground, the opposite side might rush on. Ellis, for the first time, disregarded this rule, and on catching the ball, instead of retiring backwards, rushed forwards with the ball in his hands towards the opposite goal, with what result as to the game I know not, neither do I know how this infringement of a well known rule was followed up, or when it became as it is now, a standing rule."

He adds that "Mr Ellis was high up in the school, and as to scholarship of fair average abilities. He left the school in the summer of 1825, being the second Rugby exhibitioner of that year, and was entered at Brasenose College, Oxford. He subsequently took Holy orders, and at a later period became incumbent of the church of St Clement Danes, Strand, London. He died on the continent some years ago[7]."

---

[6] Rudolph Brasch *How did sports begin?* (David McKay, 1970), and a book that often confuses urban legend and unproven theories with reality.

[7] Some additional information on WWE: He was born in Salford, just outside Manchester in 1806, and his double-barrelled name came from being born to Jim Ellis, an officer in the Dragoon Guard, and Ann Webb. His father was killed at the Battle of Albuera in 1812. It was then that Ann took him and his older brother Thomas to Rugby, where they were entitled to a place at the school if they lived within ten miles of the clock tower. William attended it from 1816 to 1825. Only one picture survives of Ellis, published in the *Illustrated London Post* following a cracking sermon he gave on the Crimean War.

The Rugby Football Union was founded in 1871, but Ellis is unlikely to have even known or particularly cared, and his death attracted no headlines. His body lay beneath a grave in the small French-Italian border town of Menton without anybody knowing anything about its significance until it was discovered by Ross McWhirter, co-editor of the *Guinness Book of Records*, in 1958. If Ellis were to come back from the dead and visit his old school, he would probably be extremely confused to see there is a statue outside bearing his name as the inventor of a sport called rugby.

Untangling the Webb

So, that's how it all started. According to Bloxam, and only according to Bloxam. Sadly, by the time he came forward, Ellis was dead, so nobody could ask the protagonist for his own version of events.

As the story was entirely based on one man's evidence, it might be interesting to also ask who this Matthew Holbeche Bloxam character was. He was at Rugby from 1813 to 1820, meaning that the Webb Ellis incident actually happened three years after he had left, so the story must have reached him second hand, quite possibly via his brother John, who was at the school at the same time as WWE.

But Bloxam did maintain close links with the school, working as a solicitor in the town, becoming a respected antiquarian, and writing a successful book on Gothic architecture. A passionate Old Rugbeian, he followed the progress of his beloved school's version of football from playground pastime to international sport, being one of the most respected voices when it came to analysing the origins of the game. But nothing raised more of a furore than his William Webb Ellis story. All of a sudden, rugby had a figurehead to turn to. A real person, a Messiah, the man who invented rugby football!

There seems to be no reason to doubt the integrity of an elderly gentleman who was simply enthused by the sudden interest in one of his most treasured possessions, his schoolboy memories. But it's odd that Bloxam knew so much about what happened to Webb Ellis after he left Rugby. He even learned of his death, yet nobody would find his grave until the best part of a century later! It all sounds like some weird in-joke made up by the two, or a nice little yarn to grab some unwarranted attention. But why would Bloxam want to put Webb Ellis on a pedestal, quite literally as it turned out, if he didn't even seem to have particularly liked the guy?

For he goes on to say that "when at school, though in a high form, Mr Ellis was not what we should call 'a swell' at least none of his compeers considered him as such. He had, however, no lack of assurance, and was ambitious of being thought something of. In fact he did an act which if a fag had ventured to have done, he would probably have received more kicks than commendations. How oft is it that such small matters lead to great results!"

In 1895, the Old Rugbeian Society decided the time had come to launch an official investigation into the Webb Ellis story, but by this time, Bloxam too had made his way up to the H-shaped goals in the sky, so he was unable to provide any further input to the story, or at least explain why he had never thought to tell it to anybody before.

The investigation was based on contacting former pupils that were old enough to remember the early days of the sport. The researchers found no fewer than seventeen, now in the twilights of their lives, and their contradicting stories reflect both the fact that it had all happened a long time ago, and also the very confused and vague nature of the (inexistent) rules that Webb Ellis had supposedly 'disregarded'.

Of the people the inquiry contacted, only one, the Reverend Thomas Harris, was old enough to have been around at the same time as the main man. Said Harris, "I remember Mr William Webb Ellis perfectly. He was an admirable cricketer, but was generally regarded as inclined to take unfair advantages at football. I should not quote him in any way as an authority."

It is interesting that Harris should mention these 'unfair advantages', for the only contemporary mention of Ellis at school comes from an 1822 letter discussing the results of the prestigious Latin Prize, in which the masters suspected that "his mother had been helping him with the composition" and as a result "Ellis got the wooden spoon[8]."

Harris adds that "as to Mr W Webb Ellis and his practices, you must observe that I was several years his junior, and had not either reasons or opportunities for closely observing his manner of play", while on the way the game itself was played he offered "picking up and running with the ball in hand was distinctly forbidden. If a player caught the ball on a rebound from the ground, or from a stroke of the hand, he was allowed to take a few steps so as to give effect to a 'Drop-kick', but no more; subject of course to interruption from adverse players."

'Forbidden' is the key word here. A popular image has been conjured up of Ellis picking up the ball and the other pupils watching aghast and thinking 'wow, I never thought of doing that'. Of course they knew how to run while carrying a ball, but they also knew the rules did not allow it. Peter Shortell makes a good point. He suggests "we should not be asking when carrying the ball was first allowed, but when it was first banned." Quite.

In any case, they would never have got far in a game played with more than one hundred on a side. "In the matches played in the lower part of the school when I was myself a junior" says Harris in a later letter, "the cry of 'hack him over' was always raised against any player who was seen to be running with the ball in his hands." Harris was a junior long before the supposed Webb Ellis incident, and from what he has to say, there is no doubt that some kind of running with the ball, however ineffective, had existed at Rugby before 1823. What's

---

[8] The mention of the 'wooden spoon' is particularly fascinating, which to this day is a booby prize awarded for coming last, most commonly in rugby's Six Nations, though it is also a firmly rooted tradition in Australian rules football. Its origins are said to go back to Cambridge University in the early 19th century, and doing badly in its *Tripos* mathematics contests, although this quote tells us that it was also used at Rugby School, though whether it was ever used in a footballing context, we do not know. The term was certainly in use by 1892, when Marshall used it to describe the miserable season the Welsh had just had.

intriguing is why Bloxam should have made such a thing out of the fact that Webb Ellis did it?

All of the other interviewees were at Rugby School in the 1830s, after Webb Ellis had left, by which time running with the ball was becoming an accepted part of the game. Thomas Hughes, an Old Rugbeian who we'll be coming back to later, wrote that "in my first year, 1834, running with the ball to get a try by touching down within goal was not absolutely forbidden, but a jury of Rugby boys of that day would almost certainly have found a verdict of 'justifiable homicide' if a boy had been killed in running in … The Webb Ellis tradition had not survived to my day" but "the practice grew, and was tolerated more and more, and indeed became rather popular in 1838–39 from the prowess of Jem Mackie, the great runner in … the question remained debatable when I was captain of Bigside in 1841–42 when we settled it … running in was made lawful with these limitations, that the ball must be caught on the bound, that the catcher was not 'off his side', that there should be no 'handing on' but that the catcher must carry the ball and 'touch down' himself."

By way of example, as most of the elderly gents were spinning the same old yarn regarding 'running in', a Mr Lushington told the investigators that "it was done in my time, that is in the autumns of 1838–39 … but I should not say done that often. I remember trying it myself on one occasion in particular, when I got particularly hacked over for my pains."

The case for Webb Ellis was not good, but the 1895 investigation was willing to hand Bloxam the benefit of the doubt. Their conclusion was that "in 1820 the form of football in vogue at Rugby was something approximating more closely to Association than to what is known as Rugby football today, that at some date between 1820 and 1830 the innovation was introduced of running with the ball, that this was in all probability done in the latter half of 1823 by Mr W Webb Ellis, who is credited by Mr Bloxam with the invention and whose 'unfair practices' were (according to Mr Harris) the subject of general remark at the time. To this we would add that the innovation was regarded as of doubtful legality for some time, and only gradually became accepted as part of the game, but obtained a customary status between 1830 and 1840, and was duly legalized … by the rules of 1846."

Where people generally rebuke the Webb Ellis myth is that he could not possibly have invented rugby, because we have so much evidence of games that involved running with the ball a long time before that. *Calcio fiorentino* certainly did, the Cornish had it in their hurling, and the Welsh had it in their *cnapan*. A case has been put forward for the Irish sport of *caid*, perhaps stretching the imagination a bit, whereby as Webb Ellis' father was stationed in Ireland once, this was how he had heard of the game, and what he was actually doing was demonstrating the art to his school chums.

And then there's camp-ball, where the player who seizes the ball "speeds home pursued by his opponents … if caught and held, he throws the ball." That quote was written in 1823, the very same year as the infamous Webb Ellis episode. Hugh Hornby makes a fascinating observation. He notes that around the 1820s there seemed to be a general shift in folk football from kicking to carrying the ball. Was the Rugby game following that trend? Hornby even notes that there were three pupils at Rugby at roughly the same time as Ellis who hailed from a town about twenty miles away called Ashbourne, the home of the now royal Shrovetide game.[9]

There could be two particular reasons why carrying was introduced (or maybe reintroduced). The first is that in the early 1820s, the playing field was extended, and the second was that a major row sparked by understandable rebellion among mistreated fags in 1822 had led to a series of expulsions and withdrawals and a rapid decline in the number of pupils (from 380 to 143, no less). That meant more space and fewer players, so there was never a more natural time to restructure a game that never had an awful lot of structure to it anyway.

Or was Bloxam's whole story part of a cover-up? Earlier we met one conspiracy theory that the whole Webb Ellis myth was dreamed up to disguise the sport's Maori influences, but there was another more likely motive. The story cropped up at the height of the dispute between northern working class professionals and the amateur old guard of the Rugby Union, a controversy that eventually led to the breakaway code of rugby league. With the middle classes losing their grip on the game, was the whole Webb Ellis thing a publicity stunt to remind the nation that Rugby School was the true and spiritual home of the game, and that its game was created by and for the upper crust? It may seem insignificant now, but at the time it was a very important issue indeed. The proletariat had no right to be messing with rugby's principles.

One thing is for sure, even if William Webb Ellis did invent running with the ball, he didn't invent rugby. The basic game was being played at the school long before he was even born, and running with the ball, though a defining characteristic, is not its be all and end all. Webb Ellis did not invent the H shaped goal, or the scrum, or the lineout, or the oval ball. And he did not invent the try, there being absolutely no truth in the legend that after performing his famous run, Webb Ellis asked his teacher if that counted as a goal, and was told no, "but it was a jolly good try." No, Webb Ellis didn't invent any of those iconic elements of rugby. The chances are he didn't invent anything at all.

Whether or not it is true, the William Webb Ellis story is one that will never go away. Thompson put it brilliantly when he said "I am pro-Ellis and conceive him to be like Voltaire's Deity. If he had not existed, it would have been necessary (and proper) to invent him[10]." The event became so entrenched in rugby folklore that 1923 was deemed rugby

---

[9] They were Barnard and Granville Dewes, and Edward Webster. It's tempting to take a shot in the total darkness here. Matthew Bloxham was writing many, many years later. He got Webb Ellis mixed up with Webster. The wrong man got the credit for creating rugby!

[10] Arthur Alexander Thompson *Rugger My Pleasure* (The Sportsmans Book Club, 1957).

centenary year, and a game was played between an England/Wales XV and a Scotland/Ireland XV on The Close in Rugby School[11].

Almost three quarters of a century later, in a small, but surely moving ceremony in August 2006, the World Cup trophy, the William Webb Ellis Trophy no less, was taken to the man himself's final resting place in the small French Vieux Château cemetery in Menton. The local and international rugby authorities were all in attendance to pay their respects to a man who died there a bachelor, in relative anonymity, leaving £9000 to charitable causes including the society for the rescue of young women and children.

May he long rest in peace. It's a nice story, and we all need something to believe in. And if that belief is in a man called William Webb Ellis, then no harm is done to anybody.

Tom Hughes's school days

We promised earlier that Thomas Hughes had more to do with the story than his contribution to the Webb Ellis research committee. Hughes had been an accomplished rugby and cricket player in his time, and went on to become an MP, was pivotal in the formation of the trade unions and founded the town of Rugby, Tennessee. But he's best known for writing a novel loosely based around his own experiences at Rugby School in the 1830s.

Published in 1857, the book was *Tom Brown's Schooldays*. At a time when novels written through the eyes of children were a rare commodity, it was a major hit on a scale comparable to the *Harry Potter* books a century and a half later. It set the tone for a flood of Victorian era books telling the tales of public schoolboy frolics as adolescents came to terms with growing up, overcoming bullies and learning to fight for each other. For an insight into the birthplace of rugby football, it is priceless. Set about ten years after William Webb Ellis was at Rugby, the whole of Chapter Five, *Rugby and Football*, describes the events before, during and after Tom Brown's first taste of the game.

Tom's sidekick in the novel, Harry 'Scud' East, provides him, and therefore us, with a detailed description. He explains how the players all wear white for the match, the author himself interjecting to comment on how confusing it all was, because now (which was 1857 for him) "each house has its own uniform of cap and jersey, of some lively colour; but at the

---

[11] There was controversy in the build-up to the game, because there were many at the RFU that felt Twickenham would have made a far more sensible venue, given the interest in the game, but the traditionalists got their way. Writing after that match, Arthur Pearson, who was at the School in the 1860s, penned a delightful article in *Rugby Football* magazine. "The match on November 1 was played in the Old School Close, where so many have played the old game who have now passed away, as also have those famous Three Trees of the old days, against whose trunks we were sometimes squeezed more tightly than was pleasant, but were a great feature of the Close in the past. And if the game has somewhat changed since those days, the old spirit of it still goes on, and long may it be so … The old game was no doubt unscientific compared with the game of the present day, but it was a glorious game, and I look back upon my last football term as one of the happiest times of my life, when I remember wondering to myself … if life could ever be so delightful again."

time we are speaking of plush caps have not yet come in, or uniforms of any sort, except the School-house white trousers[12]."

Tom is keen to play, but East tells him it wouldn't be a good idea because "you don't know the rules; you'll be a month learning them", which is pretty much still the case today. "And then it's no joke playing-up in a match, I can tell you. Quite another thing from your private school games. Why, there's been two collar-bones broken this half, and a dozen fellows lamed. And last year a fellow had his leg broken." This may be a novel, but Hughes was probably quoting from his own memories.

East (or Hughes, really) goes on to describe the posts, which are already the H shaped ones we know and love, and points out that "it won't do, you see, just to kick the ball through these posts, it must go over the crossbar; any height'll do, so long as it's between the posts. You'll have to stay in goal to touch the ball when it rolls behind the posts, because if the other side touch it they have a try at goal."

What he is explaining is what rugby now knows as a try. The *only* way of scoring in the game Tom Brown was being shown was to kick the ball over the bar and between the uprights. However, if the ball ever crossed the goal-line (or went into the end zone in American speech), then the attacking team, if they managed to touch it first, would get a free kick, or 'try' at kicking for goal. For that reason, Tom would be joining the hordes of 'goalkeeping' fags stationed behind the goal, whose job was to make sure they touched the ball down before any of the opposition could. It would not be until 1886 that winning a 'try' automatically won a point, whether or not it was successfully 'converted'.

Back to the story. "Then we fellows in quarters, we play just about in front of goal here, and have to turn the ball and kick it back before the big fellows on the other side can follow it up. And in front of us all the big fellows play, and that's where the scrummages are mostly." The 'big fellows' are the forwards, of course.

Pitch markings were not a feature yet, as East explains. "You see this gravel-walk running down all along this side of the playing-ground, and the line of elms opposite on the other? Well, they're the bounds. As soon as the ball gets past them, it's in touch, and out of play."

So, why did they call this area 'touch', as we still do today? It's because after the ball went out of bounds "whoever first touches it has to knock it straight out amongst the players-up, who make two lines with a space between them, every fellow going on his own side. Ain't there just fine scrummages then. And the three trees you see there which come out into the

---

[12] When the first England rugby team was picked, there were ten Rugbeians in the side and the white shirts they wore that day were said to be donned in honour of Rugby School. The practice would be continued to this day by most other English national sports teams, soccer included. It has been said that there was a tradition for many years that the English rugby team had to request permission from Rugby School to wear their colours, but it's probably just folk legend. It was in 1846 that the first ruling was passed at Rugby to stipulate that teams "should be distinguished by the colours of their jerseys", often regarded to be the earliest mention of the idea, although we know for sure that in a very similar sport played in Florence, they had come up with the idea some three centuries earlier.

play, that's a tremendous place when the ball hangs there, for you get thrown against the trees, and that's worse than any hack."

Later on in the chapter, Hughes describes the actual game. In fact he goes on about it for several pages. He lets his passion fly and the result is a description that's probably way too long and rambling to include in a novel, but an absolute delight for anybody with a fondness for rugby history. This is clearly not a fifteen-a-side game. "What absurdity is this? You don't mean to say that those fifty or sixty boys in white trousers, many of them quite small, are going to play that huge mass opposite[13]? Indeed I do, gentlemen. They're going to try, at any rate, and won't make such a bad fight of it either, mark my word."

The way the game pans out, it sounds more like a series of military manoeuvres than a game of football. "The sixth-form boy, who has the charge of goal, has spread his force (the goalkeepers) so as to occupy the whole space behind the goal-posts, at distances of about five yards apart. A safe and well-kept goal is the foundation of all good play … See how that youngster spreads his men (the light brigade) carefully over the ground, half-way between their own goal and the body of their own players-up (the heavy brigade). These again play in several bodies. There is young Brooke and the bull-dogs. Mark them well. They are the 'fighting brigade', the 'die-hards', larking about at leap-frog to keep themselves warm, and playing tricks on one another. And on each side of old Brooke, who is now standing in the middle of the ground and just going to kick off, you see a separate wing of players-up, each with a boy of acknowledged prowess to look to … but over all is old Brooke, absolute as he of Russia, but wisely and bravely ruling over willing and worshiping subjects, a true football king. His face is earnest and careful as he glances a last time over his array, but full of pluck and hope, the sort of look I hope to see in my general when I go out to fight … The School side is not organized in the same way. The goal-keepers are all in lumps, anyhow and nohow; you can't distinguish between the players-up and the boys in quarters, and there is divided leadership. But with such odds in strength and weight it must take more than that to hinder them from winning…"

"…The new ball you may see lie there quite by itself, in the middle, pointing towards the School or island goal." It has been said that the oval ball didn't appear until much later, but this quote surely indicates that the ball must have already assumed its characteristic shape, for how else could a spherical ball 'point'?

The game gets under way, and Hughes describes what seems little more than a marauding mass of boys chasing the ball from one end of the field to the other. "My dear sir, a battle would look much the same to you, except that the boys would be men, and the balls iron; but

---

[13] In October 1839, when Queen Adelaide (wife of William IV) visited the School, a game was played between School House, with 'only' 75 players in the side, and The Rest, who had a whopping 225. Numerically balancing the teams wasn't an issue until very late at Rugby School, and mismatches were all part of the fun. That said, once we're talking triple figures, it can't make that much differences how many players are on a side, as most of them are never likely to get near the ball anyway.

a battle would be worth your looking at for all that, and so is a football match." It feels more about 'playing at soldiers' than 'playing at ball' and takes our minds back to the North American Indians and their ball games and the words Carew used to describe the positions in Cornish hurling. Forget fertility rites. Football is a re-enactment of war!

Hughes describes the 1830s equivalents of the modern-day backs when he says "then the boys who are bending and watching on the outside, mark them: they are most useful players, the dodgers, who seize on the ball the moment it rolls out from amongst the chargers, and away with it across to the opposite goal. They seldom go into the scrummage, but must have more coolness than the chargers." Whoever invented it, running with the ball is definitely in now, and the 'dodgers' were the specialists.

And Young Brooke was one of the best dodgers of all, and gets to win the only try of the game. The ball was lingering beneath the posts and "there is a hurried rush of the School fags to the spot, but no one throws himself on the ball, the only chance, and young Brooke has touched it right under the School goal-posts." The fags get the stick they fully deserve for not touching the ball before Brooke, but there was no score yet, because a try was worth zilch unless it was converted.

And so, "Old Brooke stands with the ball under his arm motioning the School back; he will not kick out till they are all in goal, behind the posts. They are all edging forwards, inch by inch, to get nearer for the rush at Crab Jones, who stands there in front of old Brooke to catch the ball. If they can reach and destroy him before he catches, the danger is over; and with one and the same rush they will carry it right away to the School-house goal. Fond hope! It is kicked out and caught beautifully. Crab strikes his heel into the ground, to mark the spot where the ball was caught, beyond which the school line may not advance; but there they stand, five deep, ready to rush the moment the ball touches the ground. Take plenty of room. Don't give the rush a chance of reaching you. Place it true and steady. Trust Crab Jones. He has made a small hole with his heel for the ball to lie on[14], by which he is resting on one knee, with his eye on old Brooke. 'Now!' Crab places the ball at the word, Old Brooke kicks, and it rises slowly and truly as the School rush forward[15]."

Crab Jones does his job and gets "a goal in the first hour, such a thing hasn't been done in the School-house match these five years." The game goes on for several paragraphs before eventually culminating with Tom Brown himself, who is merely one of the goal-keepers,

---

[14] Another clue to the ball being oval, for there would be no need for Crab Jones to do this if the ball was spherical.

[15] There was much more ceremony to the conversion in those days. It involved the ball being kicked back into play by one of the scoring side from the point where it was touched down. As soon as it had been 'punted' the defending side charged out as the attacking side tried to make a clean catch. If the ball was caught, the catcher would 'make his mark' on the ground, beyond which the defending side could not pass, and would place the ball on the ground for the nominated kicker to hoof, hopefully, over the bar and between the uprights. All those fineries were dispensed with in the 1880s. Now it's just a matter of an unchallenged opportunity to kick the ball over the crossbar, but to a certain extent the ritual still survives in American football.

making a crunching tackle to prevent the opposition from getting a 'try at goal' just before the clock strikes five and the game ends. The match was played to the best of three goals, so 'no side' was declared and the game would carry on the day after.

The essentials of rugby were all in place. A coin was tossed to decide ends, there were half-time oranges, and the 'third half' was already an institution, with plenty of underage drinking and self-congratulatory speeches. But there was some tidying up to be done yet. Yes, players could now run with the ball, but only if they caught it directly or on first bounce, and even then there was to be no passing. A player running with the ball had no option other than to make his way up the pitch alone, which can't have been easy with a hundred or so players per side! But it was recognisably rugby. All that was needed now was a slightly more manageable number of players, and some clearer rules.

Doubting Thomas

The headmaster of Rugby School in *Tom Brown's Schooldays* was called Thomas Arnold. He was 'playing himself', for he was the real-life head from 1828 to 1841, and also one of the most important figures in the reformations made to the British education system in the 19th century. Some of these were a tad controversial for the time, but Arnold was the man who put Rugby School smack, bang on the map.

He saw the educational value of mathematics, history and modern languages, and made them part of the curriculum. He revamped the monotonous reciting of Latin and Greek verb declensions into the study of the languages in a cultural and moral context. He instituted the form system, and rather than combating the hierarchy that the boys had created amongst themselves, he turned it to his advantage and instigated the system of school prefects (praeposters) to ensure discipline. He also had huge sympathy for the poor, preached for social reform, and was one of the all-round good guys of Victorian England.

The crux of the matter is that thanks to one man's endeavours, a school that had constantly lagged behind Eton, Harrow *et al* in terms of prestige was moving up the ladder. Rugby School was all the rage. It was admired and respected, and was very much the trendsetter in the early 19th century.

But although he has often been acknowledged for his central role in the development of rugby football, to the best of our knowledge, Arnold was never particularly either for or against the game. Adrian Harvey, the debunker *par excellence* of football myths, writes that "despite the fact that Arnold wrote copiously on education, nowhere does he even mention sport having a role in education! ... Significantly enough, *Tom Brown's Schooldays*, the text that had done most to foster the idea of Arnold's interest in the educational virtues of sport, provides glaring evidence of how little attention he attached to sport, for it is noticeable that he is not even present at the sporting highlight of the year, the big end of term cricket match, having departed for his holidays! ... Although Arnold has sometimes been presented as promoting the idea that sport had a vital role in the moral education of boys, there is no evidence for this."

That's perhaps being a little hard on the man, for Harvey himself cites 1842 head boy Theodore Walrond describing Arnold's "hearty interest in the school games, which he looked upon as an integral part of education[16]" while Rugby educated Alexander J Arbuthnot, the later Secretary of State for India, went further by saying that "I have heard it said of late years that Arnold discouraged athletic games, and that a school of young prigs grew up under his influence, but I entirely disagree with this. Rugby football had a great name in my day, and Arnold encouraged us to play it. I remember his coming out in his garden, which was raised three or four feet above the level of the School field, and divided from it by a low wall, and standing there watching us[17]."

But Arnold generally left football in the hands of the people that played it, the children. He wanted them in the playground and getting proper exercise, but probably neither knew nor cared about the scoring system or the fineries of mauling and knocking on. Rather than helping to create rugby football, it might be more accurate to say that Arnold created the right conditions for it. It was not so much Thomas Arnold, but his protégés who would spread the football gospel around the country.

Codifying the customs

The writing of the first set of rules for football at rugby probably came about as a result of Arnold's sudden and unexpected death in 1842. It led unprecedented hysteria at the school, with a sudden surge of nostalgia for all the wonderful things the man had accomplished. From being a progressivist, standard-setting institution, Rugby went retro. People harked back to the good, old days when Arnold was alive and there was resistance to any tangents from the ideals the main man had popularised. Such Arnie-mania led to scores of books about his achievements and a sudden desire to put every aspect of the school's society down in words, and in 1845 that attention was finally turned to football.

Three of the school's most senior pupils were tasked with the mission of documenting written rules: 17 year old William Delafield Arnold (the late headmaster's son and later an educational administrator in Punjab, India), 16 year old Walter Waddington Shirley (who appears in one of the earliest pictures of football at the school and went on to become an ecclesiastical historian), and Frederick Hutchins (who would go on to become a successful solicitor and was probably included in the trio because of his legal skills).

Lacking models to draw upon, the 1845 *Laws of Football as Played at Rugby School* (*see Appendix Three*) are a tad unorthodox. Then again, the preface does set the tone when it says that "the following book of Rules is to be regarded rather as a set of Decisions on certain disputed points in Football, than as containing all the Laws of the Game, which are too well

---

[16] Theodore Walrond *Dictionary of National Biography* (1885).
[17] Alexander J Arbuthnot *Memories of Rugby and India* (1910).

known to render any explanation necessary to Rugbeians." This would be a little like laying down the house rules for a pool competition today, where you would hardly need to explain that you have to use the tip of the cue to hit the cueball. These rules were intended for the sole purposes of pupils playing at the school itself. All those references to 'the Close', to what happened when the ball went near the trees, and to 'the Island is all in goal' would only matter if you were playing on the Bigside field at Rugby School. Also, the original print run of just fifty copies hardly suggests they were aiming to hit the bestsellers list. In fact, several years later, in November 1858, the editor of *Bell's Life in London*, one of the foremost authorities on English sport, wrongly commented that Rugby's rules had never been put into print!

The 1845 version begins with its *Resolutions*, which are, rather than rules for the actual game, more of a set of rules for the school, and especially making sure that everybody took part. "The punishment for absenting oneself from a match, without any real or well-grounded reason, be left to the discretion of any praeposter" and "only in cases of extreme emergency … shall anyone be permitted to leave the close … till the game be finished."

Football at rugby was a far more savage affair than the game we know now, and much as some loved it, others were keen as mustard to find a way out. Even today there are plenty of British pupils that dread rugby season, and being forced to wear shorts in the middle of a freezing wet winter and be pummelled into the mud by more bullish boys. To top it off, this is followed by a communal shower and the humiliation of revealing to your classmates that you are still on the less developed side of puberty. For many kids, it is more a case of physical (and psychological) torture than education.

Forging sick notes to get out of playing games was as common then as it is now. "In consequence of the great abuse in the system of giving notes to … exempt fellows from attendance at the matches" they had to be signed by medical officers or heads of house. When you remember this was a game that actively encouraged players to kick each other in the shins, and when you learn of the 'death cart' that was used to wheel the injured off the pitch, you appreciate how, among the less athletic, those sick notes were hot property indeed. As it turns out, the rules for making sure nobody got out of playing football took up just as much space as the rules for the game itself, which is almost exactly as our pal Thomas Hughes described it.

It's curious to note that although Rugby's was by far the most successful code in exporting itself outside of the school that created it, the school itself had remarkably little to do with it. Reports on public school games were widespread in the papers long before an Old Rugbeian felt moved in 1852 to write to *Bell's Life* and say that "having often seen football matches at Eton in your paper, allow me to send you one from 'the football' school, Rugby" and Adrian Harvey notes that not even following the success of *Tom Brown's Schooldays* in 1857 was there any major move to publicise games at Rugby until reports started to be sent to *The Times* in 1866.

Rugby wasn't ready for the big stage yet. Several of its defining characteristics had yet to be institutionalised, including perhaps the most important of all... the oval ball.

All oval between us

It was at Brighton that they used to sing:

"And Eton may play with a pill if they please,
And Harrow may stick to their Cheshire Cheese,
And Rugby their outgrown egg, but here,
Is the perfect game of the perfect sphere[18]."

So, why the 'outgrown egg'? It was in 1842 that a certain William Gilbert spotted a market for flogging footballs to Rugby School boys, and moved his shoemaking business to a location close to the playing field[19], where another of his finest business lines was the manufacture of catapults (called 'tweakers' by the boys, which the little angels used for hunting rooks).

Ball-making technology was still in its infancy, and they were still using pig's bladders in those days, which our Will had down to a fine art, and he would sew four leather panels around them. Nobody had ever said that a football had to be round, so the fact that if not exactly ovoid, the ball was more of a blob didn't seem to concern anybody half as much as the fact that somebody was going to have to apply their mouth to the bladder and blow the thing up. Not nice, and Gilbert preferred to bring in volunteers for that job. But his nephew James, who carried on the business after his father's death, was "a wonder of lung strength who blew even the big match balls up tight." Bet the ladies loved him.

Yet the Gilberts were almost certainly not the inventors of the oval ball. They had a competitor, Richard Lindon, who was possibly a former apprentice under William Gilbert, and was also quick to spot the market for supplying this growing frenzy for footballs. An American called Charles Goodyear had invented vulcanised rubber in the 1850s, and it was Lindon who saw the opportunity to apply the technology to football inner tubes[20]. He had the motivation. His wife had died of a lung disorder, which was attributed to a lifetime of blowing up 'fresh green' pig's bladders that must have often carried no end of hideous diseases.

---

[18] Laurie Magnus, Robert Binney Lattimer *School: a monthly record of educational thought and progress* (1908).
[19] It is now the location of a sports shop, which also houses a small rugby football museum.
[20] Not everybody was impressed. *The Boy's book of sports, games, exercises, and pursuits Fr Warne and Co* (1869) remarked that "the old leather ball, dilated with a good ox-bladder, is decidedly the best. The newly invented vulcanized India-rubber balls are liable to get out of order – an accidental prick or cut rendering them quite useless."

Lindon's ball design was unveiled in 1862. Too late for his beloved, he also invented the hand pump, basing his idea on the ear syringe[21]. It was not just a major hit with the Rugby School boys; it was a revolution for football in general. At last here was a ball that could be made into any shape or size you fancied. And the shape that would have made the most sense would surely have been round.

So, why the hell was the Rugby ball oval? John Charles Thring, one of the forefathers of codified soccer, wrote a scathing letter to *The Field* in 1863, asking "was the oval ball an accident from want of skill in the worker in leather in Rugby, who, like the tailors, then persuaded his victims that it was the true artistic shape? Or was it designed for the sole benefit of the place-kicker, for I have yet heard that it was supposed to be good for the general game, and I can witness to its untrue rebounds."

Rugby stalwart Arthur Guillemard (later the first president of the RFU) replied in a letter of his own that "the makers in Rugby can make a ball in any possible shape," that they had won medals for their work, and supplied the likes of Marlborough, Wellington, Winchester and even Australia and New Zealand "where many people would deem the science of football quite unknown … the round ball is perhaps better for the use of some clubs who forbid carrying the ball, but I am sure that Rugbeians will never use the round balls when they can get the oval[22]."

The story goes that the boys at Rugby School were keen for their ball to be uniquely different to those used by all the other schools. So it was that Lindon came up with the oval design. But sadly for him, he failed to foresee what a major contribution his invention would make to world sport, and did nothing to patent it. Instead, it was his business rivals the Gilberts who pinched the idea. Sewing chunks of leather to porcine piss-bags may have meant pretty inauspicious beginnings for the Gilberts, but they had stumbled onto one of finest business flukes ever. Because that silly little game they were playing over the road went on to become an international phenomenon.

As rugby boomed, they flooded the market with advertising, and wherever rugby went, you could be sure that Gilbert was going to follow. Four generations oversaw the growth of the family trade as it expanded to Australasia, South Africa and beyond. Gilbert are still around today, with their name being almost synonymous with the rugby ball, though the company now also markets just about every item of rugby gear imaginable.

---

[21] Just how new Lindon's idea really was is open to debate. There is a German copperplate etching by Matthäus Merian the Elder dated to around 1615, called for some bizarre reason *The Lilies of the Valley are Often Mistaken*, that shows a game of ball being played in the background, while in the foreground a gentleman is sat holding a large ball, and another is busy inflating it with what is unmistakably some kind of hand pump. Two and a half centuries before Lindon claimed to have created something new.

[22] The original balls were a lot less oval than they are now, more plum-shape than lemon. As the years progressed, and rugby became more handling based than kicking based, the shape developed as well, though not to be regulated as oval until 1892. Throughout the early 20th century, by request of the players, rugby balls would gradually get longer and narrower.

Meanwhile, Lindon did his best to promote his balls as the true originals right up to his death in 1877, but with nothing like the commercial success of his rival. And rather than himself, it was his son Hughes John Lindon who was wrongfully accredited for many years with the invention.

It's all to do with the image of an advertisement that frequently gets reproduced in rugby histories, where the awkward wording wrongly implies that HJ Lindon was the inventor. It announces:
"H. J. Lindon,
FOOTBALL MANUFACTURER
(Successor to the late R. Lindon,)
6 Lawrence Sheriffe Street, Rugby,
Inventor of the
TRUE RUGBY BALL
ALSO
INFLATOR FOR THE SAME
which has caused the Game to become so universal."

So, while the other schools generally went for a predominantly kicking game, at Rugby they allowed something that most of the others would have considered a travesty of sporting courtesy: you could catch the ball and run with it. It also had the peculiarity of an oval ball that had to be kicked over rather than under the crossbar. Compared to football at the other public schools, it was a totally different game.

So, when the Old Rugbeians challenged the Old Etonians to a game of football in 1839, it was an accident just waiting to happen…

20 GROWN UP BOYS
Football at 19th century universities

Splendid isolation

Despite the changing attitudes to schoolboy football, which went from being condemned by the establishment to being actively encouraged and then made compulsory, there were few attempts at arranging inter-school matches. In *Eton College Magazine* (1832) it was written that "only once, indeed, has any challenge been sent, and that was from the Wykehamites, and then it was entirely impossible that the Etonians should accept it, from the absurd conditions proposed by their antagonists. That the match should be played on *Egham race course*, the players clad in *high gaiters*, or *mud boots*!" Two games between the same two schools in 1863, one by each school's rules, never got off the ground either.

"No one ever hears of two great schools contending on neutral ground in a game of football, no matter on how friendly terms they may subsist[1]" wrote Paul Ward as late as 1868. He wasn't quite right, but wasn't far off. Until the FA was formed in 1863, Adrian Harvey only has evidence of 25 matches that were ever organised between public schools[2], some of which were never actually played.

"The feud between Eton and Harrow is sufficiently well known to make an increase of hostile feeling very undesirable" wrote one Old Etonian in *The Times* in October 1863, and he had a point. The rivalry between the different schools was so intense, and violence in football and school-life in general so rife, that pitting the boys against each other was a recipe for disaster best avoided.

Perhaps the most famous attempt at an inter-school fixture was between Marlborough and Clifton in 1864. For that game, it was decided that "in accordance with the home rule, hacking over should be barred, though the Clifton regulations permitted it[3]." However, "whether it was that agreement as to no hacking over was misunderstood, or that the Clifton Twenty became irritated at being pressed, is not clear; but this is certain, that before long cries broke from the Cliftonian throats of 'hack him over!' … These suggestions were soon put into practice, and naturally provoked reprisals. A great deal of hot blood was engendered, and at one time it looked very much as if the match would degenerate into a free fight. At this juncture Boyle walked up to the Master, who was standing at the touch-line looking on. 'I think we'd better stop the game, sir, hadn't we?' 'No, no!' came the clear, decisive reply; 'they'll think we're afraid of them. Win the game first, and then talk about stopping if you like!'"

---

[1] Paul Ward *Reminiscences of Cheltenham college, by an old Cheltonian* (1968).

[2] About a third of these hardly count because they were played by old boy teams rather than the actual schools.

[3] Arthur Granville Bradley et al *A history of Marlborough college during fifty years: from its foundation to the present time* (1893).

Boyle did as he was told and scored the winner, and "there burst forth such a cheer from Marlburian throats as has never before nor since been heard on the football field … But the traditions and legends of the match lasted on for many years, and the experiences of the day led to the effectual discouragement of further contests with any alien team for some time[4]."

It would be more than two decades before the schools dared to play each other again. The honorary treasurer of the Rugby Football Union, Henry Vassall, reminisced in 1890 about how "English school authorities were long frightened by the traditions of this historic fixture[5]," which was enough to convince other schools that they were better off sticking to games among themselves.

Almost half of the games that did get played involved Westminster, who were a diamond in the rough when it came to inter-school football. Otherwise, the only other success story were the five games played between Marlborough and Rugby, two schools that played by almost identical rules anyway, which suggests that the main reason for all this self-imposed isolation was the incompatibility of the rules.

This was not helped by the snobbery of different establishments. By way of example, Harvey notes that "Harrow only recognised Eton, Winchester, Westminster and Charterhouse as public schools; Rugby only obtaining admission to this pantheon when Vaughan, an ex-Rugbeian, became Harrow's headmaster." When Westminster refused their challenge in 1866, the Shrewsbury captain retorted that the "captain of the Westminster Eleven has yet to learn the first lesson of a true public school education, the behaviour due from one gentleman to another[6]" and Harrow allegedly turned down Mill Hill's challenge with the condescending scoff that "Eton we know and Rugby we know; but who are ye[7]?"

But we also have to remember the logistics. It's 124 miles from Shrewsbury to Eton and 93 miles from Rugby to Winchester. Nowadays, there's no problem loading the kids onto the school bus and driving them off to a ground over a hundred miles away, but it was a different proposition entirely in the early 19th century, with nothing even remotely resembling a decent rail network until the 1850s. The school authorities may have started condoning football, but not to the extreme that they'd be willing to undertake operations like that, especially in times when a football teams were much bigger than they are nowadays.

So, the lack of inter-school play shouldn't come as too much of a surprise. Their different games developed in isolation. But it would be a very different story when all those pupils gathered under the same roof at university…

---

[4] But one of the combatants that day didn't seem to think it had been all that bad. "The game certainly had the appearance of a hostile encounter rather than a friendly football match" he wrote. "However, all differences and grievances were forgotten during the jovial supper with which we ended the day in the hall at Marlborough, and all finished pleasantly." Cited by EM Oakeley (ed.) in *Clifton College annals and register: 1860-1897.*

[5] Henry Vassall *Rugby Union Football (English Illustrated Magazine,* 1889-1890).

[6] *Baily's magazine of sports and pastimes* (1866).

[7] So goes the quote in so many history books, although *The Speaker* in 1890 attributed the same line to Cheltenham rejecting an offer from Clifton.

University challenges

Oxford beats Cambridge hands down when it comes to the oldest footy quote. Way back in 1303, "Thomas of Salisbury, a student of Oxford University, found his brother Adam dead, and it was alleged that he was killed by Irish students, whilst playing the ball in the High Street towards Eastgate." GAA 1, FA 0.

The statutes of St John's College, Oxford, issued on its foundation in 1555, made it clear that football would not be one of the practices it would be condoning, and corporal punishment was to be applied to any offender aged less than eighteen. But by 1584 they were all at it, when it was noted with horror how "diverse ministers adidinge in the universities, especial nonresidents, so use open plainge at football and maintininge of quarrelles to the great discredit of this universitye." And these quarrels were no idle matter, for in 1607, "the scholars of Oxford at a match of football burned the furnesses of Bullington Green containing 3 acres or thereabouts."

Something had to be done about this nonsense, and in 1636 it was. It was ordained that along with the outlawing of such indecencies as the "parade and display of guns and cross-bows, and, again, from the use of hawks for fowling … no scholars of any condition (and least of all graduates) are to play foot-ball within the University or its precinct (and particularly not in the public streets and places of the city) whether alone by themselves, or in company with townsmen." That last bit about the townsmen is interesting. It has often been suggested that the evolution of 'plebian mob football' and that of organised football within the walls of academia followed largely different courses, but here is a definite indication that the two social groups played together[8].

There is evidence of the same thing happening in 1581 at Cambridge, when a certificate states "there was a match made betwixt certain schollers of Cambridge and divers of Chesterton to play at fote ball abowt twoe yeres past, the sayd schollers resorting thither peaceably withowte anye weapons, the sayd townsmen of Chesterton had layd divers staves secretly in the church porch … and in playing did pike quarrels against the schollers & did bringe owte there staves wherewith they did so beat the schollers that divers had there heads broken[9]."

As a result of this, it was decreed in 1580 that no student "of what degree or condition soever he were, should … play at the foot-ball but only within the precincts of their several colleges, not permitting any stranger or scholars of other colleges or houses to play with them or in their company, and in no place else. And if any person being not adult shall break or violate any part of this decree and order, he shall for every default be openly corrected with the rod."

---

[8] James Walvin has a point when he suggests that the game of camp-ball in nearby East Anglia may have been the impetus for the popularity of football at Cambridge.

[9] Cited in Charles Henry Cooper, John William Cooper *Annals of Cambridge, Volume 2* (1843).

Although there were cases like that of John Narwick in 1632, who "would frequently recreate himself with bodily exercises and those violent enough, such as pitching the bar and playing at football, at which latter game, having the misfortune to break a player's collar-bone, he would never play again[10]" it was not so much the dangers of football itself as the inter-college battles that concerned the authorities. In 1595, the vice chancellor of Cambridge demanded that "the hurtfull and unschollerlike exercise of footeball and meetings tending to that ende to from henceforth utterly cease (excepte within the places severall to the Colledges, and that for them only that be of the same Colledge without noyse or outcry)."

In 1660, we learn that a student at was "in a companie that did in a riotous manner throw clotts or stones at the deputy proctor and Masters of Arts who came to prevent scholars from playing at football, and other disorderly meetings there." A 1679 reference from Magdalene College instructs that "no schollers give or receive at any time any treat or collation upon account of ye football play … further then Colledge beere or ale in ye open hall to quench their thirsts." Apart from beer, prizes or benefits for anybody purely on account of their football skills were out, but let's face it, drinking beer after playing football has never been an unpopular suggestion, especially where students are concerned.

Cambridge rules

Although football was played at British universities, it had none of the organised structure of cricket, rowing and other sports. But it was only a matter of time before it happened, and in 1839, an Old Rugbeian called Arthur Pell, who would go on to become an MP, decided to get a football team together to challenge the Old Etonians on Parker's Piece[11], an area of lawn near the centre of Cambridge.

We don't know the score, but the chances are the players didn't either. It was mayhem. Henry Charles Malden reminisced in 1897 how "an attempt was made to get up some football in preference to the hockey that was then in vogue[12] … the result was dire confusion, as every man played the rules he had been accustomed to at his public school. I remember how the Eton men howled at the Rugby men for handling the ball."

Malden had good reason to be surprised. He had been privately educated and so unlike many of his peers, did not have any personal attachment to any of the contrasting schoolboy codes. All the different school games coexisted at Cambridge. The Etonians played their

---

[10] Christopher Wordsworth *Social life at the English universities in the eighteenth century* (1874).

[11] Piece' was a common term at the time for open areas used for recreation, and in the 19th century this site was regularly used by the students for sport, generally cricket. In 1838, Dr George Elwes Corrie, Master of Jesus College, wrote that "we passed by Parker's Piece, and there saw some forty Gownsmen playing at football. The novelty and liveliness of the scene were amusing!" (Corrie M Holroyd, ed *Memorials of the Life of George Elwes Corrie* (*Cambridge Review*, 1890).

[12] This reference to hockey is especially interesting, as it suggests that hockey was, at least at Cambridge, more popular than football at the time. Although modern field hockey was an adaptation of the rules of football to stick-based games, it may have originally been the other way round.

game, and the Harrovians, Rugbeians and Wykehamists played theirs, steadfastly sticking to their old school traditions. But football culture was growing, and with that came a desire among the different old boys to replicate their cricketing contests on the football field. Working out how they were going to do that was not going to be an easy matter[13].

The next few years must have been a fascinating time at the university as the students from different schools learned about each other's takes on essentially the same sport, and started playing around with the different ideas. More than a problem, it probably caused nothing but enthralment, and we can imagine the football diehards putting more thought into the varying permutations of football than anything they were being taught in the lecture halls.

The conversations went into the small hours of the night. 'So what about Smyth-Perkins's suggestion that the sides take turns to kick the ball? Says it works wonders at Winchester', 'Bother that Godfrey Miles-Berkley, insisting on that loathsome 'bully' thing he got from Eton', 'Did you see the Charterhouse boys this afternoon, they didn't have any offside at all. I say, what a chortle it looked!', 'Golly, I hear they're allowing running in at Rugby, why, do let's run with the ball, it would be so spiffing. Belchand-Flemming says it's the way the Romans did it'.

There was an attempt around 1840, led by a former Shrewsbury pupil, Edgar Montagu, at setting up "a football club at Cambridge and drawing up rules, which were framed with the view of enabling players from other schools to join the club on fairly equal terms[14]." This club didn't last, but in 1848 it was once again Shrewsbury old boys who inspired an intrepid few to try to create a common code. John Charles Thring, the brother of the Edward Thring who was so offended by all that strumming of the one-string banjo at Uppingham, is credited with being one of the perpetrators of the first rules-writing session, along with a fellow Old Salopian, Henry de Winton. The Henry Malden who had been so riffled by the Eton v Rugby fracas was one of the chosen few who joined them on a select committee to draft the *Laws of the Cambridge University Foot Ball Club*.

Malden's letter tells the story of how "it was agreed that two men should be chosen to represent each of the public schools, and two who were not public school men for the Varsity. G Salt and myself were chosen for the Varsity. I wish I could remember the others. Burn of Rugby, was one, Whymper of Eton, I think also. We were 14 in all I believe. Harrow and Eton, Rugby, Winchester, Shrewsbury were represented. We met in my rooms after Hall, which in those days was at 4pm, anticipating a long meeting. I cleared the tables and provided pens, ink and paper. Several asked me on coming in whether an exam was on! Every man brought a copy of his school rules, or knew them by heart, and our progress in

---

[13] From a modern perspective, such insular partisanism may seem extraordinary. However, at Oxford and Cambridge today, some students play rugby league, others play rugby union, others still play soccer, and nobody is suggesting they all stop doing that and adopt a composite code.

[14] Cited in George William Fisher, John Spencer Hill *Annals of Shrewsbury School* (1899).

framing new rules was slow. On several occasions Salt and I, being unprejudiced, carried or struck out a rule when the voting was equal. We broke up five minutes before midnight."

Unfortunately no copy has survived of those original rules, and the earliest ones we can refer to today are those of 1856 (found over a century later in the Shrewsbury School library and printed in full in *Appendix Four*). There had probably been several revisions over the eight years in between, and by 1856, Thring, de Winton, Salt, Malden, Burn and Whymper had all long since graduated, and are not among the signatories.

A look at those rules shows how most of the subtleties of football played at different schools had been brushed under the carpet to produce a more streamlined game. The hots, the bullies, the mauls, the squashes, the tries on goal… all gone. This was a simple game where teams had to kick the ball into goals at either end of the pitch. What the Cambridge boys had effectively invented was soccer, although there were several differences from the way the game is played today.

The goals were two flag-posts with a string used in the place of the modern crossbar. There is nothing about the number of players on a team, nor how long a game should last. For the time being, these were issues to be sorted out on the day, as is still the case with informal soccer matches today.

The throw-in already existed, but had to be delivered at a right angle to the touchline as it still is in rugby, and the ball could be thrown however a player liked. If the ball went 'behind' the goal, then it was kicked back into play ten paces from the point where the ball crossed the line. And teams didn't change ends at half-time, they changed ends after every goal was scored.

Most forms of football at Victorian public schools allowed the ball to be caught in the air as long as it came directly from a kick without touching the ground. The Cambridge rules also allowed this, but unlike at Rugby, there was to be no running with it. And as everybody could use their hands, there was no need for goalkeepers.

There was also an offside law to prevent 'loitering', or goal-hanging as we'd call it today, whereby a player could not touch the ball unless he had at least three defenders in front of him[15], which is exactly the same law as the one being used at Eton at the time.

Rule 10 outlaws all "holding a player, pushing with the hands, or tripping up," which eliminated most of the brutality associated to the public school game. But there is no specific mention of hacking being illegal[16]. However, "any player may prevent another from getting to the ball by any means consistent with the above rules," which hints that some kind of off-

---

[15] 'Three' did not become 'two' until 1925, as it still is now, although a lot of people don't realise it, forgetting that the goalkeeper also counts as a player. If the keeper isn't there for some reason, then an attacker must have two normal defenders in front to be onside, and that's caught a few people out over the years.

[16] As the 1863 version of the Cambridge Rules states that "holding, pushing with the hands, tripping up *and shinning* are forbidden," (i.e. adding 'shinning' to the three actions that were already illegal in 1856), it is quite possible that the hacking ban was introduced after 1856.

the-ball interference was possible. As the 1863 version of the Cambridge Rules declared in capital letters: "ALL charging is legal."

There is nothing that says what happened should anybody fail to abide by any of the rules. In fact, the free kick would not become a standard part of soccer until 1876, and even then was deemed a travesty by the gentlemen amateurs. By then, cup ties had bred a win-at-all-costs mentality among the nation's footballers, but back in the 1850s it was generally assumed that no decent fellow would even dream of intentionally breaking the rules, and if by accident they did, they would simply apologise and withdraw momentarily from the game. The deliberate duping of the referee, which nowadays is almost inevitable in football, was as unthinkable back then as cheating during a round of golf today.

Malden's letter explains what happened next. "The new rules were printed as the *Cambridge Rules*, copies were distributed and pasted up on Parker's Piece, and very satisfactorily they worked, for it is right to add that they were loyally kept, and I never heard of any public school man who gave up playing from not liking the rules."

You'll miss it if you blink, but hanging on a tree just opposite the fire station in a corner of Parker's Piece there is a plaque that commemorates how "in the 1800s, students established a common set of simple football rules emphasising skill above force, which forbade catching the ball and hacking[17]."

But did the Cambridge rules really sort out the mess once and for all? That's what Malden tells us, but it seems hard to believe that the Rugbeians were so easily tamed. They had written their own rules two years earlier for a very different game that included running with the ball. It seems unlikely that they, or students that had been to schools like Marlborough and Cheltenham that also played a rugby game of sorts, would have taken much interest in the new game.

The facts suggest few problems were solved overnight. These well-meaning boys had formed a club to frame a hybrid code, but football at Cambridge seems to have remained largely segregated. In 1856, the Old Etonians at Cambridge formed their own club to play their own game, the Old Rugbeians followed suit a year later, and the Old Harrovians formed a club in 1863, all to play their own varieties of football.

The new code may have worked for some informal kickabouts on Parker's Piece, but there is no evidence that any important games were ever played by it. Other than two fixtures between Etonians and Harrovians in 1862 and 1863, Adrian Harvey has failed to find any evidence of composite games during this period, and we know that the 1862 game turned a totally blind eye to the supposedly universally accepted Cambridge Rules and was instead a surprisingly elaborate composite game of their own[18].

---

[17] The 1848 rules did not forbid either catching of the ball or hacking, although the later Cambridge Rules of 1863 did.

[18] It had very specific rules determining the size of the pitch and the goals (with a crossbar), and the length of the game (two halves of 45 minutes each, perhaps setting something of a precedent). You could charge but not

No doubt the achievements at Cambridge were something of a turning point in football, but at the time it was no bigger a matter than a few inconsequential enthusiasts arranging some innocent fun. John Venn, the creator the Venn diagrams we all learned to make at school, studied there from 1853 and 1857 and returned as a lecturer in 1862, didn't even notice it, writing in his memoirs that "I have been since informed that some devotees of what was commonly regarded as a school game occasionally indulged, in obscure places, in the peculiar art that they had acquired at Rugby or Eton. But I am certain that I never saw the game played, and that no friend of mine ever practised it. This is confirmed by my brother, who was four years my junior. He tells me that he remembers a friend coming in to Hall and relating that he had seen a number of Rugby men, mostly freshmen, playing a new game: that they made a circle round a ball and butted each other.[19]"

However, the 1863 Cambridge Rules would provide the blueprint for the first rules of the Football Association. Only a tiny part of the 1863 wording is the same as it was in 1856, so it is ambiguous whether these were an entirely new set of rules, or a development of the game invented in 1848. Certainly, the 1863 version was very different. In fact, there was some reverse evolution, for the string crossbar was gone and goals could be scored at any height, 'throw ins' were now taken with the feet, and offside was much stricter, with nobody allowed to touch the ball if they were ahead of it when it was kicked. The game had also adopted something like Eton's rouge, whereby if the ball went behind the goal, instead of a goal-kick or corner, the first player to touch it won the right to a free kick. But other aspects had moved closer to modern soccer. There was to be absolutely no touching of the ball with the arms or hands, hacking was illegal, and teams now switched ends at half-time.

Open universities

At England's other major university, Oxford, they were facing the same problems. Robert Blachford Mansfield sets the scene nicely. Having so many boys from different schools led to "amusing incidents. On one occasion, I saw a Rugby man catch the ball, and with a complacent smile was then giving a little run to give impetus to his intended kick off, when Podder, hot from Winchester, darted out, and with one dexterous turn of the leg, laid the Rugbeaian flat on the ground, and before he could scoop the mud out of his mouth … Podder had carried the ball to the other end of the ground. It subsequently appeared that by Rugby rules nobody was allowed to interfere in such a case, whereas at Winchester he who had caught the ball might kick if he could[20]."

Although Cambridge has been heralded as the place where the different schools laid aside their separate footballing identities for the sake of the common good, Harvey's findings

---

shin, there was no handling whatsoever and offside meant always having to have at least four players between yourself and the opposite goal.

[19] John Venn *Early Collegiate Life* (Heffer & Sons, 1913).

[20] Robert Blachford Mansfield *School-Life At Winchester College; Or, The Reminiscences Of A Winchester Junior Under The Old Regime, 1835-40* (1866).

suggest that "there seems to have been relatively more interaction between players from different schools at Oxford" although there is no evidence that they ever created a composite code. The closest we get to that was a game in 1862 between Harrow and Winchester old boys using the former's rules and the latter's ball.

Charles Wordsworth, the nephew of the poet William Wordsworth, instigated the first Varsity cricket match in 1827, and two years later, the same man organised the first Cambridge v Oxford Boat Race, which went on to become the two showpiece sports events of the early Victorian era. But inter-university football was another matter entirely. There was no Varsity football match until 1872, using the Rugby Union's newly published rules, and the first game using the FA's rulebook was played a year after.

In the meantime, football was developing along different paths at other universities in the British Isles. Edinburgh University probably has as long-standing a tradition of football as either of the Oxbridge institutions, and one description of the game as it was played in the 1840s is worth including for its revolting description of the ball, which was "raw bladder, fresh – but that is hardly the word – from the butcher's hands, enclosed in the leather case. The blowing of this contrivance was a disgusting operation in which a quill was used as a mouth-piece. The process was taken in turns as a necessary, but repulsive, duty – one not without risks. Consequently it was considered prudent to perform the operation of orally inflating the bag at home, because, as certainly as any one attempted to do so at school, somebody would watch his opportunity and, when the bag was three quarters filled, squash the whole thing flat. The effect of the foul blast from the unsavoury interior of the ball, thus forced down the throat of the unhappy blower, is not to be described[21]."

In March 1851, a fascinating account was published in *Bell's Life in London*. It is remarkably ahead of its time and even suggests the first 'international' between Scottish and English players. It appears in the form of a letter to the editor from 'one of England's rising generation and an admirer of her sports[22]', and a member of what he calls the "rapidly rising" University of Edinburgh Foot Ball Club. Our anonymous scribe starts by referring to an earlier battering of his own team at the hands of the 93rd Highlanders, he claims "in consequence of having to play with the men, whereas it was originally understood to be with the officers."

Unhappy with that recent experience of having to share a field with the lower ranks of British military society, their next game was "between the Scotch and English members composing this club." It was played with a massive 24 players on each side, and to the best of five 'games', although it was agreed that "at five o'clock, should the games not be finished, then the umpire should give it in favour of the side which had won most games." As well as

---

[21] Alexander Fergusson *Chronicles of the Cumming Club and Memories of Old Academy Days, 1841-1846* (1887).
[22] It's interesting that he considers football to be an English import, although Scotland played a huge part in its own in the game's historical development.

the early appearance of umpires, another ahead-of-its-time idea was a method for telling the teams apart. The teams were "distinguished on the Scotch side by a green badge and on the English by a red."

It was enough of an occasion to draw a crowd, for "nearly 500 people had collected on the links" but rather than be pleased to attract such interest, the players griped about how the onlookers "in the most unpardonable and selfish manner crowded over the grounds so that the goals and players were perfectly indistinguishable." Despite the length of the description, there are few clues to the exact nature of the game, but with just five minutes remaining, the English were two up and "had brought the ball to within a few yards of the goal, when another kick would have won it but for a Scotchman, who took the ball off the ground, and claimed a free kick, resisting every effort made to take the ball from him. The umpire, who saw the circumstance, immediately disallowed the claim[23]."

All in all, that seems like quite an organised football scene in the Scottish capital over half a decade before the formation of what has been claimed to be the oldest football club still in existence today, the Edinburgh Academicals Football Club, a group of old boys from Edinburgh schools looking in 1857 to continue the game into their adult lives. Nowadays, they play rugby, but proudly maintain the FC in their name (which is traditionally associated to soccer clubs) because they were formed before soccer and rugby were considered to be different sports.

Scottish politician and judge Sir John Hay Athole Macdonald was one of them and described the Edinburgh game in the mid 1850s as "twenty a side, and a scrum was a scrum indeed – fifteen pushing against fifteen in a tight maul, which often was immovable for several minutes. The steam rose from the pack like the smoke from a charcoal-burner's pile. It was much more straining and fatiguing than the more open game of to-day ... the breaking-up of a maul, when it came, meant vigorous kicking ahead, on the chance that ball and toe might meet. I bear the marks yet[24]."

What this chapter is shown us is that the universities provided the perfect environment for the different kinds of football to be standardised. But although they started the job, they never took it anywhere. Perhaps if they had, then something similar to the college football phenomenon in American would have occurred. But Adrian Harvey is right to muse that rather than promote a standard code, the public schools with all their "ferocious partisanship ... might well have had a profoundly negative effect on the game ... intimidating outsiders and discouraging them from creating rules to regulate football."

Outside of the elite institutions, there was not the same attachment to old school traditions. The footballers in British society at large were going to be far more receptive to the idea of

---

[23] In almost all forms of school football at the time, the ball could only be held if it was caught on the fly, not lifted from the ground, which earned the right to a free kick, unless, like at Rugby, running with the ball was allowed.
[24] John Hay Athole Macdonald *Life jottings of an old Edinburgh citizen* (1911).

developing a common set of laws that everybody could play by. And although public school old boys would play a big part that process, for now, it's time to leave the academics to their squabbles, and have a gander at what was going on in the 'real' world.

21 A QUESTION OF CLASS
19th century football in the non-academic world

Industrial disease

Things were never more glorious for Britannia and her empire than the 19th century. It's a shame so few people got the chance to enjoy it. There has almost certainly never been a more dramatic change in the history of human society than that perpetrated by the Industrial Revolution[1]. The new technology of the late 18th and early 19th centuries metamorphosed the way we worked, the way we travelled and the way we lived. Society was turned entirely on its head as mass industry swept across the country like a dark cloud of progress towards something that may or may or not have been a good thing. Nobody really knew, but the only people that were in a position to decide were those that were reaping the rewards of the Greatest of Britains – one that was becoming the wealthiest and most powerful country in the world. And they weren't going to have it any other way.

The scramble for coal led to the South Wales countryside being carved to shreds. The British steel and iron industries were booming. James Watt's steam engine as good as turned horse, wind, water and air power into things of the past. Joseph Aspdin's idea of cement meant buildings could be thrown up in no time. And despite the noble efforts of a revolutionary group called the Luddites, it would not be long before the roaring furnaces, belching chimneys and choking smog of towering mills and factories, and the claustrophobic grime of gloomy mines, would come to dominate the landscape, and the lives, of the labouring millions. The British Empire was powered by turning its ancestral homeland into an industrial machine, in which the working classes were dehumanised into expendable resources.

Cottonopolis, as Manchester was nicknamed, epitomised the transformation: "this famous great factory town. Dark and smoky from the coal vapours, it resembles a huge forge or workshop. Work, profit and greed seem to be the only thoughts here. The clatter of the cotton mills and the looms can be heard everywhere[2]."

Everything changed. Agriculture had long succumbed to automation, and the cottage industries were powerless to compete with the growing monster of mass production. Out of work, out of pocket, people flocked to the cities, where they were cooped up in disease-riddled squalor in hurriedly constructed housing, where proper water, sewage and heating systems were luxuries they would have to live without. People became commodities, pawns to be exploited, who would dedicate their lives to repeating the same menial task day after

---

[1] I say almost certainly, because it's tempting, maybe even correct, to say that the Digital Revolution we are experiencing ourselves will one day rank even higher in the history books.
[2] Johanna Schopenhauer *Sammtliche Schriften* (Frankfurt, 1830).

day, in atrocious conditions and rarely seeing the light of day. And in return they received a wage that would scarcely support themselves, let alone their families.

So the families went to work too. The population was exploding as mothers started running out of names for their children, and as there was no hope of them ever getting any kind of education, when they were barely old enough to walk both boys and girls were sent out with their fathers. Children worked the factories and the mines, where they were only slightly above the omnipresent rats in the pecking order and were treated with nightmarish and often mortal cruelty. Working 14 hour shifts or more, six days a week, they spent almost their entire childhoods atrociously undernourished and struggling to keep their eyes open, but severely beaten should they ever show signs of slacking. Injuries were common, and deaths were more of an inconvenience to the factory owner than any cause for concern.

In 1834, John Brown described how the seven year old protagonist of his book was working in a mill and once lost a finger in a machine. He was sent to have it sewn back on before being told to go straight back to work. Yet that was paradise compared to life when he was moved to a different mill, where they had to steal from the pigs to get food, where they were beaten to within inches of their lives for the smallest misdemeanours, where "the overseers toyed with the children, making them balance above the machinery that could kill or maim them if they fell[3]" and where they "died, diseased and without lament in a routine procession to the paupers corner of the local graveyard."

The Factory Acts did eventually get around to implementing laws to curb this. From 1833, for instance, no child under nine years of age could work in textile factories, and never at night, while until they turned 18, they could not work more than 12 hours a day[4]. And those, remember, were the improved conditions. And the saddest thing of all is that in many parts of this wonderful world we live in, things are no better today.

It was a bleak time for the British poor, and if the future of folk football on the village green had looked grim before, the Industrial Revolution could have been its doom. There was no time or energy left for sports, and neither was there space in the cramped industrial cities. Industry had taken over.

"Every vacant green spot has been converted into a street; field after field has been absorbed by the builder … football and cricket grounds, bowling greens … and other pastimes have been successfully parcelled out in squares, lanes or alleys … and the humbler classes who may wish to obtain the sight of a field, or inhale a mouthful of fresh air, can scarcely be gratified unless, at some expense of time and money, they make a journey for the

---

[3] John Brown *The Memoirs of Robert Blincoe* (1834), cited in a chapter on Derbyshire's Glossop North End in David Conn *The Beautiful Game? Searching for the soul of football* (Mainstream sport, 2004). Conn's book is a monumental work that describes the corruption, exploitation and manipulation that has been omnipresent in soccer since its beginnings to the present day. Read this or his other book *The Football Business* and it's enough to put you off the game for good.
[4] Such laws were only for the textile industry, and not extended to all trades until 1878.

purpose[5]" wrote Horace Smith of London, while the rector of Hircham in 1844 lamented that "they have no village green, or common, for active sports. Some thirty years ago, I am told, they had a right to a play-ground in a particular field at certain seasons of the year, and were then celebrated for their foot-ball[6]."

By 1850, the Shropshire village of Much Wenlock was advertising a football match as one of the "manly sports from England's past." In this bleak world, football was a no-go for the 19th century labourer. It was down to the lucky few at the nation's public schools to keep the momentum going. Or so the story goes. Revisionist Adrian Harvey, for one, is less convinced by the idea that the enclosure of country land, the industrialisation of the British countryside and the mass exodus of the population from rural communities to the city factories really had that dramatic an effect on football at all.

He argues that "the evidence is often sketchy, it appears there was little difference between the hours worked by industrial and agricultural workers." The seeds of the industrial revolution were already in place in the 1700s, when football was gaining rather than losing popularity, and although the long working hours in the factories did make it hard to find time to play football, and games were generally limited to public holidays, this wasn't really any different to the way it had always been.

A massive investigation was conducted into industry up and down the country by the *Royal Commission on Children in Mines and Manufactories* (1842). It does indeed reveal much about the horrifying conditions endured by children in the pits, yet also includes telling statements like one from Yorkshire claiming "the children have, on the average, not less than one unoccupied day in the last week, besides a fair proportion of time for recreation and play in the evenings and they avail themselves of these opportunities to a considerable extent from engaging in the healthful games of cricket, nor and spell[7] and football. This they are fortunately enabled to do from the circumstance of there being generally in the neighbourhood of mines a good deal of waste land."

Harvey is even less convinced by the idea that early 19th century footballers struggled to find anywhere decent to play. Lack of recreational space would have been more of a problem in the cities than in the villages, that's only logical, but in most parts of the country, it can't have been that difficult to find an empty field, park or yard to throw up a football if you really wanted to. Even the biggest cities of the early 19th century were tiny compared to our modern-day metropolises, and Harvey notes that in 1842 "in heavily urbanised Rochdale, footballers clearly regarded the availability of a playing area to be an insignificant problem, suggesting to prospective opponents that they toss for choice of grounds." In the 21st century, finding somewhere suitable to play football in inner-city areas is much more of a problem

---

[5] Horace Smith *Festivals, Games and Amusements* (1831).
[6] JS Henslow *Suggestions towards an enquiry into the present condition of the labouring population of Suffolk* (1844).
[7] Nor (or knur) and spell was a croquet-like game, and other popular Yorkshire sports were shuttlecocks and something rather curious they called 'bumball'.

than it would have been in the early 19th century. Full-size fields with the goals and pitch-markings all in place, maybe not, but they hadn't been invented yet anyway.

And not everybody left for the cities. Richard Holt, another revisionist, notices that in the 1851 census, Britain's biggest source of employment was still agriculture. Although there had been plenty of theft of the countryside going on, the old life had not disappeared entirely.

Not everything that happened in the early 19th century was bad for football, especially the vastly improved communications network. People had always led remarkably insular existences. The vast majority of the population still lived in villages of some 100 people, and often went nowhere else in their whole lives. Today it is easier to arrange an inter-continental plane trip than it was for the average person in the early 19th century to travel just twenty miles. People simply didn't have the time, the resources or much particular reason to want to make such treks, and when they did leave for the big cities or emigrated to seek their fortunes, the chances were that they would never see their homes again. William Pitt the Younger's 1803 edict on mustering to prepare for the threat of a Napoleonic invasion proclaimed that nobody was required to travel more than six miles, for this was "no more than the sturdy English peasantry were in the habit of going when led to a cricket match or other rural diversion." Even then it transpired that the 12-mile round trip in a single day had been far too optimistic.

All of this changed with the arrival of the railways. Engineers had been developing steam locomotion since the 18th century, but the earliest trains were simply used for transporting ore out of mines. It wasn't until 1825, when George Stephenson's Locomotion started chugging along the Stockton and Darlington Railway, that the potential of not just carrying goods but also paying passengers became a reality. By 1847, the country had over ten thousand miles of track, linking most of the major cities in the land. It is no coincidence that this was also the decade when football really started heading towards codification. By 1852, Winchester stated they were willing to travel as much as fifty miles for a match, something that would have been impossible a decade earlier.

The penny post, created in 1840, also meant it was now much easier for people to keep in touch. Faster and cheaper printing methods, coupled with post trains (and improved literacy), meant newspapers were suddenly a far more effective way of keeping the masses informed of everything that was going on in the outside world.

All of a sudden, the world did not seem quite as big as it used to be. Before, so scarce had been the interaction between communities that even within a single county there would be people as culturally and linguistically different as those of San Francisco, Aberystwyth and a sheep farm in the Australian outback today. This was all about to change.

In the past, representative football matches had never involved much more than one side of the town against the other, games between neighbouring parishes, between different trades or the omnipresent married men v bachelors. Mail and rail opened up a whole new land of opportunity. It was now quite feasible to arrange matches by mail or by placing announcements in the press, and then for a whole team to jump on the train in the morning, choo-choo off to a different town, play football, and be back home in time for supper. It was a totally new football culture. But the further footballers went, the more foreign the traditions became, and the same problems with conflicting rules that the public schools faced would also arise in the outside world.

Clubbing together

In Scotland, we find extraordinarily early and detailed records of a civilian football club, all thanks to the personal papers of a 17 year old trainee lawyer called John Hope, now in the National Archives of Scotland. The accounts, schedules and even a list of subscribers describe a 'Foot-Ball Club' he had formed in Edinburgh in 1824 to play on Saturday afternoons[8]. An 1825 reference mentions that they played a game involving 39 players with "such kicking of shins and such tumbling" on a field with goals marked by sticks at either end. Although tripping was illegal, players could push and hold each other, and also lift the ball. By the 1826-27 season, the club had a massive 835 members. It was no working class enterprise, with most of the players seemingly being Hope's fellow lawyer friends and other members of the Edinbourgeoisie, but they didn't have any apparent connection to the schools or university. The records are bitty, but as late as February 1841 there is one final entry concerning temporary membership, after which there is nothing. Whatever fate befell John Hope's foot-ball club, we may never know, but although the details of any other clubs around at the time have now been lost, Hope was probably was not alone in his initiative to form a local football club[9].

Looking into the commonly cited theory that football was virtually inexistent outside of the public schools between 1830 and 1859, Adrian Harvey compiled as much evidence as he could gather. Especially using *Bell's Life*, he lists references to 93 different football teams in 'wider society' over those years. He found evidence of 19 teams in Yorkshire, 14 in Lancashire and 13 in Scotland, and that's not counting the Shrovetide games, which he considers to be a different issue entirely. Just these alone are enough to tell us that there was a whole lot more football activity going on outside of academia than there was within[10].

Football was also a common inclusion at local festivals, such as Windsor (1834), Ingestrie (1834) and Richmond (1838). In rural communities, teams would just represent the village, often defined by the parish boundaries. But in the urban world, teams were usually associated to some kind of institution. Many were based around trades and workplaces, such as Deanston Cotton Mill, Edinburgh (1835), King's Guards Mill, Lancashire (1844), the

---

[8] The payments include two shillings for four bladders, one shilling for leather and pipes (which must have been used to blow them up) and 10s. 6d. to hire a local park.

[9] In Scotland, there was football played by teams from either bank of the Tweed in 1841, and also at a sports festival in Dundee in 1849.

[10] Harvey does include a few slightly less elitist schools in his calculations, which may not really belong in this part of the study, but the theory still holds true.

Edinburgh waiters (1841), Rugby tailors (1845) and Ulverston's leather workers who played against men from the other trades (1839).

Teams like Sidney Smith's Tavern in Bolton (1841) and the Cronkeysham Champions Society (1841), who were willing to change their name to the Fieldhead Lads in honour of the alehouse that patronised them, typified how publicans saw the potential gains from football, not because of the benefits for healthy exercise, but because it was a no-brainer when it came to attracting custom in much the same way as pubs install plasma screens to show live matches today. For years, publicans had been offering prizes for shooting, foot-racing, wrestling, or whatever sport tickled the local masses, and anything from food, drinks, cash and even livestock were offered as incentives to the winners.

Another major group was teams based around the military, which included the Edinburgh 93rd Highlanders (1851) and the Grenadiers 3rd Battalion in London (1859). Football clubs seemed particularly rife around the naval ports of Hampshire, where we had HMS Illustrious (1857), Parkhurst Barracks (1856) and the Winchester Garrison Officers (1859) returning from the Crimean War in search of the less life-threatening battleground of the football field.

And then there were teams like Birmingham Athenic (1842), Manchester Athenaeum (1849) and the Glasgow Celtic Society (1859), who were formed as sections of more general athletics clubs and gymnasiums. But the most common type of sports club to form football sections were the cricket teams that considered football a viable alternative to their usual game in the off-season. *The Guardian* in June 1848 mentioned that a club for playing "cricket, quoits and football" had been established in Newcastle on Tyne, which would have been along similar lines to the Great Leicestershire Cricket and Football Club (1840) and Surrey FC (1849), which was on offshoot of Surrey County Cricket Club.

Surrey FC printed their own rules in 1849, as far as we know the earliest written code outside of the academic institutions. It was no epic publication, stretching to just six points, the first three of which are merely administrative matters dealing with membership and funds, along the lines of "subscriptions of 5 shillings … shall entitle [players] to all the privileges of Surrey Football Club. That the money so subscribed shall be appropriated to the defrayal of the expenses of the club, namely, the cost of the balls and ropes, and the payment of a person who shall keep them in perfect condition. The members shall dine together at the end of the season, and any surplus in subscriptions which may then be on hand … shall be applied to such dinner."

Only the final three rules detailed the way the actual game was to be played. There were to be no more than 22 players on a team and the ball was to be "tossed up in the centre of the ground and the game determined in favour of that side which will first kick the ball over the 'goal ropes' of their opponents. Should the ball be kicked over the fence on either side of the ground, then the ball, when regained, shall be tossed up in the centre of the ground, in line with the place where it went out."

The 93 teams that Harvey encountered are only likely to represent a tiny sample of the overall number of teams that were really playing football in Britain at the time (it works out at just three new teams per year). For the whole 1830-1859 period, only two or three pub teams are identified, but there must have been dozens, nay, hundreds of others. From country villages to urban heartlands, there were probably many teams that played a lot more serious football than the Bodyguards and Fearnoughts in Rochdale (1841) or the Scottish farmers from Blairdrummond Estate who played men from the Deanston cotton mills (1835). It is just that their efforts were never recorded.

And that should come as no surprise. In a time before football codes were standardised, before there were cups and leagues, when it was just challenge matches between groups of grown up boys, football matches went ignored by the written word. Rather like we might say that fishing or pony-trekking are popular hobbies today, football was often mentioned as a common pastime, but there was little mention of specific teams, players or matches. There was as much interest in documenting their achievements as there would be in those of four businessmen enjoying a Friday afternoon round of golf today.

Most of Adrian Harvey's research was based on *Bell's Life in London*, where articles, letters and announcements were "usually written by the competitors themselves." The chances are very few early footballers ever bothered to do this, even when they were presumptuous enough to think that that anybody could possibly care. If in 1863, there was a report of the sixth "great public school match between Westminster and Harrow", but Harvey can only trace three of the previous five, then what hope for a game between the patrons of a couple of pubs in Tavistock?

At this point, historians need to stop thinking like historians and think like footballers instead. Historians are the kind of people that like to make sure everything is documented. Footballers are the kind of people that like to play football. They can't be relied on to document things, and the stattoes of the Victorian era were far too busy spotting trains and steamships to worry about football quite yet.

If football was really on the verge of extinction, then a bunch of grown men kicking a ball around would have made for quite an unusual sight. But what little press coverage of football there was is remarkably matter-of-fact about it. Compare that to other countries.

In 1888, in Arad, Romania, the mere sight of "a couple of youths running with a ball on the empty ground out of town" was enough to make the papers. In the 1880s in Seville, posters promoting the first game in the city explained that "the peculiarity of this game resides in the fact that instead of striking the ball with the hands or with bats it is instead struck by the feet and, in extreme cases, using the shoulders and head" while in Bilbao as late as 1902 the press was musing that "who knows? Maybe one day everyone here will play the game. It seems to be bringing the people together. It seems to arouse curiosity." We've got David Goldblatt to thank for these gems, and also the best of all, from a 19th century Brazilian journalist who was blissfully oblivious to the *jogo bonito* his country had coming when he reported how "a group of Englishmen, a bunch of maniacs as they all are, get together from time to time to kick around something that looks like a bull's bladder. It gives them great satisfaction or fills them with sorrow when this kind of yellowish bladder enters a rectangle formed by wooden posts."

In 19th century England, however, there was no such dumbfounded response. Football matches were so commonplace that hardly anybody ever bothered to write about them.

Making a match

There is no record of any football tournament being played prior to the 1860s. All records refer to one-off challenges, usually in the form of press announcements. Harvey provides many examples of these, which illustrate quite nicely how things worked. For instance, in *Bell's Life* in October 1842 we learn that "a meeting was held at the Clock public house, Bickenhill, Warwickshire on 15th instant, to draw up articles and decide upon the day and place for a match at football, between six gentlemen of the above parish and six gentlemen of Hampton, when it was decided to come off at Hampton in Arden, on the 2nd of November for a bottle of wine and dinner each. The length between goals to be ten score yards, width of goals ten feet, height six feet, and to be the best of three goals" or in March 1852, "the Holmfirth players will play Enderby youths at football, 10 or 12 men a side, for £20 a side, and meet them at Hyde Park, Sheffield, on Good Friday, April 9th between twelve and one o'clock. If £5 are sent to us, and articles to me, J Batty, Red Lion Inn, Jackson Bridge near Holmfirth, the match will be made."

Teams would first need to settle the basic terms, such as the date, time and venue, while in a surprisingly large number of cases they would also decide on the stakes to be won. And then they'd need to settle the rules. This principally meant deciding on two main issues. First, how many players would be on each team, Harvey noting that "there is no evidence of games being played by uneven sides." The most common number, however, was already something around ten to fifteen-a-side. And second, they needed to sort how the winner was to be decided, which would generally either be the first team to score so many goals, or for play to end by a certain time of day. Issues such as the size of the goalposts and hacking occasionally came up, but the general lack of need to go into too many details suggests that football played outside of the public schools was a much simpler affair, devoid of all the often unnecessarily complicated regulations. Here, the players just gathered on a field, decided what the goals were, and got down to getting the ball through them.

Bell's Life did offer tiny match reports. In Leicestershire "a match £5 aside, Shrove Tuesday. 15 a side, Blaby Youth v Wygston Youth, in a field near to Counsterthorpe, in the presence of several thousand people from two adjacent villages. The goals being pitched, the men stripped." And in Derbyshire, in February 1849 "10 single men of Willington v 10 single men of Egginton for £2, which was won by Willington, after one of the best games ever witnessed on the lawn at Egginton. It lasted two hours and 20 minutes and it was a fair kick and trip game[11]."

It is a futile exercise to attempt to categorise these games as rugby or soccer. Some teams edged more towards carrying and others more towards kicking, but these elements overlapped with others that would look more familiar today to Gaelic or Australian footballers. For instance, there are common references to what are called byes or by-goals, which were probably near misses along similar lines to Australian 'behinds' and Irish 'overs'.

Kicking, rather than carrying, seems to have been the most widespread method. At Rochdale in 1842, the Fear-Noughts got "the first kick", and an account the same year states the objective was for each party "by vigorous kicks to propel the ball to the hailing place behind the adversaries[12]."

But that wasn't always the case. For instance, there was one game "much in vogue in some rural districts" where "the captain gives the first kick towards the opposite bounds, the other party meeting it and returning it either by kicking, or carrying it, if preferred … but in any case whether the ball is carried or kicked out, the opposite party are privileged to throw down the ball carrier or kicker by any means in their power[13]." As the writer says, it "might be supposed that severe injuries would follow this rough practice, but it seldom is the case; and though the shins suffer severely at the time, they rarely exhibit any dangerous wounds."

The story has generally gone that 'working class' football was a wild, savage affair, and it was the public schools that civilised it. But while in earlier chapters we learned that public school football often took pride in its own brutality, in the few reports we have of football played in the adult world, there is usually far less emphasis on aggression or physicality. Surrey FC's rules firmly declared that "wilful kicking will not be allowed", and an 1839 description in *Bell's Life* tells how "many of the gentle craft were good millers, and carried on the contest toughly; but their opponents played more scientifically and outmanoeuvred them, and carried the day in triumph." In fact, many of the reports mention the presence of neutral referees or umpires long before the idea caught on among the public schools.

That's not to say that are not some reports of violence in some games, such as one between the villages of Hepworth and Holmfirth in Yorkshire 1848, with "the usual amount of contusions, bloody noses etc." But descriptions like these are much fewer and further between than one might expect, and were often written many years later after the games were really played, and no doubt spiced up with some poetic licence.

---

[11] Unfortunately, for a future game, the players expressed the hope that "the keeper will be more cautious and see that the guard dog is properly secured or a muzzle put upon him, for should he break loose again he may get his head cracked."

[12] *Chamber's Information for the People* (1842).

[13] Stonehenge *Manual of British rural sports: comprising shooting, hunting, coursing, fishing, hawking, racing, boating, pedestrianism, and the various rural games and amusements of Great Britain* (Routledge, 1861).

Golden oldies

Before the 1850s, football matches rarely amounted to anything more than these relatively informal gatherings. But as the decade wore on, more formal clubs started springing up around the country, frequently instigated by people connected in some way with the game as it was played at public schools. These people were not necessarily teaching the rest of the country how to play football, for everybody was familiar with it by now, but the involvement of the middle classes did give the formerly rustic and plebeian game an air of 'respectability'.

These were no longer games arranged as part of the village fair, the discussions of which would go no further than the local tavern. Clubs were organised in 'gentlemanly' fashion, with meetings, records, accounts and regulations, and their exploits were reported in the press along with hunting, horse-racing and cricketing feats. Football was no longer just an oral tradition – it was documented.

As a result, it is in the late 1850s that we can place almost all the different contenders for the world's 'oldest football/rugby/soccer club'. But aside from the impossibility of categorising the games they were playing, we also have to ask how exactly we define the term 'club'. The middle classes may have been formalising affairs and seeing to it that they were mentioned in the papers, but it didn't really make them any different to the neighbourhood teams that had been playing forms of football for centuries. Why are groups of gentlemen meeting for games in a London park in 1859 any more significant than the 10-a-side game at Bury Racecourse, 1755, where the winning players each took home a hat? Working class 'folk' football and middle class 'public school' football were going to meet somewhere in the middle, what Richard Slater calls "top-down bottom-up development."

The Forest Football Club, formed in 1859 and so named because they played their games at Epping Forest, London, was described by one of its founders, Charles William Alcock, as the earliest attempt to "to extend football on any definite fixed system … it was the winter of 1859–60 that really saw the first game of the great football revival. Great things it is said from trivial causes spring. The trivial cause in this instance was the humble desire of a few Old Harrovians[14] who had just left school to keep up the practice[15]."

By 1862, they had started advertising for fixtures in *Bell's Life* saying they "will be happy to make arrangements for matches to be played during the coming season on the rules of the

---

[14] Although from his assertions it has always been assumed that Forest FC were former Harrow pupils, John Blythe Smart did a little research into this, and found that only Alcock and his brother plus one other member of the original squad had ever attended Harrow at all. That said, Forest FC were unquestionably a pretty posh crowd.

[15] *The English illustrated magazine, Volume 8* (Macmillan and Co, 1891). Alcock would go on to be arguably soccer's most influential administrator of the 19th century, and his club also included AG Guillemard, one of the prominent figures in early rugby. An awful lot, sometimes too much, of what we know of soccer's early days was penned by the prolific hand of CW Alcock, and to say this was the 'first' game of football in any kind of 'revival' was a pretty broad claim.

University of Cambridge." They would later form the basis for The Wanderers[16] in 1864, a combination of old boys from the elite schools, and who won five of the first seven editions of the FA Cup, including the first ever in 1872. They're still equal eighth in the list of all-time winners, and in 1878 won the right to keep the trophy after winning it three times in succession, but graciously handed it back, on condition that nobody should ever be able to claim it outright again. But despite their early dominance, by the 1880s, the soccer rules had become so widely accepted that most public schools now had Old Boy teams of their own. Several former Wanderers were in the Old Etonians team that trounced them 7-2 in the first round of the 1879 FA Cup, and within a few years they were nothing but a memory.

The Wanderers promoted a soccer-like game, but Rugby's handling tradition was also being promoted, not by the school itself, which showed scant interest, but by its former pupils, who seemed hell-bent on convincing the nation that scrummages and running with the ball were the way ahead.

There are a number of pretenders to the title of the oldest rugby club, one of which was the Edinburgh Academicals Football Club that we met in the previous chapter. But that all sounds far too Scottish for English liking, so there is a preference for the counter-claim made by the Barnes Football Club in London. A text from 1839 tells of "persons of respectability being observed passing the ball through the streets in a game lasting around four hours when the parties retire to the public houses." This is considered sufficient evidence to believe that they are the same people that played under Ebenezer Cobb Morley from 1858, who a report in *Bell's Life* explains played on "a large field with a noble avenue of trees running through it which made a pleasant promenade for spectators and attracted many of the fairer sex." Why let a few trees on the pitch get in the way of the chance to strut your stuff in front of the ladies?

But Barnes was an offshoot of the London Rowing Club, and there is no proof that these oarsmen had anything to do with the pub clientele that had been footballing around two decades earlier, no matter how respectable they might have been. They were a snotty lot, Barnes. As well as football, they also stuck carried on rowing, built a gymnasium and organised athletics meetings, but access to these was only granted to employees of the Civil Service, former Oxbridge students or other folk of the upper crust.

Their earliest game was against Richmond in Barn Elms Park in November 1862, watched by four of five hundred spectators, and a month later they played a rematch on a very wet and muddy Richmond Park. The description of one of the goals scored as Barnes made it to the pre-arranged target of two in just twenty minutes tells how Mr Gregory "made a neat catch, about 15 yards exactly, in front of the Richmond base, and after making his mark, scored with a drop kick." That description, coupled with the use of the term 'base' for a goal, suggests they were playing to the Harrow rules, but even if they did, they didn't for long.

---

[16] For a truly brilliant history of this club, see Rob Cavallini *The Wanderers FC: five time FA Cup winners* (Dog N Duck, 2005).

Richmond went on to play a central role in the formation of the Rugby Union. In the meantime, Barnes preferred to do their dabbling down the soccer road, and played Forest FC in February 1863, where Cobb Morley was described as "a pretty and most effective dribbler." Later that year, both Forest and Barnes would be instrumental and in the formation of the Football Association, the first three secretaries of which were all Barnes men. But Barnes' love affair with soccer would not be eternal. They supposedly still exist today, playing rugby union in National Division 2 South, but even the club's website is doubtful whether they can really claim to be the same team, admitting that it is only "from the 1920s that our true history is clear."

If we are to believe the *Guinness Book of Records*, then Guy's Hospital Rugby Club[17] (from Southwark, London) is the oldest club in the world, formed in 1843. But once again, the evidence is dodgy. There isn't really any record at all of a club existing by that name until 1863, and the claim that they were any older than that comes from an 1883 fixture list, where it is noted that Guy's were celebrating their 40th anniversary. It's a good claim, but the cynics amongst us will ask whether the rumour regarding their longevity that was floating around in 1883 was actually true.

In northern England, Liverpool Football Club, who have nothing at all to do with the multiple European Cup winning soccer side from the same city, cannot make anything like as historic a claim as some of the London clubs, but if substantiated evidence is what you need, then they are older than any of them. They played their first game in December 1857. With Rugby School now linked by the new railway leading to Liverpool's port there was a profusion of Old Rugbeians in the city, including one named Richard Sykes, who provided an authentic Richard Lindon pig's bladder for the first ever recorded game of rugby not played by schools, which was organised as Old Rugbeians v The Rest, or as they far more dramatically billed it, "Rugby versus The World." So successful was the game that Liverpool FC was formed shortly afterwards. Although LFC merged with St Helens to become Liverpool St Helens Football Club in 1986, they still exist today, and proudly celebrated their 150th anniversary in 2007.

But Richard Sykes played no further part. He was actually a Mancunian, and went straight back home to form Manchester FC in 1860, who provided Liverpool's first proper opposition[18]. They were actually the first club from the city to enter soccer's FA Cup,

---

[17] Following mergers, they are now called Guy's, Kings and St Thomas' Hospitals RFC.

[18] Having been instrumental in establishing the rugby scene in the northwest, Dick Sykes then emigrated to the United States in 1883, where he founded five different towns in North Dakota, including Sykeston (named after himself, current population 150) and apparently came to own 92,000 acres of land. Sykes had not got over his rugby bug, and took his oval ball with him on his American escapades, proving instrumental in introducing Rugby football to several colleges in the Midwest. But by that time, 'British' rugby was losing ground to the new American rules.

although they eventually became Manchester Rugby Club, and still play at a reasonably high level, which is National Division Two North at the time of writing[19].

Another important addition to the rugby scene in northwest England was Sale, formed in 1861, making it the oldest football club in Britain that is still playing at the top level today. Now called the Sale Sharks as part of rugby union's peculiar wave to invent macho sounding tags to make their names more marketable, Sale's house rules outlawed any hacking, running with the ball or throwing, which was hardly rugby. And their first known game against outside opposition, in 1865 against Hulme Athenaeum, was played by the FA's soccer rules.

But there's another top flight club that predates Sale by three years. It was instigated by Wills, Hammersley and Thompson at the Parade Hotel on August 7, 1858. The Parade Hotel was in Melbourne, Australia. Melbourne FC predated the formation of any national association in England by five years, and had no option but to make up their own rules. Nowadays we call it Australian football.

Football had yet to define itself, but it was already moving abroad. 1860 saw the foundation of the first continental football team, the Lausanne Football and Cricket Club in Switzerland. Little is known about them, it is said they were made up of British students, but whatever kind of football they played, we have no idea if it was more soccer or more rugby.

Staying on the continent, arguably the oldest football club in the world is Turn und Sportverein (TSV) München 1860, the second biggest club in the Bavarian capital. They're older than their name suggests, having been formed in 1849, but were banned by the monarchy for 11 years for republican activities. But ancient though the club may be, they didn't start fielding soccer teams until 1899.

Sheffield steel

There has possibly been an unfair tendency for football historians to focus on what was going on at public schools and in London and its environs. But the north of England had a booming football tradition of its own, and the city that was at the heart of the British steel industry would go on to play an oft forgotten role in the development of soccer. In fact, if it hadn't been for what happened in Sheffield, soccer may never have survived.

Richard Sanders writes that "the bloodline connecting the modern game with that played in the Middle Ages is much stronger and broader than the early histories claimed – and that bloodline runs through Sheffield[20]." Football of sorts had been around in Sheffield for longer. There was a six-a-side game between Sheffield, dressed in green, and Norton, wearing red, way back in 1793 that ended with the Sheffielders getting their pigtails cut off and "the hostile feeling continued so that for several years afterward the people of Norton felt a dread

---

[19] Another of their claims to fame is that their Albert Neilson Hornby became the first ever player to captain England at both rugby and cricket, and his jersey, the oldest surviving England top for any code, still takes pride of place in the clubhouse.

[20] *Where it all first kicked off* in the *Yorkshire Post* (28 May 2009).

to come to Sheffield, even about their necessary business[21]." In 1831, *Bell's Life* mentions a game played in the city's Hyde Park. And in the surrounding villages, football was described in Penistone as early as 1648[22], at Holmfirth in the 1840s, and also Thurlstone, where in 1843 *Bell's Life* reported on "an excellent match of football … between six of the celebrated players of that place and six from Totties, which ended with neither party getting a goal." Were these games the basis for what would become formalised football in Sheffield?

Sheffield FC deserves a special place in any soccer history. We are not talking about either Sheffield Wednesday or Sheffield United here. Neither of the two clubs that now divide passions in the city were involved in the nativity of football[23]. We are talking about a totally different club. They may be small fries now, but formed in 1857, the Sheffield Football Club is considered the oldest surviving soccer club in the world, and in recognition of this, they are one of only two clubs to date to have been awarded the FIFA Order of Merit (the other, to the utter dismay of Barça fans, is Real Madrid). Because they steadfastly refused to embrace professionalism, they got left behind when soccer became a nationwide passion, but with a loyal hardcore of supporters, SFC are still playing today at the 1500 capacity Coach and Horses Ground, at the time of writing in the Northern Premier League Division One South.

They were formed around October 1857 when "a meeting of all the gentlemen enthusiastic for athletics, and especially as regards football, was called to form on a regular basis, The Sheffield Football Club. Games had been played before this time, but there had been no organised club for football … as no other clubs existed, no matches outside the club could be arranged, so members met at the ground in Strawberry Hall Lane to play such matches as 1st half of the alphabet v 2nd half, or Law v Medicine. There was no limit as to the time to be played, or numbers of players on each side. There were no crossbars to the goals … corner flags were the only limit on the field of play."

The origins of Sheffield FC are somewhat vague. As Adrian Harvey notes, there are four different accounts of the club's formation, all written on occasion of the club's 25th anniversary in 1907, by which time some of the finer details must have gone a bit hazy in the protagonists' memories, because the testimonies they gave are "vague and contradictory." However, much of Harvey's confusion stems from his apparent desperation to demonstrate that SFC was not a public school influenced operation, when it is patently obvious it was.

The formation of Sheffield FC was not the grandest occasion the city had ever known. The headquarters were a potting shed at the bottom of East Bank Road. That supports the popular image of Sheffield football being the northern working class' answer to the sort played by the

---

[21] Bernard Bird *Perambulations of Barney the Irishman* (1850).

[22] John Charles Shaw, one of the founders of Hallam FC, the second club to be formed in Sheffield, was born in Penistone in 1830.

[23] The Wednesday, as they were still known until the 1929–30 season, had existed as a cricket club since 1820, but didn't take up football until 1867. Meanwhile United didn't exist until 1889, when they were created to keep the Bramall Lane cricket ground open during the winter months.

toffs down south. But the early Sheffield footballers weren't short of a penny or two either. They were all riding high among the *nouveau riche* making their fortunes from the booming steel, lead and ironworks in the city. The two main instigators of the club were Nathaniel Creswick, a 26 year old solicitor who would later be knighted in recognition of his services to the volunteer movement, and a 23 year old wine merchant named William Prest, who was better known at the time for his achievements as a county cricketer for Yorkshire.

James Walvin was wrong to write that "the Sheffield club was established under the influence of Old Harrovians who persuaded local village footballers not to handle the ball." Creswick and Prest, like many of their early team-mates, attended Sheffield Collegiate School, a fairly elite institution, but where football was not played, and Harvey argues that other than one Old Rugbeian, none of original 57 members have been identified on any public school records. But then why was it stated in 1907 that "the Club was largely made up of public school boys?"

Membership of Sheffield FC was carefully vetted to make sure only proper gentlemen joined. They only allowed formally invited members of the social elite into the ground to watch their athletics meets (which aroused considerable interest, while their first attempts at football matches barely raised a murmur among Sheffield's sporting voyeurs). For a football game against Norton advertised in the *Sheffield and Rotherham Independent* of November 1861 they made it clear that "none but members and their friends may enter the ground." There can be little doubt from contemporary reports that Sheffield FC was the 'Gentlemen's Club' and they were frequently referred to as such for many years.

A report on Creswick's speech in 1907 tells how "they wrote to the leading public schools, Eton, Harrow, Winchester, Westminster, Rugby and some others, and a lot of different rules they obtained (laughter). One rule he remembered, he believed it came from Winchester, was that you could not hold and hack a man at the same time (loud laughter)." Harvey claims this quote suggests that although they did research the public school games, they took one look at them and decided they made so little sense that it would be a far better idea to work out their own. But the other 1907 histories do say that "copies of the rules in force at all the public schools were procured, and a new code, comprised of what was regarded as the best points of the whole, adopted" and another claims that "rules had to be got piecemeal – bits from the rules of each public school as the boys came in; and one law which did not last very long was that players should carry a half-crown in each hand to avoid pushing with the open hand."

It doesn't seem like there was any attempt to put any rules down in writing over the course of Sheffield's first season, but when the first AGM was held on October 21, 1858, Creswick and his committee presented a draft version, to which a series of amendments were made at that very meeting, to finally end up with eleven laws (listed in *Appendix Five*)[24].

---

[24] With Sheffield FC short of funds, the original yellow pamphlet was auctioned at Sotheby's in London in July 2011 for £881,250.

One of the 1907 accounts claims the game they invented was "half rugby and half association," although neither of those codes existed yet in 1858, and with no H-shaped goals, scrummages, hacking or running with the ball, it is hard to spot where the rugby connection lay. In its original form at least, the Sheffield version was not all that different to the Cambridge rules, in that it was essentially a kicking game, eliminated the most dangerously violent elements and also lacked the complexities that the public schools were so fond of. There could be a good reason for this. William Prest's own brother, Edward, attended both Uppingham School and Cambridge[25] at the same time as John Charles Thring, one of the framers of the original university rules. He quite probably played in some of those pioneering 'soccer' matches on Parker's Piece.

Like at Cambridge, there was a rule that catching was legal "provided the ball has not touched the ground." Like at Cambridge "no hacking or tripping up is fair under any circumstances whatever" although "pushing with the hands is allowed." Throw-ins and goal kicks were both there, and once again there was no limit on the number of players. In fact, in the early years, there are several references to what were known in Sheffield as 'odds', a handicap system whereby supposedly stronger teams would have less players to help even things out a bit.

Of particular importance is the complete absence of any offside law, which may well have been a nod to the simpler way football was played in wider society. Also, seen as a whole, it's striking just how similar the Sheffield game was to the Australian and Gaelic games in their original forms.

For their first three years, Sheffield contented themselves with playing amongst themselves and taking on the occasional military team, starting with the 58th Army Regiment in 1859. After three years of that, you'd imagine SFC would have been mighty pleased when another team formed in the city to give them some regular opposition. Hallam FC[26] grew out of the cricket club of the same name, and although they were officially founded in 1860, they may have been playing football for longer. 'The Countrymen', as they are known, also still exist, and play on their original field, Sandygate Road, making it, according to the *Guinness Book of Records*, the oldest football ground in the world.

And so it was that on a snowy Boxing Day in 1860, Sheffield and Hallam met in the first edition of the oldest surviving derby match. It was meant to be played 16-a-side, but in a tradition that would be honoured throughout the history of amateur football "owing to the severe weather several players were absent from each side[27]." Typical fair-weather northerners. For this three-hour game, the "the Sheffielders turned in their usual scarlet and white", the same colours they wear today, meaning they can also claim to have the oldest

---

[25] Not only did they share the same college, St John's, but also the same tutor.
[26] They were originally called Hallam and Stumperlowe, as some of their players were from that little hamlet.
[27] *The Sheffield Daily Telegraph* (December 28, 1860).

soccer team strip in the world. "The Sheffield Club, notwithstanding their inferior numbers, counted two goals to nothing, and went home fully satisfied with their victory."

Hallam got their revenge in March the year after with a 3-0 win, although they did have the advantage of having 18 players to Sheffield's 15. The two teams didn't play again until a few days after Christmas 1861, where there is some dispute as to whether it was a 2-2 draw or a 2-1 win to Hallam. In what could have been the world's first charity match, the game in Hyde Park was played to raise money for the Volunteer movement[28] and drew what for then was a pretty impressive crowd of 600.

Civil War was raging through America at the time, which meant there was a severe lack of cotton to supply the local mills, leading to extreme unemployment in the city. And so another charity match was played against Hallam in 1862, this time in aid of the Lancashire Relief Fund. The cause may have been good, but there was no love lost on the pitch. None other than club founder Creswick, who seems to have had something of a reputation as a troublemaker, got so wound up by being held and charged by players that he ended up punching Hallam's cutely named Waterfall in the mouth. The *Rotherham Independent* opined that "all parties were agreed that the hit was accidental" but the bleeding Waterfall felt it was time to throw aside his jacket and decide this particular encounter in a way not entirely sanctioned by Sheffield's rules. Other players, and some of the spectators, liked the idea and a near riot ensued. Once it had all calmed down, Waterfall was sent to guard the goal as punishment. They were obviously already finding it difficult to get anybody to go in goal, and that was before goalkeepers had even been invented!

A most striking innovation in Sheffield Rules football occurred in 1862. There were teething problems, and an alarming number of games were ending 0-0, which doubtlessly had something to do with the goals being so small. But rather than simply make them wider, they opted for a system of 'rouges'. In addition to the normal goal posts, which were specified as being 12 feet apart, two additional outer posts were positioned a further 12 feet to either side, and scoring in them acted as a kind of bonus, defined by the revised rules as follows:

11. A rouge is obtained by the player who first touches the ball after it has been kicked between the rouge flags, and when a rouge has been obtained one of the defending side must stand post two yards in front of the goal sticks.

12. No rouge is obtained when a player who first touches the ball is on the defending side. In that case it is a kick out as specified in law 2.

13. No player who is behind the line of the goal sticks when the ball is kicked behind, may touch it in any way, either to prevent or obtain a rouge.

14. A goal outweighs any number of rouges. Should no goals or an equal number be obtained, the match is decided by rouges."

---

[28] The Volunteer Movement was all about signing up to help prepare to defend the country against a much-feared attack from France, an invasion that never materialised.

Of course, the name 'rouge' had been heard before, and this idea for settling draws is almost identical to that described in the 1847 Eton field game rules, and it is hard to deny that that was where Sheffield got the idea from. Rouges were relatively short-lived (they were scrapped in 1868), but the concept of awarding points for 'near misses' still exists in Australian and Gaelic football, and also in Canadian football where even today the term 'rouge' is an alternative name for a single point. Eton and Sheffield may be the missing links.

Spreading the gospel

Football was on the rampage in Sheffield and its environs, where the organised form was almost certainly more widespread than anywhere else in the world (perhaps apart from Melbourne in Australia).

The Stumperlow players left Hallam in 1860 to form their own club, kicking off a Sheffield football boom. By 1861, there were at least eight teams in and around the city, there were eleven in 1862, and by March 1863, the *Sheffield and Rotherham Independent* was calling it the "now popular game", suggesting that whatever football was being played in the city before SFC came along it was, well, not popular. Nevertheless, the local sports pages were still far more concerned with developments on the cricket pitch and the racing track to bother devoting any more than the minimal column space to this growing fashion.

SFC vastly outshone the novice teams for a year or two, but it wasn't long before Hallam were more than a match for them, and by the 1862–63 season, the new Pitsmoor team was good enough to beat SFC in all three matches they played, while another club, Norfolk, was fast on its way to becoming the strongest side in the city. In part, this was probably because the other teams were getting better and better, though the official line suggested in various SFC club records is that they found these local fixtures "most unsatisfactory", and for a variety of reasons.

Partly they had themselves to blame. We learn, for instance, of a 2-0 defeat to Norton in 1863 when they had only seven men due to illness, and half the team was late for a 0-0 draw with Mackenzie in January 1864. SFC had a common complaint that when it was just to play the locals, they found it difficult to get their best men to turn out, who only really enjoyed it when they took on military teams. They also voiced their indignation at the way the local teams would borrow 'ringers' from other clubs. Adrian Harvey rejects the latter suggestion due to the lack of evidence, but knowing what informal football teams can be like even today, I'd imagine they probably had a case.

It may also have been a class thing. The *Sheffield Daily Telegraph* noted in 1865 that "the club enjoys a prestige not possessed by any of its now many rivals, and numbers amongst its members and friends the elite of the town and neighbourhood." The discussions of setting up an accident fund to cover for lost wages suffered by injured players support the idea that other clubs were less bourgeoisie, and in 1863, a Sheffielder wrote to *The Field* to suggest that if "agricultural labourers ... and the operatives of some towns and villages" were to be attracted to football, then it would be a good idea to do away with hacking. And it was a Hallamshire man, at the height of the debate regarding the formation of the Football Association in 1863, who wisely wrote to *The Field* to comment that "I would earnestly beg all … to remember that it is the interests of all classes of the people, not just the public school boys or gentlemen players only, that have to be considered."

Having set the ball rolling by drafting a formal set of rules, SFC members often acted as match officials and played leading administrative roles on the different committees that oversaw developments in the Sheffield game. But they were *laissez-faire* about sharing a playing field with the less classy clubs, especially when the more than probable risk arose of their dignity being hurt by losing to them. Football might be the great leveller, but not everybody wanted to be levelled, so they left local matches in the capable hands of a reserve team of sorts, called the Thursday Wanderers. SFC instead took a surprisingly early interest in what was happening football-wise in other cities. Aided by the development of the railway network, they were pioneers of the away trip phenomenon. Their new list of rules among their luggage, they chugged off around South Yorkshire and the North Midlands, and in doing so, started to establish a game that was essentially soccer over a considerably wide geographical area, long before the FA managed to do anything remotely comparable in the south.

The first of SFC's regular out-of-town opponents was the newly formed Nottingham FC, now known as Notts County FC and the oldest club still playing in the Football League. They were another 'gentlemen only' establishment, with many well known cricketers among their ranks, and who only played amongst themselves for the first two years, until they discovered there was a like-minded band of decent fellows in Sheffield willing to challenge them. The *Nottingham Guardian* heralded their arrival in November 1862 by reporting on a game that obviously included some kind of Sheffield influence, because the side captained by Chas Deakin won by "scoring two goals and two rouges against one and one."

Sheffield FC may have convinced their fellow citizens that their rules should be treated as gospel, but in Nottingham they found that the locals were far less keen on suddenly changing their ways to suit a bunch of Yorkshiremen. In 1865, for example, the minutes of the Sheffield FC AGM show that they had only been able to arrange a game with Nottingham after agreeing to play with the offside rule, but only in return for Nottingham dropping one of their own rules. 'Trading rules' in the build-up to matches was still one of the great charms of football, leading to plenty of arguments out on the field. In one of the Nottingham matches, Chesterman of Sheffield caused a storm when he retrieved a ball from among the crowd and promptly touched it down to claim a goal, and the ensuing dispute left the players with no option other than to abandon the match.

Another regular early opponent for SFC was Lincoln, although these games were also thwarted on several occasions by poor weather and a lack of players turning up. The Lincoln game was even more different than Nottingham's, bearing more in common with rugby than soccer, including no passing to anybody in front of the ball – but was probably more of an utter confusion than anything else. Another Sheffield away game with a fifteen from Manchester struggled to cope with the different rules used by the respective clubs, a problem that also meant Norfolk's own pioneering attempt to get some games up with Leeds, though immense fun, were somewhat chaotic. But this was some of the earliest intercity footballing contact ever to be established and such hiccups were only to be expected.

A couple of decades later, and these problems would be a thing of the past. A common code was on the way.

22 A LOAD OF OLD BALLS
Conclusions

From fertility rites to symbolic enactments of duality, and from celebrations of victories in battle to pagan head cults, theories abound for where football might have come from. But that is all they are – theories. There is virtually no evidence to support any of these ideas. Although some cultures around the world still tell legends associated to their ball games, just like the 'western' ones, these were probably added to the game rather than the game being added to them. Football, like most sports, probably started simply because it was fun and natural, driven by man's inherent desire to play, exercise, and to prove himself better than the rest.

It is no easier to plot the moment when man first played ball than it is to plot the moment when man first swam in a lake, climbed a tree or hunted a boar. He, and she, have been playing sports and games far longer than any records can account for, and would probably have worked out the basic notions of a game like football even before evolving into our modern *homo sapiens* form.

Rather than providing clues for the origins of modern football, what the first few chapters of this book tell us, in which we surveyed the ancient games played everywhere from the Americas to the Pacific Islands, is that the invention of games and amusements is common to all people. These involve running, jumping, throwing, catching, wrestling, kicking and batting, but all in slightly different combinations and adapted by different traditions, local landscapes and technological developments. As the Europeans discovered the rest of the world, they also discovered their games, which would have been both unfamiliar and familiar at the same time. As people exchanged ideas about warfare, clothing, cuisine and science, they also exchanged ideas about games. In Mesoamerica the Europeans found out about rubber, in Asia they came across hockey played on horsebacks, and in North America they were surprised that the crude and often brutal game of mob football, played a different way, could actually be an orderly, sophisticated affair of benefit to the community.

However, there is very little evidence that the game we know now as football was imported from outside of Europe. Long before meaningful cultural contact was made with the more far-lying parts world, there is ample evidence of games already being played by the Vikings, Celts, Romans, Greeks and other cultures. But we have to tread very carefully with these, because there is so little hard evidence of what they really involved. Too many bold assertions have been made that are not backed up with substantiated fact. Our ideas of 'Roman football' and 'Celtic hurling', for example, have been shaped by jumping to too many conclusions and fanciful interpretations of ancient texts and images from a modern perspective.

Football struggled to win a place among the more noble sports due to the obvious problem of the lack of decent ball. Even the ubiquitous pig's bladder encased in leather was a highly cherished object, the presentation of which, on a feast or wedding day, was attributed much ceremony. Even so, these balls would have been nothing like the durable, bouncy ones we use today. Medieval footballs were as rustic as the games that were played with them.

A far more satisfactory game could be played with a small, hard ball made of wood or stone. As a result, it does seem that the bulk of the European ball sports played before the 19th century involved batting the ball, rather than kicking it. These developed into the relatively sophisticated, and even courtly, games in the hockey, cricket, tennis and golf families. Football may have been great fun, but it was a cruder and poorer cousin in the sporting hierarchy.

It was different in Mesoamerica. Their rubber balls allowed for something very different that was enjoyed in ballparks and played a central role in Pre-Columbian society. From there, developments gradually led all the way through to Charles Goodyear and his invention of vulcanised rubber in 1855, which Richard Lindon of Rugby applied to footballs soon after. And it was precisely following those developments that football boomed. Rather like the way videogames were suddenly taken seriously with the arrival of new generation consoles, football finally had a decent ball, which would lead to very new skills and techniques. Football was not invented. It was rebranded.

Throughout the Middle Ages there had been references to football, or something very like it, being played. It was condemned by the authorities, who wanted to persuade their minions to dedicate their leisure time to more constructive purposes. And it was often condemned by the church, in times when hard labour and devout worship were encouraged above such frivolities. And the huge gatherings of entire communities to play football on feast days were a concern because of the disturbances they caused.

All that reckless barbarism on the streets tends to have been exaggerated by modern folklore and the way that almost all contemporary evidence that has survived comes in the form of condemnations of the sheer pointlessness of a bawdy, rustic practice that had no place in British society. But the descriptions of games like Cornish hurling, Welsh cnapan and East Anglian camp-ball suggest that there was a science to these games. They were far less primitive than our modern stereotypical view of the medieval peasant implies. Francis Willughby's *Book of Plaies*, written in the 1660s, shows that the basics of the modern game were well in place by the 17th century.

Scenes like those in 1772, where the Hertfordshire villages of Hitchen and Gosmore played a game where the ball was "drowned for a time in the Priory pond, then forced along Angel Street across the market place" had become less common by the 1800s, when more efficient policing coupled with increased traffic on the roads were the cause for contemporary commentators to start describing football as an ancient and disappearing custom.

"Desperate foot-ball contests, or rather cudgelling fights, under this pretence, were some years ago common … but such contests were come to be very harmlessly conducted at the time of my survey" wrote one observer in 1817[1]." Street football was incompatible with the industrial era, but as we saw in places like Alnwick, Derby and Kingston, rather than being outlawed, it simply moved from the street to delimitated fields, and played by smaller numbers out of harm's way. In some towns 'Shrovetide' football did survive, sometimes to this day, either because it was tolerated or because it defied attempts to ban it, and these rare examples are now protected as living souvenirs of Britain's traditions of old.

Although it was widely observed that football was disappearing in the early years of the 19th century, rather than the final whimper from a dying breed, as it shifted from the streets to the parks and became something a lot more innocent than the games of bygone years, it was also becoming the kind of football that the world would eventually fall in love with.

The public schools have been attributed a prominent role in making that happen, by seizing this new approach to football and nurturing it into the modern game. And although revisionists are now asserting that what the less privileged classes did for the development of football has been underestimated, we should not ignore the achievements of the upper crust on the pure basis of 21st century inverted snobbery. There is a direct and well documented relationship between the modern football codes and the public schools, who supplied many of the founding fathers. The Cambridge University rules, which formed the basis for modern soccer, were drafted by public school old boys, and Rugby School was, of course, where its rival handling code was created.

However, there was working class football in the 19th century too. It has been argued that the hardships of the Industrial Revolution made football impossible for the working man, but the conditions for the proletariat were no worse than they had always been. Only a few games were ever documented, but there were obviously thousands of others that went unreported. It was not until the involvement of middle class gentlemen in football administration from the 1850s that matters were put down on paper and a more formal structure was created for the game. But much of that structure may well have drawn inspiration from the working classes, or was perhaps crafted for their benefit by championing simplicity as opposed to the often absurd complexities of the public school games, something that was particularly apparent in Sheffield, where 'standardised' football was implemented on a large scale for the first time England.

This was something made possible by the vast improvements in communications in the mid 19th century. Football had previously been a localised affair, with little need for a national standard. But as Sheffield discovered on their pioneering trips away from South Yorkshire, inter-provincial matches were going to need a common rulebook.

By 1860, football was at a crossroads. It was already firmly ingrained in the culture of the Anglosphere, but unlike sports like cricket, there was no universally accepted set of rules. It

---

[1] John Farey *General view of the agriculture and minerals of Derbyshire* (1817).

was not even clear whether players could run with the ball, or whether they should be limited to only kicking it, and the levels of tolerated violence varied tremendously. In 1863, the Football Association was about to be created to lay the foundations for what, though not entirely through its own doing, would eventually become recognisable as the soccer played and watched by millions all around the world today.

Convincing everybody to play by their rulebook was not going to be easy. By the time the FA had done its job, it was too late for the isolated colony of Victoria in Australia. They had already jumped the gun and created a game of their own. Unimpressed with soccer, the Rugby Football Union would soon be appearing with rules for a more physical carrying game, and later still, the Northern Union would branch off in yet another direction. Rugby football players in the United States and Canada decided even more wholesale changes were needed. In Ireland, such was the adversity to being 'obliged' to play by rules created in England that the Gaelic Athletic Association decided that their country should have a national alternative too.

In volume two, we'll be examining how and why there were so many different fortunes for the same old game.

APENDIXES

Appendix One: The Eton field game (1847)

1. The game begins strictly at half past twelve, unless previously agreed on.

2. At the expiration of half the time, goals must be changed, and a bully formed in the middle.

3. Play is to cease at half past one, or punctually at the expiration of the hour agreed on.

4. To prevent dispute it is better to appoint, before the game begins, two umpires: one chosen by each party; and a referee to be agreed on by both parties, whose decision, if the umpires differ, is to be final.

5. It will be the duty of the umpires to enforce the rules: to decide on disputes that arise; to break a rouge or bully, when necessary, and to see fair play for both parties.

6. If a player shall have begun the game and shall be hurt, or otherwise disabled from going on, no substitute may take his place.

7. If a player be not present, when the game begins, no substitute may play, until he comes, but the game must proceed without him.

8. The goal sticks are to be seven feet out of the ground; a goal is gained when the ball is kicked between them provided it is not over the level of the top of them.

9. The space between each goal stick is to be eleven feet.

10. A rouge is obtained by touching the ball first, after it has been kicked behind.

11. When a rouge has been obtained the ball must be placed one yard from the centre of the goal; and no player is to touch the ball, or let it rest against his foot, until the player, who has obtained the rouge, has kicked the ball himself.

12. No player may run behind the goal sticks before the ball be kicked behind, either to prevent or obtain a rouge.

13. Should the player, who has prevented the rouge have been behind the ball, a player of the opposite side may touch it, and obtain a rouge.

14. If a ball go behind the goal sticks and without being touched, be kicked before them again, any player of the opposite side, if he can touch it first, may obtain a rouge.

15. If the ball be kicked behind by a cool kick, that is, when no one of the opposite side be bullying the kicker, no rouge, whoever touches it, can be obtained.

16. If a rouge be obtained before the time for leaving off expires, and the time expires, before the rouge is finished, the said rouge must be played out, until either a goal be obtained, or the ball be kicked outside the side sticks, or behind the goal sticks.

17. No rouge, or goal obtained after the time expires is admissible, except in the case of Rule 16.

18. The Bully, or Rouge must be broken, immediately a player falls on the ball, and formed anew.

19. No crawling on the hands and knees with the ball between the legs is allowed.

20. If a player falls on a rouge, or bully, although not on the ball, and calls 'Man Down' or calls for 'Air', the said Bully, or Rouge must be broken, and formed anew.

21. The umpires must use their discretion on the 15th, 18th and 20th Rules: and may make a player get up from the ground, if he has fallen, without breaking the rouge.

22. Hands may only be used to the stop the ball, or touch it when behind. The ball must not be carried, thrown or struck by the hand.

23. A rouge may be obtained by touching the ball, when on the line of the goal sticks.

24. No player, if behind, before the ball, may pick it up, or carry it to one of his own side to touch, but must leave it where it stopped.

25. The ball is dead when outside, or on a line with the side sticks, and must not be kicked.

26. When the Ball is dead, it must be thrown in, or a bully formed parallel to the place where it stopped: these are to take place alternately.

27. If the Ball bounces off a bystander or any other object, outside the line of the side sticks, it may be kicked immediately on coming in.

28. If the Ball, when kicked out, bounds from any object without coming in, it must be put in parallel to the place, where it struck that object.

29. A player is considered to be sneaking when only three, or less than three, of the opposite side are before him and may not kick the ball.

30. One goal outweighs any number of rouges. If each party has an equal number of goals, that party wins, which has the majority of rouges in addition to the goals. If no goals are obtained, the game is decided by rouges.

31. These Rules may be altered and revised in any way by the Keeper of the Field at any future time, with the approbation of the first four choices

32. Should the decision be equally divided, the first keeper must have the casting vote.

33. No person can keep the field two football terms running unless it is mutually agreed on.

34. No Keeper of the Field can keep the Wall during the same term.

Appendix Two: Harrow football (1858[1])

1. The Choice of Bases is determined, in House Matches by tossing; but in the ordinary School Games that Side has the Choice, on which the Head of the School (or in his absence the Highest in the School present) is playing.

2. The Bases are 12 ft. in width, and the distance between them, in House Matches, must not be greater than 150 yds. The width of the ground must not be more than 100 yds.

3. The Ball must be kicked off from the middle of the ground, halfway between the two Bases.

---

[1] This date appears on the manuscript, but is not necessarily the date the rules were written.

4. If when the Ball is kicked, from Hand or otherwise, any one on the same side, but nearer the opposite Base, touches or kicks the Ball, he is said to be Behind, only if one of the opposite Side be between him and the party who kicked the Ball. Any one who is thus Behind is considered as being virtually out of the Game, and must wait till the Ball has been touched by one of the opposite side: nor must he interfere with any one of the opposite Side, or in any way prevent or obstruct his catching the Ball.

5. The Ball may not be caught off any other part of the Body but the leg below the knee, or foot; but if after being kicked, it hits any other part of the Body, before falling to the ground, it may then be caught.

6. Whoever catches the Ball is entitled to a free kick if he calls Three yards; but whoever catches the Ball, and does not call Three yards, is liable to have it knocked out of his hands.

7. The Ball, when in Play, must never be touched by the hand, except in the case of a Catch, as above stated.

8. All Charging is fair, but neither Holding nor Tripping is allowed.

9. If the Ball is kicked beyond the prescribed limits of the Ground, it must be kicked straight in again; and then must not be touched by the Hands, or Arms below the Elbow.

10. When the Ball goes behind the Line of either of the Bases, it must be kicked straight in (as by Rule 9), and then must not be touched by any one belonging to the Side, behind whose Base it was kicked, until it has been touched by one of the opposite Side.

11. Bases can only be obtained by kicking; but when any one catches the Ball near the opposite Base, he may jump the Three yards and go back to get a free kick: or if he catches it at so short a distance from the Base that he can carry it through by jumping the Three yards, he may do so.

12. All Shinning and Backshinning is strictly prohibited.

13. After a Base has been obtained, the two Sides change their respective Bases.

14. There must always be two Umpires in a House Match.

15. The above Rules should be put up conspicuously in every House at the beginning of every Football Quarter, and new Boys should be required to make themselves thoroughly acquainted with them.

Appendix Three: Laws of Football as Played at Rugby School (1845)

i. FAIR CATCH is a catch direct from the foot.

ii. OFF SIDE. A player is off his side if the ball has touched one of his own side behind him, until the other side touch it.

iii. FIRST OF HIS SIDE, is the player nearest the ball on his side.

iv. A KNOCK ON, as distinguished from a throw on, consists in striking the ball on with the arm or hand.

v. TRY AT GOAL. A ball touched between the goal-posts may be brought up to either of them, but not between. The ball when punted must be within, when caught without the line of goal: the ball must be placed-kicked and not dropped, even though it touch two hands, and it must go over the bar and between the posts without having touched the dress or person of any player. No goal may be kicked from touch.

vi. KICK OFF FROM MIDDLE, must be a place.

vii. KICK OUT must not be from more than ten yards out of goal if a place-kick, not more than twenty-five yards, if a punt, drop, or knock on.

viii. RUNNING IN is allowed to any player on his side, provided he does not take the ball off the ground, or take it through touch.

ix. CHARGING is fair, in case of a place kick, as soon as a ball has touched the ground; in case of a kick from a catch, as soon as the player's foot has left the ground, and not before.

x. OFF SIDE. No player being off his side shall kick the ball in any case whatever.

xi. No player being off his side shall hack, charge, run in, touch the ball in goal, or interrupt a match.

xii. A player when off his side having a fair catch is entitled to a fair knock on, and in no other case.

xiii. A player being off his side shall not touch the ball on the ground, except in touch.

xiv. A player being off his side cannot put on his side himself, or any other player, by knocking or throwing on the ball.

xv. TOUCH. A player may not in any case run with the ball in or through touch.

xvi. A player standing up to another may hold one arm only, but may hack him or knock the ball out of his hand if he attempt to kick it, or go beyond the line of touch.

xvii. No agreement between players to send the ball straight out shall be allowed on big side.

xviii. A player having touched the ball straight for a tree, and touched the tree with it, may drop from either side if he can, but the opposite side may oblige him to go to his own side of the tree.

xiv. A player touching the ball off his side must throw it straight out.

xx. All matches are drawn after five days, but after three if no goal has been kicked.

xxi. Two big-side balls must always be in the Close during a match or big-side.

xxii. The direction of sending into goals rests with the heads of sides or houses.

xxiii. No football shall be played between the goals till the Sixth match.

xxiv. Heads of sides, or two deputies appointed by them, are the sole arbiters of all disputes.

xxv. No strangers, in any match, may have a place kick at goal.

xxvi. No hacking with the heel, or above the knee, is fair.

xxvii. No player but the first on his side, may be hacked, except in a scrummage.

xxviii. No player may wear projecting nails or iron plates on the heels or soles of his shoes or boots.

xxix. No player may take the ball out of the Close.

xxx. No player may stop the ball with anything but his own person.

xxxi. Nobody may wear cap or jersey without leave from the head of his house.

xxxii. At a big-side, the two players highest in the school shall toss up.

xxxiii. The Island is all in goal.

xxxiv. At little sides the goals shall be four paces wide, and in kicking a goal the ball must pass out of the reach of any player present.

xxxv. Three Præpostors constitute a big-side.

xxxvi. If a player take a punt when he is not entitled to it, the opposite side may take a punt or drop, without running if the ball has not touched two hands.

xxxvii. No player may be held, unless he is himself holding the ball.

Appendix Four: Laws of the Cambridge University Foot Ball Club (1856)

1. This club shall be called the University Foot Ball Club

2. At the commencement of the play, the ball shall be kicked off from the middle of the ground: after every goal there shall be a kick-off in the same way.

3. After a goal, the losing side shall kick off; the sides changing goals, unless a previous arrangement be made to the contrary.

4. The ball is out when it has passed the line of the flag-posts on either side of the ground, in which case it shall be thrown in straight.

5. The ball is behind when it has passed the goal on either side of it.

6. When the ball is behind it shall be brought forward at the place where it left the ground, not more than ten paces, and kicked off.

7. Goal is when the ball is kicked through the flag-posts and under the string.

8. When a player catches the ball directly from the foot, he may kick it as he can without running with it. In no other case may the ball be touched with the hands, except to stop it.

9. If the ball has passed a player, and has come from the direction of his own goal, he may not touch it till the other side have kicked it, unless there are more than three of the other side before him. No player is allowed to loiter between the ball and the adversaries' goal.

10. In no case is holding a player, pushing with the hands, or tripping up allowed. Any player may prevent another from getting to the ball by any means consistent with the above rules.

11. Every match shall be decided by a majority of goals.

Appendix Five: Sheffield Rules Football (1858)

1. The kick off from the middle must be a place kick.

2. Kick out must not be more than 25 yards out of goal.

3. A fair catch is a catch from any player provided the ball has not touched the ground or has not been thrown from touch and is entitled to a free-kick[2].

4. Charging is fair in case of a place kick (with the exception of a kick off as soon as a player offers to kick) but he may always draw back unless he has actually touched the ball with his foot.

5. Pushing with the hands is allowed but no hacking or tripping up is fair under any circumstances whatever[3].

6. No player may be held or pulled over.

7. It is not lawful to take the ball off the ground (except in touch) for any purpose whatever.

8. The ball may be pushed or hit with the hand, but holding the ball except in the case of a free kick is altogether disallowed[4].

9. A goal must be kicked but not from touch nor by a free kick from a catch.

10. A ball in touch is dead, consequently the side that touches it down must bring it to the edge of the touch and throw it straight out from touch.

11. Each player must provide himself with a red and dark blue flannel cap, one colour to be worn by each side.

---

[2] Amended from the original rule that a fair catch was only valid if it was a catch direct from the foot of the opposite side. Now they were allowing catches when the ball was kicked by a team-mate too.

[3] The original rules had not allowed pushing with the hand.

[4] Different to the original law, which said that the ball could only be stopped by the hand, but not pushed or hit, if it was bouncing. If it was rolling, it could only be kicked.

INDEX

BIBLIOGRAPHY

Where a source material is used for a very specific detail, it is mentioned as a footnote to the text itself. The source materials detailed in this bibliography are those that have been used more generally as primary sources either throughout the book, or throughout particular sections. Where relevant, and to avoid overloading the text with footnotes, only the name of the author(s) is included in the main body of the book.

Alcock, Charles William *Football: the association game* (G Bell & Sons, 1906).

Bailey, Steven *Football at Winchester, Eton and Harrow* (in *The Sports Historian*, May, 1995).

Bairner, Alan (editor) *Sport and the Irish* (University College Dublin Press, 2005).

Baker, William J *Sports in the Western World* (Rowman and Littlefield, 1982).

Beers, William George *Lacrosse: the national game of Canada* (Dawson Brothers, 1869)

Birley, Sir Derek *Sport and the Making of Britain (International Studies in the History of Sport)* (Manchester University Press, 1993).

Blainey, Geoffrey *The Origins of Australian Football* (Scwartz Publishing, 2003).

Blanchard, Kendall *The anthropology of sport: an introduction* (Bergin & Garvey, 1984)

Brasch, Rudolph. *How Did Sports Begin? A look at the origins of man at play* (David McKay Company, 1970).

Collins, Tony; Martin, John and Vamplew, Wray *Encyclopedia of traditional British rural sports* (Routledge, 2005).

Corry, Eoghan *An Illustrated History of the GAA* (Gill & MacMillan, 2005).

Cronin, Mike; Murphy, William; Rouse, Paul *The Gaelic Athletic Association* 1884-2009 (Irish Academic Press, 2009).

Crowther, Nigel B *Sport in Ancient Times* (Praeger Publishers, 2007).

Culin, Stewart *24th Annual Report of the Bureau of American Ethnology: Games of North American Indians* (1907). (Reissued in 1994 by University of Nebraska Press).

Curry, Graham *Football: A Study in Diffusion* (University of Leicester, 2001).

Davis, Parke H *Football, the American intercollegiate game* (Scribner's sons, 1912).

De Burca, Marcus *Michael Cusack and the GAA* (Anvil Books, 1989).

De Moore, Greg *Tom Wills – His Spectacular Rise and Tragic Fall* (Allen & Unwin, 2008).

Dolan, Paddy and Connolly, John *The Civilizing of Hurling in Ireland* (Dublin Institute of Technology, 2009).

Du Chaillu, Paul B *The Viking Age: The Early History, Manners, and Customs of the Ancestors of the English-Speaking Nations* (John Murray 1889).

Dunning, Eric and Sheard, Kenneth *Barbarians, Gentlemen and Players: A Sociological Study of the Development of Rugby Football* (Martin Robertson, 1979).

Eisen George and Wiggins, David Kenneth *Ethnicity and sport in North American history and culture* (Praeger Paperback, 1995).

Fabian, AH & Green, G (eds) *Association Football Vols 1 to 4* (Caxton, 1960).

Flannery, Michael *The true history of golf* (*Golf International Magazine*, 2009).

Fremantle Media *History of Football, The Beautiful Game* (2004 video).

Gardiner, E Norman *Athletics in the Ancient World* (Clarendon Press, 1971).

Giller, Norman *Football and all that: an irreverent history* (Hodder & Stoughton, 2004).

Goldblatt, David *The Ball is Round* (Penguin, 2006).

Gorn, Elliott J and Goldstein, Warren *A Brief History of American Sports* (University of Illinois Press, 1993).

Grow, Robin *More than a game: The real story of Australian Rules Football* (Melbourne University Press, 1998). Edited by Rob Hess and Bob Stewart.

Guttmann Allen *Sports: The First Five Millennia* (University of Massachusetts Press, 2004).

Guttmann, Allen and Thompson, Lee *Japanese Sports: A History* (University of Hawaii Press, 2001).

Hampson Ditchfield, Peter *Old English Sports* (1891).

Harris, Harold Arthur *Sport in Greece and Rome* (Cornell University Press, 1972).

Harris, Tim *Sport: Almost Everything You Ever Wanted to Know* (Yellow Jersey Press, 2007).

Harvey, Adrian *Football: The First Hundred Years, The Untold Story* (Routledge, 2005).

Henderson, Robert *Bat, Ball and Bishop: The Origin of Ball Games* (University of Illinois Press, 1947).

Holt, Richard *Sport and the British: a modern history* (Oxford University Press, 1990).

Hone, William *The Every Day Book* (1825) and *Hone's Table Book* (1841).

Hornby, Hugh *Uppies and Downies: The Extraordinary Football Games of Britain* (English Heritage, 2008).

Hurley, John W *Shillelagh: The Irish Fighting Stick* (Caravat Press, 2007).

James Riordan, Robin E Jones *Sport and physical education in China* (Spons Architecture, 1999).

Jarvie, Grant *Sport in the Making of Celtic Culture* (Leicester University Press, 1999).

Jusserand, Jean-Jule *Le sport et les jeux d'exercice dans l'ancienne France* (Plon, 1901).

King, Seamus J *A History of Hurling* (Gill & Macmillan Ltd, 2005).

Leatherdale, Clive (ed) *The book of football: a complete history and record of the association and rugby games* (Republished by Desert Island Books, 1996, originally serialised 1905-06).

Levinson, David and Christensen, Karen *Encyclopedia of World Sport, From ancient times to the present* (Oxford University Press, 1999).

Lipoñski, Wojciech *World Sports Encyclopedia* (MBI Publishing Company, 2003).

Macrory, Jennifer *Running with the ball: The Birth of Rugby Union* (Collins Willow, 1991).

MacLennan, Hugh D, *Shinty!* (Balnain Books 1993), *Not an Orchid* (Kessock Communications 1995), *Shinty in England, Pre-1893* (*Sports Historian*, November, 1999) and *Shinty's Place and Space in World* (*The Sports Historian*, May, 1998).

Magoun, Frances Peabody Jr *History of Football from the Beginning to 1871* (Heinrich Poppinghays OHG, 1938) and *Football in Medieval England and Middle-English literature* (*The American Historical Review*, vol 35, no 1, 1929).

Mahon, Jack *A History of Gaelic Football* (Gill & Macmillan, 2000).

Malcolmson, Robert W *Popular Recreations in English Society 1700-1850* (Cambridge University Press, 1980).

Mangan, JA *Sport in Europe: politics, class, gender* (Frank Cass, 1999), *Athleticism in the Victorian and Edwardian Public School: The Emergence and Consolidation of an Educational Ideology* (Frank Cass, 2000) and *The Cultural bond: sport, empire, society* (Gainsborough House, 1992).

Marples, Morris. *A History of Football* (Secker and Warburg, 1954).

Marshall, Francis *Football* (Cassell and company, 1892) with **Arthur G Guillemard**, **G Rowland Hill** and **Arthur Budd** contributing particularly relevant chapters.

Mason, Nicholas *Football!: The story of all the world's football games* (Drake Publishers, 1875).

MacDonald, Rev J Ninian *Shinty: A Short History of The Ancient Highland Game* (R Carruthers, 1932).

McCarthy, Daniel *Citizen Cusack and Clare's Gaelic Games* (in *Clare History & Society*, Geography Publications, 2008).

Midwinter, Eric *Parish to Planet: How football came to rule the world* (Know the Score, 2007).

Miller, Stephen G *Ancient Greek Athletics* (Yale University Press, 2004).

Nelson, David *The Anatomy of a Game: Football, the Rules, and the Men who Made the Game* (University of Delaware Press, 1994).

Northern Bullants FC *Our Game: The Melbourne Rules* (www.northernbullants.com.au).

Owl Historian *Sheffield fan-site* at www.btinternet.com/~a.drake/2003sheffhist.htm.

Oxendine, Joseph B *American Indian Sports Heritage* (University of Nebraska Press, 1988).

Peek, Hedley, Earl of Suffolk and Berkshire, and Aflalo, FG *The Encyclopaedia of Sport* (GP Putnam & sons, 1898) .

Rice, Jonathan *Start of Play: The curious origins of our favourite sports* (Prion Books Ltd, 1998).

Rouse, Paul *How Dublin saved hurling: the 1880s and the making of a modern game* (Seminar held in Dublin City Library and Archive, 11th September, 2010).

Sanders, Richard *Beastly Fury: The strange birth of British football* (Bantam Books, 2009).

Shaw Fairman, Patricia *The bewties of the fut-ball: Reactions and references to this boisterous sport in English writings, 1175 -1815* (University of Oviedo, 1994).

Shearman, Montagu *Athletics and football* (Longmans, Green and Co, 1888).

Shortell, Peter *The William Webb Ellis Myth* (www.pshortell.demon.co.uk).

Smith, William *A Dictionary of Greek and Roman Antiquities* (John Murray, 1875).

Society of North American Hockey Historians and Researchers. *The History of Hockey.* Available online at www.sonahhr.com.

Strutt, Joseph *The Sports and Pastimes of Rural England* (1801).

Taylor, Matthew *The association game: a history of British football* (Pearson Education Limited, 2007).

Tokovinine, Alexandre *The Royal Ball Game of the Ancient Maya* (http://www.mayavase.com/alex/alexballgame.html).

Tranter, Nigel *Sport, economy and society in Britain 1750-1914* (Cambridge University Press, 1998).

Trueman, Nigel *Rugby Union History* (www.rugbyfootballhistory.com).

Walvin, James *The People's Game* (Revised from 1975, Mainstream, 1995).

Wilkins, Sally E D *Sports and games of medieval cultures* (Greenwood Press, 2002).

Percy M Young *A History of British Football* (Stanley Paul, 1968).

ABOUT THE AUTHOR

Mike Roberts was born in Aberystwyth, Wales in 1970, and later lived in Okehampton, Devon. He studied at Christ Church University, Canterbury and after moving to Barcelona in 1992 to work at the Olympic Games, he decided to make the Catalan city his home.

He is currently working as a translator for FC Barcelona and the Universitat Autònoma de Catalunya, and recently retired after fifteen years as secretary of the Barcelona International Football League.

Having played rugby at school and soccer as an adult, and followed both sports intently, in the cosmopolitan city of Barcelona, he was drawn into the worlds of what until then had been less familiar football codes to him, particularly Gaelic and American football, and his interest in these was intensified by writing for his self-published sports magazine and also working for a sports travel company.

What started as basic historical research for background articles soon ignited a spark in Roberts' curious mind. Despite all he had been told about Gaelic football, the pieces didn't quite seem to fit. The more he dabbled, the more he came to question the authenticity of several of the generalised claims about ancient ball games and the origins of the modern codes. He also came to realise that no matter how academic the research into different sports, among historians there was widespread lack of knowledge, or of willingness to recognise, the common bond between all the different codes of football. Instead, in each code's self-congratulatory quest to build its individual identity, an inaccurate picture of football's true origins was being presented.

This, his first book, is the result of ten years of dedicated research. In compiling it, he is indebted to the painstaking work of greater historians than he, and hopes he has managed to produce a comprehensive review of the literature as it stands today to paint an accurate and unbiased picture of how all the world's different football cultures link together as the same old game.

Disclaimer

All of the information published in this book is, to the best of my knowledge and following extensive research and verification, correct. However, in such an ambitious project, and with new evidence emerging every week, it is only natural that there may be errors. I would be delighted if readers could bring any of these to my attention in order for them to be corrected in future editions.

Likewise, as often as possible or necessary, all sources have been given. I would be grateful for any information regarding erroneous or missing sources, and to rectify them in future editions, and apologise for any inconvenience unwittingly caused.

Lightning Source UK Ltd.
Milton Keynes UK
UKOW05f2001181217
314719UK00005B/504/P

9 781461 093190